TEEN
Health
COURSE 2

TEEN Health

COURSE 2

Mary Bronson Merki, Ph.D.

Glencoe McGraw-Hill

New York, New York
Columbus, Ohio
Woodland Hills, California
Peoria, Illinois

Meet the Author

Mary Bronson Merki has taught health education in grades K–12, as well as health education methods classes at the undergraduate and graduate levels. As Health Education Specialist for the Dallas School District, Dr. Merki developed and implemented a district-wide health education program, *Skills for Living,* which was used as a model by the state education agency. She also helped develop and implement the district's Human Growth, Development, and Sexuality program, which won the National PTA's Excellence in Education Award and earned her an honorary lifetime membership in the state PTA. Dr. Merki has assisted school districts throughout the country in developing local health education programs. In 1988 she was named the Texas Health Educator of the Year by the Texas Association for Health, Physical Education, Recreation, and Dance. Dr. Merki is also the author of *Glencoe Health,* a high school textbook adopted in school districts throughout the country. She currently teaches in a Texas public school, where she was recently honored as Teacher of the Year. Dr. Merki completed her undergraduate work at Colorado State University in Fort Collins, Colorado. She earned her master's and doctoral degrees in health education at Texas Woman's University in Denton, Texas.

Editorial and production services
provided by Visual Education Corporation, Princeton, NJ.

Design by Bill Smith Studio, New York, NY.

Glencoe/McGraw-Hill

A Division of The **McGraw·Hill** Companies

Send all inquiries to:
Glencoe/McGraw-Hill
21600 Oxnard Street, Suite 500
Woodland Hills, California 91367

ISBN 0-02-653128-3 (Course 2 Student Text)
ISBN 0-02-653129-1 (Course 2 Teacher's Wraparound Edition)

Printed in the United States of America.

6 7 8 9   003   06 05 04 03 02 01 00

Health Consultants

Unit 1
Choosing a Healthy Life

Becky J. Smith, Ph.D.; C.H.E.S.
Reston, Virginia

Robert Frye, M.P.H.
Health Education Consultant
Apex, North Carolina

Alice B. Pappas, Ph.D.; R.N.
Associate Professor
Associate Dean for Academic Affairs
Baylor University School of Nursing
Dallas, Texas

Unit 2
Nutrition and Fitness

Cathy Strain, M.S.; R.D.; C.D.
Associate Professor
Marian College
Indianapolis, Indiana

Kim Shibinski, M.S.
Department of Physical Education and Health
    Promotion
Columbia College
Columbia, South Carolina

Ronald G. Knowlton, Ph.D.
Professor and Chair, Physical Education Department
Southern Illinois University
Carbondale, Illinois

Unit 3
Understanding Yourself and Others

Janice Livingston, R.N.; M.Ed.; M.S.; A.R.N.P.
Professor
Central Florida Community College
Ocala, Florida

Howard Steven Shapiro, M.D.
Assistant Professor of Psychiatry
University of Southern California School of Medicine
    and Senior Attending Physician
Cedars Sinai Medical Center
Los Angeles, California

E. Laurette Taylor, Ph.D.
Associate Professor
Department of Health and Sport Sciences
The University of Oklahoma
Norman, Oklahoma

Unit 4
Protecting Your Health

Robert D. Russell, Ed.D.
Professor of Health Education Emeritus
Southern Illinois University
Carbondale, Illinois

Richard L. Papenfuss, Ph.D.
Associate Professor of Health Education
Arizona Health Sciences Center
University of Arizona
Tucson, Arizona

David M. Allen, M.D.
Infectious Disease Associates
Dallas, Texas

Mark Dignan, Ph.D.; M.P.H.
Chair, Center for Community Studies
AMC Cancer Research Center
Denver, Colorado

Unit 5
Personal Safety

Richard J. Shuntich, Ph.D.
College of Social and Behavioral Sciences
Department of Psychology
Eastern Kentucky University
Richmond, Kentucky

David Sleet, Ph.D.
Associate Director for Science
Unintentional Injury Prevention
Centers for Disease Control and Prevention (CDC)
Atlanta, Georgia

Teacher Reviewers

Reviewer for Entire Book

Pamela R. Connolly
Subject Area Coordinator for Health Education,
    Pittsburgh Catholic Schools
Oakland Catholic High School, Diocese of Pittsburgh
Pittsburgh, Pennsylvania

Unit 1
Choosing a Healthy Life

Beverly J. Berkin, C.H.E.S.
Health Education Consultant
Bedford Corners, New York

Lori Hart
Health Educator
West Shore Middle School
Milford, Connecticut

Unit 2
Nutrition and Fitness

Robert Wandberg, Ph.D.
Health Education
John F. Kennedy Senior High School
Bloomington, Minnesota

Debra C. Harris, Ph.D.
HPE Department Chair, HPE Teacher
West Linn High School
West Linn, Oregon

Unit 3
Understanding Yourself and Others

Betty Anne White
Health & Physical Education Teacher
Bryan Station Traditional Middle School
Lexington, Kentucky

Donna Breitenstein, Ed.D.
Professor & Coordinator of Health Education,
Director of NC School Health Training Center
Appalachian State University
Boone, North Carolina

Unit 4
Protecting Your Health

Deborah L. Tackmann, B.S.; M.E.P.D.
Health Education Instructor
North High School
Eau Claire, Wisconsin

Peggy V. Johns
Supervisor, Pre-K–12 Health Education
Pinellas County Schools
Largo, Florida

Beverely J. Berkin, C.H.E.S.
Health Education Consultant
Bedford Corners, New York

Lynn Westberg
Health Education Department Head
Kearns High School
Kearns, Utah

Unit 5
Personal Safety

Debra Penland Forbes
Health Educator
Pleasanton Unified School District
Pleasanton, California

Contents

Unit 2
Nutrition and Fitness

Unit 4
Protecting Your Health

Unit 4
Protecting Your Health

Unit 5
Personal Safety

Features

Health Lab

Life Skills

Making Healthy Decisions

Personal Inventory

People at Work

HEALTH UPDATE

CON$UMER FOCU$

Teens Making a Difference

Myths and Realities

Sports and Recreation

Personal Trainer

Unit 1
Choosing a Healthy Life

1

Chapter 1

A Healthy Foundation

Student Expectations

After reading this chapter, you should be able to:

① Describe what it means to be healthy.

② Recognize the factors that influence your health.

③ Explain how you can keep track of your own health status.

④ Identify skills that will help you stay healthy.

Megan: Where's Brittany? I thought she was going to help put up posters for the jazz band competition.

Dee: She's home sick.

Rafael: Again? She was out a couple of days last week. What's going on?

Dee: I think she's way too busy. She's on the basketball team, she babysits twice a week, and she volunteers for almost every school project. It's starting to get to her, I think.

Megan: She never even has time to sit down with us and eat lunch anymore. She just grabs a drink and runs off somewhere. No wonder she's sick all the time.

Rafael: I think I'll stop by and see her on my way home. Maybe I can help her figure out how to make some changes in her schedule.

in your journal

In each chapter, you will be asked to write entries in your journal. These are your private reflections and thoughts and are for your use only. Read the dialogue on this page. Have you ever wondered if you should take better care of your health? Start your private journal entries on your overall health and wellness by answering these questions:

▶ What advice would you give to Brittany?

▶ What does being healthy mean to you?

▶ What steps do you take to protect your health?

▶ What kinds of health habits would you like to improve?

When you reach the end of the chapter, you will use your journal entries to make an action plan.

Your Health and Wellness

This lesson will help you find answers to questions that teens often ask about personal health and wellness. For example:

▶ **What does it mean to be healthy?**

▶ **How can I keep my physical, mental/emotional, and social health in balance?**

▶ **What is the relationship between health and wellness?**

Words to Know

health
emotions
wellness

Being Healthy

What does it mean to be healthy? Think about that question as you read about Roy and Karen. Roy is on the track team. He is in excellent physical shape. Yet he finds he has trouble controlling his temper. As a result, his friendships rarely last. Karen is a good student. She also writes for the school newspaper. She often stays up late studying, however, and sometimes skips breakfast. As a result, Karen feels tired much of the time. How would you rate Roy's and Karen's health?

Good health involves every part of your life. **Health** is *a combination of physical, mental/emotional, and social well-being.* Your physical health has to do with the condition of your body. Your mental/emotional health involves your thoughts and **emotions,** which are *feelings such as love, joy, or fear.* Your social health involves the ways in which you relate to other people. Each of these aspects of health deserves a closer look.

Your Physical Health

Maintaining physical health involves taking care of your body. There are many ways to do this.

■ Eat a well-balanced diet.

  ■ Stay fit through regular exercise.

    ■ Get at least eight hours of sleep each night.

      ■ Keep your body, teeth, and hair clean.

        ■ Have regular medical and dental check-ups.

          ■ Avoid tobacco, alcohol, and drugs.

PHYSICAL HEALTH

Your Mental/Emotional Health

Maintaining mental and emotional health means taking care of your mind. Here are some ways to keep yourself mentally and emotionally healthy.

CONNECTION
Tap into the Web for health resources geared to your interests and concerns.

http://www.glencoe.com/sec/health

- Face problems with a positive and realistic attitude.

- Express your feelings clearly and calmly to others.

- Set priorities so that you will not be overwhelmed by school, responsibilities at home, or athletic activities.

- See your mistakes as opportunities to learn, grow, and change.

- Recognize your weak areas and try to improve them.

- Develop effective decision-making skills.

MENTAL/EMOTIONAL HEALTH

- Use your talents effectively.

- Accept responsibility for your actions.

- Stand up for your beliefs and values.

- Remain open to learning new information.

Your Social Health

Maintaining social health means taking care of the ways in which you get along with other people. You can do this in the following ways.

- Have a friendly, open attitude toward other people.

- Learn to communicate effectively.

- Respect and care for family members.

- Be a loyal, truthful, and dependable friend.

- Honor other people's feelings.

- Respect other people's property.

- Learn to disagree without arguing.

- Learn to resolve conflicts effectively.

- Give support and help when it is needed.

SOCIAL HEALTH

in your journal

Reread the guidelines for mental and emotional health. In your journal, make a list of the guidelines that you follow regularly. Make a second list of the guidelines that you do not follow regularly. Write a paragraph about the positive effects you would receive if you began following the guidelines that you do not follow now.

Staying in Balance

It's easy to concentrate on one aspect of health and neglect the others. That's what happened to Roy and Karen, the teens you read about at the beginning of the lesson. A totally healthy person, however, keeps physical, mental/emotional, and social health in proper balance. To help you achieve a balance of the three aspects of health, think of your health as a triangle with equal sides, as shown in **Figure 1.1.** To achieve and maintain *total* personal health, make sure that you give attention to all three sides of your health triangle.

Figure 1.1
The Health Triangle
You can keep your health in balance by thinking of it as a triangle with three sides.

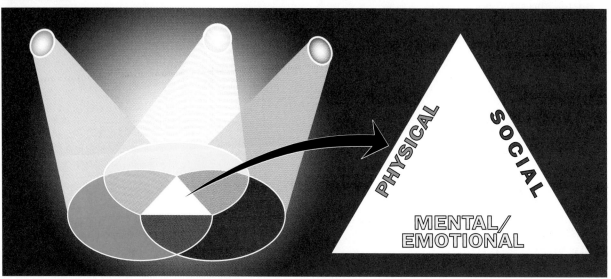

What Is Wellness?

Keeping the three parts of your health triangle in balance is the best way to achieve **wellness,** *an overall state of well-being involving regular behaviors that have a positive result over time.* How do health and wellness relate to each other? Think of health as a snapshot—a picture of how you are doing physically, mentally, emotionally, and socially at a particular moment. Your level of wellness, on the other hand, is more like a film that shows how these aspects of health interact over a period of time. The choices about health that you make every moment become part of your long-term level of wellness.

What does it mean to have a high level of wellness? **Figure 1.2** shows one way to understand levels of wellness. It shows various conditions and circumstances and where they might be placed on a wellness meter. Most people would prefer to enjoy a high level of wellness. The decisions you make now can help you maintain or achieve that goal throughout your life.

Figure 1.2
Measuring Your Level of Wellness
Where would you place yourself on this wellness meter?

Using complete sentences, answer the following questions on a separate sheet of paper.

Reviewing Terms and Facts

1. **Vocabulary**   Define the term *emotions*.

2. **Vocabulary**   Explain the meaning of *wellness*. Then use the term in an original sentence.

3. **List**   Identify the three aspects of health that must be balanced in order to achieve wellness.

4. **Restate**   Explain the relationship between health and wellness.

Thinking Critically

5. **Analyze**   Reread the descriptions of Roy and Karen on page 4. Explain why their health triangles seem to be out of balance. Draw a diagram to illustrate each situation.

6. **Explain**   Many of the health guidelines in this lesson (pages 4 and 5) are related to each other. For example, developing effective decision-making skills will help you avoid using tobacco, alcohol, and drugs. Select guidelines from two different aspects of health. Explain how the guidelines are related.

Applying Health Concepts

7. **Health of Others**   Based on what you have learned, make a poster to persuade younger students to make the right choices to achieve lifelong wellness. Use specific facts from the lesson to make your poster as informative and helpful as possible.

Influences on Your Health

This lesson will help you find answers to questions that teens often ask about what affects their health. For example:

▶ How do heredity and my environment affect my health?

▶ How do the people around me affect my health?

In your journal, list three things that influence your health. Are the influences positive or negative?

What Affects Your Health?

As you have learned, the choices you make and the ways you think and act have a strong effect on your total health. These are parts of your life over which you have quite a bit of control. There are, however, outside factors that influence your health. To make the best choices, you will need to understand what these factors are and what you can do about them.

Putting the Puzzle Together

Every person is an individual. Each life unfolds in its own way, guided and molded by both personal choices and outside factors. Think of a person as a one-of-a-kind jigsaw puzzle. The factors that influence that person's health are the pieces of the puzzle. Each person's puzzle has different pieces that, when put together, form a unique picture, as shown in **Figure 1.3.**

Figure 1.3
Pieces of a Puzzle

Many elements come together to create the person you are.

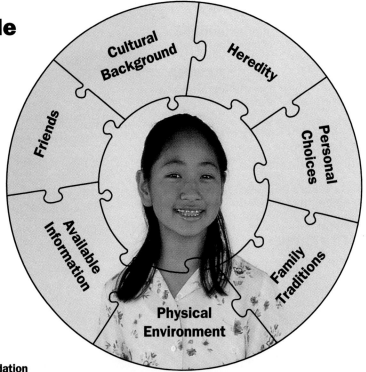

Heredity and Environment

Heredity (huh·RED·i·tee) is *the passing on of traits from biological parents to children.* Some traits passed on through heredity are the following:

Certain traits are passed on from parents to children.

- Skin, eye, and hair color

- Body build

- Growth patterns

- The tendency to get certain diseases

Hereditary traits are "built in"—you can't choose them or avoid them. However, recognizing the traits that you have already inherited from your parents can help you make crucial decisions about your health. If, for example, members of your family have had a high number of dental cavities, you should pay extra attention to your dental care. Similarly, people who know that heart disease or cancer has affected several family members should learn all they can about reducing their own risks of developing these particular diseases.

Your **environment** (en·VY·ruhn·ment) is *all the living and nonliving things that surround you.* Part of your environment is your physical environment, including:

- **Your home, neighborhood, and school.** Do you live in a large city or a small town? Are you surrounded by farms, by other homes, or by shops and restaurants?

- **The air you breathe and the water you drink.** Is the air clean, or do you live an area with heavy pollution? Does your water come from a well or is there a public water supply?

Like your hereditary traits, choices about where you live and the school you attend may be beyond your control. You still have choices to make, however. You can decide to be as healthy as possible within your physical environment. This involves recognizing characteristics of your environment that can be harmful to your overall health and taking steps to protect yourself. For example, if you live in a hot, sunny climate, you will need to take special precautions to protect your skin from the sun. Think also about how you affect the environment that you share with others. Are there ways that you and your family, for example, can avoid contributing to air or water pollution?

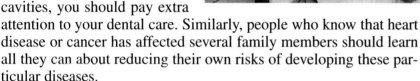

Social Studies Connection

Environmental Features ACTIVITY!

Describe the geography of the area where you live. Is there a body of water nearby? Are you in a city? Is the area mountainous or flat?

Based on your description, write ten features of your physical environment that might influence the health of people living there. For at least two of the features, tell how a person in your area can behave to prevent illness or injury.

Other Influences

Along with your heredity and physical environment, many other factors in your life influence your health and your health choices. **Figure 1.4** illustrates some of the most important factors.

Figure 1.4
Influences on Your Health Choices

How will knowing about these influences affect the decisions you make about your health?

Your family's cultural background and traditions influence many aspects of your health, such as the foods you eat, the holidays you celebrate, and the goals you have.

Your friends can have a major influence on the decisions you make. Such influences can be either positive or negative. A friend who urges you to smoke may have a very negative influence on your health. A friend who listens to you and encourages you will probably have a strong positive influence on your health.

Books, magazines, newspapers, television and radio programs, and the Internet can also have a tremendous influence on your health choices. Just remember to evaluate the source of any message. Commercials, for example, are there to convince you to buy—not just to provide information.

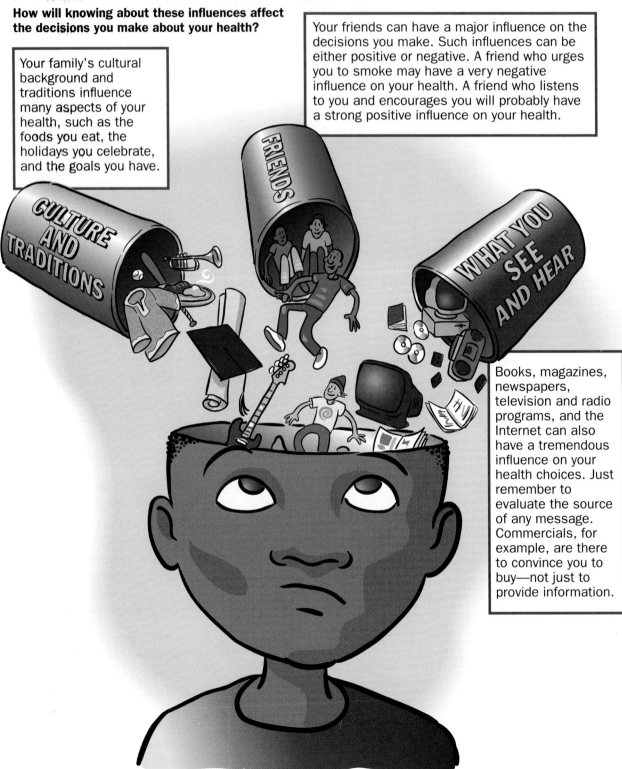

Using complete sentences, answer the following questions on a separate sheet of paper.

Reviewing Terms and Facts

1. **Vocabulary** Define the terms *heredity* and *environment.*

2. **Restate** Describe how you can use information about hereditary traits to make health decisions.

3. **List** Identify three factors, other than heredity and physical environment, that can have an influence on a person's health.

Thinking Critically

4. **Explain** Why are there laws about allowable levels of environmental pollution?

5. **Evaluate** Choose one of the categories of influences in **Figure 1.4.** Describe a possible positive and a possible negative health influence in that category.

Applying Health Concepts

6. **Personal Health** With a group of four students, create a skit about the factors that influence personal health. Create a scene or a series of scenes in which a teen is influenced by one or more of the factors described in **Figure 1.4.** Show how the teen responds and how it affects his or her health. Perform your skit for the class.

HEALTH LAB

Influences on Health

Introduction: Recognizing the factors that influence your health can provide valuable background information as you make choices and take actions that affect your overall health and wellness.

Objective: With a group of three to five classmates, design, conduct, and analyze the results of a survey about how people view influences on their health.

Materials and Method: As a class, come up with a list of 15 to 20 factors that might have an influence on people's health. (Possible factors to include are diet, religious beliefs, inherited tendencies toward disease, the opinions of friends, air quality, or neighborhood crime.) Work with your own group to create a short survey that asks people to choose from this list the five most important influences. Suggest that people then rank the factors they have chosen from 1 to 5 in order of importance. Conduct the survey on students and adults outside your class.

Observations and Analysis: After conducting your survey, analyze the results. You may want to display the results in graph form. Which factors do the people you surveyed consider most important? Which do they consider least important? How do your results compare with the results of your classmates? In what areas do you think people should be more aware of the influences on their health? How could health professionals help people become more aware of how to make wise choices about health?

TEEN HEALTH DIGEST

Sports and Recreation
A Champ with a Sense of Balance

In 1996, at the age of 15, California teen Michelle Kwan won the World Figure Skating Championship. Such early success might tempt an athlete to focus solely on his or her sport. Yet Kwan realizes that there is more to life than her skating career.

Kwan, an excellent student, gives careful attention to her tutored courses in biology, algebra, English, French, and history. She also understands the importance of her social health. She remains physically and emotionally close to her family. Kwan depends on her parents for comfort and advice.

Michelle Kwan looks forward to putting her skates away someday and going to college. "A lot of skaters look at skating and nothing else," she says. "Hello! There's a life in between!"

CON$UMER FOCU$
Handwashing for Health?

Q. Do those antibacterial soaps I see advertised really work? Can I protect myself against germs by using them?

A. Yes and no. The soaps really *do* contain ingredients that kill bacteria. They do an especially good job on the germs that produce odor, and they can also kill some of the germs that spread illness. To get the full benefits, however, you have to wash in the right way. That means rubbing your hands briskly under warm water for at least 20 seconds. Even after rinsing, your hands may retain an antibacterial coating that protects against future germs.

Try This:

Use a timer to practice washing your hands in the way described. Try to use the method each time you wash.

HEALTH UPDATE
Young and Healthy

Young Americans are eating in ways that reduce their cancer risk. A 1996 American Cancer Society report showed that the students surveyed were doing better than adults in some areas of nutrition. "The proportion of students who ate at least five servings of fruits and vegetables daily doubled between 1993 and 1995," the report noted.

The American Cancer Society recommends having at least five servings of fruits and vegetables daily as well as limiting fat intake and getting regular physical activity. These guidelines are also recommended for preventing other diseases, such as heart disease and diabetes.

Try This: For the next five days, write down how many times you eat fruits and vegetables, as well as how much you eat. If you aren't getting enough of these foods, make a plan to get what you need.

Myths and Realities
The More I Exercise, the Hungrier I Get

Q. I thought that exercise would dull my appetite, but I'm actually hungrier after I exercise. Is that unusual?

A. The answer seems to depend on whether you are male or female. Recent studies in England and elsewhere found that although exercising seemed to make men lose their appetites, it had the opposite effect on women. Exercising remains a crucial element of any weight management program. If exercising gives you an appetite, however, be sure to snack on healthful, low-calorie foods.

Personal Trainer
Safe Video Routines

You say your friend bought an exercise video and the two of you want to try it out? Keep these tips in mind.

1. **Protect your feet.** If the video includes jumping exercises, be sure you wear athletic shoes. Don't exercise in socks or bare feet.
2. **Clear an area.** Make sure you have cleared enough space in front of the TV. Try to exercise away from tables, lamps, and other furniture.
3. **Don't overdo it.** Don't worry about keeping up with the instructor on the tape. You haven't been doing this as long as he or she has.
4. **Don't forget to pause.** The beauty of a video is that you can stop anytime. Stop if you feel any pain or if you feel you are exercising too hard.

What's Your Health Status?

This lesson will help you find answers to questions that teens often ask about the status of their health. For example:

► Why should I check my health status?

► What do I need to do to be healthy?

► How can I plan for a high level of wellness?

Words to Know

prevention
risk behavior
self-assessment

Q & A

Listen to Grandma!

Q: When I was little, my grandmother used to make chicken soup to help me get better from a cold. Aren't cold medicines more reliable than chicken soup?

A: Your grandmother is in good company. Chicken soup is a folk remedy all over the world, from Italy to Greece to China. Scientists comparing various liquids have found that chicken soup actually seems to have a beneficial effect on colds.

Where You Are and Where You're Going

As you have learned, your heredity, environment, and the people with whom you interact are all major influences on your overall health and wellness. However, such factors are not the *only* influences. In fact, the most important influence on your health is *you*.

One of the keys to overall wellness is the prevention of health problems. **Prevention** involves *taking steps to make sure that something unhealthy does not happen.* For example, you wash your hands to prevent illnesses caused by germs. Most importantly, prevention involves avoiding risk behaviors. A **risk behavior** is *an action or choice that may cause injury or harm to you or others.* Smoking cigarettes is a risk behavior because it can lead to lung disease and many types of cancer. Riding a bike without a helmet is a risk behavior because it can lead to head injury.

When you were a young child, you depended on trusted adults such as parents, teachers, and counselors to "set the rules." Now that you are a teen, you are taking a more active role in the choices that you make for your own safety and wellness. One of the most effective ways to begin taking that active role is **self-assessment,** or *careful examination and evaluation of your own patterns of behavior.* Honest self-assessment can give you a clear picture of your health status.

As a teen, you can have a positive influence on the health choices of young children.

14

Personal Inventory

Use this self-assessment form to examine your health status. It should help you evaluate how your choices and actions influence your health and wellness.

On a separate sheet of paper, write yes or no to tell whether each statement describes you.

Physical Health

1. I get at least eight hours of sleep each night.

2. I eat a well-balanced diet, including a healthful breakfast every day.

3. I wear a seat belt in cars and protective gear when bicycling or playing sports.

4. I keep my body, teeth, and hair clean.

5. I do not use tobacco, alcohol, or drugs.

6. I exercise regularly.

7. I do not skip meals or use harsh diet plans to try to lose weight.

8. I have regular check-ups with my doctor and dentist.

9. I am aware of hereditary illnesses within my family and take steps to protect my health.

10. I do not plan to engage in sexual activity before marriage.

Mental/Emotional Health

1. I generally like and accept who I am.

2. I can accept helpful criticism.

3. I can express my feelings clearly and calmly, even when I'm angry or sad.

4. I do not blame others for my mistakes.

5. I accept that I will make mistakes, and I try to learn from them.

6. I can stand up for my own values.

7. I can face problems calmly.

8. I have at least one hobby that I enjoy.

9. I enjoy learning new information and acquiring new skills.

10. I feel that people like me.

Social Health

1. I have at least one or two close friends.

2. I respect and care for my family.

3. I have a friendly, open attitude when I meet new people.

4. I work well in a group.

5. I feel that my friends know that I am truthful and dependable.

6. I can disagree without arguing.

7. I am willing to give and get support from others when needed.

8. I am a good listener.

9. I can confidently say no when people ask me to do something harmful or wrong.

10. I respect the right of others to have opinions that may differ from mine.

Give yourself one point for every yes. Total the number of yes responses in each of the three areas. Then check your score with the following ranking.

In each section, a score of 9–10 is very good, 7–8 is good, and 5–6 is fair. If you scored 0–4 in any area, you need to take a more active role in avoiding risk behaviors that can harm your health.

Improving Your Health

The Personal Inventory on the previous page is just one way you might assess your own health status. Here are some other ways.

■ Talk with a trusted adult, such as a parent.

■ Discuss your health status with a health care professional.

■ Ask your school nurse for information about health care topics.

■ Read recommendations in health books and publications from groups such as the American Heart Association or the American Cancer Society, paying attention to how closely your health behaviors follow their recommendations.

All of these methods have the same goal—to help you understand the choices you are making right now and how those choices will affect your level of wellness. Your ultimate goal is to make choices that will increase your overall level of wellness.

What Have I Learned?

Through self-assessment you can learn about your own behaviors and possible risks you are taking. Part of this process involves making judgments. Look again at the Personal Inventory in this lesson. You will notice that the risks represented in the statements are not all equal. For example, skipping breakfast one morning is a poor health choice, but it is not a choice that will put your life in danger. Not wearing a seat belt, however, *is* life threatening. Every time you ride in a car without wearing a seat belt you are in danger of being seriously injured or killed.

What's next? You've assessed the status of your health. You've found some areas in which you could improve. You've thought about which areas are the most essential for you to work on right away. Now you're ready for the next and most important step. You're ready to use the information in a positive way by making a personal wellness contract.

Doctors, school nurses, and other health professionals can point you to good sources of accurate and reliable health information that will help you make wise choices.

Creating a Personal Wellness Contract

To help you create a wellness contract, ask yourself the following questions and jot down all the ideas you have for possible answers.

- According to my self-assessment, what positive behaviors am I engaged in regarding my health?
- What risk behaviors are putting my health in jeopardy?
- What additional health issues do I want to work on?
- Which areas should I work on first?
- How might changing some of my behaviors make me happier and healthier?
- What specific steps might I take to change each behavior?

Look back at the ideas you have written. Use those ideas to make a personal wellness contract. Think of this as a real contract—an agreement you will abide by—with yourself. In the contract, specify what you will do in order to improve your health and wellness. **Figure 1.5** shows one form that this contract might take.

Q&A

It's Never Too Late

Q: Most mornings, I'm too rushed for breakfast! What can I do?

A: Try a piece of whole wheat bread and this instant, delicious shake, mixed in a blender or shaken in a lidded jar:

8 ounces plain nonfat yogurt

1 banana, chopped or mashed

1 cup orange juice

Figure 1.5

A Personal Wellness Contract

What is the value of writing down your promises and dating the contract?

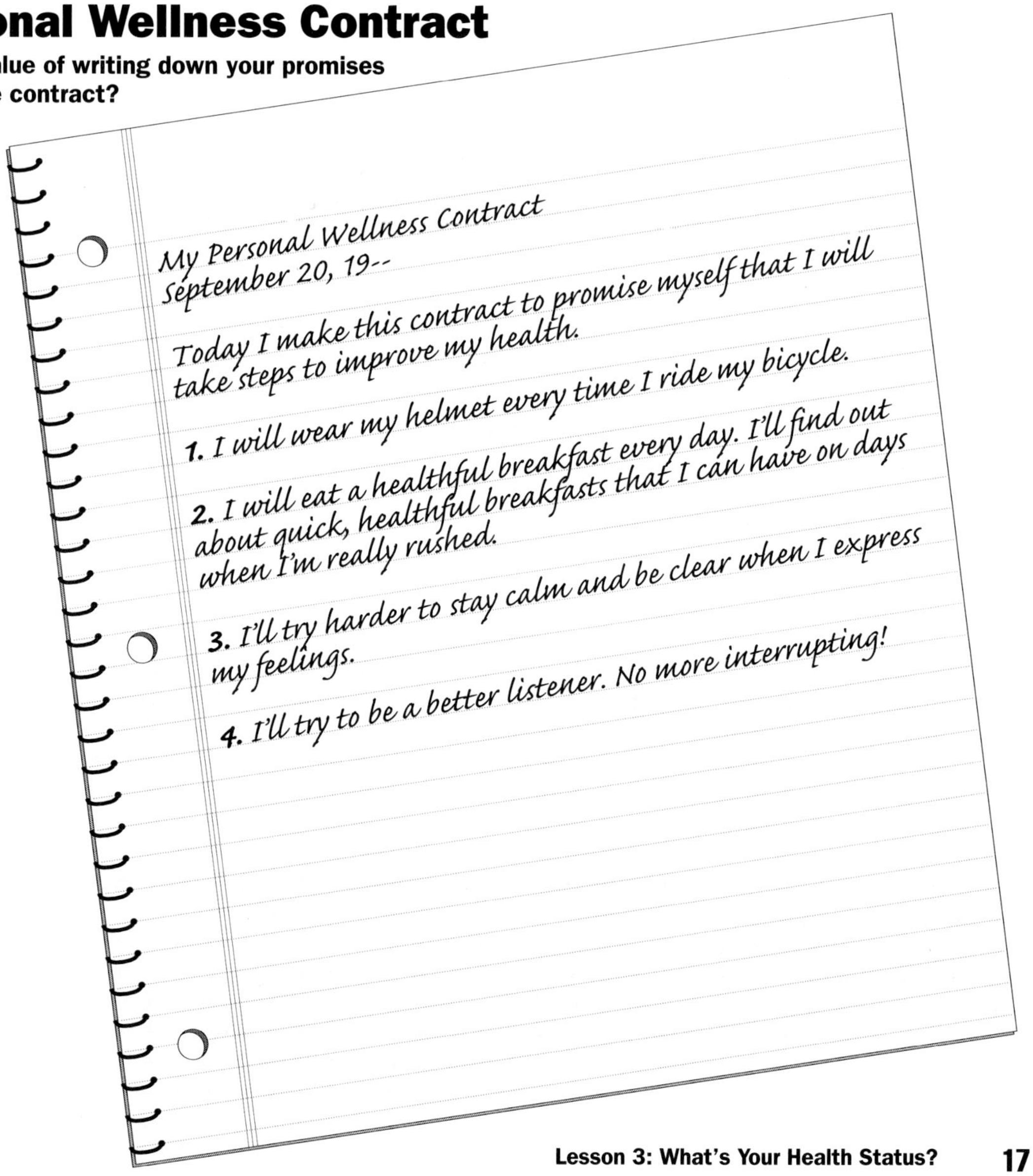

My Personal Wellness Contract
September 20, 19--
Today I make this contract to promise myself that I will take steps to improve my health.
1. I will wear my helmet every time I ride my bicycle.
2. I will eat a healthful breakfast every day. I'll find out about quick, healthful breakfasts that I can have on days when I'm really rushed.
3. I'll try harder to stay calm and be clear when I express my feelings.
4. I'll try to be a better listener. No more interrupting!

Control the Clock! ACTIVITY!

Do you ever feel that you don't have time to manage all your activities and responsibilities? Try taking control of the clock! Make a daily schedule. Give yourself a realistic amount of time for each task that you must do, and don't forget to schedule in a reward—time for fun and relaxation after those tasks are completed. Experiment with your daily schedule until you find the right balance of task time and reward time.

Using the Contract

The rest is up to you! Stick to your contract and take an active role in improving your health. Try sharing your contract with a friend, and ask your friend to share his or hers with you. How can the two of you help each other to fulfill the contracts? By following through, you can become positive influences on each other's health.

A friend's encouragement can have a powerful effect.

Lesson 3 Review

Using complete sentences, answer the following questions on a separate sheet of paper.

Reviewing Terms and Facts

1. **Vocabulary**   Define the term *risk behavior.* Give two examples.

2. **List**   Identify two ways, other than a personal inventory, to perform self-assessment.

3. **Recall**   What is the purpose of a personal wellness contract?

Thinking Critically

4. **Describe**   Choose a sport or other physical activity that you enjoy. Describe specific preventive steps you might take to avoid injuries or accidents in that activity.

5. **Recommend**   Reread the contract shown on page 17. What specific steps might the teen take to try to stay calm and be clear when expressing his or her feelings?

Applying Health Concepts

6. **Personal Health**   For the next week, keep a log of your progress as you work to fulfill your contract with yourself. Describe specific actions or choices you take, and tell whether or not you feel that they are helpful.

7. **Growth and Development**   Make a poster that would help early elementary children (ages six to eight) become aware of the factors that influence their health. The poster could for example, talk about healthful eating habits or safety on bicycles. If you choose to discuss negative influences, avoid making the poster frightening for this age group.

Building Health Skills

This lesson will help you find answers to questions that teens often ask about taking charge of their health. For example:

▶ **What steps can I take to be in charge of my own health?**

▶ **What skills can I develop in the three areas of health?**

▶ **How can I avoid health risks?**

Taking Charge of Your Own Health

Making a personal wellness contract is the first step in taking charge of your own health. The next step is to *follow* the plan. To do that, you will need to understand and practice specific skills. One way to think about the skills is to remember the health triangle. Some skills are most important for your physical health. Others will help improve your mental/emotional health. Still others will enhance your social health. This lesson provides an overview of these skills. The rest of the textbook explains how they can be used in your daily life.

Skills for Building Physical Health

You can develop many skills that will help you build and maintain physical health. Some of these skills will protect you from immediate illness or injury. Others will increase your level of physical wellness far into the future.

Staying Safe

Take safety precautions to avoid risks that can lead to injuries. For example, obey traffic rules when bicycling, riding in a car, or walking along the side of a road. Don't go out alone after dark.

Staying safe also involves practicing personal **hygiene** (HY·jeen), or *cleanliness*. Daily hygiene includes care of the skin, teeth, nails, and hair. A clean body is the best line of defense against germs that cause illness.

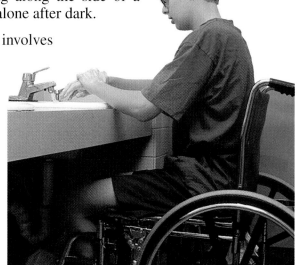

Words to Know

hygiene
self-management
values
refusal skills

Cultural Connections

Yoga for Fitness and Relaxation

Yoga is a system of mental and physical exercise. It was developed centuries ago by Hindus in India. In Sanskrit, the classical language of India, yoga means "discipline." Most yoga exercises are simple to do and combine coordinated movements and postures with breathing techniques and meditation. Many people throughout the world practice yoga to improve fitness, reduce tension, and improve overall health.

Washing your hands is one of the simplest and most effective ways to prevent the spread of illness.

Knowing Yourself

ACTIVITY!

In William Shakespeare's classic drama "Hamlet," a character gives the following advice to a young man: "To thine own self be true." In more modern and informal language, this sentence might translate to "Be honest with yourself."

Write a letter to a student who is younger than you and share this advice. Point out the positive effects it can have on emotional and mental health. Include examples to make your meaning clear.

Eating Well and Staying Fit

Other important physical skills involve choosing healthful foods and staying active. Learn as much as you can about food and good health. Eat a balanced diet that is rich in whole grains, fruits, vegetables, lean meats, and dairy products. Avoid foods that are high in fat. In addition, put your body to work every day. Whenever possible, walk! Choose the stairs instead of the escalator. Join a sports team or start a regular exercise group with your friends.

Skills for Building Mental and Emotional Health

The following skills are ones that will help you mentally and emotionally. They will allow you to understand yourself and others. They will also give you access to information available from experts in health. Finally, the skills in this section will help you feel good about yourself and about what you can do with your life.

Knowing Yourself

Get into the habit of honest self-assessment. Examine and evaluate your choices and actions. Understand that everyone—including you—makes mistakes. Don't let mistakes get you down, however. Use them instead in a positive way—to learn, grow, and change.

LIFE SKILLS
Becoming Media Literate

*A*n important point to remember whenever you are gathering facts is that not all information is equally valid. In other words, not all sources of information—books, articles, and data on the Internet—can be trusted. Here are some tips to follow when gathering information.

▶ DO learn to use such research tools as the library computer or card catalog, *The Reader's Guide to Periodical Literature*, and Internet search engines. These tools will help you find information from a variety of useful sources. A teacher or librarian can show you how to begin.

▶ DO check your sources. Check the credentials of the author and any people whom the author quotes. Are these people experts on the topic

presented? Then check the accuracy of the author's sources and findings. Is the information based on reliable scientific studies or reports?

▶ DON'T randomly surf the Internet, or gather health-related information from a public message board or chat room.

Locating Helpful Information

Today's world provides access to all kinds of information. Develop good fact-finding skills so that you can gather the information you need to make healthful decisions. Are you aware of the resources available at home, at school, and in your community for valid health information? **Figure 1.6** summarizes some of them.

Figure 1.6
How to Find the Facts
Many information sources are available to you.

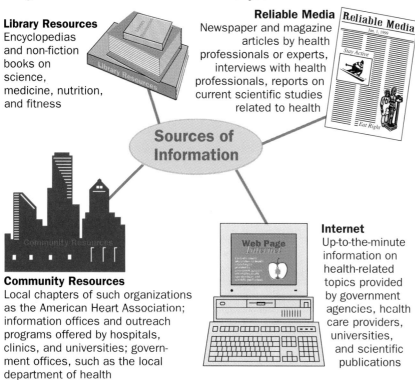

Library Resources
Encyclopedias and non-fiction books on science, medicine, nutrition, and fitness

Reliable Media
Newspaper and magazine articles by health professionals or experts, interviews with health professionals, reports on current scientific studies related to health

Sources of Information

Community Resources
Local chapters of such organizations as the American Heart Association; information offices and outreach programs offered by hospitals, clinics, and universities; government offices, such as the local department of health

Internet
Up-to-the-minute information on health-related topics provided by government agencies, health care providers, universities, and scientific publications

Q & A

Who Do I Believe?

Q: It seems like every time one report comes out telling me that something is bad for me, a couple of months later another researcher finds something different. Who do I trust?

A: It's not unusual for two scientists performing the same types of experiments to come up with conflicting results. In today's world, news travels so quickly that sometimes preliminary results are reported as final. Also, in a quick "sound bite," full explanations of a study are impossible. What does this mean? Before making any changes in your lifestyle, check out the information with a health professional. He or she can probably put the information in the proper perspective.

Make sure that your information is coming from experts whom you can trust.

▶ DO seek information from the Web sites of such reliable sources as universities, libraries, and government agencies such as the Centers for Disease Control and Prevention (CDC), the National Institutes of Health (NIH), and the Environmental Protection Agency (EPA).

▶ DO seek information from reliable media sources such as *Consumer Reports* and the news and science sections of responsible newspapers.

▶ DO seek information from such television sources as news, science, or health-related programs.

▶ DO seek information from the Web sites and printed materials of recognized national organizations such as the American Cancer Society, the American Medical Association, and the American Heart Association.

▶ DON'T seek factual information from advertisements in newspapers and magazines or on television, or from any Internet Web site that offers a product for sale.

▶ DO run a "back-up" check on the reliability of any source of information by getting the advice of a trusted adult, such as a parent, a teacher, or a librarian.

Follow-up Activity

Select a health-related topic, such as immunization, bicycle safety, air pollution, or dietary fiber. Then use the tips listed above to find reliable sources of information on your topic. Make a chart to report on and evaluate at least five sources that you find.

Sometimes the hardest thing to do when someone disagrees with you is to stay cool. Everyone's opinions are influenced by facts as well as emotions. During a disagreement, strong emotions like fear or pride can ignite a discussion just as a match ignites paper. Remain aware of your emotions and the roles they play in your approach to disagreements. Preventing a fire is often much easier than putting one out!

Having a Healthy Attitude

Develop the skill of **self-management,** *the ability to take care of your overall health and to take control of your behavior and actions.* Start building self-management skills by learning to like and accept yourself. Take pride in your strengths and accomplishments, and be aware of the things about yourself that you'd like to improve upon. After all, everybody has both strengths and weaknesses. Instead of dwelling on the weaknesses, focus on developing the strengths.

Remember that no one leads a totally trouble-free life. Everyone must face problems, stress, and occasional conflicts. However, you can prevent some problems by identifying and avoiding unnecessary risks and risk behaviors. You can manage other problems by learning how to stay calm as you recognize, discuss, and solve them.

Taking Responsibility

Now that you are a teen, you are taking more and more responsibility for yourself. Being responsible means taking charge. For example, it means completing necessary tasks such as schoolwork and household chores without being reminded to do so. It also means making decisions that uphold your **values,** *the beliefs that guide the way a person lives, such as beliefs about what is right and wrong and what is most important.*

Skills for Building Social Health

Do you stop and think about how important your family and friends are? They are the people you spend time with and who share your interests and ideas. They can be valuable resources because they can help and guide you in making good decisions. Your relationships with family and friends depend on good social skills. People with good social skills communicate effectively, know how to say no, and have a positive attitude.

Being able to talk openly and honestly with friends becomes more important in the teen years.

Listening and Talking

Communication skills involve much more than being able to speak clearly. People also get their messages across by facial expressions, tone of voice, and choice of words. People even communicate by the way they listen. Effective communication skills are one way to prevent misunderstandings. Skills in communication will allow you to give support to others when they need it. In addition, effective communication skills will allow you to express your own feelings clearly.

Refusal Skills

A very important group of health-building skills includes **refusal skills,** which are *ways to say no effectively.* Understanding and respecting your values—what's right and wrong and what's important to you—will help you to say no when you need to. If a friend urges you to do something that you feel is wrong, your values will help you to refuse. True friends will respect your decision.

Making a Difference

Learning how to be a positive, reliable influence on someone else's life is extremely valuable. Each time you help a friend develop a new skill, make a healthy decision, or prevent or manage a problem, you make a positive difference in that friend's life.

in your journal

Reread the Personal Wellness Contract you created in Lesson 3. In your journal, write how you might change or add to your contract in order to improve it. Explain what specific health-building skills you might work on in order to strengthen your overall health status.

Helping someone else makes you feel good about yourself.

Review

Using complete sentences, answer the following questions on a separate sheet of paper.

Reviewing Terms and Facts

1. **Vocabulary** Define the term *hygiene.* Then give two examples of important steps to take each day for personal hygiene.

2. **List** Identify three reliable sources for factual information related to health.

3. **Explain** Explain the roles of values and self-management in helping a person to be emotionally healthy.

Thinking Critically

4. **Describe** Select one of the health-building skills summarized in this lesson. Write a short paragraph that describes how developing the skill can help a person gain a high level of physical, mental/emotional, or social health.

5. **Integrate** Think of a situation in which you would use skills from each of the three aspects of health (physical, mental/emotional, social). Describe the situation.

Applying Health Concepts

6. **Consumer Health** Make a list of five community resources for reliable health-related information. Combine your list with those of your classmates to create a class list of community information sources. Ask a school administrator how your class list of resources might be used by others in your school.

Chapter 1 Review

Chapter Summary

▶ **Lesson 1** Health is a combination of physical, mental/emotional, and social well-being. A person can achieve a high level of wellness by taking care of these three aspects of health over time.

▶ **Lesson 2** Each person's overall health is influenced by factors such as heredity and environment as well as culture and family traditions, friends, and available information.

▶ **Lesson 3** Individuals should practice self-assessment to check the status of their own health and avoid risk behaviors.

▶ **Lesson 4** Developing specific health-building skills is important in taking effective control over personal health and wellness.

Reviewing Key Terms and Concepts

Using complete sentences, answer the following questions on a separate sheet of paper.

Lesson 1

1. What is the meaning of the term *health?*

2. Describe a high level of wellness.

Lesson 2

3. Provide examples of the ways both heredity and environment can influence a person's overall health.

4. Describe how you can exert control over one outside influence on your health.

Lesson 3

5. What is *prevention?*

6. How does self-assessment help you to create a personal wellness contract?

Lesson 4

7. What does *self-management* mean?

8. Describe what is meant by the term *refusal skills.*

Thinking Critically

Using complete sentences, answer the following questions on a separate sheet of paper.

9. **Analyze** How might high personal levels of wellness among individuals benefit society as a whole?

10. **Synthesize** Imagine that you are a teen who moves from a small town to a large city. What environmental changes might you experience, and how might those changes affect your overall health?

11. **Infer** What effect do a person's values have on her or his physical, mental/emotional, and social health?

12. **Explain** Discuss the role that taking responsibility for your actions plays in achieving a high level of wellness.

Your Action Plan

To achieve a high level of wellness, it is important to assess your own health habits. You have begun that work in creating a personal wellness contract. Now it is time to extend your work.

Step 1 Review the journal entries that you created throughout Chapter 1. Summarize your entries, highlighting points that will help you strengthen your personal wellness contract.

Step 2 Based on your summary, write a thoughtful letter to yourself, describing what you need to work on.

Use the letter to make a weekly schedule. Provide time, each day of the week, to achieve the steps in your personal wellness contract. When you feel you have achieved a goal, check it off and reward yourself for what you have accomplished. Enjoy a movie or spend some time just doing what you want.

In Your Home and Community

1. **Personal Health** Select one family member or friend as a wellness partner. Using your own personal wellness contract as a model, encourage your partner to create a similar overall plan and daily schedule. Set aside time to work on your plans together.

2. **Community Resources** Conduct research on one health-related group in your community. Through a telephone interview, find out how that group promotes wellness in your community. Report on your research in your class.

Building Your Portfolio

1. **List of Health Tips** Create a list of Top Ten Tips for Achieving Wellness. Be sure that the tips cover the three aspects of health and that they represent what you feel are the most important highlights. Add the list to your portfolio.

2. **Profile** Write a profile for an imaginary person—The Healthiest Person Alive. Describe his or her qualities in ways that show how the individual has achieved a superior level of wellness. Add the description to your portfolio.

3. **Personal Assessment** Look through all the activities and projects you did for this chapter. Choose one or two that you would like to include in your portfolio.

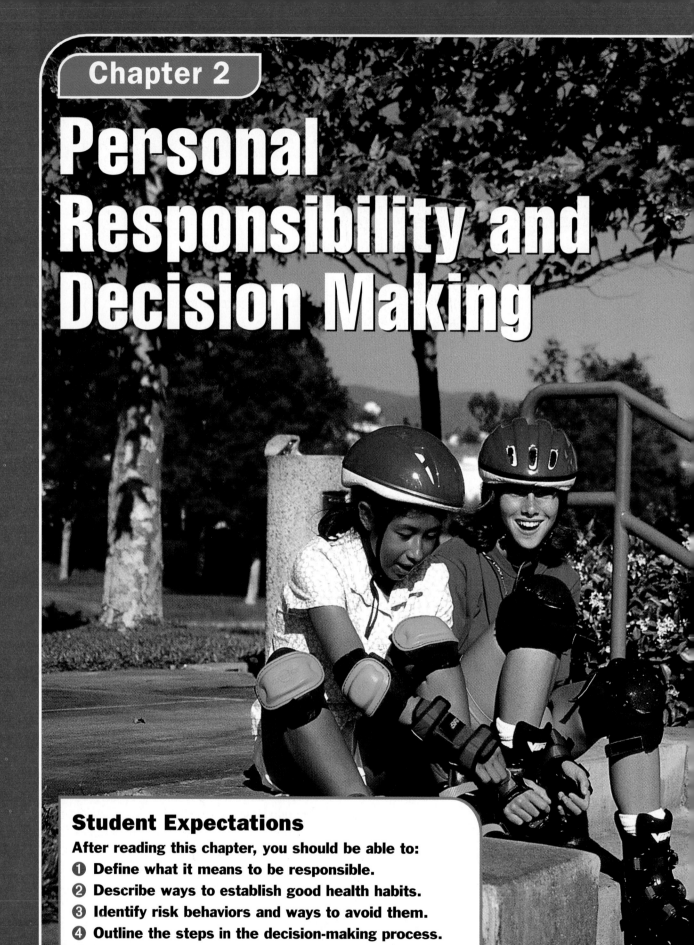

Personal Responsibility and Decision Making

Student Expectations

After reading this chapter, you should be able to:

1. Define what it means to be responsible.
2. Describe ways to establish good health habits.
3. Identify risk behaviors and ways to avoid them.
4. Outline the steps in the decision-making process.
5. Explain the process of setting goals.

Melissa: Come on, David. Put on your helmet and let's get going. I have to be home for dinner at six, and I want to have lots of time for skating.

David: How can you two wear these helmets? I think I'll just leave mine off. I feel like such a dork in it.

Kendra: You'll look like a bigger dork if you fall and smash your head on the pavement!

Melissa: Yeah, David. My cousin wasn't wearing a helmet when she fell off her bike. She hit her head really hard and had to stay in the hospital for a whole week. The doctor said she was lucky to be alive.

David: All right, I'll wear it, but it's such a pain to put on all of this safety gear.

Kendra: Just think of it as a habit like brushing your teeth or wearing a seat belt. Pretty soon you'll just do it without even thinking!

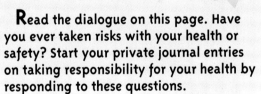

in your journal

Read the dialogue on this page. Have you ever taken risks with your health or safety? Start your private journal entries on taking responsibility for your health by responding to these questions.

▶ How would you have convinced David to wear his helmet?

▶ What choices have you made that show that you take responsibility for your own health?

▶ How do your health decisions affect your friends and family members?

When you reach the end of the chapter, you will use your journal entries to make an action plan.

Taking Responsibility for Your Actions

This lesson will help you find answers to questions that teens often ask about showing responsibility. For example:

▶ **What does it mean to be responsible?**

▶ **What responsibilities do I have for my own health?**

▶ **What responsibilities do I have for the health of others?**

Words to Know

responsibility
consequences

Being Responsible

Do you think you are a responsible person? What does it really mean to be responsible? **Responsibility** is *the ability to make choices and to accept the results of those choices.* One aspect of being responsible involves living up to what is expected of you. For example, at home you may be expected to keep your room clean, wash the dishes, or help care for a younger brother or sister. At school you are expected to participate in class and turn in your homework on time. Showing responsibility also means helping others and being dependable and reliable.

As you grow up, you take on greater responsibility. You also gain more freedom. You have probably noticed that people expect more of you now than they did a few years ago. With this added responsibility usually comes greater freedom and the opportunity to make your own decisions. For example, your parents probably expect you to keep track of your own school assignments, but they may also allow you to make more of your own decisions about clothing purchases. They may expect you to be responsible for the way your friends behave when they are at your home, but they may also allow you to stay at home without supervision for longer periods than before.

It is easier to act responsibly when you believe that your efforts can make a difference. For example, suppose that you are upset with a decision your parents have made. You might choose to talk calmly with them instead of getting angry and slamming the door. You will be more likely to make this decision if you believe that talking will help them to understand your point of view. In many parts of your life, recognizing the benefits of responsible action will help you choose positive behavior.

Sometimes you can see the positive results of your actions right away.

Responsibility for Your Own Health

As a teen, you have an important responsibility: your own health. Accepting this responsibility means that you will make decisions that will promote your good health. These decisions involve

- your physical health.
- your habits.
- the activities in which you participate.
- your mental and emotional health.
- your social health.

Healthful decisions will promote your overall wellness. Making these decisions shows that you take your own health seriously. With a high level of wellness, you will be able to make positive contributions to your family, friends, and community.

Making Positive Choices

To be responsible, you need to make positive choices. Every day you are presented with many options. Some decisions, such as what to eat for lunch, may seem routine. You know that other decisions, such as choosing not to smoke cigarettes, will have lifelong benefits. Whether they are large or small, however, all choices that affect your health are important.

As a teen, you can make wise choices that will have a positive effect on many areas of your health. Five of these areas are shown in **Figure 2.1.** In each of these areas, you will make better choices if you seek reliable information. For example, consider choices about diet. You could read a book on nutrition, search the Internet for nutritional information, or take an after-school class on preparing healthful snack foods. Applying what you learn to your everyday eating habits will help you stay healthier.

*inter*NET
CONNECTION
Check cyberspace for ideas on how to manage habits, risks, and goals responsibly.
http://www.glencoe.com/sec/health

Figure 2.1
Making Healthful Choices

Can you think of other areas in which you could make positive health choices?

Sleep

Hygiene

Prevention/ Risk Protection

Exercise

Diet

Knowing and Using Your Abilities

Another way in which you can take responsibility for your health is to use your abilities to their best advantage. Let's say, for example, that you often help prepare meals for your family. You can use your cooking ability to make sure that the meals taste good and are nutritious. If you are good at communicating, you can use this ability to join a peer counseling program. If you are naturally athletic, you can use this ability to teach younger neighbors specific sports skills.

How do you know what your abilities are? Think about the activities that you enjoy. Which ones do you think you are best at? Which ones do you receive compliments on? Ask family members and friends for their opinions. In what areas do they think you are skillful?

In addition to using your own abilities, you can also make use of the abilities of others. Everyone needs help and encouragement from other people. You have access to many people who can assist you. Look to the following people for advice, answers to questions, and help in managing aspects of your health:

- Family members—parents, grandparents, aunts and uncles, older brothers and sisters

- Educational leaders—teachers, guidance counselors

- Health care professionals—pediatrician, your family's physician, school nurse, psychologist

- Members of the clergy—priest, minister, rabbi, mullah

- Other trusted adults—neighbors, scout leaders, coaches, friends of the family

LIFE SKILLS
Skills in Leadership

As you get older, you will probably take on more leadership roles. For example, you might head a peer mediation team or help organize a fund-raiser for the American Heart Association. Skills in leadership will help you do these jobs effectively. What are the qualities of a good leader? Here are five key leadership skills:

▶ **Ability to communicate clearly.** Effective leaders make clear what is needed and how it might be done. Remember, however, that good communication involves listening as well as speaking.

▶ **Ability to identify the strengths of others.** Effective leaders understand that every person is different. They recognize what each person can contribute and work to encourage all.

▶ **Ability to be assertive.** Effective leaders are assertive—they stand up for themselves in a respectful way. Assertive people express their feelings politely, but without apologizing.

▶ **Ability to solve problems.** Good leaders look for solutions to problems. They search for solutions that will satisfy as many people as possible.

Responsibility for the Health of Others

Besides being responsible for your own health, you also have a responsibility for the health and well-being of others. Many of your actions and the choices you make affect other people. You might think of any action you take as a stone skipping across a pond. This concept is illustrated in **Figure 2.2.**

Figure 2.2
Actions Have Effects

Your actions may affect the health of others. Those effects may in turn create additional effects. Think about the following example.

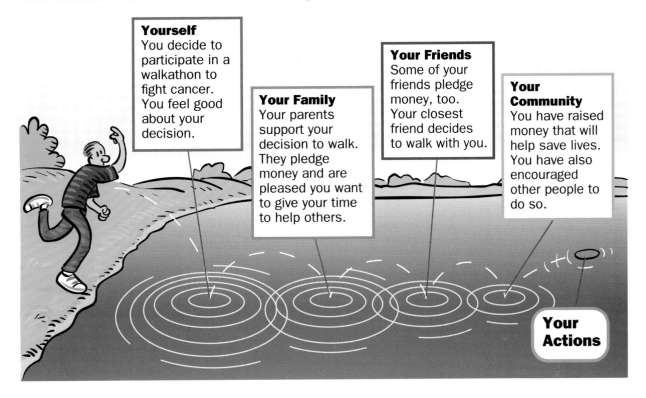

Yourself
You decide to participate in a walkathon to fight cancer. You feel good about your decision.

Your Family
Your parents support your decision to walk. They pledge money and are pleased you want to give your time to help others.

Your Friends
Some of your friends pledge money, too. Your closest friend decides to walk with you.

Your Community
You have raised money that will help save lives. You have also encouraged other people to do so.

Your Actions

▶ **Ability to control emotions.** Good leaders can communicate their feelings calmly. Everyone feels strong emotions such as fear and anger, but effective leaders are able to control the way they express these emotions.

Follow-up Activity

Identify a health-related activity that might be accomplished in your school or community. Write a short story about a person who takes a leadership role in that type of activity. Show how the main character displays at least three of the skills described in this feature.

What's Luck Got to Do with It?

Can you make your own luck? Psychologists believe that there is some truth in this idea. People who believe that bad things "just happen" to them, for example, are less likely to make an effort to improve their lives. One way to make your own luck is to learn from experience. If, for example, you seem to be involved in many arguments, stop and think about why this might be happening. Is it bad luck, or are you taking unnecessary chances—for example, by stopping to watch or take sides in a fight between classmates? By taking action to protect yourself, you may change your luck.

Living with Consequences

As you have just seen, your actions have effects on both yourself and others. Even when choices are made without thinking, they have **consequences,** which are *the effects or results of actions.* Consider Ryan's story. Ryan was expected to mow the lawn on Saturday. He was playing basketball at a friend's house, however, and forgot. Ryan's brother, Scott, got stuck mowing the lawn instead. Ryan's parents decided that he would have to take over one of Scott's responsibilities, which was to baby-sit their younger sister on Sunday. As a result, Ryan wasn't able to play in his softball game. His teammates had to find a last-minute replacement for him. Ryan's action (forgetting to mow the lawn) had consequences that affected several people. These people included Ryan, his brother, his parents, his sister, and his softball teammates.

Consequences may be positive or negative. In some cases, the same action can have both positive *and* negative consequences. Suppose that you and your friend both tried out for the lead role in the school play. Your friend gets the part—a positive consequence for her. You are happy for her (a positive consequence), but you are also personally disappointed (a negative consequence).

Accepting the consequences of your actions is an important part of becoming an adult. Being responsible involves both enjoying the positive consequences of your actions and accepting the negative ones. For example:

- Taking responsibility allows you to take credit for a positive outcome, but it also means that you may have to take the blame for a negative one.

- Taking responsibility means that you can be proud when you live up to your ideals, but that you will feel disappointment when you do not.

- Taking responsibility means that you can feel good when you make a friend happy, but that you will feel sad when you disappoint someone.

One of the benefits of taking responsibility is that it allows you to enjoy the positive feelings that come with success.

Factors You Can't Control

No matter how responsible you are, some things are beyond your control. Your heredity and your environment may be such factors. You may have a tendency toward certain diseases because of your heredity. Your environment may contain pollution or be prone to tornadoes. In addition, other people's decisions, actions, and errors are generally beyond your control.

Becoming a mature adult involves recognizing all that you can accomplish. It also includes realizing that you cannot control everything. Luck and chance, however, are not the deciding factors in your life. You can manage your life by following these rules:

- **Be careful.** First, do all you can to protect yourself against illness and accidents. Don't take unnecessary chances. For example, wear a bike helmet, practice good hygiene, and never drive with someone who has been drinking.

- **Be prepared.** If you know how to handle emergencies, you will be better able to deal with them if they occur. Know what to do if you or another person should become ill or experience an injury.

Taking a class in first aid is one way to show responsibility for yourself and others.

Review

Lesson 1

Using complete sentences, answer the following questions on a separate sheet of paper.

Reviewing Terms and Facts

1. **Vocabulary**   Define the term *responsibility*. Give three examples of responsibilities that a teen might have at home.

2. **List**   Name five areas of health in which you can make positive choices.

3. **Vocabulary**   Explain the meaning of the term *consequences*. Then use the term in an original sentence.

4. **Identify**   List three factors over which you do not have control.

Thinking Critically

5. **Explain**   Describe a situation in which you saw positive consequences of an action you took.

6. **Evaluate**   Suppose that you decide to join a soccer team. You will have practice several times a week and games on the weekends. Outline the possible positive and negative consequences of your decision.

Applying Health Concepts

7. **Health of Others**   Make a poster that shows ways in which teens can make wise choices about their own health. Include at least one example from each of the following areas: physical health, habits, activities, mental and emotional health, and social health.

Recognizing and Managing Habits

This lesson will help you find answers to questions that teens often ask about personal habits. For example:

▶ **What is a habit?**
▶ **How can I establish good health habits?**
▶ **How can I change harmful habits?**

Words to Know

habit
life-threatening
life-altering

What Is a Habit?

A **habit** is *a pattern of behavior repeated frequently enough to be performed almost without thinking.* Everyone has habits. Some habits, such as hair twirling or finger tapping, are minor and do not affect your health. Others, such as daily bathing and regular exercise, form an important part of the responsible lifestyle that you create for yourself.

Because habits are such a normal part of your day-to-day life, you may not even be aware of them. Habits, however, grow in strength with frequent repetition. Good habits that are formed early in life can have lifelong benefits. Making a habit of eating plenty of fruits and vegetables, for example, can help you stay well and even help prevent certain diseases. On the other hand, harmful habits formed early in life can be difficult to change. That's why it is a good idea to start thinking about your habits now.

Although you may not realize it, your habits affect other people as well. Your harmless finger tapping may annoy a classmate. Suppose, on the other hand, that you make it a habit to be supportive of your friends or to greet people in a friendly manner. This behavior helps you socially because it enables you to be a good friend. It also helps other people by making them feel comfortable and relaxed.

Greeting people in a friendly manner is a good habit to form.

Forming Healthful Habits

The key to establishing good health habits is repetition. The more often you perform an action, the more natural it will seem. Soon the action will become a part of your everyday life—something you don't even think about anymore. **Figure 2.3** illustrates how to form a healthful habit, such as exercising for 20 minutes each day.

Figure 2.3
Developing a Habit
Here are the steps you can take to form a healthful habit.

1 Choosing
The first step is to decide what you want to achieve. Having a clear idea of the end result you want will help you reach it. Wanting to be in better shape or to become skilled at a sport are examples of good goals.

2 Remembering
At first, you may have to make a real effort just to remember to perform the action. Reminders from parents, teachers, and friends can be helpful. Making your own reminder list or schedule can also keep you on target.

3 Performing
The next step is to make an effort to do a good job of performing the action. This can take time and energy. You need to make a commitment to yourself to stick with it.

5 Growing
Your overall feeling of well-being increases. In addition, your confidence grows because you know that you are in control of this area of your health.

4 Repeating
As time passes, you get used to remembering and performing the action. It becomes more and more natural. You may begin to plan around your exercise sessions. You know that you are doing something good for your health.

Changing Harmful Habits

Everyone has habits that they would like to break. Perhaps you interrupt people when they are talking, or you put off doing your homework until the last minute. Although these behaviors may be bothersome to you or to others, they are not life-threatening. A **life-threatening** habit is one that *may cause death*. Riding in a car without fastening your seat belt is a life-threatening habit. Using tobacco, drinking alcohol, and taking other drugs are also life-threatening habits. They can also become addictions. With an addiction, a person develops a physical or psychological need for a substance.

It is important to learn how to break habits that may threaten your health or life. If you have developed habits that could become a serious problem, such as smoking, drinking, or using drugs, you should talk to a parent or another trusted adult. It is very difficult to break this type of habit on your own. You can, however, work toward changing other, less serious behaviors. Here are some tips to follow.

- **Identify the habit.** If you don't know what your harmful habits might be, ask a family member or friend. If you have more than one harmful habit, choose the one that you would most like to change. Trying to change all of your habits at once may cause you to become frustrated and give up.

- **Analyze the habit.** Think about your habit. Why do you do it? When do you do it? Try to change the cause of the behavior. Maybe you don't wear your bicycle helmet because you are always in a rush. If you start allowing yourself a few extra minutes, you will have time to put on your helmet.

Getting Accustomed ACTIVITY!

A custom is similar to a habit, except that it is usually associated with a cultural group. In the United States, for example, it is common to shake hands when you are introduced to a person. In other societies, such as Japan, the custom is to bow.

Look in a reference source to find out about the customs of other cultures that affect health. Share your findings with the class.

HEALTH LAB

The Effects of Repetition

*I*ntroduction: The more often you perform a task, the easier it is to do. The principles demonstrated in this simple experiment can be applied to forming and practicing healthful habits.

Objective: Work with a partner to repeat a difficult task until it becomes easier. In this way, you will see how habits can be formed.

Materials and Method: Each set of partners will need a stopwatch or a watch with a second hand, sheets of unlined paper, pencils, and a mirror. On separate sheets of paper, each of you should draw a simple maze using parallel lines.

Photocopy or trace each maze on four more sheets of paper so that each partner has five copies of the same maze.

Put one copy of your maze on a desk. Hold a small mirror in front of the maze while your partner sits opposite you. Experiment with tilting the mirror until your partner can see the maze in the mirror. He or she should then solve the maze while looking at the mirror image only. (Make sure that the person is not looking down at the maze itself.) Use the stopwatch or watch to see how long it takes your partner to trace the maze correctly with a pencil.

- **Consider the future.** Ask yourself this question: Could this habit eventually hurt me or someone else? Thinking about the possible consequences may help you realize the importance of kicking the habit now.

- **Set goals.** Set a short-term goal. You might decide, for example, that you will eat a healthful breakfast every morning. At the end of several weeks, reward yourself if you have reached your goal. As each week goes by, it will be easier to follow your new, healthful habit.

- **Ask for help.** Perhaps you can ask a friend to give you a secret signal when she sees you biting your nails. Maybe your parents can avoid keeping candy in the house, so that you will not be tempted to eat it. Allow others to offer their encouragement.

- **Find a substitute behavior.** If you usually eat chips or ice cream when you are doing homework, try snacking on apple slices or carrot sticks instead. Over time, you will associate these more healthful foods with homework time.

- **Be patient.** Keep in mind that you have probably been practicing your harmful habit for awhile. It will take time to break the habit. If you slip back into an old behavior, don't be too hard on yourself. Just get back on track and try not to slip again!

Finding a substitute activity can help you form a new, more healthful habit.

Repeat the test with the other four copies of the maze, keeping track of the time it takes to complete each test. Then switch places so that you are completing your partner's maze while he or she is holding the mirror and timing you.

Observations and Analysis:
After you and your partner have completed your tests, discuss your findings with the class. Was the maze easier to finish after you had done it several times? Did you complete it faster each time? What does this experiment suggest to you about how repetition can help you establish good habits?

Going Too Far

Even good habits can become harmful. People sometimes become too strongly focused on a certain behavior. For example, a person may be overly concerned with cleanliness and germs. That person might wash his hands over and over again or take many showers in one day. Another person may become so worried about getting cavities that she brushes her teeth until her gums bleed. A focus that is normal for one teen may become harmful for another. For instance, teens are typically concerned about their looks. Sometimes, however, a teen becomes so anxious about weight loss and exercise that little else seems important. Such an intense focus can lead to serious health problems.

Don't be afraid to ask for help in breaking a habit that you think may be taking over your life. A counselor will listen to your concerns and be ready to help.

Actions that begin as habits sometimes take control of a person. The individual may not feel able to change the habit. In these cases, the habit can become **life-altering,** or *capable of changing a person's day-to-day existence.* If you think that you or a friend might have a life-altering habit, it is best to talk to a parent or another trusted adult. In many cases, professional help is needed to break the habit.

Lesson 2 Review

Using complete sentences, answer the following questions on a separate sheet of paper.

Reviewing Terms and Facts

1. **Give Examples**   List two examples of healthful habits and two examples of harmful habits.

2. **Identify**   List the five steps to developing a healthful habit.

3. **List**   Identify five tips for changing a harmful habit.

4. **Vocabulary**   Explain the difference between *life-altering* and *life-threatening* habits.

Thinking Critically

5. **Hypothesize**   Why might it be a good idea to examine your own habits?

6. **Analyze**   What kinds of harmful habits do you think are most common among people your age? Choose two of these habits and explain how they could negatively influence a person's future health.

Applying Health Concepts

7. **Consumer Health**   Examine products (in a store or in magazine advertisements) that claim to help people stop harmful habits such as nail biting or overeating. Are the claims believable? How do the products say they will work? Do you think that the products could be harmful? Write a short report about what you have found.

Health Risks and Your Behavior

This lesson will help you find answers to questions that teens often ask about taking risks. For example:

▶ **What is a risk behavior?**

▶ **How do I know if something is really a risk?**

▶ **What are cumulative risks?**

▶ **How can I avoid unnecessary risk behaviors?**

Recognizing Risks

Risks—the chances that something harmful may happen—come in many forms. You are probably aware of the risks associated with using alcohol and other drugs. Did you know, however, that you also create health risks by eating foods that are high in fats and by not getting enough exercise? An important part of taking responsibility for your health is avoiding risk behaviors. As you learned in Chapter 1, a risk behavior is an action or choice that may cause injury or harm to you or to others. Harmful habits usually include several risk behaviors.

Health risks may have a variety of consequences. Some consequences affect only you and may not be especially dangerous. If you skip breakfast one morning, for example, you will probably feel hungry and have little energy. However, your actions will most likely not have major consequences for you or anyone else. Some risk behaviors, on the other hand, carry very undesirable consequences. These consequences may include serious injury and **mortality** (mor·TA·luh·tee), or *death.*

Consider Ben's story. One of his friends invited him to go in-line skating. Ben was showing off, and he lost his balance and shattered several bones in his wrist. Because of his risk behavior, Ben suffered serious consequences:

■ **Physical consequences.** Ben now has a badly broken wrist. It was painful when it occurred and for some time afterward. He will have to wear a cast for many weeks.

You should pay attention to warnings that tell you about how to avoid risk behaviors.

in your journal

Have you ever chosen to engage in a risky recreational activity? Describe the risk in your journal. Did the risk have physical, academic, social, or financial consequences? Explain how you could avoid taking that risk in the future.

■ **Social consequences.** Ben will have to sit out the rest of the basketball season. His team, on which he plays forward, is disappointed.

■ **Mental and emotional consequences.** Ben feels depressed about not playing basketball and sorry about disappointing his team. He feels foolish about showing off.

■ **Academic consequences.** Ben had to take several days off from school after he broke his wrist. He did poorly on several tests because of the work he missed.

■ **Financial consequences.** Ben's parents had to pay for expensive medical care. Their insurance covered most costs, but some were not covered.

In addition, some risks are illegal. Suppose, for example, that a person climbs over a fence to get into a construction site. That person is taking a health risk by being in a dangerous area. He or she is also committing a crime by breaking into private property. Legal consequences may result.

Who's Taking Chances?

Are teens taking risks? The answer seems to be yes. A survey sponsored by the Centers for Disease Control (CDC) asked more than 10,000 high school students about risk behaviors they had engaged in, either at one time or within a specified period preceding the survey. **Figure 2.4** shows some of the results for ninth graders—the youngest group of students surveyed.

Figure 2.4
Youth Risk Behavior, 1995

These graphs show the percentage of ninth graders surveyed who had engaged in these risk behaviors. How could taking each of these risks harm a person's health?

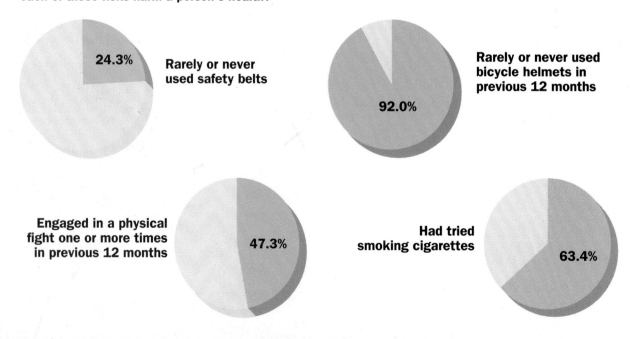

24.3% Rarely or never used safety belts

92.0% Rarely or never used bicycle helmets in previous 12 months

Engaged in a physical fight one or more times in previous 12 months 47.3%

Had tried smoking cigarettes 63.4%

Is It Really a Risk?

Why do teens take risks? Some young people take risks because they believe that nothing bad can happen to them. Others may question whether certain actions are really risks. They may believe, for example, that people who are involved in accidents are just unlucky. This idea is **subjective,** which means that it *comes from a person's own views and beliefs, not necessarily from facts.*

When considering risks, it is much better to use **objective** information, which is *based on facts.* The following is an example of subjective versus objective thinking.

■ Subjective (involving a person's own views): "Lots of people smoke cigarettes, so how can it be harmful?"

■ Objective (based on facts): "Smokers are ten times more likely to get lung cancer than nonsmokers."

Objective information can help you act responsibly so that you can prevent many injuries and illnesses. Looking out for **hazards,** or *potential sources of danger,* is a good habit to develop. Hazards occur in many different forms, including high levels of dietary fat, the violent behavior of others, and alcohol use. If you are aware of hazards, you can take precautions against them. A **precaution** is *an action taken to avoid danger.*

Some hazards or risk factors by themselves may not seem very dangerous. If, for example, your blood pressure is a little high, you may not be especially worried about your health. However, if you have high blood pressure and you are overweight, your risk for heart disease increases. If you don't get much exercise, your risk increases even more. The greater the number of risk factors you have, the more likely you will be to develop a particular disease.

Groups of risks like the ones just mentioned are called **cumulative** (KYOO·myuh·luh·tiv) **risks.** These are *related risks that increase in effect with each added risk.* Cumulative risks are associated with injuries as well as diseases. Riding a bicycle without a helmet, for example, is *one* risk factor. If you are also riding on a busy street (second risk factor), and it is raining (third risk factor), your chance of serious injury increases greatly.

| What potential hazards and health risks are obvious in this picture?

Avoiding Risks

The best way to prevent the problems associated with risks is to act safely and practice healthful habits. For example, although riding in a car can be risky, choosing to ride with a responsible driver and to wear a seat belt reduces many of those risks. Although walking home from school could put you at risk of physical attack, choosing a safe route and walking with a friend makes such problems much less likely. **Figure 2.5** presents other ways to avoid risks. Getting in the habit of asking yourself these questions will help you make decisions that are good for your health.

Figure 2.5
How to Avoid Risks

Think of each of these attitudes and actions as a piece of armor to help protect you against risks that could threaten your health and your life.

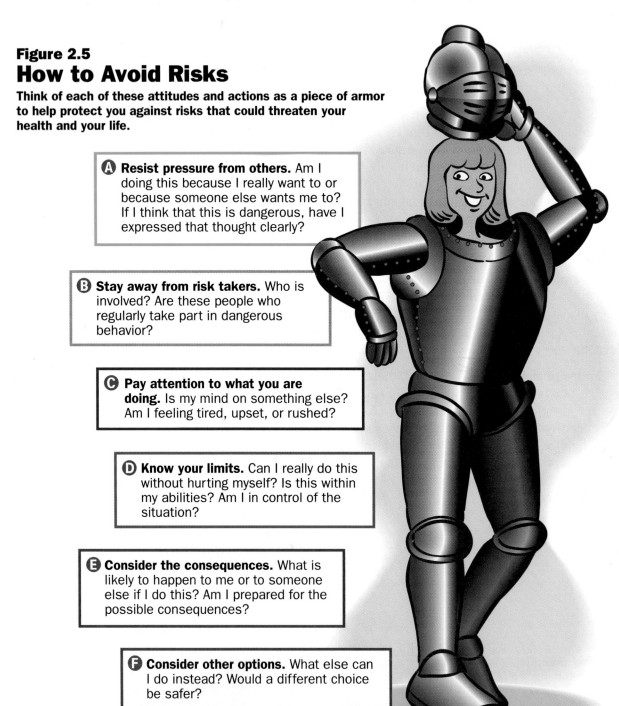

Ⓐ Resist pressure from others. Am I doing this because I really want to or because someone else wants me to? If I think that this is dangerous, have I expressed that thought clearly?

Ⓑ Stay away from risk takers. Who is involved? Are these people who regularly take part in dangerous behavior?

Ⓒ Pay attention to what you are doing. Is my mind on something else? Am I feeling tired, upset, or rushed?

Ⓓ Know your limits. Can I really do this without hurting myself? Is this within my abilities? Am I in control of the situation?

Ⓔ Consider the consequences. What is likely to happen to me or to someone else if I do this? Am I prepared for the possible consequences?

Ⓕ Consider other options. What else can I do instead? Would a different choice be safer?

Managing Your Life

Part of being responsible means taking an active role in managing your own health. You can still have fun and enjoy life while considering your own safety and the safety of others. After all, most accidents and injuries don't "just happen," and they are not caused by luck or fate. If you act responsibly and avoid risks, you can prevent most injuries. By practicing good health habits, you can prevent many illnesses.

in your journal

Think about the ways to avoid risks that you learned in this lesson. In your journal, make a list of the health and safety rules that you already follow. Then make a list of the risk behaviors that you would like to change. Describe how you will change just one of these behaviors.

Learning how to play a sport correctly is one way to decrease risks.

Review
Lesson 3

Using complete sentences, answer the following questions on a separate sheet of paper.

Reviewing Terms and Facts

1. **Identify**   List five types of consequences that may result from risk behavior.

2. **Compare**   What is the difference between *subjective* and *objective* information about risks?

3. **Vocabulary**   What is the difference between a *hazard* and a *precaution?* Give one example of each.

4. **Vocabulary**   Define the term *cumulative risks.* Then give an example of cumulative risks.

5. **Recall**   Identify four ways to avoid risks.

Thinking Critically

6. **Predict**   What might the consequences be if a person went for a boat ride and did not wear a life jacket?

7. **Describe**   How do risk factors become cumulative risks?

Applying Health Concepts

8. **Growth and Development**   With one of your classmates, plan a skit for younger children. Show them how they can reduce risks while doing the following: crossing the street, bicycling, and riding in a car.

TEEN HEALTH DIGEST

Sports and Recreation
A Camp for Kids

Andrea Jaeger became a professional tennis player when she was only 14 years old. In the early 1980s, she was one of the world's top ten female players. After 1984, however, a shoulder injury caused Jaeger's tennis game to decline.

In 1989, Jaeger was hit by a drunk driver. While recovering from the accident, she had time to think about her life. She realized that visiting sick children had always been rewarding to her. That was when Jaeger decided to start the Kids' Stuff Foundation. Through it, she opened a camp for children who have life-threatening illnesses.

Each year, 100 children spend a week at

the camp in Aspen, Colorado. They take part in such activities as horseback riding, white-water rafting, and crafts. At camp, the kids can forget about their problems and just have fun. Making the children happy makes Andrea Jaeger happy, too.

Teens Making a Difference

Y.O.U.T.H. Matters

Helping others is important to Lenti Smith. At an early age, this teen realized that she could do more with an organization than she could by herself. Smith and some friends started Youth Organization Unites to Help (Y.O.U.T.H.).

Y.O.U.T.H has sponsored many projects to help others. The group has visited elderly people in nursing homes and recorded books on tape for people who are visually impaired. Group members have also collected canned goods for hurricane victims and picked up litter.

Try This: *List some projects in your community that could be done by a group. Share your ideas with your class, and consider making one a class project.*

HEALTH UPDATE

Is Your Heart at Risk?

Do you enjoy foods such as fast-food cheeseburgers and milkshakes? If you think that you don't have to worry about your diet until you get older, think again. Recent studies show that young people with diets high in fatty foods increase their risk of heart disease in adulthood. Changing bad eating habits now can help you lead a longer and healthier life.

Try This:

Divide a sheet of paper into two columns. In the first, list fatty foods that you like, such as ice cream. In the second, list more healthful choices, such as nonfat frozen yogurt.

CON$UMER FOCU$

Are Air Bags Safe?

Q. I've been hearing news reports about the dangers of car air bags. Aren't air bags supposed to save lives?

A. Between 1986 and 1996, air bags saved more than 1,600 lives. However, air bags have also caused some injuries and deaths. Most of the problems occurred when people were not wearing seat belts and when small children were in the front seat. To stay safe, follow these rules when riding in a car.

- *Always* wear your seat belt.
- Whenever possible, sit in the back.
- If you must sit in the front, push the seat back as far as you possibly can.
- Make sure that children aged 12 and under sit in the back. Small children should be in safety seats.

4 Making Responsible Decisions

This lesson will help you find answers to questions that teens often ask about decision making. For example:

▶ **What kinds of decisions affect my health?**

▶ **How do my values affect my decisions?**

▶ **What are the steps in the decision-making process?**

Words to Know

decision making
criteria

Teen Issues

Silent Decisions, ACTIVITY! Poor Decisions

In a recent antidrug campaign aimed at parents of teens, this message was used: Silence is acceptance. What do you think is meant by this? Can silence be a type of decision—one you have not made very well? For instance, suppose that several of your friends are making fun of another student. You don't join in, but you don't stop them, either. How does this example illustrate the meaning of "Silence is acceptance"? Write a paragraph explaining your answer, and tell how the decision-making process could have helped you make a better decision.

Facing Decisions

Although you may not even realize it, you use decision-making skills every day. **Decision making** is *the process of making a choice or finding a solution.* You make decisions in every area of your life—your health, family, friends, school, activities, and so on. The decisions you make can expose you or others to risks, or they can decrease the risk of accident or injury. Learning how to make wise decisions is part of becoming a responsible adult.

Minor and Major Decisions

Many of the decisions you make are simple, and you make them almost automatically. These are minor decisions. They often involve only you, and they have few possible negative consequences. Minor decisions might include what to wear or whether to walk or ride your bike to school.

From time to time, you will be faced with major decisions. Major decisions in your future might include choices about your education or whether you will enter military service. These kinds of major decisions require serious thought and should be made in an orderly way.

When making any decision, you should always consider the possible consequences, or results of your actions. On the surface, for example, choosing whether or not to wear a bicycle helmet may seem like a minor decision. Yet it involves major health risks and consequences. Because you risk serious injury or even death by not wearing a helmet, this choice is an important one.

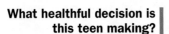

What healthful decision is this teen making?

Thinking About Values

When making decisions, you will want to consider your values, or beliefs. Values such as honesty and self-respect are an important part of your personal identity and self-image. If you make a choice that goes against your values, your actions will have a negative effect on your self-image. On the other hand, making decisions based on your values will help you feel good about yourself.

For example, keeping promises and being honest are important values. Suppose that you have promised your parents that you will attend all of your scheduled track practices. One day, however, a couple of your friends tell you about their plans to meet at one person's house after school. They ask you to come along. In order to go, you would have to miss practice. When you point this out, one friend suggests that you could just tell your parents that you went to the friend's home *after* track practice. By following this advice, you would go against your own values. You would probably feel guilty. Following your values—telling your friends that you'll come along another day—will make you feel good about keeping your promises.

Where do values come from? People develop values from many sources:

- **Family.** You learn values from your parents, grandparents, older brothers and sisters, and other relatives. If your family values physical fitness, for example, you will probably also value it.

- **Religious beliefs.** Some of your values, especially about what is right and wrong, may be based on your religious beliefs.

- **Cultural heritage and the society in which you live.** You may share values with other members of the cultural group to which you belong. In addition, you may share the values of people in your society. Many Americans share a belief in democracy and personal freedom.

- **Personal experiences.** All the places where you have lived, the people you have known, and the things you have accomplished influence your values.

Cultural Connections

Your Values and You ACTIVITY!

An important part of the decision-making process is considering your values. Some of your values come from your cultural heritage. Talk to your parents or other relatives about your family's cultural heritage. Find out more about customs and values from your cultural background by looking in reference books.

Your choice of profession may be based on what is important to you. Many physicians chose medicine because they value helping others.

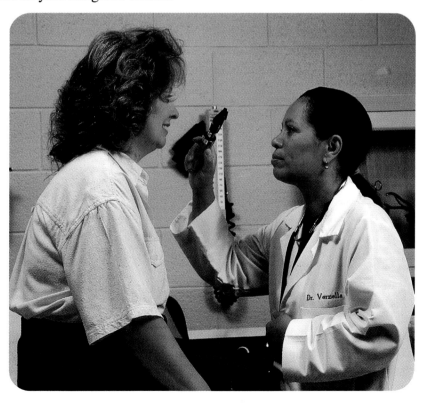

Making Choices

ACTIVITY!

Choose a story you have read in language arts class or a television drama or movie you have seen recently. Think about one character in that story, drama, or film who was faced with an important decision. How did that person make a choice? Did he or she carefully consider the options, or was the decision made on impulse? What were the consequences of the choice? Write several paragraphs describing the choice you would have made if faced with the same decision.

Warnings are put up in order to protect your health and safety. What risks might these teens be taking by ignoring this warning?

in your journal

List a decision you might make in the next month—to attend a particular party or to join a sports team, for example. Then list at least three values that might be used as criteria in your decision-making process. Tell which value or values will be most important to you in making this decision.

Applying Criteria

Your values provide you with **criteria** (kry·TIR·ee·uh), or *standards on which to base your decisions*. When making a decision, you can use these criteria to evaluate the situation. After you make a choice, you can also use your criteria to evaluate the outcome of your decision.

Consider this situation. You place a high value on your health and safety. You also try to do what is right. Some of your friends want you to go swimming with them in a lake at night. Swimming is prohibited in this lake at night because no lifeguards are on duty. On the basis of your values, you could evaluate the situation by applying the following HELP criteria:

- **H (Healthful).** Might swimming here lead to an injury?

- **E (Ethical).** Something that is ethical is what you consider right, according to your values and morals. Is it right to go swimming here?

- **L (Legal).** Since swimming is prohibited at night, am I breaking the law by swimming here?

- **P (Parent approved).** Would my parents approve of my swimming here?

In this case, using the above criteria to evaluate the situation would help you make the decision not to join your friends—and, in fact, to try to convince them to swim in a safer place or choose another activity.

The Decision-Making Process

The decision-making process doesn't have to be overwhelming. It can be easier if you break it down into the six steps illustrated in **Figure 2.6.** The next time you are faced with a decision, try asking yourself the questions shown in this illustration. Although you will normally use this skill only on major decisions, start practicing with small ones. Then, when you need to make an important choice, you will be familiar with the steps.

Figure 2.6

The Steps of the Decision-Making Process

There are six steps in the decision-making process.

1 **State the Situation**
What is the problem? How did the problem occur? Who is involved? How much time do I have to make my decision?

2 **List the Options**
How could I solve the problem? What are my choices? With whom can I talk about the problem?

3 **Weigh the Possible Outcomes**
What are the consequences of each option? How will my choice affect me both now and in the future? Whom else will it affect, and how?

POSSIBLE OUTCOMES

4 **Consider Your Values**
How does each of my options fit in with my value system? How will my values influence my decision?

5 **Make a Decision and Act**
What choice shall I make? What do I need to do to follow through on my decision?

ACT!

6 **Evaluate the Decision**
What were the consequences of my decision? Did the results turn out as I planned? If I had to do it again, would I make the same choice?

DECISION

Chains of Decisions

In many cases, you will make decisions that lead to other decisions. These chains of decisions are a natural part of life. If you decide to join the basketball team, for example, you may also have to make decisions about other activities. Basketball practice may take place at the same time as your gymnastics lessons. Should you drop gymnastics, or can you take lessons at a different time? Weekend basketball games may conflict with your responsibilities at home. How will you get your chores done? You may have to decide on ways to rearrange your weekend schedule.

With practice, decision making will become easier. The six-step process will help you make wise choices. Every time you successfully make an important decision, you show that you are a mature and responsible individual.

Part of the decision-making process involves balancing family responsibilities with the other things you want to do.

MAKING HEALTHY DECISIONS
Making a Difficult Choice

Justina has been offered a fantastic opportunity. Her aunt is going to Paris, France, on vacation. She would like Justina to come along. Justina has begun taking French this year in middle school and is very excited about the idea of going to Paris.

Unfortunately, the two-week period when her aunt is going to Paris is the same two-week period when she usually goes to summer camp. For the past three years, Justina and her friend Alison have gone to camp together. Alison and Justina were best friends in Indiana, where Justina used to live before her family moved here to Florida.

Justina's parents want to leave the decision about what to do up to Justina. However, she doesn't know what she wants to do. On one hand, she looks forward to camp every year. Most years, the weeks at camp are the best part of her summer. It is the only time that she gets to see Alison anymore. To make it more difficult, Justina knows that Alison is expecting her to go.

On the other hand, a trip to Paris is a once-in-a-lifetime opportunity. Justina will disappoint her aunt and miss out on going if she goes to camp. Justina decides to use the six-step decision-making process to solve her problem:

❶ **State the situation**

❷ **List the options**

❸ **Weigh the possible outcomes**

Using complete sentences, answer the following questions on a separate sheet of paper.

Reviewing Terms and Facts

1. **Give Examples** What are two examples of minor decisions and two examples of major ones?

2. **Identify** List four sources from which people get their values.

3. **Vocabulary** Define the term *criteria.* Then use it in an original sentence.

4. **List** What are the six steps of the decision-making process?

Thinking Critically

5. **Explain** Why should you think about your values before making a major decision?

6. **Predict** What might the consequences be of deciding not to study for a test?

7. **Analyze** Which of the six steps in the decision-making process do you think is most important? Explain your answer.

Applying Health Concepts

8. **Health of Others** Think about how you might adapt the decision-making model for younger children, ages nine to ten. Make a colorful poster that could help them work through a similar process, but on a simpler level. Share your poster with your class.

④ **Consider your values**

⑤ **Make a decision and act**

⑥ **Evaluate the decision**

Follow-up Activities

1. Apply the six steps of the decision-making process to Justina's story.

2. What types of values are involved in Justina's decision?

3. With a partner, role-play a scene in which Justina discusses her decision either with Alison or with her aunt. (The discussion should be with whichever person she will have to disappoint.)

5 Setting Goals and Making Action Plans

This lesson will help you find answers to questions that teens often ask about goals and action plans. For example:

▶ **What are the benefits of setting goals?**

▶ **Why do I need both short-term and long-term goals?**

▶ **What is an action plan?**

Words to Know

self-esteem
long-term goal
short-term goal
action plan

? Q&A

Career Goals

Q: My best friend has always liked animals and knows that he wants to be a veterinarian. My career goals seem to change from one week to the next. Is that unusual?

A: Not at all. During the teen years, you are developing your interests, skills, and abilities. As these change, your goals and ambitions change, too. Many people do not make a career choice until after they finish high school or college.

What short-term goal do you think this teen has set for herself?

Why Have Goals?

You may wonder why having goals is important. Goals help give direction to your behavior and a pattern to your decisions. A goal is also one way to measure your success. You can look at goals as milestones on a journey. They allow you to evaluate how far you have traveled and how far you have left to go.

Some goals may be easy to achieve, while others are very challenging. Suppose, for example, that your goal is to improve your grade in science class. Getting an A on one science project may not be a problem for you. Getting an A in science for the whole year, however, may be very difficult. In either case, achieving the goal that you have set for yourself is a rewarding experience.

Goals and Self-Esteem

Merely having goals won't make you reach them automatically. You will have to put in both thought and effort to achieve what you want. When you set a goal, you make a promise to yourself that you will work to reach it. Part of that work involves planning. The rest involves carrying out your plans and overcoming any obstacles that may come along.

Although it may sometimes seem difficult to achieve your goals, your efforts will be worthwhile. Meeting your goals will have a positive effect on your **self-esteem,** or *confidence in yourself.* Knowing that you have reached some goals in the past will help you improve your self-esteem. It will also give you the confidence to try to reach new goals in the future. Suppose, for instance, that you have achieved a goal of learning to control your temper. Next, you might feel ready to work with a peer mediation group to help others work out their disagreements in healthy ways.

Types of Goals

Time is an important element in the process of setting goals. Some goals will take much longer to achieve than others. A **long-term goal** is *a goal that you plan to reach over an extended length of time.* Examples of long-term goals include getting into college or becoming a professional golfer. These goals would take months or even years to achieve. Long-term goals, however, usually mean much more to you than other goals.

Some goals do not take much time. A **short-term goal** is *a goal that you can reach right away.* Examples of short-term goals include writing a book report or cleaning your room. Setting a series of short-term goals is a good way to achieve a long-term goal. If your long-term goal was to save money to go on the eighth-grade class trip, you could follow the steps shown in **Figure 2.7** on the next page.

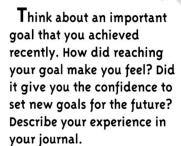

in Your Journal

Think about an important goal that you achieved recently. How did reaching your goal make you feel? Did it give you the confidence to set new goals for the future? Describe your experience in your journal.

Teen Issues

Conflicting Goals

At any given time, you probably have several goals that you would like to achieve. Sometimes you may find that two or more of these goals are in conflict. For example, you may not be able to take both karate and guitar lessons. When this happens, it is helpful to make a list of your goals and number them in order of their importance to you.

You may not reach all of your goals, but every success makes you feel good about yourself.

Figure 2.7
Achieving a Long-Term Goal

Reaching a long-term goal involves setting and meeting many short-term goals. This teen plans to work on her goal over the course of one year.

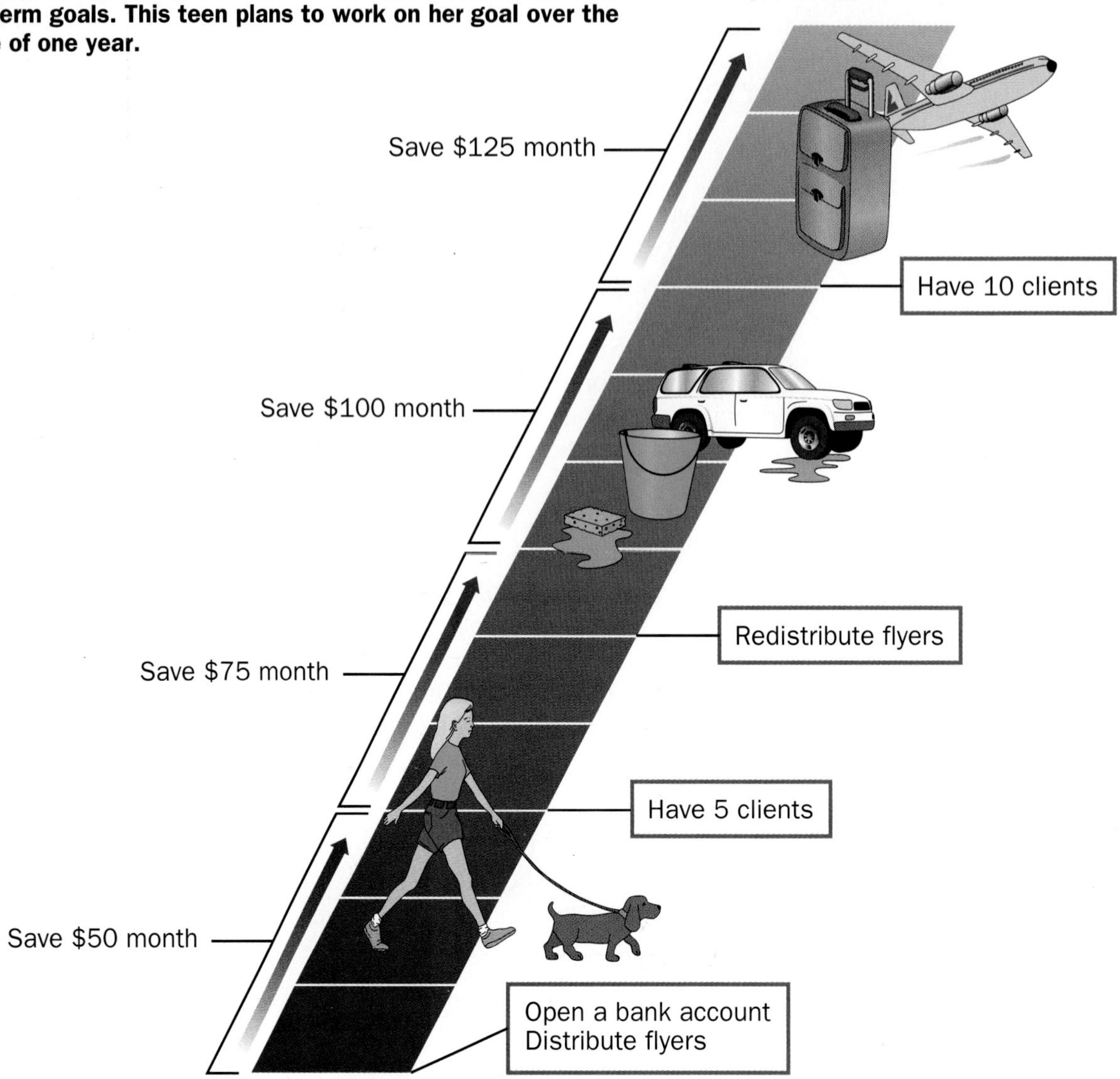

Long-Term Goal: To save enough money to go on the eighth-grade class trip.

Save $125 month

Have 10 clients

Save $100 month

Redistribute flyers

Save $75 month

Have 5 clients

Save $50 month

Open a bank account
Distribute flyers

Start a car-washing and dog-walking service.

Goal, Plans, Action!

Imagine that you are a film director shooting a new movie. The actors are ready, the stage is set, and the cameras are rolling. There's only one problem—there's no script! Everything comes to a standstill because no one knows what to do next. In much the same way that a director needs a script to shoot a movie, you need an action plan to achieve your goals. An **action plan** is *a series of steps for reaching your goal.*

Creating an action plan is the first step you should take after you decide on a goal. Your action plan will help you organize your efforts, manage your time, and achieve the results you want. **Figure 2.8** describes this process.

Figure 2.8

Creating an Action Plan

An action plan is like a script. Just as a script tells film actors what to do next, your action plan will provide step-by-step instructions for achieving your goal.

Step 1 Decide on your goal and write it down.

Step 2 List the steps you will take to reach your goal.

Step 3 Identify sources of help and support.

Step 4 Set a specific time period to reach your goal.

Step 5 Set up checkpoints to see how well you are doing.

Step 6 Reward yourself after you have achieved your goal.

My Action Plan

1 Goal: To be able to run three miles without stopping to walk or rest.

2 (a) I will begin by running/walking 1 mile, working up to 3 miles of running and walking.
(b) First, I will increase the mileage I cover, and then I will concentrate on walking less and running more.

3 Sources of help: my brother and my friend (who will exercise with me).

4 I have eight weeks to work toward my goal.

5 In two weeks: run/walk 2 miles. In four weeks: run/walk 3 miles. In six weeks: run 2 miles; run/walk 1 mile. In eight weeks: run 3 miles without walking or stopping.

6 If I achieve my goal, I will buy myself a video game.

Review

Using complete sentences, answer the following questions on a separate sheet of paper.

Reviewing Terms and Facts

1. **Restate**   What is the purpose of setting goals?

2. **Vocabulary**   Define the term *self-esteem.* Use it in an original sentence.

3. **Identify**   Give examples of two long-term goals and two short-term goals.

4. **List**   Identify the six steps involved in creating an action plan.

Thinking Critically

5. **Predict**   What might happen if you never set specific goals for yourself?

6. **Analyze**   Why is it a good idea to break down a long-term goal into a series of short-term goals?

Applying Health Concepts

7. **Personal Health**   Think of a short-term goal that you would like to achieve. Following the steps to create an action plan, describe how you would go about reaching your goal.

Chapter 2 Review

Chapter Summary

▶ **Lesson 1** Becoming a teen means taking more responsibility for your behavior. The choices you make may have consequences that will affect your own health and the health of other people.

▶ **Lesson 2** Establishing good health habits during the teen years will have benefits that last a lifetime. Harmful habits, on the other hand, can be life-altering or life-threatening.

▶ **Lesson 3** You can protect your health by recognizing risks and avoiding them whenever possible.

▶ **Lesson 4** You are faced with a variety of decisions every day. By using the six steps of the decision-making process, you will be able to make responsible choices.

▶ **Lesson 5** Setting short-term and long-term goals helps give direction to your life. Creating an action plan will help you achieve your goals.

Reviewing Key Terms and Concepts

Using complete sentences, answer the following questions on a separate sheet of paper.

Lesson 1

1. In what areas are you responsible for your own health?

2. Explain ways in which your actions can affect the health of others.

Lesson 2

3. Provide two examples of ways your habits affect other people.

4. Explain the importance of repetition in establishing good health habits.

Lesson 3

5. What is the meaning of the term *mortality?*

6. Give an example of a subjective statement about a risk and an objective statement about the same risk.

Lesson 4

7. What does *decision making* mean?

8. What does it mean to consider possible outcomes when you are making a decision?

Lesson 5

9. What is the difference between a short-term goal and a long-term goal?

10. What is an action plan?

Thinking Critically

Using complete sentences, answer the following questions on a separate sheet of paper.

11. **Analyze** Explain how avoiding risk behaviors is an essential part of taking responsibility for your own health.

12. **Infer** Name some lifelong benefits of developing the habit of exercising on a regular basis.

13. **Synthesize** Describe how you could use the six-step decision-making process to choose a long-term goal.

Your Action Plan

An important part of achieving overall wellness is taking responsibility for your own health.

Step 1 Review your private journal entries for this chapter. Do you always act responsibly? Do you have some habits and behaviors that you would like to change?

Step 2 Decide on a long-term goal you would like to achieve. You might want to watch less television and exercise more.

Step 3 Now write down short-term goals that will help you achieve your long-term goal. For instance, your short-term goals might be to restrict your television watching to one hour a day and to walk a mile three times a week.

Step 4 Plan a schedule for reaching each short-term goal. You might make a list of programs you will give up and write down when you will walk.

Your reward for reaching your long-term goal will be a feeling of well-being and the knowledge that you have made healthful choices.

In Your Home and Community

1. **Community Resources** Learn about an organization in your community, such as Alcoholics Anonymous or Gamblers Anonymous, that helps people overcome habits that have taken over their lives. Report on how the organization encourages people to break their habit.

2. **Health of Others** Ask permission from your parents to schedule a family meeting. As a group, choose one goal that everyone in your home would like to accomplish. Then create an action plan to achieve the family's goal.

Building Your Portfolio

1. **List of Potential Hazards** Make a list of potential hazards in your home and school. Next to each hazard, write at least one precaution that you could take to avoid the risk of accident or injury. Add the list to your portfolio.

2. **List of Tips for Decision Making** Talk to a parent or other adult who must make many decisions. Ask the person for tips about how to make important choices. Add the list of tips to your portfolio.

3. **Personal Assessment** Look through all the activities and projects you did for this chapter. Choose one or two that you would like to include in your portfolio.

Chapter 3

Being a Health Care Consumer

Student Expectations

After reading this chapter, you should be able to:

❶ Identify factors that influence your consumer decisions.

❷ Explain how to compare and choose personal products.

❸ Describe how to keep your teeth, skin, and hair healthy.

❹ Explain how to take care of your eyes and ears.

❺ Compare different sources of health care.

Media Messages

The various methods for communicating information are called **media. Mass media** are *media that can reach large groups of people.* Here are some examples of mass media:

- Newspapers and magazines
- Television and radio
- Movies
- Books
- Recordings
- The Internet

*inter*NET
CONNECTION
Surf the net for consumer tips on products and services to keep you healthy and safe.
http://www.glencoe.com/sec/health

All of these media are very powerful. They can convey facts and opinions to you and to millions of other people around the world. They can entertain and amuse you. They often try to persuade you to think or act in a particular way. Sometimes they can do all of these things at once.

Figure 3.1
Why Do You Buy?

Many different factors affect your decision to buy a product or use a service.

Hey! Aren't those the shoes Gail Devers wore when she ran in the Olympics?

Yes. My older sister suggested I buy them.

But those aren't the ones I saw advertised in this month's *Sports Today.*

Nearly everybody on my team wears the ones you're talking about. But I chose these instead.

I heard they're pretty expensive.

They are, but the salesperson showed me how well made they are. These shoes are going to have to last a couple of seasons.

1 **Your Values.** Your personal beliefs about what is important play a big part in your purchasing decisions.

2 **Your Family Background.** Your culture and family help shape your buying decisions.

3 **The Power of Advertising.** Commercials and **advertisements**, *messages designed to get consumers to buy a product or service,* have a strong influence on your buying choices. Remember that ads are sales tools, meant to persuade you to buy a product or service.

4 **The Influence of Your Peers.** The opinions of friends may be the first factor you consider when making a buying decision. However, what's right for someone else isn't necessarily right for you.

5 **The Cost of a Product or Service.** Price can be a determining factor. However, more expensive does not necessarily mean better. Wise consumers shop for both quality and value.

6 **The Advice of Salespeople.** Store employees can help you make a purchasing decision, but the final choice should be based on your own needs and wants—and on facts. Remember that salespeople will tell you anything just to make the sale.

Before buying or using a health product, ask yourself whether a change in your lifestyle or diet could produce the same results you're hoping to get from that product. For example, including enough milk and other dairy products in your diet will eliminate the need for calcium supplements. List some changes you could make in your own lifestyle or diet that would benefit your health.

Advertising is a central part of most media. Magazines overflow with advertisements. Television programs are interrupted by commercials. More and more advertising appears on the Internet.

Advertisements can be very useful. They can make you aware of various products and provide information for your purchasing decisions. However, advertisements can also be misleading. They may exaggerate positive aspects of a product and omit negative ones. They may blend fact and opinion in such a way that you can't distinguish between the two. To make wise purchasing decisions, you need to know the facts. You must also recognize the difference between your needs (the goods or services you must have to live) and your wants (the goods and services you would like to have but that aren't essential). Sometimes advertisements try to convince you that your wants and your needs are the same thing.

What kinds of information do you think are being communicated to this teen through this magazine?

LIFE SKILLS

Being a Wise Consumer of Health Information

*E*very day you're bombarded with information about health care products. This information comes from many sources: newspapers and magazines, television and radio, friends and family. To protect yourself, be skeptical. Don't believe everything you read or hear, no matter how much you may *want* to believe it. Here are some guidelines to help you become a wise information consumer.

▶ Be wary of any product that promises "miracle" results in "no time at all." Body building, weight loss, and other physical changes do not occur overnight. Also, be wary of vague claims, such as "increased energy."

▶ Don't rely on information printed on packages and in pamphlets and mail-order catalogs. Such data may not be reliable. Similarly, don't believe testimonials attributed to "thousands of satisfied customers." Rarely, if ever, can you talk to any of

these individuals to find out how satisfied they really were.

▶ Beware of products claiming "scientific breakthroughs." True breakthroughs are rare and would be reported in the news.

▶ Remember that medical studies differ. Some involve a small number of patients who were observed for a short time. They are less reliable than long-term studies that involve more patients.

▶ When you read a research report, ask yourself if a clear cause-effect relationship has been established. Some studies "suggest" a link, but don't actually prove it.

▶ Don't start—or stop—using a product or medicine just because of research findings reported in the media. Discuss the findings with your doctor, or consult other reliable, factual reference

Understanding Advertising Methods

Whether in print or on television or radio, advertisements usually fall into one of two groups: informational ads and image ads. Both types of advertisements have the same basic purpose: to convince you to buy a product or service.

Informational ads rely mainly on facts. They may use statistics or charts to back their claims, or they may include the words of experts in the field. Ads that use phrases such as "nine out of ten doctors recommend" or "90 percent more effective" are usually informational ads.

A special kind of informational ad is the infomercial. An **infomercial** (IN·foh·mer·shuhl) is *a longer TV commercial whose main purpose appears to be to present information rather than to sell a product.* Infomercials report on everything from political candidates to the latest in home workout equipment. Many are misleading because they look like other types of television programs. An infomercial *is* an advertisement, however, even if it resembles a factual account or a scientific explanation.

Image ads link a product or service to a desirable image. They may feature a glamorous model or famous athlete giving an **endorsement** (en·DOR·smuhnt), *a statement of approval.* Image ads may show carefree skiers or blissfully happy couples. Their message—stated or implied—is usually the same: *This could be you!*

Language Arts Connection

Article or Advertisement? ACTIVITY!

Sometimes the line between magazine articles and advertisements becomes unclear. Perhaps you have read magazines that include "special sections" that provide information and sell products at the same time. A section on fitness, for example, may give helpful exercise hints while suggesting the use of exercise equipment made by a certain manufacturer. Critics say that these types of advertisements are misleading. What do you think? Look for examples of this kind of special section in magazines. How are they like advertisements? How are they like articles?

sources. Try to identify two or more separate research studies that reach the same conclusions.

▶ Watch for studies that add to—or contradict—previous information. Some side effects may not become known for years. Substances that seem safe at first may later be taken off the market.

▶ Scan the fine print on bottles and packages to find out if a product's health claims have been reviewed or approved by the Food and Drug Administration. Remember, however, that not all products are regulated in this way.

Follow-up Activity

Compare the packaging of nonprescription cold remedies. What claims do the various products make? Which statements are factual? Which are nothing more than advertising? Which words—such as new or improved—do you see repeatedly? Summarize your findings in a brief report.

Being an Aware Consumer

Being a consumer is a little like being a detective. You examine the claims that manufacturers make about the products that are available to you and ask questions. Avoid accepting advertising at face value. **Figure 3.2** suggests some questions to ask yourself when evaluating advertisements.

Figure 3.2
Analyzing Advertising Claims

Some advertisements don't make their claims openly—they just imply that something is true. Learn to ask the right questions.

Ask yourself: Can this claim be true, or is it an exaggeration? Even if many people do use this product, does that mean it's what I want?

Ask yourself: Is this claim based on fact or emotional appeal? What does it really mean? Does my social life really depend on what brand of sugarless gum I use?

New **Fresh** is the best deodorant there is!

Ask yourself: What does "best" really mean? What factual proof does the manufacturer provide that this product is better than others?

Ask yourself: Can any article of clothing help me play "like a pro"? What does an endorsement from a paid celebrity or actor mean? Does this perhaps only raise the price of the product?

Lesson 1 Review

Using complete sentences, answer the following questions on a separate sheet of paper.

Reviewing Terms and Facts

1. **List** Identify six factors that influence your buying decisions.

2. **Vocabulary** Explain the term *mass media.* Give two examples.

3. **Vocabulary** What is an *endorsement?*

Thinking Critically

4. **Analyze** Where might you look to find factual information about a product or service? List two possible places to look.

5. **Create** Examine several advertisements and think of two questions you might ask yourself before buying the advertised products.

Applying Health Concepts

6. **Consumer Health** Choose an advertisement for a personal care or health product from a magazine aimed at teens. Write a paragraph explaining how the advertisement tries to persuade readers to buy the product.

Buying Personal Products

This lesson will help you find answers to questions that teens often ask about buying personal products. For example:

▶ **What factors should I consider when choosing personal products?**

▶ **What information can I find by reading product labels?**

▶ **How can I choose personal products wisely?**

Words to Know

quackery
comparison
   shopping
discount store
generic products
warranty

Decisions, Decisions

Consumers spend millions of dollars each year on personal products, which include toothpaste, shampoo, and skin creams. Companies spend millions of dollars, too—trying to convince you to buy *their* products. How can you choose wisely? First, remember that you must take responsibility for collecting information and evaluating products. **Figure 3.3** shows important questions you should consider when making choices.

Figure 3.3
Choosing Personal Products Wisely

Products lined up on store shelves may *look* good, but wise consumers are not fooled by appearances. They ask smart questions and think carefully about the answers.

☑ Does the product offer the results I am looking for?

☑ Is the product safe? Can it harm me—or others?

☑ What benefits can I realistically expect from the product?

☑ Is the product worth the price? Is there an equivalent product that costs less?

☑ What sets the product apart from other, similar products?

☑ Have I used other items made by the same company? Was I satisfied?

I cost less!

I'll make you more popular!

Don't leave the store without checking me out!

Here's the finest money can buy!

I'm on sale today!

Unrealistic Images

Magazine advertisements and television commercials frequently show very thin models with perfect-looking hair, skin, and teeth. Even these models, who are real people, may not look this way in real life. Photos may be altered or touched up in a variety of ways. Discuss with your classmates why such ads are not just unrealistic but potentially harmful to a teen's self-image.

Wise Buying

Quackery (KWAK·uh·ree) is *the sale of worthless products and treatments through false claims.* Such products and treatments may be advertised in the mass media, sold through the mail, or offered over the phone. Their makers may claim that they cure or prevent diseases or other health problems. While some such products and treatments may not be completely worthless, their value is far less than the seller claims. Here are some tips to help you avoid quackery and be a wise buyer of health products.

■ Remember that product claims that sound too good to be true usually are. Be especially careful of claims concerning beauty aids, diets, and "miracle" products.

■ Don't be taken in by impressive-sounding words, "secret ingredients," or glowing testimonials by unknown people. Such advertising techniques may reflect nothing more than the creativity of advertisement writers.

■ Beware of "free" samples for which you're asked to send money "to cover shipping and handling costs."

■ Check with your doctor, a pharmacist, or another reliable source of information before buying or using products. This is especially important for products that you take into your body, such as dietary supplements.

Be a cautious consumer. "Amazing" products may not work, and some may even be harmful. Investigate before you buy.

Math Connection

Using Unit Pricing

Because product packages contain varying amounts, making price comparisons can be tricky. Always check the unit price. For example, a 6-ounce package selling for $3 has a unit price of $0.50 per ounce: $3.00 divided by 6. An 8-ounce package selling for $3.60 has a unit price of $0.45 per ounce: $3.60 divided by 8. Larger packages often have a lower unit price than smaller ones.

Reading Product Labels

The labels that appear on personal products include valuable information. If you pay careful attention to this information, it will help you make smart buying decisions. Labels can also help you make safe use of the products you buy.

Figure 3.4 shows the kinds of information that labels typically provide and suggests how you can use that information wisely. If any information on a product label seems confusing or incomplete, speak with your doctor or pharmacist or check with the manufacturer.

Figure 3.4
Label Information

Product labels can tell you a great deal, so you should take the time to read them.

Control number
If a problem develops, the manufacturer may ask you to provide this identifying number.

Directions for use
Read and follow directions carefully for best results.

Product name
Don't rely solely on a product's name to determine its purpose. Read the label.

Product's intended use
Be sure that the product's purpose suits your needs.

Warnings
To protect yourself and others, pay close attention to warnings. Even safe products can be hazardous if they are not used properly.

Amount in container
When comparing prices, be sure to compare equal amounts.

Manufacture's name and address
Contact the manufacturer if you have a problem or question. Some product labels also include phone numbers.

Ingredients
If two brands have the same ingredients listed in the same order, they will probably have the same effects. If you are allergic to a particular substance, you will want to see if the product contains it.

MAKING HEALTHY DECISIONS
Reaching a Purchasing Decision

*K*im takes physical fitness seriously. She is a member of the track team at school, and she has decided to buy in-line skates to help her stay in shape at home.

After shopping around, Kim has narrowed down her choice to two models. One model has every feature she wants. It's manufactured by a company that Kim knows has an excellent reputation. The XL-62s, however, have one big drawback—their price. The skates are very expensive.

By contrast, the MX-25s are much more reasonably priced. However, they lack the extra padding that Kim wants. In addition, she's never heard of the company that makes these skates. A salesperson has assured her, though, that the company does make a high-quality product.

To make her decision, Kim uses the decision-making process:

❶ **State the situation**
❷ **List the options**
❸ **Weigh the possible outcomes**
❹ **Consider your values**
❺ **Make a decision and act**
❻ **Evaluate the decision**

Follow-up Activities

1. Apply the six steps of the decision-making process to Kim's dilemma.

2. List at least three other actions Kim could take before making a final decision. Explain how each action would help Kim make a good decision.

Wise consumers gather information before making a purchasing decision. Think of a hair styling or personal care product you would like to buy. In your journal, list some sources of information about the product. Put a check next to sources you consider particularly reliable.

Comparison Shopping

Make a habit of **comparison** (kuhm·PEHR·i·suhn) **shopping,** or *comparing products, evaluating their benefits, and choosing the products that offer the best value.* Consider these factors:

- **Cost.** Compare prices of the same brand in different stores. Check newspapers for sales. Look for **discount stores,** *stores that offer special reduced prices.* Also look for **generic** (juh·NEHR·ik) **products**—*goods sold in plain packages at lower prices than brand name goods.* Generic products can save you money when they are equal in quality to brand-name items.

- **Features.** Avoid paying for features that you don't need. However, *do* pay for features that you will find especially useful.

- **Quality.** Well-made products generally outlast those that are poorly made. A cheap product is no bargain if it falls apart.

- **Warranty.** Before you buy a costly product, ask about the **warranty.** A warranty is *a company's or store's written agreement to repair a product or refund your money if the product does not work properly.*

Find out about store policies *before* you buy. For example, will the store return your money if you're dissatisfied with a product, or only give credit?

Lesson 2 Review

Using complete sentences, answer the following questions on a separate sheet of paper.

Reviewing Terms and Facts

1. **Vocabulary** Define the term *quackery.*
2. **Give Examples** List two ways in which the information on product labels can help you.
3. **Vocabulary** What is a *warranty?*

Thinking Critically

4. **Apply** Choose a shampoo or sunblock that you use and explain what factors you considered in selecting that brand.

5. **Analyze** How might *not* reading a product's label be dangerous?

Applying Health Concepts

6. **Consumer Health** Choose two leading brands of the same product, such as toothpaste or deodorant. Make a chart comparing the two based on what you've read in this lesson. Use your chart to explain why you would choose one over the other.

Caring for Your Teeth, Skin, and Hair

This lesson will help you find answers to questions that teens often ask about teeth, skin, and hair. For example:

▶ **How can I keep my teeth healthy?**

▶ **How should I clean and protect my skin?**

▶ **How do I care for my hair?**

Words to Know

fluoride
plaque
tartar
cavity
epidermis
melanin
dermis
pores
dandruff
head lice

Healthy Teeth

If you're like most teens, you pay attention to your appearance. You probably spend time—and money—making sure that your teeth, skin, and hair look their best. Such personal care is important, not just because it makes you feel good about how you look, but because it is sensible personal hygiene.

Think about your teeth for a moment. Clean, healthy teeth not only add to your smile but also enable you to chew food and speak clearly. **Figure 3.5** shows how a tooth looks inside and out.

Figure 3.5
The Parts of a Tooth

Understanding what's inside your teeth will help you take care of them more effectively.

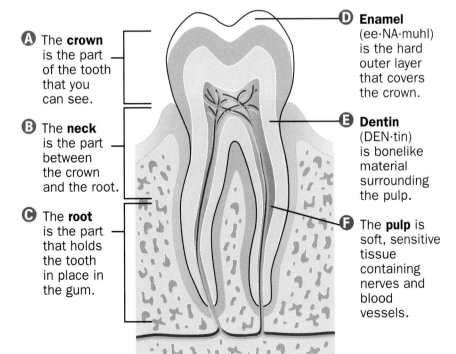

A The **crown** is the part of the tooth that you can see.

B The **neck** is the part between the crown and the root.

C The **root** is the part that holds the tooth in place in the gum.

D **Enamel** (ee·NA·muhl) is the hard outer layer that covers the crown.

E **Dentin** (DEN·tin) is bonelike material surrounding the pulp.

F The **pulp** is soft, sensitive tissue containing nerves and blood vessels.

Did You Know?

Hard as . . . Teeth?

Tooth enamel is the hardest substance in the human body. It's so hard that a dentist's drill must turn at a rate of more than 8,000 times per second in order to drill into a tooth.

Caring for Your Teeth

Caring for your teeth means keeping them clean and healthy. If you neglect your teeth, you allow the process of tooth decay to begin. This process is shown in **Figure 3.6.**

To fight tooth decay and keep your teeth and gums in good shape, follow these guidelines:

■ **Brush your teeth regularly.** Brush at least twice a day. If possible, brush as soon as possible after each meal. If you can't brush after every meal, at least rinse your mouth with water. Regular brushing is especially important if you wear braces, which can trap bits of food. Choose a toothpaste that contains **fluoride** (FLAWR·eyed), *a substance that helps teeth resist decay.* Use a soft-bristled toothbrush, and replace it with a new one every few months. You should also replace your toothbrush after you have had a bad cold or a sore throat.

Sweet Talk

Limiting your intake of foods that are high in sugar will reduce your likelihood of getting cavities and also help you control your weight. If you chew gum, chew sugarless gum. Make a list of healthful snacks you might eat in place of sugary treats.

Figure 3.6
What Causes Tooth Decay

Decay is a process that can damage or even destroy teeth. You can prevent this process by taking care of your teeth.

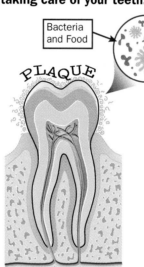

1 Bacteria in your mouth, often combined with food, leave *a thin, sticky film* called **plaque** (PLAK) on your teeth. If plaque is not cleaned away, it becomes **tartar** (TAR·ter), *a hard material that threatens gum health.* Tartar must be removed by a dentist or dental hygienist.

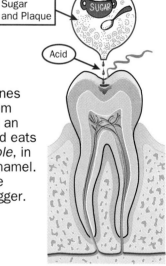

2 Plaque combines with sugar from foods to form an acid. The acid eats a **cavity** or *hole,* in the tooth's enamel. Over time, the cavity gets bigger.

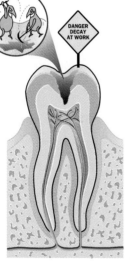

3 The decay spreads, invading the tooth's dentin.

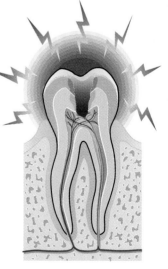

4 The decay then spreads to the pulp. If the cavity exposes a nerve, you are likely to have a toothache.

- **Use dental floss.** Floss at least once a day to clean between your teeth. **Figure 3.7** shows you how. Floss can remove trapped food that brushing alone cannot reach. Floss comes in several different types. Your dentist can recommend the best type for you.

- **Cut down on sugar.** Limit your intake of foods that are mostly sugar, such as candy and cookies.

- **Eat a balanced diet.** Include plenty of healthful foods, such as fruits and vegetables, and foods high in calcium, such as milk and cheese. You can have regular snacks, but don't snack all day. Constant eating will bathe your teeth in cavity-producing acids.

- **Have regular dental checkups.** Visit your dentist regularly. Most dentists see their patients twice a year. Your dentist and dental hygienist can help you keep your teeth clean. They can also spot tooth and gum problems before they become serious. Dental clinics offer full dental services for those who cannot afford a private dentist.

in Your Journal

How well do you take care of your teeth? In your journal, list the actions you always take now to keep your teeth healthy. Then make a second list of actions you can take in the future to improve your approach to tooth care.

Figure 3.7
Brushing and Flossing Your Teeth

Proper brushing and flossing will keep your teeth healthy. The first photo shows a person's teeth after he has just chewed a special tablet that reveals areas of the teeth that need cleaning. After proper brushing and flossing, his teeth are bright and clean.

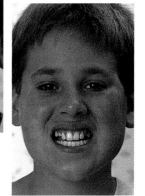

Before

After

How to Brush
A Brush the outer surfaces of your upper and lower teeth. Use a combination of up-and-down strokes and small circular or side-to-side strokes.

B Thoroughly brush all chewing surfaces.

C Brush the inside surfaces of your upper and lower teeth.

D Brush your tongue.

E Rinse your mouth.

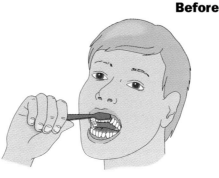

How to Use Dental Floss
A Wrap about 18 inches of floss around the middle finger of each hand.

B Grip the floss tightly between thumb and forefinger.

C Slide the floss back and forth between teeth until it touches your gumline.

D Forming a *C* with the floss around each tooth, keep sliding the floss back and forth gently as you move it up and down along the side of the tooth.

E Do the same for all of your teeth, using a clean section of floss for each one.

F When you've finished, rinse your mouth.

Healthy Skin

Your skin is an organ of your body, like your lungs or heart. In fact, the skin is the largest body organ. Because it performs several key functions, it is also one of the most important. **Figure 3.8** describes some of these functions.

Figure 3.8
Your Skin's Functions
Your skin serves many important functions.

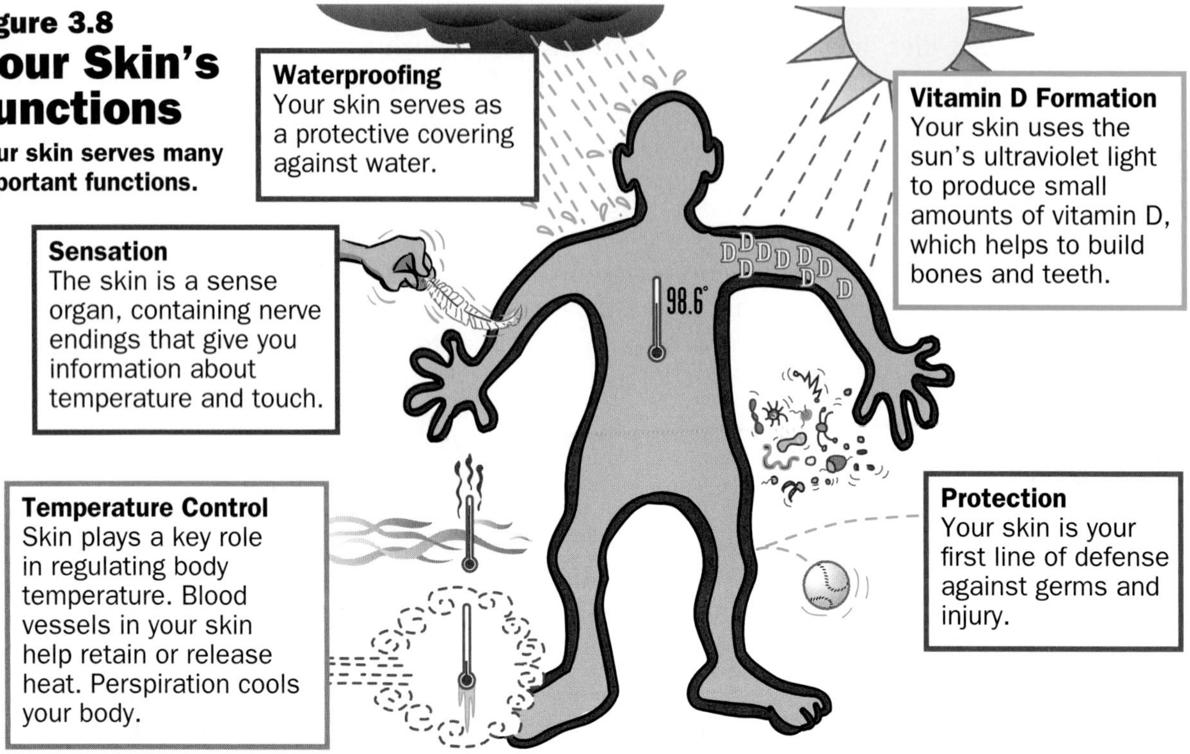

Waterproofing
Your skin serves as a protective covering against water.

Sensation
The skin is a sense organ, containing nerve endings that give you information about temperature and touch.

Temperature Control
Skin plays a key role in regulating body temperature. Blood vessels in your skin help retain or release heat. Perspiration cools your body.

Vitamin D Formation
Your skin uses the sun's ultraviolet light to produce small amounts of vitamin D, which helps to build bones and teeth.

Protection
Your skin is your first line of defense against germs and injury.

HEALTH LAB

How Well Do Sunscreens Protect?

Introduction: Using sunscreen or sunblock lotion helps protect against the effects of the sun. Not all lotions protect equally.

Objective: Compare the protection offered by three sunscreen lotions with different SPFs, or sun protection factors.

Materials and Method: You'll need three different lotions: one with an SPF of 2–4, one with an SPF of 15, and one with an SPF of 30 or more. You'll also need masking tape; a clear plastic folder; photographic developing paper; 3 tablespoons of concentrated dechlorination solution (about 18 percent sodium thiosulfate); 1 cup of distilled water; a shallow plastic pan; and tweezers.

Divide the clear top sheet of the folder into three equal parts with strips of masking tape. Coat each part with a different lotion. Keep track of which lotion you apply to which part.

In a darkened room, slide a sheet of developing paper into the folder. The glossy side should face up, under the top sheet. Place the closed folder, lotion side up, outside in sunshine for 5 to 10 minutes.

Combine the dechlorination solution and distilled water in the pan. Next, use tweezers to put the exposed developing paper into the solution for 3 seconds. Take the paper out, rinse it with cold water, and let it dry.

Observations and Analysis: Observe the differences in color among the three sections of the paper. Which lotion provided the most protection? Which provided the least? What happened to the paper under the masking tape?

The Inside Story

Your skin is composed of two main layers. The **epidermis** (e·puh·DER·mis) is *the outermost layer of skin.* New cells made in the epidermis continuously replace old cells, which are lost from the surface of the skin. Cells in the epidermis make **melanin** (MEL·uh·nin), *the substance that gives your skin its color.*

Beneath the epidermis is the **dermis** (DER·mis). The dermis is *the skin's inner layer that contains blood vessels, nerve endings, and hair follicles.* The dermis also contains two kinds of glands. Sweat glands let perspiration escape through **pores,** or *tiny openings in the skin.* Oil glands produce oils to keep skin soft. Under the dermis is a layer of fat tissue. **Figure 3.9** shows the parts of the skin.

Figure 3.9
Parts of the Skin
The skin is constantly replacing and repairing itself.

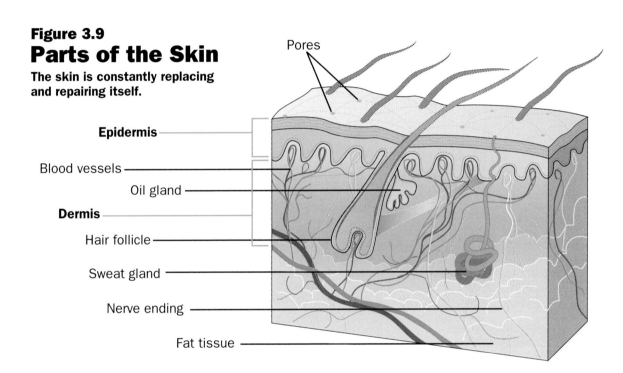

Pores

Epidermis

Blood vessels

Oil gland

Dermis

Hair follicle

Sweat gland

Nerve ending

Fat tissue

Caring for Your Skin

Taking care of your skin helps you stay healthy and keeps you looking your best. Here are some skin care tips:

- **Keep clean.** Take a bath or shower daily. Keeping your skin clean is particularly important during your early teen years, when sweat glands become more active. Bacteria mixing with perspiration can cause an unpleasant odor, especially under your arms, where there are many sweat glands. Washing with soap removes bacteria and excess oils from your skin. You can also combat body odor by using a deodorant or antiperspirant.

- **Take care of yourself.** Eat a healthful diet. Foods such as milk, green and yellow vegetables, and eggs are high in vitamin A, a vitamin that helps your skin stay healthy. In addition, get regular exercise and plenty of rest.

Have You Heard the Expression . . . ?

ACTIVITY!

Many common expressions refer to teeth, skin, or hair. For example, people escape "by the skin of their teeth" or "get into each other's hair." Make a list of expressions you've heard that use these words. See if you can figure out how these expressions may have come to have these meanings.

■ **Guard against the sun.** Ultraviolet light from the sun can damage your skin and increase your risk of getting skin cancer. Experts warn that one severe sunburn during the first 15 years of life can double the risk for skin cancer. Try to keep out of the sun between 10:00 a.m. and 3:00 p.m., the period when ultraviolet rays are most intense. If you do spend time in the sun, use sunscreen or sunblock lotion to protect your skin. Choose a lotion with an SPF (sun protection factor) of 15 or higher. Follow the instructions on the label carefully.

Keep in mind that the sun does not affect everyone equally. For example, fair-skinned people, whose skins have less melanin, will get sunburned more easily than darker skinned people. Also, remember that ultraviolet rays are invisible. They are present—and dangerous—even on overcast days.

Acne

Many teens have to cope with a skin condition called acne. This condition occurs when active oil glands cause pores to become clogged. Pimples, whiteheads, or blackheads may result. Acne often appears on the face, but may also affect the neck, back, and shoulders.

To fight acne, gently wash the affected area at least twice daily with mild soap and warm water. Avoid touching, picking at, or rubbing the area, and don't apply heavy makeup or creams. If you are concerned about your skin, talk with your doctor or other primary health care provider, who may refer you to a dermatologist (duhr·muh·TAH·luh·jist), a physician who specializes in treating the skin and its diseases.

Figure 3.10
Hair Structure

Hair grows from structures called follicles (FAH·li·kuhlz). Your body has about 5 million hair follicles, about 100,000 of which are in the scalp.

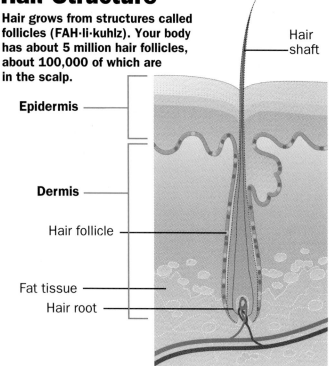

Epidermis

Dermis

Hair follicle

Fat tissue

Hair root

Hair shaft

Healthy Hair

Your hair is one of the first features people notice. Keeping it clean and healthy is well worth the time and effort you invest. Hair care is an important part of good personal grooming.

Hair color comes from melanin, just as skin color does. Whether your hair is straight, wavy, or curly depends on the shape of the hair shaft, the part of the hair that you can see (see **Figure 3.10**). This visible portion is made of dead cells. New hair cells grow beneath the skin surface.

Caring for Your Hair

Daily brushing keeps your hair healthy by removing dirt. Brushing also spreads oils down hair shafts, making hair shiny. You should also wash your hair regularly, using a gentle shampoo. How often you should wash depends on whether your hair tends to be dry or oily. Most people need to wash their hair at least twice a week. If possible, allow your hair to air dry. Blow dryers can make your hair brittle, particularly if you use a high-heat setting.

Several problems can occur with the hair and with the scalp, the skin beneath the hair. One is **dandruff,** *a flaking of the outer layer of dead skin cells on the scalp.* This condition is usually caused by dry skin. You may be able to control dandruff through regular shampooing. Special dandruff shampoos are also available. In certain cases, your doctor may prescribe a medicated shampoo.

Another hair and scalp problem involves **head lice,** *parasitic insects that live in the hair and cause itching.* Head lice are very easy to catch from other people. To avoid the problem, don't share combs, brushes, or hats with others. If you do get head lice, you'll need to use a special shampoo to kill them. You'll also have to wash all bedding, towels, and clothes that you have used. Other members of your family, even pets, may need to be treated, too.

Teens often try out different hairstyles as a means of self-expression.

Review

Lesson 3

Using complete sentences, answer the following questions on a separate sheet of paper.

Reviewing Terms and Facts

1. **Vocabulary** Define the terms *plaque* and *tartar.*

2. **Recall** Describe five of the functions of the skin.

3. **Vocabulary** What are the *epidermis* and *dermis?*

Thinking Critically

4. **Hypothesize** A friend tells you, "I don't have to go to the dentist because I've never had a cavity." Do you agree or disagree with the conclusion your friend has made. Why?

5. **Apply** You're going to vacation at the beach. What actions can you take to protect your skin?

Applying Health Concepts

6. **Growth and Development** Head lice spread easily among groups of younger children, especially in schools. Work with a partner to create a poster for children, suggesting ways to avoid getting head lice.

7. **Consumer Health** Compare three brands of shampoo sold in stores. How are they alike? How do they differ? Prepare an oral or written report explaining how a consumer might go about deciding which of those three brands to buy.

Caring for Your Eyes and Ears

This lesson will help you find answers to questions that teens often ask about caring for their eyes and ears. For example:

▶ How can I keep my eyes healthy?
▶ What should I know about wearing glasses or contacts?
▶ How can I protect my ears from loud noises?

Words to Know

cornea
iris
pupil
lens
retina
optic nerve
optometrist
ophthalmologist
astigmatism
decibel

How Your Eyes Work

Your eyes tell you about the world—about light, darkness, shapes, colors, and movement. The data gathered by your eyes is interpreted by your brain, allowing you to recognize your friend coming toward you in the hallway or the words on this page. To see how your eyes work, look at **Figure 3.11.**

Figure 3.11
The Eye

The eye is like a camera. It takes in light and focuses it to create an image. This image is sent to the brain, which "develops" the picture.

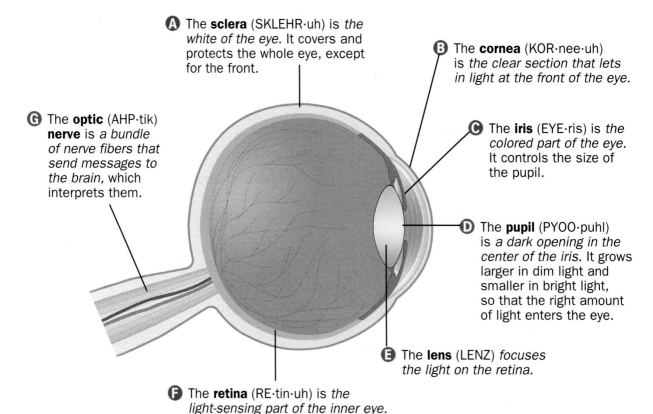

A The **sclera** (SKLEHR·uh) is *the white of the eye.* It covers and protects the whole eye, except for the front.

B The **cornea** (KOR·nee·uh) is *the clear section that lets in light at the front of the eye.*

G The **optic** (AHP·tik) **nerve** is *a bundle of nerve fibers that send messages to the brain,* which interprets them.

C The **iris** (EYE·ris) is *the colored part of the eye.* It controls the size of the pupil.

D The **pupil** (PYOO·puhl) is *a dark opening in the center of the iris.* It grows larger in dim light and smaller in bright light, so that the right amount of light enters the eye.

E The **lens** (LENZ) *focuses the light on the retina.*

F The **retina** (RE·tin·uh) is *the light-sensing part of the inner eye.*

Caring for Your Eyes

Because your eyes tell you so much about your world, you will want to protect them. To care for your eyes, follow these tips.

- Make sure that you have enough light. Read and watch television in a well-lighted room. If necessary, use a reading lamp.

- Avoid having too much light. Sit at least 6 feet away from the television set. Do not look directly at the sun or at any other bright light. When you are outside, wear sunglasses that protect your eyes from ultraviolet (UV) rays.

- Don't rub your eyes. If dirt gets into your eyes, rubbing them may scratch the cornea. Instead, rinse your eyes with cool water.

- Protect your eyes from injury. Wear protective equipment when playing sports, such as baseball or hockey, that could result in eye injury. Also, wear protective glasses or goggles if you work with power tools or chemicals.

- Have your eyes examined regularly by an eye care professional. An **optometrist** (ahp·TAH·muh·trist) *is trained to examine the eyes for vision problems and to prescribe corrective lenses.* An **ophthalmologist** (ahf·thahl·MAH·luh·jist) is *a physician who specializes in the structure, functions, and diseases of the eye.* If you wear either glasses or contact lenses, you should have your eyes checked once a year. Otherwise, have them checked every two years.

in your journal

Do you think that you take good care of your eyes? Name one habit you have now that promotes good eye care. Then list two things you might start doing immediately that would help you take better care of your eyes.

Problems with Vision

When you have your eyes examined, the doctor will check for several possible problems. Your vision will be tested with an eye chart, and the parts of your eye will be examined to see if they are working properly. The doctor will also check for glaucoma (glaw·KOH·muh), a disease in which fluid builds up in the eyes, causing pressure that can destroy the optic nerve.

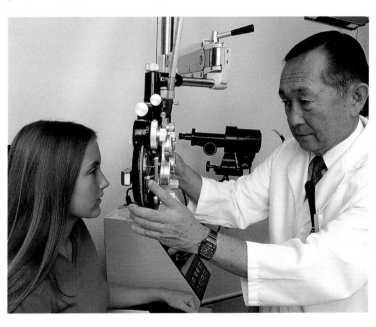

Regular eye checkups can detect vision problems before they become serious.

Three common problems that may be detected are nearsightedness, farsightedness, and astigmatism. With nearsightedness, only objects close to the eye can be seen clearly. Farsightedness is just the opposite. Faraway objects are seen clearly, but nearby objects appear blurry. **Astigmatism** (uh·STIG·muh·tiz·uhm) is *an eye condition in which images are distorted.* Both faraway and close-up objects appear wavy or blurry.

Q & A

Contact Solutions

Q: I'd like to get contact lenses. What kinds of lenses are there, and which is best?

A: There are three basic types of contact lenses. Rigid gas-permeable (or "hard") lenses are easy to take care of, but many people find them uncomfortable. Soft lenses are easier to get used to, but they are harder to clean. Extended-wear lenses are worn for 30 days and then thrown away. However, it is possible to forget about them and wear them too long. If you are not sure which type is best for you, ask your doctor.

Correcting Vision Problems

Many vision problems can be corrected with eyeglasses or contact lenses. Both types of lenses correct the focusing problems of the eye. Eyeglasses, however, are mounted on frames, while contact lenses rest on the cornea. If you wear contact lenses, it is important to care for them properly. Here are some points to remember.

■ Clean your lenses every day. Different types of lenses require different methods of cleaning. Follow your doctor's instructions for proper cleaning and storage of your lenses.

■ Always wash your hands before you handle your lenses.

■ Always remove your contact lenses before going to sleep, unless you have been told by your eye doctor that it is safe to wear them to bed.

■ Replace your lenses if they are torn, cracked, or warped. Damaged lenses can scratch the cornea of your eye. These scratches can lead to eye infections or even to blindness.

How Your Ears Work

Your ears allow you to hear and help you keep your balance. Their structure is quite complex. **Figure 3.12** shows the structures of the ear, which are usually organized into three parts. The way these parts work together is explained below.

■ The outer ear is shaped like a cup to pick up sound waves, which are vibrations in the air. The sound waves travel through the external auditory canal.

■ In the middle ear, these waves make the eardrum vibrate. The vibrations of the eardrum move three tiny bones called the hammer, the anvil, and the stirrup. These bones carry the vibrations to the oval window.

■ In the inner ear, the oval window causes the fluid in the cochlea (KOK·lee·uh) to move. Tiny hairs lining the cochlea vibrate in response, sending electrical messages to the auditory nerve. These messages travel to the brain, which identifies the sound.

Figure 3.12
The Ear

Some of the structures of the ear are not directly concerned with hearing. The Eustachian (yoo·STAY·shuhn) tube leads from the back of the eardrum to the throat. This tube keeps the air pressure equal on both sides of the eardrum. The semicircular canals are filled with fluid and tiny hairs. These hairs send messages through nerves to the brain, helping your body keep its balance.

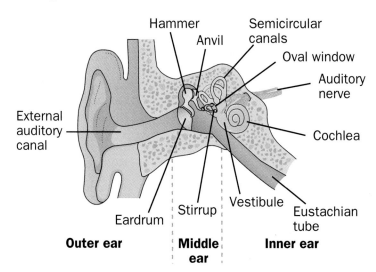

Caring for Your Ears

One way to care for your ears is to protect them from loud sounds. *The unit for measuring the loudness of sound waves* is the **decibel.** Normal conversation is about 60 decibels. Sounds over 125 decibels are loud enough to be painful. Lower levels of sound can also harm the ears if the sounds continue for a long time. Some tips for protecting your ears from noise and preventing other problems include the following.

■ Keep the volume fairly low on your radio and television. This is especially important if you are using headphones.

■ Wear ear plugs or other hearing protection if you are going to be exposed to loud, prolonged noise, such as the noise from a power lawnmower.

■ Clean the outside of your ear with a wet washcloth. Do not put a cotton swab or any other object into your ear canal. If ear wax builds up and becomes a problem, see a doctor to have it removed.

■ On cold days, wear earmuffs or a hat that covers your ears. Cold air can irritate your middle ear. It can also cause frostbite on your outer ear.

■ See a doctor promptly if you have pain in the ear, an ear infection, or a hearing problem.

Science Connection

Over There

How do you tell which direction a sound comes from? The sound reaches the closer ear about 1/1500 of a second sooner than it reaches the ear that is farther away. Also, the sound is slightly louder in the closer ear. These small differences are analyzed by the brain instantaneously.

Adjust the volume on headphones or earphones to avoid ear damage.

Review

Lesson 4

Using complete sentences, answer the following questions on a separate sheet of paper.

Reviewing Terms and Facts

1. **Vocabulary**   Identify the *cornea, iris, pupil, lens,* and *retina.*

2. **Define**   Explain what an *optometrist* and an *ophthalmologist* are.

3. **Vocabulary**   What is a *decibel?*

Thinking Critically

4. **Evaluate**   What kinds of factors might you consider when you choose an eye care professional?

5. **Relate**   What types of activities or situations in your life might be harmful to your hearing? What could you do to protect your hearing?

Applying Health Concepts

6. **Consumer Health**   Write an advertisement for sunglasses, ear plugs, or any other type of protective eyewear or earwear. Explain what the product does and why it is important to use it. Include an illustration if you wish. Display the advertisement in your classroom.

TEEN HEALTH DIGEST

People at Work

Open Wide . . .

Job: Dentist

Responsibilities: To care for patients' teeth, gums, and mouths; teach patients how to keep their teeth healthy; fill cavities; repair or remove teeth; replace missing teeth.

Education and Training: Six to ten years beyond high school, including four years at dental college.

Workplace: Dentists may practice individu-

ally or as a group. Many have the help of a dental assistant or dental hygienist.

Positive: High prestige; good earning potential; can set own work schedule.

Negative: Long hours standing up; must deal with patients who are nervous or upset; contact with patients' germs.

Try This:

Gather some information on the history of dentistry. Compare the role of dentists in the past with the way they work today.

HEALTH UPDATE

Decay? No Way!

Keeping your teeth clean and limiting sugary snacks will help you fight the battle against tooth decay. Another way to protect your teeth is with dental sealants.

Dental sealants are plastic coatings that your dentist can apply to the chewing surfaces of your teeth. They form a protective covering, shielding tooth enamel from the effects of decay-causing bacteria.

Sealants are not put on all tooth surfaces, so you'll still need to practice good dental hygiene. However, sealants are one possible way that you can keep cavities at bay.

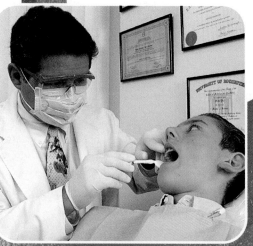

Fashion Statement or Health Risk?

In recent years, body piercing has become increasingly popular. Many people are not aware, however, of the health risks associated with body piercing.

Piercing equipment must be sterile to avoid causing infection. A minor infection that develops after a piercing can be controlled by cleansing the pierced area properly with an antibacterial soap or other cleanser. Equipment that is not sterile, however, can create much more serious problems. These include the passing on of viruses such as HIV, which causes AIDS, and the hepatitis virus.

Because of the potential dangers, some states are working to set health standards for piercing. These standards would regulate techniques and require piercing specialists to be licensed.

Myths and Realities

Seeing the Light

Q. I've heard that indoor tanning, using a sunlamp or tanning bed, is a safe way to get a tan. Is that true?

A. No. The light rays from sunlamps and tanning beds actually penetrate your skin more deeply than the burning rays of the sun. Studies have shown that indoor tanning devices may cause early aging and skin cancer. In fact, cancer from indoor tanning devices can be more severe—and grow faster—than cancer from sunlight. Your eyes can also be damaged by this type of light.

Teens Making a Difference

A Teen for Others

Most voluntary health groups could not work successfully without thousands of dedicated volunteers. One such volunteer is Stephen Massey, a student from Arizona. He has been a volunteer for the March of Dimes Birth Defects Foundation since he was in eighth grade. Massey has done everything from collecting items for mothers and babies who live in crisis centers to helping organize a walkathon fund raiser. His work paid off: in that walkathon, his high school raised more than $21,000, the most collected by any high school.

Try This:

Interview someone who works as a volunteer for a health organization. Ask the person what kind of tasks are involved, and why he or she decided to volunteer.

5 Health Care Providers

This lesson will help you find answers to questions that teens often ask about health care. For example:

► **What kinds of health care workers can help me stay well?**

► **Where can I find help if I become ill or injured?**

► **Why is health insurance important?**

primary care
   provider
specialist
health insurance
managed care
health
   maintenance
   organization
   (HMO)
Medicare
Medicaid

Prevention and Treatment

When was the last time you visited a doctor? Perhaps you had a bad cough and a fever, or maybe you sprained your ankle playing sports. Doctors treat these and many other kinds of illnesses and injuries. Doctors and other health professionals also try to *prevent* illness and injury. Health care workers, including dental hygienists, nurses, counselors, health teachers, and dietitians work to educate people and help them stay healthy. In addition, there are many voluntary organizations—such as the American Heart Association and the American Cancer Society—that offer health-related information and services. People donate time and money to these groups. The donated funds help to pay for medical research.

When you become ill or have an injury, you probably seek health care at a doctor's office, clinic, or hospital. Any of a wide range of health care workers may help you. Some provide general care, while others have special training to handle particular medical problems.

in your journal

Washing your hands is one way to prevent the spread of germs. What other kinds of "preventive medicine" do you practice? In your journal, make a list of everyday actions you can take that will help keep yourself and others healthy.

Medical research goes on in many different settings to help prevent and cure disease.

General and Specialized Care

Primary care providers are *the doctors and other health professionals who provide checkups and general care.* For some problems, a doctor may suggest a **specialist** (SPE·she·list). A specialist is *a doctor trained to treat particular types of patients or health matters.* **Figure 3.13** shows some common specialists.

Figure 3.13
Medical Specialists
Which of these specialists are already familiar to you?

Specialist	Specialty
allergist	asthma, hay fever, and other allergies
cardiologist	the heart, its functions, and its diseases
dermatologist	the skin and its diseases
gynecologist	women's health care and diseases
ophthalmologist	the eye, its functions, and its diseases
orthodontist	irregularities of the teeth and jaw
orthopedist	bones, joints, and muscles and their injuries and diseases
pediatrician	infant and child health care and diseases
plastic surgeon	cosmetic surgery to repair damage
psychiatrist	mental and emotional problems
urologist	the urinary system and its diseases

Health Care Facilities

Health care is available in many different places. In addition to doctors' offices, clinics, and hospitals, health care facilities include the following.

- Birthing centers are an alternative to hospitals for giving birth.

- Nursing homes take care of sick, disabled, and elderly people who require special care. Assisted living (or assisted care) facilities are residences for people who need extra help with bathing or other tasks of daily living.

- Drug treatment centers offer help to people with drug-related problems.

- Rehabilitation centers aid people who need special help to recover from serious illness or injury.

- Hospices provide care and support for terminally ill patients.

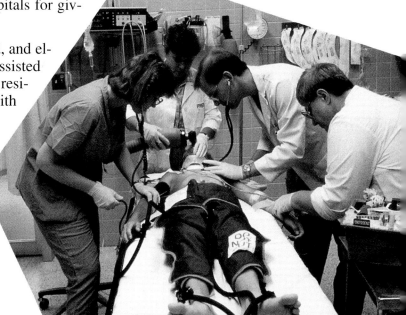

Hospital emergency rooms provide immediate medical care, especially for victims of accidents or sudden illnesses.

Paying for Health Care

Health services are available in many forms. Doctors may work on their own in a private practice or join with others to create a group practice. They may also work for clinics. Medical care is often very expensive. Surgery and hospital stays, for example, typically cost thousands of dollars.

A number of factors account for the rising cost of health care. High-technology equipment and advanced medical procedures, such as organ transplants, are very expensive. Providing care for people with AIDS has made enormous demands on the health care system. In addition, health care providers and medical facilities pay high insurance premiums to protect themselves against possible lawsuits. Drug companies invest huge sums of money to develop and test new medicines and treatments.

You may be surprised at how many different health care providers you and your family have called upon. With other family members, brainstorm a list of health care workers who have served your family over the past five years. Which of these workers are specialists?

Health Insurance

To pay for health care, many people buy **health insurance** (in·SHUR·uhns). This is *a plan in which people pay a set fee to an insurance company in return for the company's agreement to pay some or most medical costs.* People may buy health insurance on their own or as part of a group. Group insurance is offered mainly through people's employers. Some companies pay all or part of the cost of health insurance for their workers. An employee's health insurance may also cover some of the medical expenses for the employee's family.

Many people receive health services through **managed care** plans. Such plans *emphasize preventive medicine and work to manage the cost and quality of health care.* A common form of managed care is the **health maintenance** (MAYN·tuh·nuhns) **organization,** or **HMO.** An HMO *offers its members the services of many different types of health care providers.* Members pay a monthly or yearly fee instead of paying for individual services.

Modern medical technology helps doctors diagnose and treat patients. However, this new equipment is costly.

Millions of Americans, however, are not covered by health insurance. Their employers may not offer it—or may pay only a small part of the cost—and they cannot afford insurance on an individual basis. The government and the health care industry are looking for ways to make health care more affordable. None of the types of health insurance currently available is perfect. A lower cost usually means fewer services, while the higher cost of private insurance is out of reach for millions of American families.

Government Programs

Federal, state, and local governments each play a role in health care. For example, all states and most cities have health departments. These departments work to maintain community health standards. They also provide health-related information and services to the public.

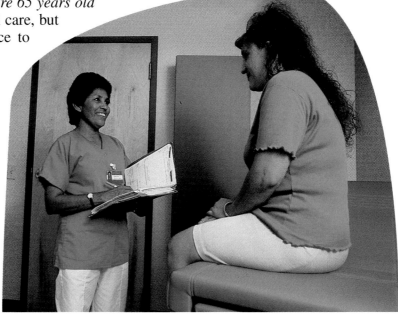

Local health department workers promote community health by talking with people and distributing information.

The federal government has two insurance programs to help pay the cost of health care. **Medicare** (MED·i·kehr) *provides health insurance to people who are 65 years old or over.* Medicare covers hospital care, but patients must buy other insurance to pay doctors' bills and other costs.

Medicaid (MED·i·kayd) is *a public health insurance program for low-income families and individuals.* In general, Medicaid offers coverage for young children, people whose personal or family income is below a certain level, and people who are disabled. The federal and state governments both support this program. Because Medicaid programs are run by state governments, however, rules vary from state to state.

Review

Lesson
5

Using complete sentences, answer the following questions on a separate sheet of paper.

Reviewing Terms and Facts

1. **Vocabulary** What is the difference between a *primary care provider* and a *specialist?*

2. **List** Identify three factors that help explain the rising cost of health care.

3. **Vocabulary** What is a *health maintenance organization (HMO)?*

4. **Recall** Describe two health insurance programs provided by the federal or state governments.

Thinking Critically

5. **Explain** How do primary care providers and specialists work together to treat patients?

6. **Analyze** Why is it important for a family to be covered by health insurance?

Applying Health Concepts

7. **Personal Health** Draw a map of the route from your home to the nearest hospital emergency room. How could you get there in a hurry if you had to?

8. **Health of Others** Contact the American Heart Association, the American Diabetes Association, or another voluntary health organization. Ask about the organization's purpose and activities. Share the information with your class.

Chapter 3 Review

Chapter Summary

▶ **Lesson 1** To make wise consumer choices, you need to gather and evaluate information and recognize how advertising and other factors influence your decision making.

▶ **Lesson 2** Always compare personal products carefully before you buy. Product labels provide helpful information.

▶ **Lesson 3** Caring for your teeth, skin, and hair involves brushing and flossing, regular dentist visits (teeth); good hygiene, protection from the sun (skin); and regular shampooing (hair).

▶ **Lesson 4** Caring for your eyes and ears includes regular eye checkups and protecting your ears from loud sounds.

▶ **Lesson 5** Many different health care professionals treat illnesses and injuries and work to prevent them. Health insurance helps people pay for health care.

Reviewing Key Terms and Concepts

Using complete sentences, answer the following questions on a separate sheet of paper.

Lesson 1

1. What can you do to be a wise consumer?

2. What is an *infomercial?*

Lesson 2

3. What is *comparison shopping?*

4. How can knowing about discount stores and generic products help you get good value for your money?

Lesson 3

5. What actions can you take to prevent cavities?

6. What is *melanin?*

Lesson 4

7. What is the *optic nerve?*

8. Describe nearsightedness, farsightedness, and astigmatism.

Lesson 5

9. If you were ill or injured, where could you go for medical care? Give several examples.

10. What is *managed care?*

Thinking Critically

Using complete sentences, answer the following questions on a separate sheet of paper.

11. **Synthesize** How can analyzing advertising claims help you make wise purchasing decisions?

12. **Apply** Describe two potentially serious health consequences that might result from having poor consumer skills.

13. **Explain** How are healthy teeth the result of both good hygiene and good diet?

14. **Predict** How might allowing eye or ear problems to go untreated affect other areas of your health?

15. **Assess** Do you think that companies should be required to provide health insurance for employees and their families? Why or why not?

Your Action Plan

Worthwhile goals always require effort. For example, it takes effort to stay healthy and to look your best. It also takes effort to be a wise consumer.

Step 1 Review your journal entries for this chapter. What do they suggest about personal goals you might set for yourself?

Step 2 Set some short-term and long-term personal goals for yourself. A possible short-term goal might be to compare at least three different brands before making your next product purchase. A long-term goal might be limiting your skin's exposure to the sun.

Step 3 Alongside each of your goals, list specific steps you can take to accomplish the goal.

Periodically, check your progress. Feel good about what you've accomplished, and make note of what you still need to do.

In Your Home and Community

1. **Health of Others** Find out from your teacher, school nurse, or school counselor what opportunities you might create to help younger students learn how to take proper care of their teeth, skin, hair, eyes, and ears. For example, students from your school might conduct a "Care for Yourself" clinic for elementary school children. The clinic could combine live demonstrations with informative posters and handouts.

2. **Consumer Health** Prepare a "Smart Shopper" newsletter for your local community. Include tips for comparison shopping, analyzing advertisements, and reading product labels. Find out how you can post or distribute your newsletter.

Building Your Portfolio

1. **Analysis of Advertisements** Clip several magazine advertisements for personal products. Attach each ad to a sheet of paper. Below the ad, write your analysis of how the advertiser is trying to persuade you to buy the product. Add your analyses to your portfolio.

2. **Careers in Health Care** A variety of careers exist in the health care field. Check the employment section of the newspaper, or look at the *Occupational Outlook Handbook* at the library. Choose two health care jobs that sound interesting. Research their qualifications and responsibilities, and write a summary of your findings. Put the summary in your portfolio.

3. **Personal Assessment** Look through all the activities and projects you did for this chapter. Choose one or two that you would like to include in your portfolio.

Unit 2
Nutrition and Fitness

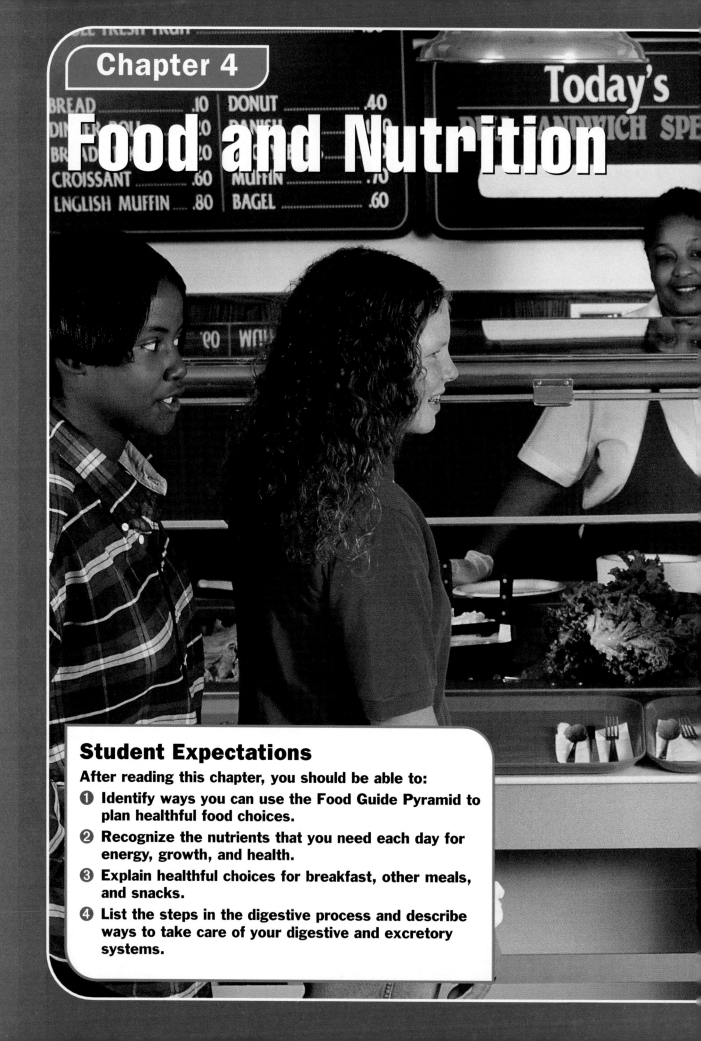

Chapter 4
Food and Nutrition

Student Expectations

After reading this chapter, you should be able to:

① Identify ways you can use the Food Guide Pyramid to plan healthful food choices.

② Recognize the nutrients that you need each day for energy, growth, and health.

③ Explain healthful choices for breakfast, other meals, and snacks.

④ List the steps in the digestive process and describe ways to take care of your digestive and excretory systems.

CROISSANT EXTRA
POTATO SALAD
COLE SLAW
SALAD BAR .... PER OUNCE

Teen Chat Group

LaShawna: I don't know what I want. What are you two getting?

Jessica: I'm getting the salad.

Tiffany: Oh, no! Now *I* have to get something healthy, too.

LaShawna: I don't even know what's healthy anymore. One week some food is really bad for you, and the next week it's okay. I'm just going to eat what I like.

Tiffany: Sounds good to me!

Jessica: I know what you mean, LaShawna, but it's not really that hard. I try to eat fruits and vegetables whenever I can. I like them anyway. You know I'm not a fanatic about what I eat—I still eat dessert.

Tiffany: Then *I'm* getting a burger. It's what I want. What about you, LaShawna?

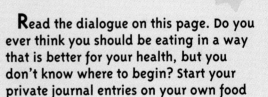

Read the dialogue on this page. Do you ever think you should be eating in a way that is better for your health, but you don't know where to begin? Start your private journal entries on your own food choices by responding to these questions.

▶ What would you say if you were eating lunch with these girls? What might you order?

▶ What influences the choices you make about the foods you eat?

▶ How might your eating habits affect the way you look and feel? How much thought do you give to meal planning?

When you reach the end of the chapter, you will use your journal entries to make an action plan.

The Food Guide Pyramid

This lesson will help you find answers to questions that teens often ask about their daily diets. For example:

▶ **What influences my diet?**

▶ **How can I use the Food Guide Pyramid to plan a healthful diet?**

Words to Know

nutrition
diet
Food Guide
   Pyramid
nutrients
calories

Food in Your Life

Food provides your body with the fuel it needs to grow and work properly. After you eat, your body breaks down the food and uses it to build and repair body cells and provide you with energy. **Nutrition** (noo·TRI·shuhn) is the term for *the process of taking in food and using it for growth and good health.* This is the main reason why people need to eat—to fulfill the body's physical needs. Eating satisfies social needs, too, however. Mealtimes can provide a chance to enjoy the company of family members and friends. Eating also has an emotional element. Babies, for example, learn to associate feeding with feelings of closeness. The choices you make about food, therefore, have an impact on every area of your life.

What Influences Your Food Choices?

Traditions and ethnic background have an influence on food choices. How do your family's traditions and background affect your food choices?

Now that you are a teen, you make more of the decisions about your **diet,** *all the things you regularly eat and drink.* Many factors influence these choices, including:

■ **Sensory appeal.** The ways that foods look, taste, smell, and feel influence what you choose to eat.

■ **Geography.** The land, climate, and agricultural products of your region influence your food choices and food availability.

■ **Your Cultural and Family Background.** You may make certain food choices because they are part of your family's cultural or ethnic background.

■ **Advertising.** Food advertisements are designed to influence you to choose one food over another.

The Food Guide Pyramid

There are many ways to combine different foods to create a wholesome and delicious diet. **Figure 4.1** shows the **Food Guide Pyramid,** *a guide for making healthful daily food choices.* The Food Guide Pyramid was developed by the U.S. Department of Agriculture. It puts foods into groups on a diagram, based on the substances they provide to the body. One of the benefits of such a guide is that you can see at a glance the variety of foods you need for good health.

*inter*NET
CONNECTION
Research the fat in fast foods, or find simple but delicious-and-nutritious recipes by weighing on to the Web!
http://www.glencoe.com/sec/health

Figure 4.1
The Food Guide Pyramid: A Guide to Daily Food Choices

The Food Guide Pyramid is an excellent tool for planning your food choices each day. At the narrowest part of the pyramid are foods you should eat only in small amounts. As the pyramid gets wider, the suggested number of servings from each food group increases.

KEY

○ Shows the amount of naturally occurring and added fats in each group

▽ Shows the amount of added sugars in each group

These symbols show that fats and added sugars come mostly from foods in the pyramid tip. The substances can, however, be part of or added to foods in the other food groups as well.

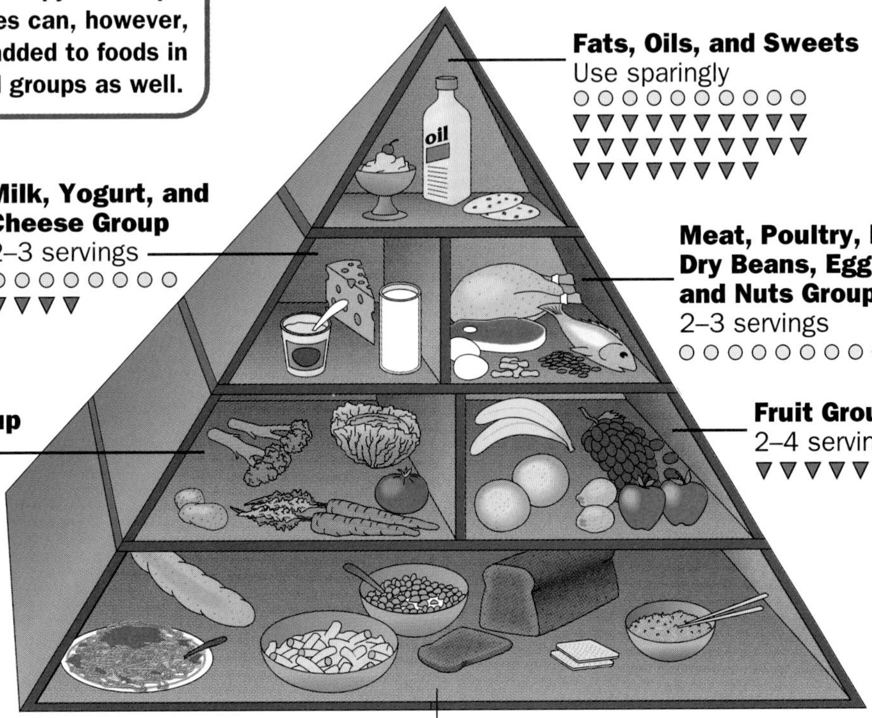

Fats, Oils, and Sweets
Use sparingly

Milk, Yogurt, and Cheese Group
2–3 servings

Meat, Poultry, Fish, Dry Beans, Eggs, and Nuts Group
2–3 servings

Vegetable Group
3–5 servings

Fruit Group
2–4 servings

Bread, Cereal, Rice, and Pasta Group
6–11 servings

Lesson 1: The Food Guide Pyramid **93**

Getting What You Need

The Food Guide Pyramid shows a suggested range of servings for foods within each of the five major food groups. The number of servings you need depends on your energy needs. Your energy needs depend on your age, gender, and activity level. **Figure 4.2** shows the recommended daily servings in each group for teen girls and for teen boys. **Figure 4.3** shows what this means in terms of an actual day's menu.

Figure 4.2
Recommended Daily Servings

Daily servings should always take into account your energy needs, and should be based on *calorie intake* and *activity level*.

Food Group	Sample Serving Sizes	Teen Girls	Teen Boys
Milk, Yogurt, and Cheese	1 cup (8 oz.) milk or yogurt 1½ oz. natural cheese 2 oz. processed cheese	3 or more servings	3 or more servings
Meat, Poultry, Fish, Dry Beans, Eggs, and Nuts	2–3 oz. cooked lean meat, poultry, or fish The following are equivalent to 1 oz. meat: 1 egg, ½ cup cooked dry beans, 2 Tbs. peanut butter, ⅓ cup nuts	2 servings	3 servings
Vegetables	½ cup cooked or raw chopped vegetables 1 cup raw leafy vegetables ¾ cup vegetable juice	4 servings	5 servings
Fruits	1 medium apple, banana, orange ½ cup chopped, cooked, or canned fruit ¾ cup fruit juice	3 servings	4 servings
Breads, Cereals, Rice, and Pasta	1 slice of bread or 1 muffin 1 oz. ready-to-eat cereal ½ cup cooked cereal, rice, or pasta	9 servings	11 servings

Figure 4.3
A Day's Menu

This menu fulfills the recommended daily servings from the Food Guide Pyramid for a teen girl.

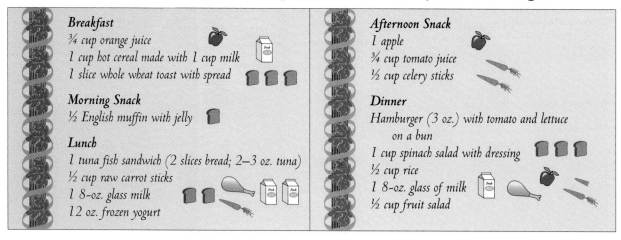

Breakfast
¾ cup orange juice
1 cup hot cereal made with 1 cup milk
1 slice whole wheat toast with spread

Morning Snack
½ English muffin with jelly

Lunch
1 tuna fish sandwich (2 slices bread; 2–3 oz. tuna)
½ cup raw carrot sticks
1 8-oz. glass milk
12 oz. frozen yogurt

Afternoon Snack
1 apple
¾ cup tomato juice
½ cup celery sticks

Dinner
Hamburger (3 oz.) with tomato and lettuce
on a bun
1 cup spinach salad with dressing
½ cup rice
1 8-oz. glass of milk
½ cup fruit salad

Eating a Variety of Foods

Using the Food Guide Pyramid can help you get enough **nutrients** (NOO·tree·ents)—*the substances in foods that your body needs in order to grow, have energy, and stay healthy.* Of course, many of the foods you eat will be made from several food groups—beef stew, for example, will have both meat and vegetables. Even within a food group, different foods have different amounts of nutrients. It's a good idea, therefore, to eat many different types of foods over time from every group. Your meals will also be more interesting that way.

Foods that are high in sugars and fats—represented by the tiny tip of the Food Guide Pyramid—are generally low in other nutrients. Additionally, these foods are high in **calories** (KA·luh·reez), which are *units of heat that measure the energy available in foods.* A diet that is high in calories often leads to weight gain and other types of health problems. Most 11- to 14-year-olds need about 2,200 to 2,500 calories per day.

in your journal

List the foods that you ate yesterday—breakfast, lunch, snacks, and dinner. Evaluate your daily food choices, using the Food Guide Pyramid and the Recommended Daily Servings chart on page 94. Give specific suggestions for improving your daily diet, based on your findings.

What food groups are represented in this meal?

Review
Lesson 1

Using complete sentences, answer the following questions on a separate sheet of paper.

Reviewing Terms and Facts

1. **Vocabulary** Define the term *Food Guide Pyramid,* and explain how it can be used to plan a healthful diet.

2. **List** Identify the five major food groups in the Food Guide Pyramid, and list the range of servings recommended daily for each one.

3. **Restate** Foods provide *nutrients* and *calories.* Define each term.

Thinking Critically

4. **Differentiate** List two factors that may influence a person's food choices.

Describe how these influences could be negative as well as positive.

5. **Explain** Reread the menu in Figure 4.3 on page 94. How might this menu be adapted to the recommended daily number of servings for an active teen boy? Describe additions you could make to the menu.

Applying Health Concepts

6. **Personal Health** Create a three-day menu for yourself that satisfies recommendations and is both varied and appetizing. Share your menu with a classmate.

Nutrients for Health and Wellness

This lesson will help you find answers to questions that teens often ask about the nutrients in the foods they eat. For example:

▶ What nutrients do I need in order to be healthy?
▶ What substances should I limit in my diet?
▶ How can I use nutrition labels to make wise food choices?

Words to Know

carbohydrates
proteins
vitamins
minerals
fats
fiber
saturated fats
cholesterol
unsaturated fats

The Six Major Nutrients

Using the Food Guide Pyramid to plan your daily diet is the best way to make sure that you are getting all the nutrients you need in order to build and repair your body and to provide enough energy to help you feel fit and well. **Figure 4.4** shows the six categories of nutrients. Each plays an important role in maintaining your health and wellness.

Figure 4.4
The Six Types of Nutrients
These are the major nutrient catagories.

Carbohydrates (kar·boh·HY·drayts) *are the starches and sugars that provide the body with most of its energy.*

Simple carbohydrates are sugars. Some sugars are found in fruits, milk, and honey. Table sugar is processed from sugar cane or sugar beets.

Complex carbohydrates include the starches found in breads, pasta, rice, and such starchy vegetables as potatoes and corn. Your body breaks down starch and converts it to sugar.

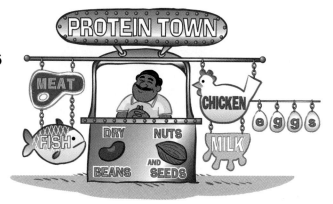

Proteins (PROH·teenz) *are essential nutrients used to repair body cells and tissues.* Proteins are made up of a group of 22 chemicals called amino (uh·MEE·noh) acids. Your body can make many of them on its own, but essential amino acids can be obtained only from some foods.

Complete proteins are found in foods—such as milk, eggs, and fish—that come from animals. They contain all 9 of the essential amino acids.

Incomplete proteins are found in foods—such as dry beans and grains—from plants. Such foods do not contain all the essential amino acids. People who do not eat foods that come from animals can get all the amino acids that they need by eating a variety of plant-based foods.

Vitamins are *substances that help to regulate the body's functions.* Vitamins also help the body use other nutrients. Some help fight infection. Fruits, vegetables, and whole-grain breads are good vitamin sources.

Water-soluble vitamins, including vitamin C and many B vitamins, dissolve in water. Because the body gets rid of extra amounts of these vitamins in urine, water-soluble vitamins must be replaced each day.

Fat-soluble vitamins, including vitamins A, D, E, and K, dissolve in fat. The body can therefore store these vitamins until they are needed. Fruits and vegetables, whole-grain breads and cereals, and fortified milk are the best sources of vitamins.

Minerals are *substances that strengthen the muscles, bones, and teeth; enrich the blood; and keep the heart and other organs operating properly.*

The minerals calcium and fluoride are particularly important for strong bones and teeth. Iron is needed for building and strengthening red blood cells. Potassium, sodium, and chloride help regulate the water balance in body tissues. Milk, meat, fish, spinach, fruits, and dry beans are rich sources of minerals.

Fats are *sources of energy that also perform other functions, such as vitamin storage and body insulation.* Fats keep the skin healthy as well.

Food energy that is not used by the body, however, is stored as body fat. Too much body fat puts stress on the skeleton and the heart. This is one reason why fats should be eaten in small quantities. Fats are found in meat, butter, margarine, cooking oil, whole milk, egg yolks, cheese, and most salad dressings.

Water is essential to survival. At birth, water makes up 75 percent of your total body weight; by adulthood, it makes up 60 percent. Water helps break down food, carries nutrients throughout the body, removes wastes from the body, and keeps the body at a comfortable temperature.

You should drink six to eight glasses of water each day. You can obtain additional water from many foods, including fruits and fruit juices, celery, milk and cabbage.

Your Bones Need Calcium!

The disabling bone disease called osteoporosis (ahs•tee•oh•puh•ROH•suhs) affects about 25 million Americans. Osteoporosis causes bones to become brittle, leading to fractures and spinal injuries. Recent studies indicate that Caucasian and Asian-American women are at the highest risk for developing this disease. An adequate supply of calcium, especially in the teen years when so much of the skeleton is developing, is very important. Start protecting yourself today by eating more calcium-rich foods, such as milk, yogurt, broccoli, and calcium-fortified cereals and fruit juices. In addition, make sure that you engage in regular physical activity.

Guidelines for Healthful Choices

To help you plan a healthful diet, the United States government has created a series of dietary guidelines. These guidelines are designed to help you to meet the Recommended Dietary Allowances, often abbreviated as RDAs, a set of measured amounts of particular nutrients that will meet the needs of most healthy people. RDAs are figured based on a person's gender, age, and activity level. By following dietary guidelines and using the Food Guide Pyramid, you will get the nutrients you need. The major points covered by the guidelines are explained on these pages. How well do you follow these guidelines in your diet?

Vary Your Diet

You already know that the most healthful diet consists of many different foods, chosen from the five basic groups. By varying your diet and following Food Guide Pyramid recommendations for food choices and servings, you can get the right amounts of the nutrients you need. No one food or food group can supply all that your body needs for growth and good health.

Manage Your Weight Through Exercise

Physical activity has many benefits. One of these benefits is to burn off the calories you consume every day. (Chapter 5 discusses physical activity and weight management.) Try to get at least 30 minutes of moderate physical activity most days of the week. Everything from brisk walking to in-line skating and dance—even cleaning your room—will provide you with exercise.

Eat Plenty of Grains, Vegetables, and Fruits

Foods in the three groups at the bottom of the pyramid provide energy as well as vitamins and minerals for healthy eyes, skin, bones, and blood. Additionally, many of these foods are good sources of **fiber,** *the part of grains, fruits, and vegetables that the body cannot break down.* Examples of fibrous parts of foods include apple and potato skins and the tough outer coating on kernels of corn and wheat. Many types of beans are also high in fiber. Although your body does not use fiber for energy, fiber helps you move food and wastes through your system. It also helps prevent some diseases, such as cancer. You should eat at least 20 grams of fiber each day to keep your digestive system healthy.

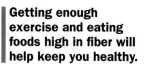
Getting enough exercise and eating foods high in fiber will help keep you healthy.

Cut Down on Fats

Fats are an essential nutrient, and you need them in your diet. However, no more than 30 percent of your daily calories should come from fat. No more than 10 percent of your total calories should come from saturated fats. **Saturated fats** are *fats found mostly in meats and dairy products.* They include the fats in meats, poultry, and eggs, as well as those in milk and butter. Physicians suggest that people go easy on saturated fats because they tend to raise the body's level of **cholesterol** (kuh·LES·tuh·rawl), *a waxlike substance used by the body to build cells and make other substances.* The body produces all the cholesterol it needs, so including large amounts of cholesterol in your diet can contribute to heart disease and stroke. **Unsaturated fats,** *liquid fats that come mainly from plants,* are found in olive oil and canola oil. You can cut down on cholesterol by choosing foods that contain unsaturated fats. A high-fiber and low-fat diet is linked to a lower risk for some types of cancer.

Avoid Too Much Added Sugar

Most people enjoy the sweet taste that sugar naturally gives to such foods as apples and strawberries. Sugar is a simple carbohydrate that the body uses for energy. Consuming too much added sugar (or carbohydrates in any form), however, can lead to tooth decay. Foods at the tip of the pyramid are high in fats and added sugars and low in other nutrients. They should be eaten sparingly.

Cut down on your sugar intake by not adding table sugar to fruit desserts or breakfast cereal and by avoiding sugary snacks such as cookies and candy. Remember to check canned and processed foods for hidden sugars. **Figure 4.5** shows some of the names of various sugars as they appear on food labels.

Watch Sodium and Salt

Sodium is a mineral that the body needs in small amounts to help regulate fluids. In the diet, its most common form is sodium chloride, commonly called table salt. Although each person's daily intake of salt should be no more than a teaspoonful, most people consume far more than that. Like sugar, salt or other high-sodium ingredients are often added to processed foods.

Cut down on sodium and salt by seasoning your food with herbs and spices rather than with table salt. Read nutrition labels on packaged foods to choose those with less sodium. In addition, go easy on salty snacks such as potato chips and salted peanuts.

Figure 4.5
Other Names for Sugar

If a food has one of these substances early in the ingredients list, or if several appear within the list, the food is likely to be high in added sugars.

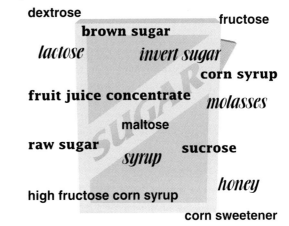

dextrose
fructose
brown sugar
lactose
invert sugar
corn syrup
fruit juice concentrate
molasses
maltose
raw sugar
syrup
sucrose
honey
high fructose corn syrup
corn sweetener

Reading a Nutrition Facts Label

The Nutrition Facts label found on most food packages is another tool to help you make smart food choices. Learn to use this resource to evaluate packaged foods before you buy them. **Figure 4.6** shows the information that appears on a Nutrition Facts label. The illustration also shows how you can use this label to make wise choices.

The percentages shown on the label are based on amounts called Daily Reference Values. Daily Reference Values are guidelines concerning the amounts of certain nutrients that are part of a healthy diet.

LIFE SKILLS

Making Healthful Choices at Fast-Food Restaurants

*I*n the United States in 1995, on any given day, 57 percent of Americans ate at least one meal or snack away from home. The same study found that when children and teens ate out, they did so in fast-food restaurants more than 80 percent of the time. Fast-food restaurants can offer benefits to teens: enjoyable food at reasonable prices, quick service, and an informal and convenient place to gather with friends. However, many fast-food meals are high in saturated fat, cholesterol, sodium, sugar, and calories.

How can you make healthful choices at fast-food restaurants? Follow these tips.

▶ **Have food you like, but have it in a different way.** Ask the server to hold (leave out) the creamy spread on your sandwich. Pass up the french fries for a plain baked potato, or have a small order of fries.

▶ **Take advantage of items on the menu with lower amounts of fat.** Try the salad bar, and use the low-fat dressing. Instead of having a sandwich with meat that has been fried, choose meat that has been grilled or baked.

▶ **Try a new drink.** Many fast-food restaurants offer fruit juices and low-fat or skim milk.

▶ **Eat your vegetables.** If you order a pizza, top it with green peppers, mushrooms, onions, or broccoli.

▶ **Be creative about dessert.** For less fat, try frozen yogurt rather than ice cream. Or choose fresh fruit from the salad bar.

Follow-up Activity

Think about a fast-food restaurant that you enjoy. What do you usually order? Write down your order, and then analyze its nutritional value. What foods might you substitute, or what cooking methods might you avoid?

Figure 4.6
Reading a Nutrition Facts Label
Most processed foods now carry this label. You may also see such labels on or displayed near fruits, vegetables, meats, poultry, and fish.

The amount of calories, **Ⓐ** nutrients, and other substances is based on one serving of the package's contents. Also shown is the serving size. Measures are shown in both standard and metric units.

One serving contains this many **Ⓑ** calories. Next to this amount is the number of calories from fat.

Major nutrients are measured in **Ⓒ** grams (g) or milligrams (mg) and the percentage of daily values. On labels from larger containers, like this one, additional information is provided at the bottom of the label.

Ⓓ This shows the amount of total fat, as well as of saturated fat, in one serving. Less than 0.5 grams is rounded to 0.

Ⓔ This shows the amounts of these substances in one serving of the food.

Ⓕ This shows the percentage of daily values for selected vitamins and minerals in one serving of the product.

Nutrition Facts
Serving Size ½ cup (114g)
Servings Per Container 4

Amount Per Serving

Calories 90   Calories from Fat 30

	% Daily Value*
Total Fat 3g	5%
Saturated Fat 0g	0%
Cholesterol 0mg	0%
Sodium 300mg	13%
Total Carbohydrate 13g	4%
Dietary Fiber 3g	12%
Sugars 3g	
Protein 3g	

Vitamin A	80%	Vitamin C	60%
Calcium	4%	Iron	4%

* Percent Daily Values are based on a 2,000 calorie diet. Your daily values may be higher or lower depending on your calorie needs:

		Calories	2,000	2,500
Total Fat	Less Than		65g	80g
Sat Fat	Less Than		20g	25g
Cholesterol	Less Than		300mg	300mg
Sodium	Less Than		2,400mg	2,400mg
Total Carbohydrate			300g	375g
Fiber			25g	30g

Calories per gram:
Fat 9   Carbohydrate 4   Protein 4

Review

Using complete sentences, answer the following questions on a separate sheet of paper.

Reviewing Terms and Facts

1. **List**   Identify the six major types of nutrients.

2. **Restate**   What are RDAs?

3. **Vocabulary**   Explain what is meant by the term *fiber,* and describe its value to the body.

Thinking Critically

4. **Compare and Contrast**   State the difference between saturated and unsaturated fats, including the foods each come from.

5. **Explain**   How can the Food Guide Pyramid help you avoid having too much fat and sugar in your diet?

Applying Health Concepts

6. **Consumer Health**   Study the Nutrition Facts panel on a package or can of food. Which of the dietary guidelines apply to this food? Write a short report in which you list your findings and explain the product's nutritional value.

7. **Growth and Development**   Find out more about vitamin D. Discover which foods contain moderate to high amounts of this vitamin and how it affects growth and development. Then find out what conditions might result from having too little vitamin D in the diet. Write a paragraph summarizing your findings.

Healthful Meal Planning

This lesson will help you find answers to questions that teens often ask about planning meals. For example:

▶ **Why is breakfast so important?**
▶ **How can I plan nutritious meals?**
▶ **What snacks will provide important nutrients?**

Words to Know

glucose
nutrient density

Cultural Connections

A European Breakfast

To add some fun and variety to breakfast, try these foods, which are traditional parts of breakfast in many parts of Europe:

▶ Crusty rye or French bread
▶ Thin slices of low-fat ham and cheese
▶ Granola mixed with yogurt and honey
▶ Chunks of fresh fruit topped with a sprinkling of cinnamon or nutmeg

Find out about breakfast foods from other parts of the world. Report on your findings to your class.

If you get into the habit of eating a good breakfast now, you'll probably continue that habit into adulthood.

The Importance of Breakfast

When you get up in the morning, at least 10 or 12 hours may have passed since you last ate. You need a new supply of nutrients to build and repair cells. Your body also needs to be resupplied with energy. When the body breaks down carbohydrates, it converts them to a sugar called **glucose** (GLOO·kohs). This sugar is *the body's main source of energy.* Because your body cannot store extra reserves of glucose, you need to resupply it in the morning.

Several 1995 nutritional studies clearly showed that eating a healthful breakfast helps teens to think and work better. Students who eat breakfast have a longer attention span and a more positive attitude toward school. What's a good breakfast? Fortunately, you have a number of delicious choices.

■ The best breakfasts are high in complex carbohydrates. Toast, bagels, English muffins, and waffles are good choices. To cut down on fat, top them with yogurt, fruit spreads, cottage cheese, or applesauce rather than with butter or margarine.

■ If time is short, choose easy-to-prepare items, such as fresh or canned fruits, yogurt, and ready-to-eat cereals. Look for cereals made from whole grains or fortified with vitamins and minerals. You can top ready-to-eat cereals with dried fruits or chopped nuts, too.

■ Take something with you. Celery stuffed with peanut butter or a lowfat cheese stick along with fruit or vegetable juice are good choices.

- If you aren't hungry, at least drink a glass of milk or juice. Remember, however, that cereal with milk or a piece of fruit will provide more lasting energy than just milk or juice.

- Finally, you don't have to eat traditional breakfast foods. A bagel pizza or a reheated plate of spaghetti will provide you with an excellent start to the day.

Planning Your Other Meals

A good breakfast sets the pattern for good nutrition all day. The Food Guide Pyramid can help you make healthful meal and snack choices. What kinds of ground rules will help you get the nutrients you need and enjoy your food, too? Here are a few suggestions.

- **Eat regular meals.** Avoid skipping meals. People who skip meals often overeat at another meal.

- **Watch portion sizes.** Suggested portion sizes may be smaller than you think. For example, one serving of meat is only 2-3 ounces, which is about the size of a deck of cards. (The palm of your hand is also a good, easy guide for meat serving size). Many people eat a cup of pasta at one sitting. Keep in mind that this represents *two* servings—not one—from the bread, cereals, rice, and pasta group.

- **Eat less of the "pyramid tip" foods, but don't feel forced to cut them out entirely.** After all, you eat for enjoyment as well as for good nutrition. It's okay to have a soft drink or candy occasionally.

- **Plan and make healthful lunches.** If you pack your own lunch to take to school, try to make nutritious food choices. For example, using whole-wheat bread instead of white bread for sandwiches will provide more fiber. If you use mayonnaise or butter on a sandwich, use a small amount. Add moisture with lettuce leaves and tomato slices. If you like luncheon meats, try turkey, chicken, or low-fat ham to cut down on fat.

- **Achieve balance over time.** Balance your nutrients and food groups over several days or a week. If you eat a lunch that is high in fats one day, make sure that dinner and perhaps the next day's choices are low in fats.

Many teens enjoy planning and making some of their own meals.

Smart Snacking

Between meals during the day, many people like to have a snack. Unfortunately, they may reach for snack foods that are high in calories, fat, and sugar, and low in nutrients. A healthful diet includes snacks with high **nutrient density,** *the amount of nutrients in a food relative to the number of calories.* **Figure 4.7** shows a comparison of various snack foods, based on nutrient density.

Figure 4.7
Snacks and Nutrient Density

It is fairly easy to substitute snacks with high nutrient density for those with lower nutrient density.

Snacks with LOW Nutrient Density (high in calories, low in nutrients)	Snacks with HIGH Nutrient Density (low in calories, high in nutrients)
potato chips	pretzels
candy bars	raisins
soft drinks	mixed vegetable juice
ice cream	low-fat frozen yogurt
chocolate chip cookies	graham crackers
dips made with sour cream	dips made with salsa

MAKING HEALTHY DECISIONS
Making Breakfast Important

Jameel has begun to take more of an interest in his diet since he entered middle school. One area in which he has seen improvement is breakfast. He and his parents used to have daily arguments about his refusal to eat in the morning. Now, although his choices aren't always standard breakfast foods, he eats a nutritious breakfast every day.

Jameel's best friend, Raymond, has the same arguments with his parents that Jameel used to have. He either eats nothing at all or grabs a doughnut or a toaster pastry. Jameel would like to encourage his friend to eat more healthful breakfasts, but he isn't sure how to introduce the subject. Then he remembers the six-step decision-making process he learned in school.

① **State the situation**
② **List the options**
③ **Weigh the possible outcomes**
④ **Consider your values**
⑤ **Make a decision and act**
⑥ **Evaluate the decision**

Follow-up Activities

1. Apply the six steps of the decision-making process to Jameel's situation.
2. With your classmates, role-play a number of different decisions that Jameel might make. Discuss these role plays.

Think of your total daily snacks as a fourth meal, a fourth chance to provide your body with the nutrients it needs. If you often look forward to snack time for an energy boost, what should you reach for? Studies indicate that the best energy snacks combine complex carbohydrates with small amounts of protein. Be creative by combining foods that you enjoy from these two food groups. Here are a few examples:

- Chunks or slices of unpeeled fresh fruit or vegetables dipped in low-fat yogurt

- A bowl of whole-grain cereal with skim milk

- Popcorn topped with Parmesan cheese

- Whole-wheat crackers spread with peanut butter

- A microwaveable soft pretzel and a stick of string cheese

- Half of a pita pocket stuffed with low-fat turkey

in your journal

From the snacks you have read about in this lesson, or from your own knowledge of healthful snacks, write a weekly "snack plan" for yourself, with the goal of making this part of your diet more healthful.

These snacks are both nutritious and delicious.

Review   Lesson 3

Using complete sentences, answer the following questions on a separate sheet of paper.

Reviewing Terms and Facts

1. **Recall**   Why is breakfast so important?

2. **List**   Suggest two tips for planning meals other than breakfast.

3. **Vocabulary**   Define the term *nutrient density.*

4. **Explain**   Which two nutrient categories can be combined for a high-energy snack?

Thinking Critically

5. **Infer**   Why do you think that people do not need to cut out foods from the pyramid tip entirely?

6. **Evaluate**   How does technology affect the way people eat? Describe how the technology available today affects your meal planning choices.

Applying Health Concepts

7. **Health of Others**   Using what you have learned, write an advertisement for a healthful breakfast or snack. Combine words and pictures to persuade readers that your featured foods are healthful, easy to prepare, and delicious.

Lesson 3: Healthful Meal Planning   105

TEEN HEALTH DIGEST

Teens Making a Difference

Strength in Numbers

Along with their regular classes, students at the William Penn Charter School in Philadelphia can take a course in helping others. As part of a program led by James Ballengee, Director of Service Learning, teens spend at least 40 hours each year helping people in need.

Once a month, a group of students spends four to five hours on a Saturday helping out at a shelter and soup kitchen for homeless men. Another group volunteers for Philabundance, a nonprofit agency that picks up surplus foods from restaurants, caterers, and hotels and de-livers it to shelters and other resources for needy people.

Jeff Riddle, a staff member at Philabundance, knows that he can count on the Penn Charter students to help out. "Jim Ballengee's students define the term *youth in action!*" he said. One week, Philabundance learned that someone wanted to donate 10,000 pounds of sweet potatoes. The potatoes would have spoiled if they had been left on the truck for very long. A call to Mr. Ballengee brought a team from Penn Charter. They spent most of a day unloading, sorting, and repacking the potatoes for distribution.

Try This: *Find out about a group in your community that fights hunger. Ask what opportunities there are for teens to help.*

Myths and Realities

The Truth About Sugar

Q. I hear parents talk about how sugar affects their kids and makes them act wild. Is that really true?

A. Despite what many people believe, sugar does not seem to cause hyperactive behavior. One study of 23 children conducted over nine weeks, for example, found no link between sugar consumption and boisterous behavior. Eating a lot of sugar can cause other problems for children, however. It promotes tooth decay and can lead to excessive weight gain. Children who are severely overweight may experience health problems such as diabetes or high blood pressure when they reach adulthood.

HEALTH UPDATE

Safe Fruits and Vegetables

Fruits and vegetables are an important part of a healthful diet. However, you should know that some of today's farming and food production methods may expose foods to dangerous germs that can make people ill.

To protect yourself, rinse produce thoroughly, especially if you plan to eat it without cooking it. Raw meat, poultry, seafood, and eggs may also contain harmful germs. If you are preparing those foods, therefore, wash your hands and any utensils thoroughly before working with other foods.

Personal Trainer

Make a Commitment with Calcium!

Getting enough calcium is crucial for strong bones. Just consuming calcium alone, however, does not make bones as dense as they could be. You also need physical activity.

What kind of activity will help you use the calcium you consume? Weight-bearing exercise, which puts stress on your bones, makes them grow stronger. There are many forms of weight-bearing exercise, including

- brisk walking.
- dancing.
- stair climbing.
- jumping rope.

CON$UMER FOCU$

Good Bargains, Good Nutrition

Smart shoppers save money by buying foods that are on sale. However, you should be careful *not* to buy perishables—foods that may spoil, such as meats, dairy products, and fresh fruits and vegetables—in such large quantities that you can't use them up while they are still fresh. Make sure you read the expiration, or "Use by," date on packaged sale items. Such dates tell you the *last* date that the product is considered fresh.

Try This:

Help a family member with a shopping trip by checking store advertisements and coupons ahead of time and suggesting bargains.

The Digestive and Excretory Systems

This lesson will help you find answers to questions that teens often ask about how their bodies break down and use food. For example:

▶ **Why does food have to be digested?**

▶ **How does digestion work?**

▶ **How are waste products removed from the body?**

Words to Know

digestion
digestive system
saliva
stomach
small intestine
liver
pancreas
excretory system
excretion
kidney
colon

Energy for Life

Food provides nutrients that the body needs in order to grow, develop, and stay healthy. Before the body can use the nutrients from food, it must break food down into smaller parts. **Digestion** (dy·JES·chuhn) is *the process by which the body breaks food down into smaller components that can be absorbed by the bloodstream and sent to each cell in your body.* The process of digestion is accomplished by your **digestive** (dy·JES·tiv) **system,** *a series of organs that work together to break down foods into substances that your cells can use.*

How Digestion Works

Think for a moment about what happens in a typical factory. Raw materials, such as logs or iron ore, enter the factory. Inside, processes occur that change the material into another form. For example, logs might be ground into pieces to make paper, or iron ore might be melted to make steel. At some point, usually, chemicals are added. The end product is stored for later use, and waste materials are thrown away.

Digestion is similar in some ways. It involves both physical changes, such as the crushing of food by the teeth, and chemical changes, such as the transforming of food by body chemicals called *enzymes.*

It takes anywhere from 16 to 24 hours for your body to process food into energy and get rid of waste products.

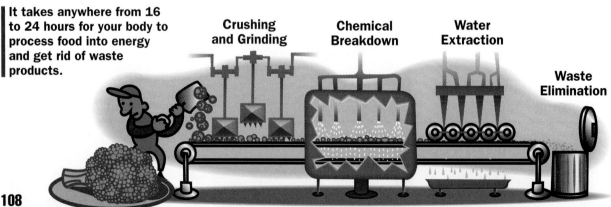

Crushing and Grinding   Chemical Breakdown   Water Extraction   Waste Elimination

The Mouth and Throat

Does your mouth ever water when you sit down to eat, or when you smell something delicious roasting in the oven? That "water" is **saliva** (suh·LY·vuh), *a digestive juice produced by the salivary glands in your mouth.* It starts to flow as a physical signal from your body that it is ready to begin the digestive process. **Figure 4.8** shows the first steps in digestion.

Figure 4.8
The Beginning of Digestion
The process of digestion begins in the mouth.

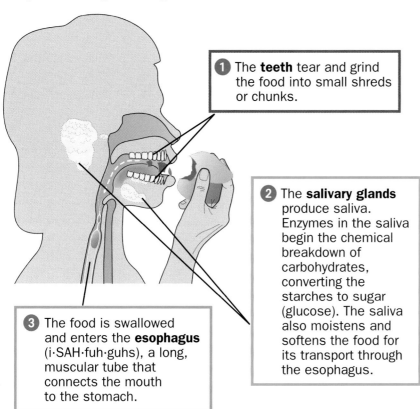

❶ The **teeth** tear and grind the food into small shreds or chunks.

❷ The **salivary glands** produce saliva. Enzymes in the saliva begin the chemical breakdown of carbohydrates, converting the starches to sugar (glucose). The saliva also moistens and softens the food for its transport through the esophagus.

❸ The food is swallowed and enters the **esophagus** (i·SAH·fuh·guhs), a long, muscular tube that connects the mouth to the stomach.

The esophagus is located right next to the trachea (TRAY·kee·uh), or windpipe. The trachea is the passageway through which air gets to your lungs. The passages up to the nose are at the back of your throat. Getting food into your air passages could cause you to choke. For that reason, two flaps of skin close airways when you swallow. The uvula (YOO·vyuh·luh) closes the airway to the nose. The epiglottis (e·puh·GLAH·tis) closes the airway to the lungs, as shown in **Figure 4.9.**

Figure 4.9
When You Swallow
Before you swallow, the passages to the nose and lungs are open. When you swallow, these passages are automatically closed.

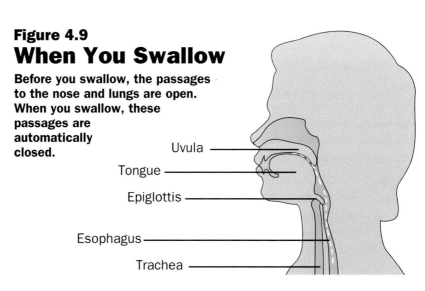

Uvula

Tongue

Epiglottis

Esophagus

Trachea

Q & A

Baby Talk

Q: Why do babies sometimes spit up milk after feeding?

A: Between the stomach and the esophagus there is a muscle designed to keep the food in the stomach. In young babies, this muscle is not mature. The gases that normally build up in the stomach during feeding create pressure. That pressure—a burp—forces some of the milk in the baby's stomach past the muscle and up the esophagus. Over the first year of life this muscle gradually strengthens. Spitting up does not usually happen after the age of one.

The Stomach and Small Intestine

Figure 4.10 shows the path that food takes during the next part of the digestive process. Once food enters the esophagus, muscles lining the walls of the esophagus contract and relax, moving the food along until it reaches the **stomach,** *a muscular organ in which some digestion occurs.* The stomach holds and processes the food for up to four hours. During this time the stomach's strong muscular walls churn and mix the food. When this part of the digestive process is complete, the food resembles a fairly thin soup, called chyme (KYM).

Figure 4.10
The Digestive System

Most of the process of digestion goes on in the small intestine.

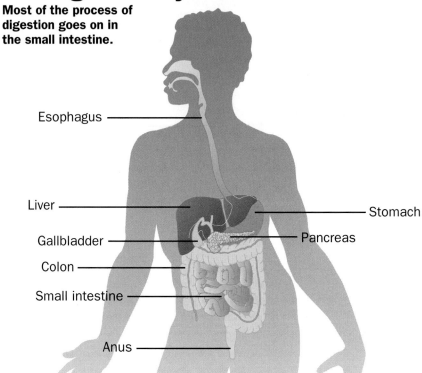

Esophagus

Liver

Gallbladder

Colon

Small intestine

Anus

Stomach

Pancreas

HEALTH LAB
The Digestion of Protein

Introduction: During digestion, organs of the digestive system secrete enzymes to break down proteins. Once proteins are broken down, their amino acids can flow into the bloodstream and be used by the body.

All plants and animals contain enzymes. In this experiment, you will use the enzyme *papain* (puh·PAY·uhn), a protein-splitting enzyme that comes from the papaya fruit. You will also use gelatin, a substance made from a strong protein called *collagen* (KAH·luh·juhn). In meat, collagen is a tough material found in tendons and ligaments.

Objective: Observe how enzymes break down proteins during digestion.

Materials and Method: Work with a partner or small group. You will need a package of flavored or unflavored gelatin; a measuring cup; a spoon for stirring; water; two petri dishes or other shallow, nonmetallic containers; measuring spoons; and unflavored meat tenderizer made from papain.

Follow the package directions to make the gelatin. Pour the gelatin into each shallow container, to a depth of about ½ inch. Label one container A and the

Next the food moves to the **small intestine,** *a coiled tube, about 20 feet long, where most of the digestive process takes place.* Three other organs help the small intestine in the digestive process:

- **Liver.** The **liver** is *the body's largest gland, which secretes a liquid called bile that helps to digest fats.* The liver also helps to regulate the level of sugar in the blood, breaks down harmful substances such as alcohol, and stores some vitamins.

- **Gallbladder.** After the liver produces bile, it sends it to the gallbladder (GAWL·bla·der), which stores this bile until it is needed.

- **Pancreas.** The **pancreas** (PAN·kree·uhs) is *a gland that helps the small intestine by producing pancreatic juice, a blend of enzymes that breaks down proteins, carbohydrates, and fats.*

When food has been completely broken down, nutrients are absorbed through the walls of the small intestine into the bloodstream. Blood carries the nutrients to body cells. **Figure 4.11** shows this absorption process.

Liver Damage

One of the functions of the liver is to act as a "detox center" for poisons that enter the body. For this reason, overconsumption of alcohol can damage the liver over time. A condition called cirrhosis (suh·ROH·sis) can occur, in which liver cells are destroyed and replaced by scar tissue. If excessive drinking continues, the condition can cause death.

Figure 4.11
Nutrient Absorption

The walls of the small intestine are covered with fingerlike projections called villi (VI·ly). Digested material is absorbed into the villi, which allow it to enter the bloodstream.

Blood vessels

Villi

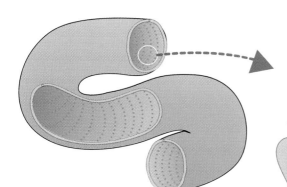
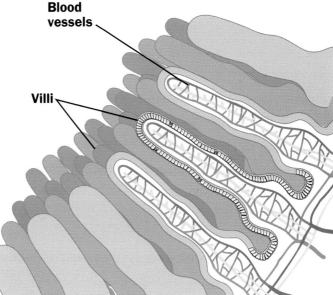

other container B. Allow the gelatin to set until firm. With the measuring spoons, sprinkle about 1 teaspoon of the meat tenderizer on the top of the gelatin in dish A. Wash your hands thoroughly. (**NOTE:** Do not eat the gelatin in either dish.) Wait one-half hour to make your observations.

Observations and Analysis:
Observe dish A and dish B. Compare the appearance of the gelatin. What was the effect of the papain on the gelatin? What conclusions can you draw regarding the effect of human digestive enzymes on meat and poultry?

Note that papain is an ingredient in meat tenderizer, a substance that chefs sometimes sprinkle on tough

meats before cooking them. How do you think papain makes meat tender?

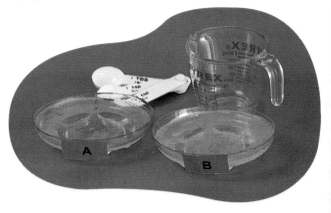

Removing Wastes

Although digestion is complete, the body still has tasks to perform. As food is being broken down, the body separates out the parts that it cannot use. Those wastes must then be removed from the body.

The body produces three kinds of wastes. Solid wastes are made up of foods that the body could not break down, including fiber. Liquid wastes and carbon dioxide gas are wastes produced by cell activity. Your **excretory** (EK·skruh·tor·ee) **system** is *the system that removes wastes from your body and controls water balance.* Your lungs perform some functions of the excretory system by getting rid of carbon dioxide gas when you exhale. Your skin also gets rid of some wastes through sweat. The major organs of the excretory system, however, are the kidneys, bladder, and colon. These remove most of the liquid and solid wastes from your system.

The Kidneys, Bladder, and Colon

Approximately 60 percent of your body is water, and most waste materials are dissolved in it. **Excretion** (ek·SKREE·shuhn) is *the process by which the body gets rid of liquid waste materials.* **Figure 4.12** shows the process of filtering, storing, and excreting liquid wastes.

Figure 4.12
The Process of Excretion
Your kidneys and bladder get rid of liquid wastes.

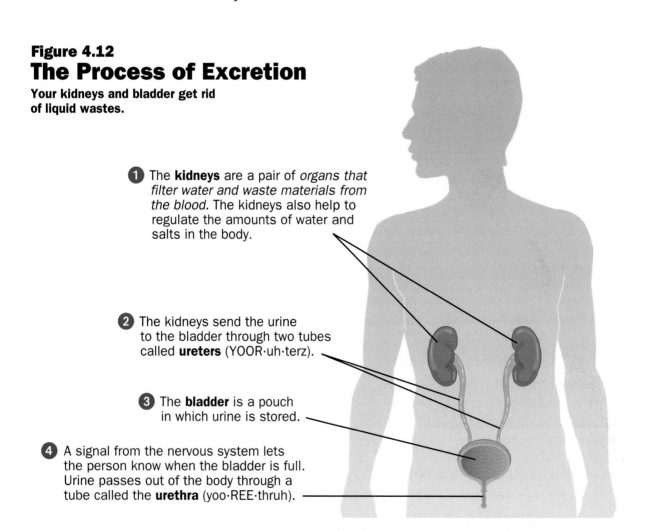

❶ The **kidneys** are a pair of *organs that filter water and waste materials from the blood.* The kidneys also help to regulate the amounts of water and salts in the body.

❷ The kidneys send the urine to the bladder through two tubes called **ureters** (YOOR·uh·terz).

❸ The **bladder** is a pouch in which urine is stored.

❹ A signal from the nervous system lets the person know when the bladder is full. Urine passes out of the body through a tube called the **urethra** (yoo·REE·thruh).

The body sends a mixture of water and undigested solid wastes, into the **colon** (KOH·luhn), or large intestine, *a storage tube for solid wastes.* Most of the water is absorbed by the colon and returned to the body. The remaining solid wastes become material called feces. When the colon becomes full, strong muscles in its walls contract. This movement pushes the feces out of the body through an opening called the anus.

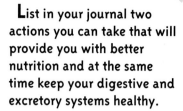
Caring for Your Digestive and Excretory Systems

Good health habits are essential to the care of the digestive and excretory systems. Follow these guidelines.

- Eat a balanced diet, based on the Food Guide Pyramid.

- Eat plenty of foods that are low in fat and high in fiber.

- Drink six to eight glasses of water every day.

- Eat at regular times each day.

- Always chew your food slowly and carefully.

- Brush and floss your teeth at least twice a day and have regular dental checkups. Your teeth are important to the digestive process.

- Be active! Participate in moderate physical activity most, if not all, days of the week.

Fiber-rich foods are particularly important to the health of your digestive and excretory systems.

Review Lesson 4

Using complete sentences, answer the following questions on a separate sheet of paper.

Reviewing Terms and Facts

1. **Vocabulary**   Define the terms *digestive system* and *excretory system.*

2. **Recall**   How do the liver, gallbladder, and pancreas aid in the digestive process?

3. **Restate**   What does the colon do?

Thinking Critically

4. **Explain**   Describe possible consequences for the rest of the body of a digestive system that is not working properly.

5. **Hypothesize**   Choose two of the tips for caring for your digestive system, and explain why you think each might be beneficial.

Applying Health Concepts

6. **Personal Health**   Make a diagram or flow chart to show the passage of food from the time it enters the mouth to the time that its undigested parts are excreted from the body.

Chapter Summary

▶ **Lesson 1** Basing your food choices on the Food Guide Pyramid helps you plan meals that provide the nutrients you need each day.

▶ **Lesson 2** The body needs a daily supply of the six major nutrients: carbohydrates, proteins, vitamins, minerals, fats, and water. Although fats are needed for overall health, they should be eaten sparingly.

▶ **Lesson 3** Breakfast is an important meal because it refuels the body with energy. Wise planning decisions such as eating regular meals and achieving balance over time in your meal and snack choices will help you get the nutrients you need.

▶ **Lesson 4** In order to use food, the body must digest it—break it down into tiny particles that can be absorbed by the blood—and excrete waste products.

Reviewing Key Terms and Concepts

Using complete sentences, answer the following questions on a separate sheet of paper.

Lesson 1

1. Define the terms *diet* and *nutrition,* and explain the relationship between them.

2. Which food group should be the source of the largest number of servings each day?

Lesson 2

3. Define *cholesterol.* What is the role of cholesterol in your health?

4. List three pieces of information listed on a Nutrition Facts panel of a food label.

Lesson 3

5. Define *glucose.*

6. What does it mean to achieve balance in your food choices over time?

Lesson 4

7. Explain the role of saliva in digestion.

8. Briefly describe the processes of digestion and excretion after the food leaves the stomach.

Thinking Critically

Using complete sentences, answer the following questions on a separate sheet of paper.

9. **Explain** Use what you have learned about nutrients to show why the sections of the Food Guide Pyramid vary in size.

10. **Evaluate** Analyze the nutritional value of each of the following breakfast menus. Then suggest several foods that might be substituted to make each menu more nutritious and lower in fat.

    Breakfast #1: orange juice, two fried eggs with bacon, whole-wheat toast

    Breakfast #2: whole-grain cereal with whole milk and sliced peaches, white toast with butter and jelly, water

11. **Describe** Explain the value of a high-fiber, low-fat diet.

Your Action Plan

The decisions you make about your diet will affect your health and energy level, both now and in the future.

Step 1 Look over your journal entries from Chapter 4. What do you need to do to improve your nutrition? Use your journal entries to set a long-term goal. You might decide to follow the Food Guide Pyramid in making food choices or to increase or decrease the amount of a particular nutrient in your diet.

Step 2 Describe steps you can take to reach your long-term goal. For example, you might decide to begin eating breakfast or making your lunch every day instead of buying it.

Set specific dates to assess your progress. On those dates, write a paragraph in your journal that describes how you feel about achieving your goals.

In Your Home and Community

1. **Health of Others** Offer to make dinner for your family one night at home. Plan a healthful menu that you think everyone will enjoy. Go over it with a parent or guardian to make sure that person approves. Then make the meal and serve it to your family. If you like the results, you may decide to do this on a regular basis, monthly or even weekly.

2. **Growth and Development** Talk with a preschool teacher in your area about the concepts the school teaches to young children about nutrition. Offer to make some colorful posters, shoot a video, or take some photographs to enliven his or her next lesson.

Building Your Portfolio

1. **Illustration of the Food Guide Pyramid** Create your own version of the Food Guide Pyramid. Draw the outline on a large piece of poster paper, and use pictures from magazines or pictures you draw to illustrate the sections. Do additional research to find out some of the main nutrients that are found within each food group (for example, calcium in the milk, yogurt, and cheese group).

2. **Nutrient Advertisement** Create an advertisement for a food or a particular nutrient. Show how you would promote the value of that food or nutrient. Add the advertisement or its description to your portfolio.

3. **Personal Assessment** Look through all the activities and projects you did for this chapter. Choose one or two that you would like to include in your portfolio.

Chapter 5

Physical Activity and Weight Management

Medical Center
Cancer Benefit

5K Walk/Run
Registration →

Student Expectations

After reading this chapter, you should be able to:

❶ Define what it means to be fit.

❷ Describe how the circulatory system works.

❸ Explain how the skeletal and muscular systems work.

❹ Describe how to plan a fitness program.

❺ Identify healthful attitudes for and principles of weight management.

Teen Chat Group

Stephan: James! Are you here for the cancer research benefit, too?

James: Yeah. It's my first. I hope I can do the whole five kilometers.

Krystina: It's not that hard. Just remember to pace yourself. Are you going to walk or jog?

James: I'm going to jog until I get tired and then walk for a while. I jog every morning now, so I want to see how far I can go.

Stephan: This is my first time, too. I decided to get involved because my grandfather was diagnosed with cancer earlier this year. I thought maybe this could help him and be good for me at the same time.

Krystina: You won't regret it. I did it last year. It's great to know there's something you can do to make a difference.

James: Come on, let's head for the starting line.

in your journal

Read the dialogue on this page. Have you ever thought about how your personal fitness could make a difference to others? Start your private journal entries on fitness by responding to these questions:

► What does being fit mean to you?
► What activities could help you stay fit?
► How do you think fitness is related to weight management?

When you reach the end of the chapter, you will use your journal entries to make an action plan.

1 Physical Fitness and You

This lesson will help you find answers to questions that teens often ask about physical fitness. For example:

▶ **What does it mean to be fit?**

▶ **How will fitness help me?**

▶ **What kinds of activities will help me be fit?**

Words to Know

fitness
exercise
body composition
strength
endurance
aerobic exercise
anaerobic exercise
flexibility

Your Total Health

Fitness for Others **ACTIVITY!**

When you are fit, it will not only improve every area of your life, but it can also help the people around you. A fit person can respond effectively to emergencies. If, for example, you are with a friend who experiences a sudden injury, you will be able to run for help. Knowing first aid is another way to be prepared for an emergency. Find out where you can learn first-aid procedures in your area.

Fitness for Life

What does it mean to be fit? **Fitness** is *the ability to handle the physical work and play of everyday life without becoming overly tired.* Being fit also means that you have energy in reserve to meet unexpected demands. Think about all the different things you do each day: going to school, taking part in after-school activities, doing chores. You're fit if you can meet all these demands—as well as extra challenges, such as having to run for the bus or spend an evening waiting on tables for a school fundraising dinner.

Do you think that you are fit? How might you raise your level of fitness? **Exercise** is *physical activity that develops fitness.* By exercising, you become more fit. When you exercise regularly, you find that you are able to get through each day with energy to spare. The more demanding your activities are, the more you must exercise to stay fit. A soccer player, for example, needs to do wind sprints to be fit to play in games. Developing the habit of exercising and keeping fit can help you remain healthy throughout your life.

Physical activity is one way for people of different ages to stay fit and enjoy one another's company.

What Fitness Does For You

The benefits of fitness are much more than just physical well-being. Being fit also helps you mentally and emotionally as well as socially. Fitness is an excellent way to keep your health triangle in balance. Take a look at **Figure 5.1** below. Do you see how the benefits of fitness in one area of health lead to benefits in the other areas as well?

*inter*NET
CONNECTION
Shape up with healthy ideas on the Web, like customized meal and fitness plans to help achieve your goals.
http://www.glencoe.com/sec/health

Figure 5.1
The Benefits of Fitness
Staying fit is a way of life.

Benefits to Physical Health

Higher energy level
Decreased risk of getting certain diseases
Better performance of heart and lungs
Improved strength and endurance
Improved posture
Greater freedom of movement
Better coordination
Better sleep
Better weight control

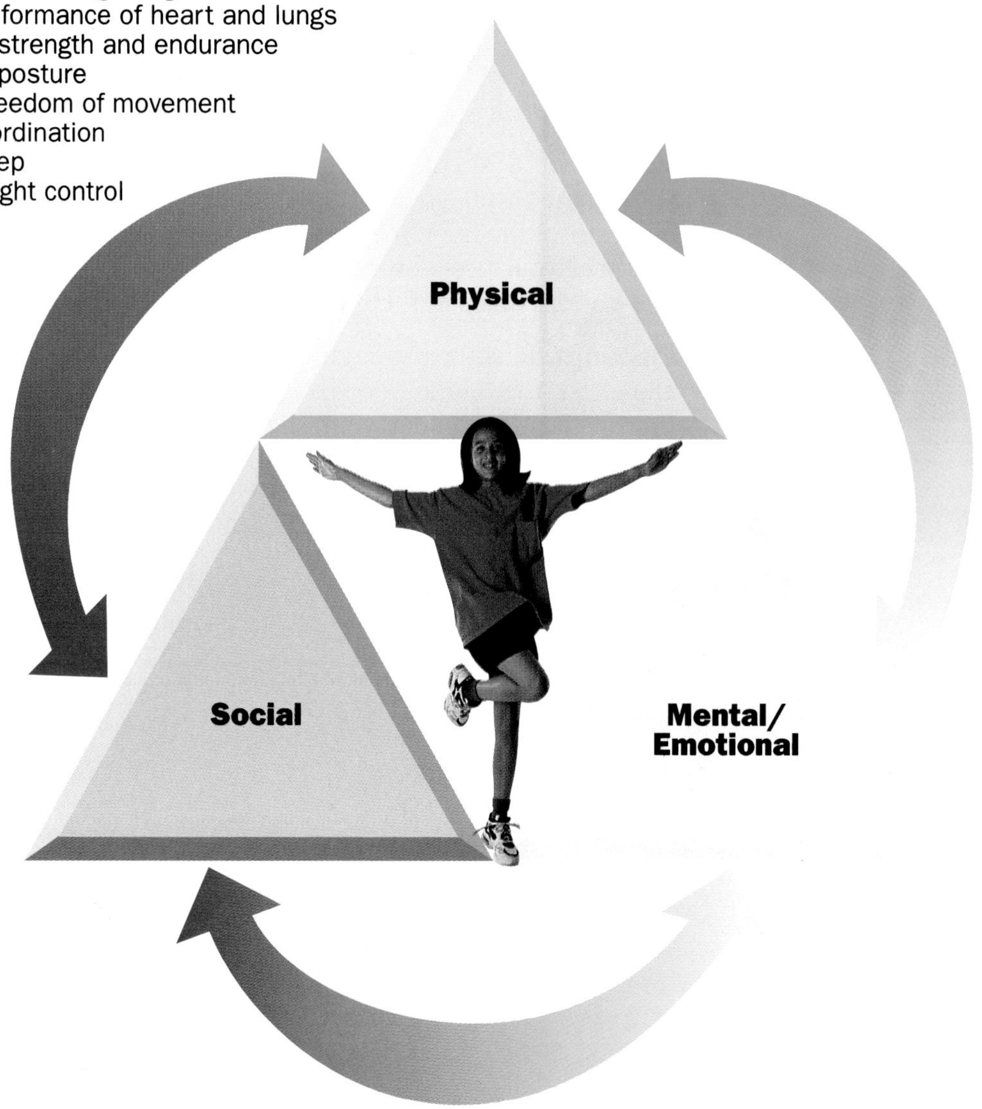

Physical

Social

Mental/ Emotional

Benefits to Social Health

Additional chances to meet new people
Opportunities to share common goals with others
Greater ability to interact and cooperate with others
Opportunities to use talents to help others
Ability to work more efficiently

Benefits to Mental/Emotional Health

Enhanced self-esteem
Sharpened mental alertness
Reduced stress
More relaxed attitude
More enjoyment of leisure time

Q: I haven't jumped rope since I was little. How do I find a rope the right size for me?

A: Hold the handles of the rope together and step with one of your feet on the middle of the rope. The handles should reach to about the middle of your chest.

To build your strength, gradually increase the number of repetitions you do at each exercise session.

The Elements of Fitness

When you exercise, you develop three elements of fitness: strength, endurance, and flexibility. Another aspect of fitness is **body composition**—*the proportions of fat, bones, muscle, and fluid that make up body weight.* By eating a nutritious diet that is low in fats and getting plenty of exercise, you will keep your body composition within healthful limits.

Strength

Strength is *the ability of your muscles to exert a force.* In fitness, strength is measured by the most work your muscles can do at a given time. By exercising to build strength, you can more easily lift heavy objects without injury or strain. You will also be more skilled in the sports and other activities in which you participate. Here are three standard strength-training exercises:

■ **Curl-ups.** Curl-ups, also called crunches, strengthen your abdominal muscles. Strong abdominal muscles take some of the strain off the muscles of your back. To do curl-ups, lie on your back, bend your knees, and put your hands on the floor at your sides. (For a slightly easier exercise, cross your hands over your chest.) Roll yourself up far enough so that your shoulder blades clear the floor, then lower yourself to the floor again. Make sure that your heels do not come up off the floor. When you do this exercise, be careful to avoid pulling forcefully on your neck.

■ **Push-ups.** Push-ups strengthen the muscles of your upper arms and chest. Lie on the floor face down, with arms bent and hands flat on the floor under your shoulders. Press your whole body upward until your arms are straight, lower your body to the floor again, and repeat. Keep your legs and back straight throughout the exercise. For a somewhat easier exercise, bend your knees and rest them on the floor. Push up only your hips and upper body. Be sure to keep your back and upper legs straight.

■ **Step-ups.** This exercise strengthens leg muscles. Step up onto a step with your left foot, bring the right foot up, step down with the right foot, then bring the left foot down. Repeat, alternating legs.

LIFE SKILLS
Everyday Fitness

*I*t's good to have a regular exercise routine to improve your strength, endurance, and flexibility. However, you can also include activities in your day-to-day life that will help you become fit. These activities shouldn't replace vigorous activities such as swimming laps or jogging with a friend, but they can help you to develop a more active lifestyle. Try some of the following ideas:

▶ Use your bicycle for transportation, making sure that you ride in safe areas. Wear your backpack and take your bike for local errands.

▶ When you get together with your friends, take a walk instead of sitting around someone's house.

▶ Plan family outings that include walking, riding bikes, or playing active games.

Endurance

Endurance (in·DUR·uhnts) is *your ability to perform vigorous physical activity without getting overly tired.* There are two basic types of endurance. Muscle endurance is the measure of how long a group of muscles can exert a force without tiring. Heart and lung endurance is the measure of how effectively your heart and lungs work during exercise and how quickly they return to normal.

The best way to build endurance is through **aerobic** (e·ROH·bik) **exercise**—*nonstop, rhythmic, vigorous activity that increases breathing and heartbeat rates.* Aerobic exercises include running, bicycling, and swimming. (The other type of exercise is **anaerobic** (an·e·ROH·bik) **exercise,** *intense physical activity that requires short bursts of energy,* such as weight lifting or sprinting.)

To build your endurance, it is best to perform aerobic exercises for at least 20 minutes, at least three times a week. Doing this will raise your heart and breathing rates enough to benefit your cardio-vascular system. The following exercises will build endurance:

- **Walking/Jogging.** Begin by walking briskly, working up to a 20-minute walk. Then alternate jogging with walking until you can jog or run the entire time.

- **Jumping Rope.** Alternate jumping rope with running in place. When you jump, protect your joints from strain by raising your feet only enough to clear the rope—no more than two inches off the floor.

- **Swimming.** Swim near the surface of the water. The lower you are, the harder you have to work. Gradually increase your swimming time to 20 minutes of sustained laps at a steady pace.

Swimming is a total body workout that is easy on the joints.

- ▶ Enjoy nature in your leisure time. Try hiking or bird watching instead of just going to a movie or renting a video.

- ▶ Go window shopping. Even during bad weather, you can get a lot of walking done in the mall.

- ▶ Take the stairs whenever possible instead of riding the elevator or the escalator. For your own safety, however, stay out of empty stairwells in buildings.

Follow-up Activity

Think of other ways to make your lifestyle more active. Make entries in your journal or calendar any time you try one of these physical activities. Write about how you feel. Do you feel stronger or better about yourself? Do you feel as if you have more energy? Share what you've been doing with your friends and family members.

Flexibility

Flexibility is the *ability to move joints fully and easily.* Some people are more naturally flexible than others, but everyone benefits from increased flexibility. By doing regular, gentle stretching, bending, and twisting, you will feel more comfortable, improve your posture, and reduce your risk of injury during strength or endurance training. **Figure 5.2** offers tips for safe stretching.

Figure 5.2
Safety in Stretching
Stretching should be gentle, not forced.

A Wear loose-fitting, comfortable clothing.

B Stretch to a point where you feel a gentle pull. Do not force your muscles to stretch too far. Hold there for a count of 15 or 20.

C Do not bounce or jerk to try to get more of a stretch. This can cause an injury.

D Stretch both sides of your body equally.

Lesson 1

Review

Using complete sentences, answer the following questions on a separate sheet of paper.

Reviewing Terms and Facts

1. **List** Identify the three elements of fitness.
2. **Explain** What is body composition?
3. **Vocabulary** Define *endurance,* and identify the two types.
4. **Vocabulary** Describe *aerobic exercise,* and give two examples.

Thinking Critically

5. **Describe** Explain how the three parts of the health triangle may be linked through fitness.

6. **Compare and Contrast** Reread the descriptions of the strength and endurance exercises. In what ways are they similar? How are they different?
7. **Design** Create a workout that includes exercises that develop each of the elements of fitness.

Applying Health Concepts

8. **Consumer Health** Interview a health club employee or another exercise professional. Ask questions about exercise equipment for use at home. What products are helpful, and which may be harmful? Present your report to the whole class.

The Circulatory System

This lesson will help you find answers to questions that teens often ask about the heart and about blood circulation. For example:

▶ **What does the circulatory system do for the body?**

▶ **How does blood circulate through the body?**

▶ **How can I keep my circulatory system healthy?**

Transporting Materials Through the Body

Part of being fit involves having a healthy circulatory system. The **circulatory system** is *the group of organs and tissues that transport essential materials to body cells and remove their waste products.* This system consists of the heart, the blood vessels, and the blood itself. The **cardiovascular** (KAR·dee·oh·VAS·kyoo·ler) **system** is *another name for the circulatory system. Cardio-* refers to the heart and -*vascular* means having to do with vessels.

The heart is a muscle that pumps blood throughout the network of blood vessels. Blood flows through three types of blood vessels, as shown in **Figure 5.3.**

> ### Words to Know
>
> **circulatory system**
> **cardiovascular system**
> **artery**
> **capillary**
> **vein**
> **pulmonary circulation**
> **systemic circulation**
> **plasma**
> **blood pressure**

Figure 5.3
The Circulatory System

There are three types of blood vessels: arteries, capillaries, and veins (VAYNZ).

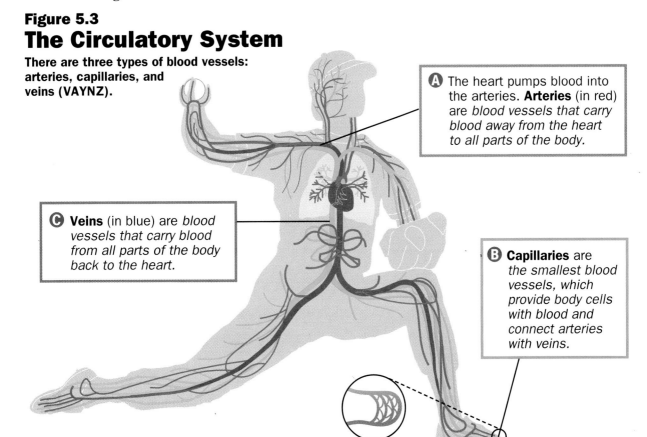

A The heart pumps blood into the arteries. **Arteries** (in red) are *blood vessels that carry blood away from the heart to all parts of the body.*

C **Veins** (in blue) are *blood vessels that carry blood from all parts of the body back to the heart.*

B **Capillaries** are *the smallest blood vessels, which provide body cells with blood and connect arteries with veins.*

Constant stress can harm the heart and blood vessels. You can reduce stress by using effective time management skills and having people you can talk with when you have problems.

In your private journal, write about your feelings when you experience stress. Imagine how these feelings might affect your circulatory system. Then make a list of actions you can take to keep stress to a minimum in your life.

Circulation Through the System

The cardiovascular system transports blood along a pathway that includes two types of circulation. **Pulmonary** (PUL·muh·nehr·ee) **circulation** *carries blood from the heart, through the lungs, and back to the heart.* This stage of circulation allows the blood to become enriched with oxygen before it is sent throughout the body. **Systemic** (sis·TE·mik) **circulation** *sends oxygen-rich blood to all the body tissues except the lungs.* Take a look at **Figure 5.4.** It shows how these two types of circulation work together to keep your body cells supplied with nutrients and free of waste products.

Figure 5.4
How Circulation Works

Oxygen-rich blood coming from the lungs is circulated through the heart and pumped to body tissues. This blood returns to the heart depleted of oxygen and is pumped to the lungs.

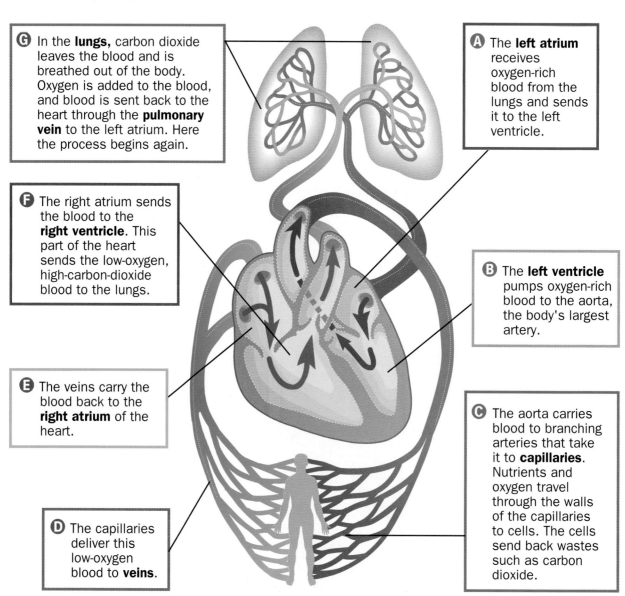

G In the **lungs,** carbon dioxide leaves the blood and is breathed out of the body. Oxygen is added to the blood, and blood is sent back to the heart through the **pulmonary vein** to the left atrium. Here the process begins again.

F The right atrium sends the blood to the **right ventricle**. This part of the heart sends the low-oxygen, high-carbon-dioxide blood to the lungs.

E The veins carry the blood back to the **right atrium** of the heart.

D The capillaries deliver this low-oxygen blood to **veins**.

A The **left atrium** receives oxygen-rich blood from the lungs and sends it to the left ventricle.

B The **left ventricle** pumps oxygen-rich blood to the aorta, the body's largest artery.

C The aorta carries blood to branching arteries that take it to **capillaries**. Nutrients and oxygen travel through the walls of the capillaries to cells. The cells send back wastes such as carbon dioxide.

The Blood

Blood performs many important functions in the body. Many of the functions of the blood have to do with transporting substances through the system or protecting the body against harm. The blood does all of the following.

- Blood delivers oxygen from the lungs to all body parts.
- Blood transports carbon dioxide to the lungs for removal.
- Blood transports other wastes to the kidneys for removal.
- Blood delivers nutrients, such as vitamins and sugars, to cells.
- Blood carries special cells that fight germs in the body.
- Blood carries hormones, the messenger chemicals that regulate body processes.
- Blood promotes healing by clotting at wounds.

Parts of the Blood

Over half of the volume of blood is made up of plasma. **Plasma** (PLAZ·muh) is *a yellowish fluid, the watery portion of blood.* The rest of the volume of blood is made up of three kinds of cells: red blood cells, white blood cells, and cell fragments called platelets (PLAYT·luhts). Each of these cell types is shown in **Figure 5.5.**

Q & A ?

Tough Guys

Q: How do platelets make blood clot?

A: When a break occurs in the skin, platelets immediately begin to clump together. They also release chemicals to create a sticky mesh that traps even more blood cells. Eventually the clot hardens into a scab. This gives the skin and blood vessel wall time to heal.

Figure 5.5
Plasma and Blood Cells

Each element of the blood helps the body in a different way.

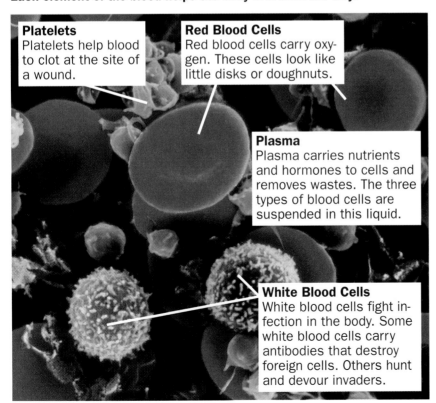

Platelets
Platelets help blood to clot at the site of a wound.

Red Blood Cells
Red blood cells carry oxygen. These cells look like little disks or doughnuts.

Plasma
Plasma carries nutrients and hormones to cells and removes wastes. The three types of blood cells are suspended in this liquid.

White Blood Cells
White blood cells fight infection in the body. Some white blood cells carry antibodies that destroy foreign cells. Others hunt and devour invaders.

Science Connection

Ups and Downs   **ACTIVITY!**

Blood has to flow against gravity in some parts of the body. How do you think this affects you? To find out, try this experiment.

Stretch one arm up so that your hand is held high above your head. Let the other arm hang down so that your hand is held low by your side. Hold this position for a minute, then examine your hands. What differences can you detect?

Blood Pressure

Blood pressure is *the force of blood pushing against the walls of the blood vessels.* A blood pressure reading consists of two numbers, usually written in this way: 120/80. The first number is the pressure at its highest point, when the heart contracts and forces blood into the arteries. The second number is the lowest point of pressure, when the heart relaxes to refill with blood.

A blood pressure reading can reveal how your circulatory system is working. A high reading means that your heart is working harder than it should be. High blood pressure may also indicate that the blood vessels are not as elastic as they should be.

Blood Types

Not all blood is the same. The four types— A, B, AB, and O—are classified according to the type of red blood cells they contain. Some blood types can be mixed, while others cannot. When blood types that are not compatible are mixed, the chemicals in one type of blood clump together and block the blood vessels. That is why hospitals make sure of a person's blood type before allowing one person to receive blood from another. In most cases, the blood given should be the same type as the recipient's blood. A person can, however, receive a different, compatible blood type in an emergency. **Figure 5.6** shows compatible blood types.

Blood may also contain a chemical called an Rh factor. Most people are Rh-positive, meaning that their blood has this chemical. Some are Rh-negative, meaning that their blood does not contain the chemical. People with Rh-positive blood can receive blood from people who are either Rh-positive or Rh-negative. People who are Rh-negative, however, can accept blood only from others who are Rh-negative.

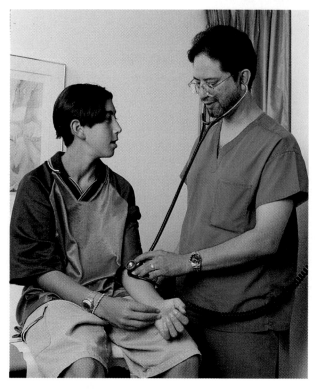

A normal blood pressure reading for teens is about 110/70.

Did You Know?

Where Do Blood Cells Come From?

Many red blood cells and most white blood cells are made in the bones. In the center of many bones there is fatty tissue called bone marrow. New blood cells are manufactured there and then released into the bloodstream.

Figure 5.6
Blood Type Compatibility

Type A blood has substances called A antigens (AN·ti·jenz). Type B blood has B antigens. Type AB has both A and B antigens, and type O has no A or B antigens.

Type	Can Receive	Can Donate To
A	O, A	A, AB
B	O, B	B, AB
AB	all	AB
O	O	all

Caring for Your Circulatory System

You can take care of your circulatory system in several ways. First, you can eat a balanced diet that is low in fats. You should also try to avoid tension, because tension can put strain on your heart and blood vessels. Two conditions that can harm your circulatory system are being overweight and smoking. Excess weight makes your heart work harder. Cigarette smoke contains chemicals that keep your blood from carrying oxygen effectively.

Staying fit is an important way to keep your circulatory system healthy. When you exercise vigorously, blood is pumped around your body faster than when you are at rest. This supplies extra oxygen and nutrients to cells. How else does fitness help this system?

- Exercise makes the muscle fibers in your heart stronger and thicker. This makes your heart more powerful and able to work more efficiently. Your heart actually has to beat less often.

- When you are exercising vigorously, blood flushes through your arteries. This may help reduce clogging by fatty materials.

- Fitness helps you stay at your ideal weight. Being overweight increases your risk for heart disease.

Handball is ranked high, along with jogging and swimming, in terms of its cardiovascular benefits.

Review

Lesson 1

Using complete sentences, answer the following questions on a separate sheet of paper.

Reviewing Terms and Facts

1. **Describe**   What does the circulatory system do?

2. **Vocabulary**   List and define the three kinds of blood vessels.

3. **Identify**   Name the two types of circulation.

4. **List**   What are the components of blood?

Thinking Critically

5. **Analyze**   Describe ways that the circulatory system and the digestive and excretory systems work together.

6. **Describe**   How does the circulatory system help fight disease?

7. **Explain**   Why is it important for hospitals to know the blood types of patients?

Applying Health Concepts

8. **Health of Others**   With a group, create an advertisement or commercial for physical fitness. Do research that will help you to promote the idea that being physically fit protects and improves the circulatory system. Try to convince others that exercise will offer them long-term health benefits.

The Skeletal and Muscular Systems

This lesson will help you find answers to questions that teens often ask about how the body supports itself and moves. For example:

▶ What do the skeletal and muscular systems do for the body?

▶ How do bones and muscles work together to allow movement?

▶ How can I keep my skeletal and muscular systems healthy?

Words to Know

skeletal system
muscular system
joint
cartilage
ligament
tendon
contract
extend

in your journal

Write down three exercises that you do or that you would like to begin doing. Describe the effects that these exercises might have on your bones, joints, or muscles.

Support and Movement

Whether you are taking a leisurely walk or playing a game of baseball, you depend on your skeletal and muscular systems to support you and help you move. The **skeletal system** is the *framework of bones and other tissues that support the body.* Your skeletal system supports your body, protects major organs and other soft parts of your body, and helps to make it possible for you to move.

Muscles provide the power to move the body. The **muscular system** *consists of tissues that move parts of the body and operate internal organs.* For example, your leg muscles help you run and your stomach muscles help you digest food.

There are 206 bones—of many shapes and sizes—and more than 600 muscles in an adult human body. The skeletal system consists of bones, joints, and connecting tissues.

The Bones and the Joints

Bones are made of living tissue and, like other organs, are supplied by blood vessels. They do more than just support and protect your body. Bones store calcium and other minerals. In addition, the inner part of bones, called the marrow, makes new blood cells.

Joints are *places where two or more bones meet.* Some joints are immovable, such as those in the skull. Others allow a wide range of movement. **Figure 5.7** on the next page identifies some of the major bones in the skeletal system and describes several types of joints.

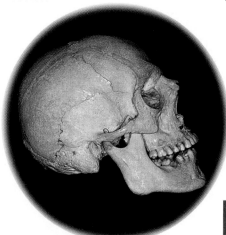

In adults the joints in the skull are fused, protecting the brain.

Figure 5.7

The Skeletal System

Here are some of the major bones and joints of the skeletal system.

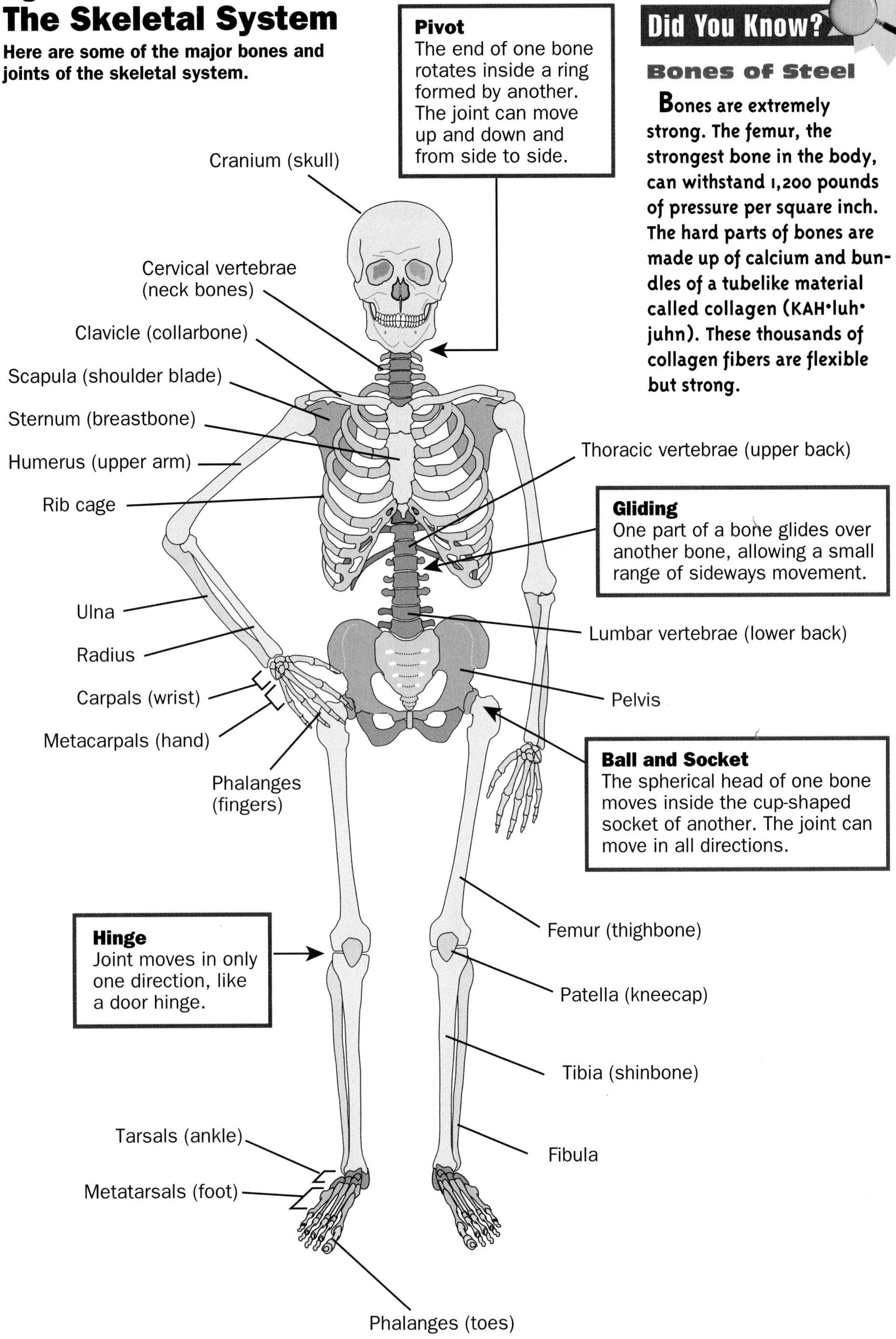
Pivot
The end of one bone rotates inside a ring formed by another. The joint can move up and down and from side to side.
Cranium (skull)
Cervical vertebrae (neck bones)
Clavicle (collarbone)
Scapula (shoulder blade)
Sternum (breastbone)
Humerus (upper arm)
Rib cage
Thoracic vertebrae (upper back)
Gliding
One part of a bone glides over another bone, allowing a small range of sideways movement.
Ulna
Radius
Carpals (wrist)
Metacarpals (hand)
Phalanges (fingers)
Lumbar vertebrae (lower back)
Pelvis
Ball and Socket
The spherical head of one bone moves inside the cup-shaped socket of another. The joint can move in all directions.
Hinge
Joint moves in only one direction, like a door hinge.
Femur (thighbone)
Patella (kneecap)
Tibia (shinbone)
Tarsals (ankle)
Metatarsals (foot)
Fibula
Phalanges (toes)

Did You Know?

Bones of Steel

Bones are extremely strong. The femur, the strongest bone in the body, can withstand 1,200 pounds of pressure per square inch. The hard parts of bones are made up of calcium and bundles of a tubelike material called collagen (KAH•luh•juhn). These thousands of collagen fibers are flexible but strong.

Q: How come I can't move some of my fingers without moving others?

A: Each finger is connected to muscles in your forearm with tendons. However, there is also a connection between the tendons of your middle finger and those of your ring finger. This connection makes it hard to move those two fingers separately. You can demonstrate this by placing your hand palm down on a table with the middle finger curled under. Try to lift each of your fingers. You probably won't be able to lift your ring finger.

Connecting Tissues

Cartilage (KAR·tuhl·ij), ligaments (LI·guh·ments), and tendons (TEN·duhns) are connecting tissues. They link bones and muscles so that the two can work together to move parts of the body. **Figure 5.8** describes the types of connecting tissue.

Figure 5.8
Connecting Tissues

Connecting tissues join bones to muscles and other bones.

Tissue Type	Description	Job
Cartilage	Strong, flexible tissue that covers the ends of bones; also supports some structures	Allows joints to move easily, cushions bones, supports soft tissues (in nose and ear)
Ligaments	Strong bands of tissue that hold bones in place at the joints	Hold bones in place, support joints
Tendons	Strong, flexible, fibrous tissue that joins muscle to muscle or muscle to bone	Move bones when muscles contract

Muscles

Muscle is tissue that responds to messages from the brain and **contracts** (kuhn·TRAKTS), or *shortens,* to cause movement. Some muscles are voluntary, or under your control, such as the muscles in your arms and legs. Others are involuntary and move without your being aware of it. These include the muscles of internal organs and blood vessels. There are three main types of muscle tissue, as shown in **Figure 5.9. Figure 5.10** shows some of the major muscles of the body.

Figure 5.9
Types of Muscles

Here are the three types of muscles, shown as magnified under a microscope.

Skeletal Muscle
Muscles of this type are voluntary and are attached to the bones.

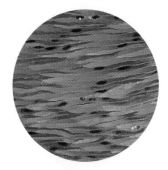

Cardiac Muscle
This type of muscle, found only in the heart, is involuntary. It contracts and relaxes about 70 times per minute, pumping blood to all parts of your body.

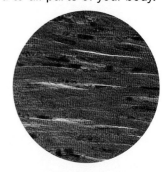

Smooth Muscle
Muscles of this type are involuntary and are found in internal organs such as the stomach.

Figure 5.10
The Muscular System

These are some of the main skeletal muscles of your body.

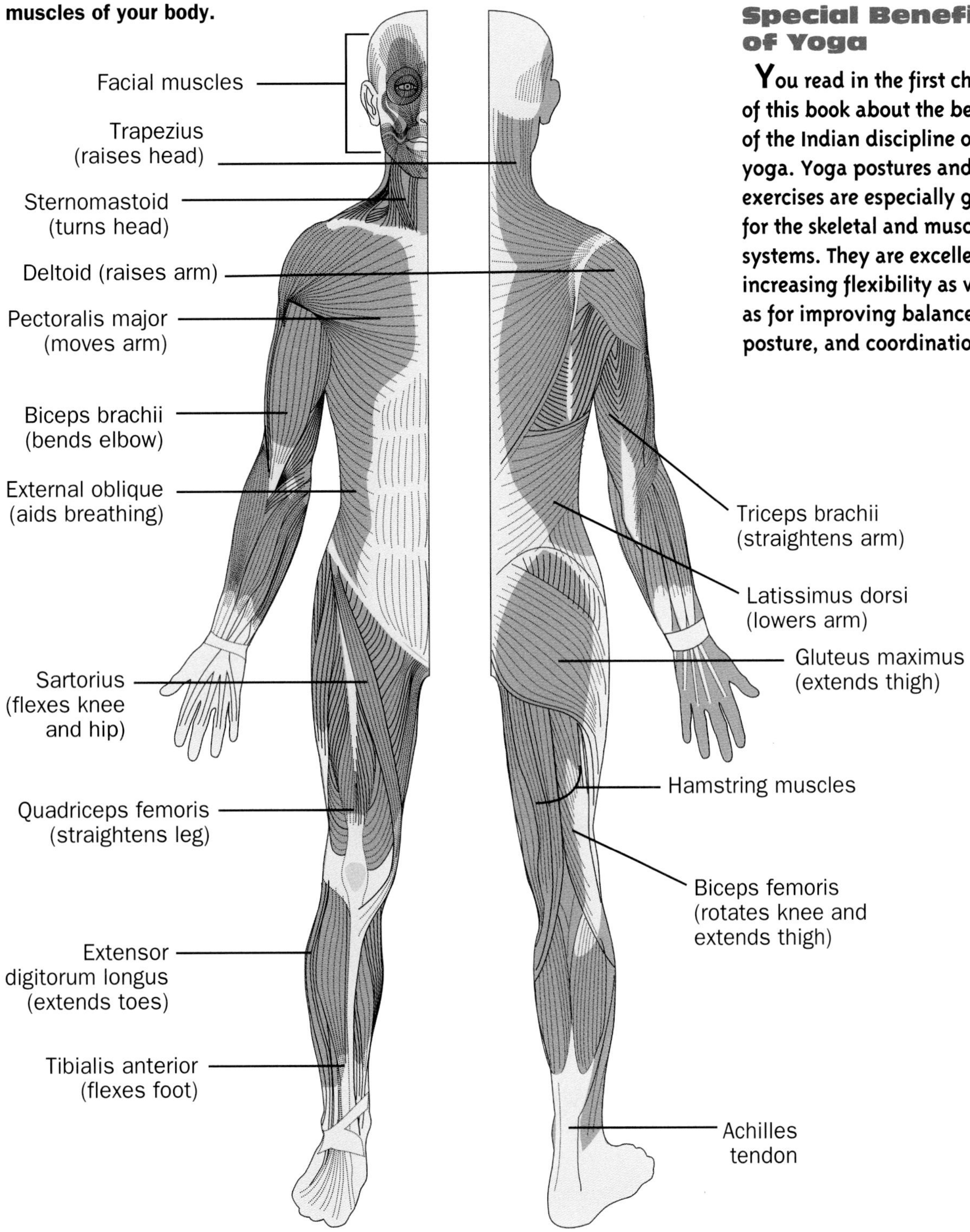

Facial muscles

Trapezius (raises head)

Sternomastoid (turns head)

Deltoid (raises arm)

Pectoralis major (moves arm)

Biceps brachii (bends elbow)

External oblique (aids breathing)

Sartorius (flexes knee and hip)

Quadriceps femoris (straightens leg)

Extensor digitorum longus (extends toes)

Tibialis anterior (flexes foot)

Triceps brachii (straightens arm)

Latissimus dorsi (lowers arm)

Gluteus maximus (extends thigh)

Hamstring muscles

Biceps femoris (rotates knee and extends thigh)

Achilles tendon

Cultural Connections

Special Benefits of Yoga

You read in the first chapter of this book about the benefits of the Indian discipline of yoga. Yoga postures and exercises are especially good for the skeletal and muscular systems. They are excellent for increasing flexibility as well as for improving balance, posture, and coordination.

Working Together for Movement

Skeletal muscles work in pairs to move bones. Each member of the pair is connected to the bone that is to be moved. When one muscle contracts, the other muscle **extends,** or *lengthens.* The muscles switch roles to move the bone back to its original position. **Figure 5.11** shows this process in the arm.

Figure 5.11
Muscles and Bones Work Together

Muscle pairs are said to work in opposition. This means that to create movement, two muscles must do opposite things.

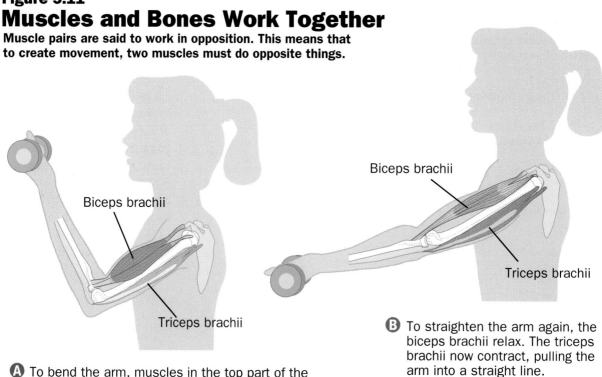

Biceps brachii

Biceps brachii

Triceps brachii

Triceps brachii

Ⓐ To bend the arm, muscles in the top part of the arm—especially the biceps brachii—contract, or shorten, pulling the bone of the lower arm upward. At the same time, the triceps brachii—on the other side of the arm—must relax and extend, or lengthen.

Ⓑ To straighten the arm again, the biceps brachii relax. The triceps brachii now contract, pulling the arm into a straight line.

HEALTH LAB
Pulling Pairs

Introduction: What makes your arm bend? Bend your elbow, bringing your hand close to your shoulder. With your other hand, feel your biceps, the muscle in the front of your upper arm. Then straighten your arm, feeling your triceps, the muscle at the back of your upper arm. Can you feel how the muscles are working?

Objective: With a partner, create a model to explore how paired muscles cause bones to move.

Materials and Method: You'll need two cardboard rectangles, each about 7 inches by 3 inches; a hole punch, a brad, scissors, and two large rubber bands. Overlap the ends of the rectangles and connect them with the brad. Punch two holes in each piece of cardboard, as shown in the diagram. Then cut the rubber bands, run them through the holes as shown, and retie them.

Pull on each rubber band to make the "arm" bend. Try pulling on one rubber band, then the other. What happens?

Observations and Analysis: Observe how the model works. Then think about how this applies to the more complex muscles in your arm. Could you have made the model move by pushing on the rubber bands instead of pulling them? How is this also true of the way muscles allow movement?

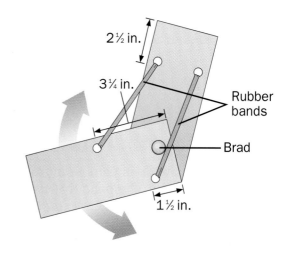

2½ in.

3¼ in.

Rubber bands

Brad

1½ in.

Caring for Your Skeletal and Muscular Systems

Follow these tips to keep your skeletal and muscular systems healthy.

in your journal

Look back at what you wrote in your journal entry at the beginning of this lesson. In what ways were you correct? Now that you know more about how your muscles and bones work, describe what is happening in these systems when you engage in a physical activity.

- **Exercise regularly.** Exercises that build strength will make your bones and muscles stronger. Exercises that build endurance will make muscles more efficient and will also strengthen the muscles in your heart. Exercises that increase flexibility will make it easier for you to move and may prevent injuries.

- **Eat a nutritious diet.** Include foods that are rich in calcium and vitamin D for bone growth and strength. Carbohydrates will give your muscles energy, and proteins will build muscle tissue.

- **Watch your posture.** Sit and stand in a correct but relaxed manner, so that bones, joints, and muscles maintain proper placement.

- **Treat injuries promptly.** If you hurt yourself, see a physician. Avoid putting stress on an injured body part.

Many teens enjoy gymnastics, which has many fitness benefits.

Review
Lesson 3

Using complete sentences, answer the following questions on a separate sheet of paper.

Reviewing Terms and Facts

1. **Vocabulary** Describe the skeletal system and the muscular system, and tell how they work together.

2. **List** Name three types of joints, giving an example of each.

3. **Identify** What are the three types of connecting tissue?

4. **Vocabulary** Use the words *contract* and *extend* in a sentence together.

Thinking Critically

5. **Analyze** How might a muscle injury affect a bone, and how might a bone injury affect a joint or muscle?

6. **Hypothesize** Why do you think there are more muscles than bones in the body?

Applying Health Concepts

7. **Health of Others** With a small group, create a skit in which you show ways to care for the skeletal and muscular systems. You may want to use pantomime to show good exercise and diet habits, with a narrator providing an explanation.

8. **Growth and Development** Children's bones are softer and more flexible than those of adults. They are less likely to break because they are able to bend slightly. Do some research to find out what causes bones to grow harder and more brittle over time. Present your findings to the class.

TEEN HEALTH DIGEST

CON$UMER FOCU$

Don't Fall for These Ads

"You don't have to be a doctor or a scientist to spot a phony diet ad," says Richard Cleland, a lawyer with the Federal Trade Commission's division of advertising practices. "Ads that use testimonials where people have lost 15 pounds in the first week or claims that a product works by a secret formula or is the result of some new scientific breakthrough are simply not credible."

When a product claim sounds too good to be true, it probably is.

That goes especially for diet plans that say that you can eat unlimited amounts of certain foods. If you take in more calories than you use up, you'll gain weight—no matter where the calories came from.

Remember: you didn't gain weight overnight, and you aren't going to lose it that way, either. But you can damage your future health through poor choices. Make sure that your weight-loss program is good for your total health.

Try This: List at least three other claims diet ads might make that should tip off a consumer.

Personal Trainer

Water Workout

This water exercise builds strength in your abdominal and back muscles. Don't forget to warm up with easy swimming before trying it!

In deep water, face the pool side and hold onto it with both hands. Raise both legs out to your sides, then bring them together, crossing them over each other. Continue raising and crossing, alternating which leg is in front.

You could also try walking through waist-high water, taking giant steps. This exercise builds abdominal, back, and leg muscles.

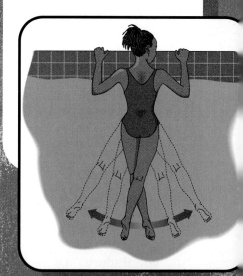

Myths and Realities

Realistic Expectations

"If I buy that fitness video and do all the exercises, will I look like the model on the box?" Some people think so. When the results don't measure up, disappointment can rob them of their enthusiasm for fitness.

Peg Jordan, a California researcher, explains that unrealistic goals can chip away at self-esteem and actually prevent people from forming healthful habits. Exercising to improve your total fitness is a healthy, realistic goal. Hoping to look like a professional fitness trainer who works out for a living is not.

Balance and common sense are the keys to setting your fitness goals. You don't need to look like a model to have a fit, healthy body.

Try This: Ask friends what fitness videos they have used or like. Find out the reasons for their comments.

HEALTH UPDATE

Time to Eat

According to Roberta Schwartz Wennick, a registered dietitian, eating the right foods at the right time is an important part of your exercise schedule. You can make the most of your fitness routines by following a few of Wennick's guidelines.

- If you exercise early in the morning—eat a light breakfast *about a half hour* before exercising.
- If you exercise in the middle of the day—have a light lunch or snack *about one hour* before exercising.
- If you exercise at night—eat dinner *about one to two hours* before exercising.

Sports and Recreation

Maine's Main Woman

Cindy Blodgett is so popular at the University of Maine that boys and girls all over the state wear basketball jerseys with her number—14—on them.

"She's a great role model for kids because of her personality and the fact that she's an excellent student," says her coach, Joanne Palombo-McCallie.

Kids aren't her only fans. Two of her team's most prominent supporters are the horror writer Stephen King and his wife, Tabitha King, who wrote a biographical book about Cindy.

The 5'9" point guard led the nation in scoring in the 1996 season. As a high school player in Clinton, Maine, Cindy led her team to four state championships. She was recruited by many colleges but chose to stay in her home state. The people of Maine support her in return.

Planning a Fitness Program

This lesson will help you find answers to questions that teens often ask about setting up their own fitness programs. For example:

▶ What do I need to think about when I plan a fitness program?
▶ How should I plan my workouts?
▶ How can I assess my progress?

in your journal

List three reasons why you might want to increase your level of fitness. If you are happy with your fitness level, list three reasons why you are satisfied.

First Things First

Perhaps you've decided that a fitness program will benefit your circulatory, skeletal, and muscular systems. What's next? First of all, think about your goals. What do you want to achieve? You may want to increase your endurance or develop specific skills for a team sport. You may just want to feel healthier. Having a specific goal to work toward can inspire you to stick with your fitness program—and help you know when you've accomplished something.

Selecting the Right Exercises

You also need to consider the practical aspects of your workout. What kind of exercises do you want to do? Do you need to buy equipment? When and where will you exercise? You need to plan a program that is convenient, affordable, and enjoyable for you.

There are many different activities from which you can choose. Ideally, you will want to work on strength, endurance, and flexibility. What types of exercise will help you most? **Figure 5.12** shows how some common forms of exercise measure up in these three categories.

Figure 5.12
Types of Physical Activity
Which type of exercise offers the highest level of benefit in all three categories of fitness?

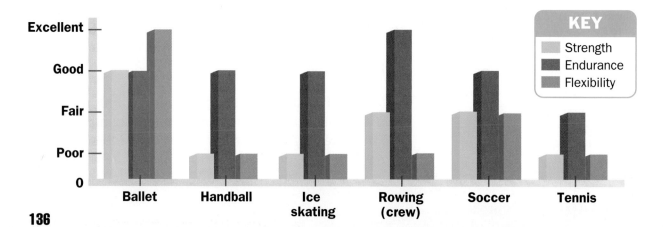

Thinking About Safety

You must also think about your safety when you work out. You can exercise safely by taking sensible precautions. **Figure 5.13** lists some of the most important safety issues. Consider these points as you plan your program.

Figure 5.13
Safety Issues

Think about your total health when you plan for fitness.

Choose Safe Places and Times
Soft, even surfaces will be easier on your bones and muscles. Be careful about exercising outdoors alone, especially in a deserted place or at night. If possible, take along a couple of friends.

Dress Appropriately
Loose-fitting clothing is best for exercising. If you will be exercising outdoors at night, wear light-colored clothing and reflective coverings. This will make you more visible to others.

Choose Good Equipment
Good equipment is not necessarily the most expensive. Take special care, however, that your shoes or skates provide good support and are comfortable. Wear appropriate equipment for your activity.

Think About the Weather
When it is cold, wear several thin layers of clothing. As your body warms up, you may want to remove one layer. Always protect your skin from freezing temperatures. On extremely hot days, shorten your outdoor workout, and remember to apply sunscreen. Always drink plenty of fluids.

Listen to Your Body
A little discomfort when beginning new exercises or increasing intensity is normal. Pain is *not* normal, however. If you feel pain, stop exercising. If the pain continues, see a doctor. Also, don't exercise if you feel sick. You'll get well sooner if your body uses its energy for healing.

Making a Schedule

Making a schedule will help you exercise consistently. Write out a weekly plan that includes your school physical education classes and your activities before and after school. Then make a wall chart or calendar to remind yourself of what you'll do and when you'll exercise each day. Keep track of the amount of time you spend exercising each day and each week.

Be flexible, however. You don't have to write a plan for six months in advance. Your goals and needs may change as your fitness develops. Be willing to try new activities. In fact, varying your workout will help prevent boredom.

When astronauts are in space for long periods of time, they lose bone and muscle mass. The problem is caused by the weightlessness of space, where gravity has little or no effect. Scientists are working on exercises especially for astronauts that emphasize aerobics and endurance training as well as strength-building.

Planning Your Workout

Plan your exercise session to include a beginning warm-up, the workout activity, and a cool-down period. You may choose an aerobic workout to develop overall fitness and endurance or do strength-building exercises. If you do both, do the strength training after the aerobic work. After aerobic exercise, your muscles will work more smoothly.

Warm-Up and Cool-Down

A **warm-up** routine is *gentle exercise you do to prepare your muscles for vigorous activity.* Warm-up exercises bring blood into muscles, supplying them with nutrients and oxygen. Your muscles and tendons actually become warmer, so that they are more flexible. Warming up also allows you to increase your heart rate gradually and safely. Spend about ten minutes on your warm-up, which should consist of easy aerobic exercise—a brisk walk or some gentle body exercises.

Stretching should be done *after* you are warmed up. **Figure 5.14** shows two stretching exercises. You will also want to do some stretching after your **cool-down.** The cool-down stage involves *gentle exercises that let your body adjust to ending a workout.* If you stop exercising abruptly, your muscles may tighten, or you may feel faint. Continue the movements of your workout in a slower fashion. After running, for example, jog and then walk for about ten minutes to cool down. Cooling down brings your blood circulation back to normal and lowers your body temperature.

Figure 5.14
Stretching Exercises
These exercises will stretch the muscles of your upper body and your legs.

A Lean against a wall for support. Keep your arms straight while moving your upper body downward. Keep your knees slightly bent, and keep your hips over your feet.

B Stand close to a wall and lean toward it, placing your palms flat against it. Keep one leg bent and the other extended. Keeping the heel of the extended leg on the ground, move your hips forward until you feel a stretch in the calf muscle.

Your Workout

To meet your workout goals, you need to pay attention to the frequency, intensity, and duration of your workout sessions. All of these factors should increase over time.

- **Exercise frequency** means *how often you work out each week.*

- **Exercise intensity** means *how much energy you use when you work out.*

- Exercise time, or duration, is how long each workout lasts.

Figure 5.15 shows how you can work with these factors to reach your fitness goals.

Teen Issues

Do What You Like [ACTIVITY!]

The exercise plan that will help you the most is the one you can stick to and enjoy. Talk to people you know who are physically active. Ask them what motivates them to exercise. Share your findings with the class.

Figure 5.15
Meeting Your Goals
Over time, frequency, intensity, and time should all progress.

Frequency. Gradually increase your exercise frequency. Begin by working out two or three times a week. Work up to exercising every day. Remember that you will probably want to vary your routine from day to day.

Intensity. You can increase your intensity by working harder. You may try to bicycle 3 miles in less time than you did the week before. You might also include more hills in your route.

Time. Begin by exercising in 10- to 15-minute sessions. Increase the duration of individual workouts. Gradually, work up to 30 or 45 minutes of exercise at each session.

Your Target Heart Rate

You can measure your exercise intensity, or find out how hard you're really working, by figuring out your target heart rate. Your **target heart rate** is the *number of heartbeats per minute you should aim for during vigorous exercise for cardiovascular benefit.* Your target heart rate is usually a range, not a single number. If you are just starting to exercise, you should try to reach the lower part of the range. As you become more fit, try to attain higher levels. Do not, however, go beyond the top of your range. To find your target heart rate, do the following:

- Subtract your age from 220. This is your maximum heart rate.

- Multiply by 0.6 for the low end of your heart rate range.

- Multiply by 0.8 for the high end of your heart rate range.

To check your actual heart rate, take your pulse for 15 seconds in the middle of an exercise session, then multiply the number of pulse beats by four. Where are you within your range?

Checking Your Progress

You've established your fitness program and followed your weekly schedule. How are you doing? How do you feel? Look back at your original goals. Are you achieving them? The following tips can help you assess your program and your progress.

■ If you've been working out for four to eight weeks, you should see some results. You may feel stronger, be more flexible, or have more endurance. Keeping a fitness log as you go will help you see how far you have come.

■ If you feel that you're not any closer to your goal, think about whether you have been keeping to your schedule. If not, how can you make sure that you do? If you have stuck to your schedule, you may need to reevaluate your goal. Is it realistic? Maybe you need more time than you thought.

■ If you've already achieved your goal, it's time for you to set a new, more challenging one.

A family member may be able to help you reach your fitness goals.

Q & A

RICE is Nice

Q: I pulled a muscle in my leg while exercising. A friend of mine told me to use RICE. What is it?

A: RICE is a way to help people remember four rules for treating an injury: Rest, Ice, Compression, and Elevation. The first letter of each word, put together, spells RICE. First, rest by stopping your exercise program. Use ice to keep swelling down and reduce blood flow to the area. Compression means putting pressure on the injured area to reduce swelling, as with a wrapped bandage. Elevation involves raising the injured part, also to reduce swelling. Check with a doctor or trainer before trying this method.

Lesson 4 Review

Using complete sentences, answer the following questions on a separate sheet of paper.

Reviewing Terms and Facts

1. **List**   Identify five safety precautions you should take when exercising.

2. **Describe**   What is the purpose of a warm-up?

3. **Explain**   Define *cool-down,* and identify its purpose.

4. **Vocabulary**   Define *exercise frequency* and *exercise intensity.*

Thinking Critically

5. **Apply**   What are some factors you would need to consider when planning your exercise program? Explain why each factor is important.

6. **Hypothesize**   List three factors that you think might make the difference between a successful exercise program and one that a person tries and then abandons.

Applying Health Concepts

7. **Personal Health**   Create a fitness log that you could use for an exercise program. Be ready to explain how you would use such a log to monitor your fitness program.

Weight Management

This lesson will help you find answers to questions that teens often ask about managing their weight. For example:

▶ **How do I know what is a healthy weight for me?**

▶ **How can I manage my weight through diet and exercise?**

▶ **Why are eating disorders dangerous, and how can I recognize them?**

Wellness and Weight Management

Knowing and maintaining the weight that is right for you is an important part of your total health. To some extent, your ideal weight—the weight that is right for you—is determined by your height, age, and gender. Heredity also plays a part. You have a particular body type, and the weight that is right for you may not be ideal for your friend of the same height and age.

Your ideal weight is a range, not a single number. While your weight is one way to measure your health, many other factors—such as good nutrition, avoidance of risks, and overall fitness—also affect your level of wellness.

Your Body Mass Index

One way to determine your ideal weight is the Body Mass Index, or BMI. The **Body Mass Index** is *a measure of weight based on comparing body weight to height.* Calculating your BMI can help you see whether you are in a healthy range. **Figure 5.16** on the next page shows you how to calculate this number.

Words to Know

Body Mass Index (BMI)
obesity
eating disorder
anorexia nervosa
bulimia nervosa

in your journal

Write a journal entry about weight. Discuss your own feelings about weight. Why do you think there is so much emphasis on this subject in the United States? See what conclusion you can draw about a healthy approach people can take toward weight.

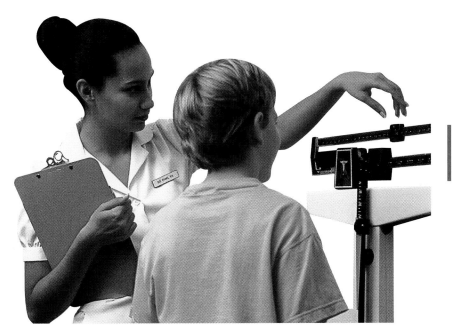

If you are not sure whether your weight is right for you, talk with a health professional.

Figure 5.16
Body Mass Index

To find your Body Mass Index, find your height in column A. Then find your weight in column B. Using a ruler, place it on the illustration so that the edge of the ruler lines up with both your height and your weight. The point at which the ruler intersects the scale in column C is your BMI. Generally, a BMI of over 25 indicates that you are overweight. This is only an approximation, however. A doctor can perform more precise tests of body composition.

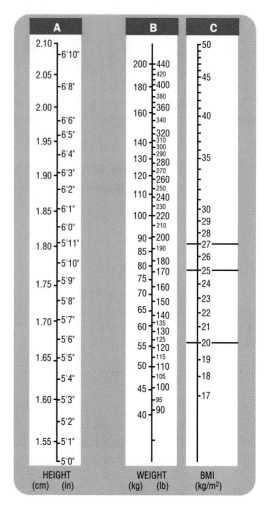

A	B	C
HEIGHT (cm) (in)	WEIGHT (kg) (lb)	BMI (kg/m²)

Did You Know?

Another Health Risk ACTIVITY!

Another risk related to being overweight is the risk of developing diabetes. This disease is characterized by difficulties in converting food into energy. Do some research to find out about this link, and write a one-page report displaying your findings.

Weight and Good Health

Many people think about their weight only in terms of how they look. Being underweight or overweight, however, can also create health risks and problems. If you weigh too little, you may experience fatigue, irritability, sleeping problems, or dry skin. Women who are too thin may experience problems with their reproductive systems.

Being overweight has other consequences. Obesity is especially dangerous. **Obesity** is *weighing 20 percent more than your ideal weight.* Excess weight creates a number of health risks.

■ Your skeletal and muscular systems have to bear more weight than they should. Muscle and joint problems may result.

■ Your heart must work harder. People who are obese have a higher risk of heart disease and stroke.

■ Higher rates of certain cancers are associated with a diet high in fats. Such a diet may lead to obesity.

■ People who are obese have a lower life expectancy than people who maintain their ideal weight.

Nutrition and Exercise

Staying at your ideal weight involves both good nutrition *and* adequate exercise. The food you eat affects your weight, but so does your activity level. By developing healthy eating and exercise habits, you can control your weight.

Figuring Out Calories

Your body runs on energy from food, much as a car runs on energy from gasoline. A calorie is a unit of heat that measures the energy available in foods. Your body needs a certain amount of energy just to stay warm and to build and repair tissues. It needs additional energy for the activities you engage in each day.

The calories in food are converted by your body to a type of energy that your cells can use. If more of this energy is produced than your cells require, the body converts the calories into body fat. Fat is stored energy, ready for use at a later time. (Every 3,500 calories that are stored rather than used become one pound of body fat.) To achieve your ideal weight, keep the following points in mind.

■ To maintain your weight, you must take in the same number of calories each day that you use for energy.

■ To gain weight, you must take in more calories than you use.

■ To lose weight, you must take in fewer calories than you use. Your body will then turn to reserves of fat for the extra calories it needs to function. As this fat is used up, it will disappear.

You can see that if losing weight is your goal, you can approach it by consuming fewer calories *and* increasing your activity level. That way you will use more calories every day than you take in, and excess body fat will be burned up. **Figure 5.17** shows how many calories are burned during some common activities.

Q & A

Fat Versus Calories **ACTIVITY!**

Q: Will low-fat products help me control my weight?

A: Not by themselves. Weight management involves eating sensibly and exercising regularly. Many people believe that if they eat low-fat foods, they will lose weight no matter how much they eat. However, food labeled "low-fat" may still be high in calories.

With a partner, check out the nutrition labels on packages of five low-fat snacks. Make a chart showing the actual calorie count for each snack serving, and share your results with the class.

Figure 5.17
Calories Burned in Selected Activities

The number of calories burned is calculated for a 100-pound person performing the activity for one hour. The longer you perform an activity, the more calories you burn.

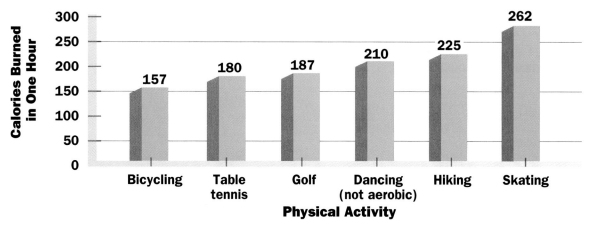

Managing Your Weight

How can you manage your weight effectively? You will need to keep track of the number of calories you take in and the number you use up. **Figure 5.18** gives tips for gaining or losing weight in healthful ways.

Figure 5.18
Tips for Weight Management
These tips can help you lose or gain weight in a healthful way.

To Lose Weight

Ⓐ Do not try to lose more than 1–2 pounds per week.

Ⓑ Eat smaller servings of food with fewer calories. Follow Food Guide Pyramid guidelines, choosing foods high in complex carbohydrates and fiber.

Ⓒ Avoid fried foods. Choose broiled, baked, or steamed foods instead.

Ⓓ Increase the amount of exercise you get. Include exercises that build muscle, because your body will burn more energy supporting a pound of muscle than it will supporting a pound of fat.

Ⓔ Eat slowly. Less food will satisfy you if you take more time to eat.

Ⓕ Don't skip meals. Always eat breakfast to give you energy for the day. Avoid eating within two hours of bedtime, however.

Ⓖ Avoid extreme diets. They can seriously damage your health.

To Gain Weight

Ⓐ Eat larger servings of nutritious foods.

Ⓑ When choosing foods for weight gain, concentrate on complex carbohydrates and some dairy products, but not items high in fat.

Ⓒ Continue to exercise so that the weight you gain is muscle not fat. Exercises that build strength and endurance are good choices.

Ⓓ Eat healthful snacks between meals. Avoid eating too close to mealtimes, however.

MAKING HEALTHY DECISIONS

Helping a Friend with an Eating Disorder

Chantal and Tamara have been taking ballet classes together since first grade. In the past three months, Chantal has noticed that Tamara is steadily losing weight. Tamara is always tired, too. As Chantal thinks back, she realizes that Tamara has been making constant comments about being too fat. In fact, Chantal realizes that she hasn't seen Tamara eat anything for a long time.

When Chantal asks Tamara about her weight, Tamara gets angry and tells Chantal that everything is fine. Chantal has to make a decision. Should she do something, and if so, what? Chantal uses the six steps of the decision-making process.

❶ **State the situation**

❷ **List the options**

❸ **Weigh the possible outcomes**

❹ **Consider your values**

❺ **Make a decision and act**

❻ **Evaluate the decision**

Follow-up Activities

1. Apply the six steps of the decision-making process to Chantal's situation.

2. With a classmate, role-play Chantal talking the problem over with Tamara or with an adult.

3. Discuss the situation in a small group. Should Chantal try to talk to Tamara again before going to an adult? What do you think a teen should do when a friend's health seems threatened?

Eating Disorders

Many teens are concerned about their weight. Some, however, develop **eating disorders,** which are *extreme eating behaviors that can lead to serious illness or even death.* These disorders are dangerous to mental and emotional health as well as to physical health.

■ **Anorexia nervosa** (an·uh·REK·see·uh ner·VOH·suh) is *an eating disorder in which a person has an intense fear of weight gain and starves himself or herself.* People who have anorexia nervosa often become dangerously thin. They may see themselves as overweight no matter how thin they are.

■ **Bulimia nervosa** (boo·LEE·mee·uh ner·VOH·suh) is *an eating disorder in which a person repeatedly eats large amounts of food and then purges.*

Why some teens and adults develop eating disorders is not clear. Several factors may be at work, however, including life stresses, a desire for control or perfection, and depression. Our society's emphasis on appearance, especially for girls and women, may also play a part. No matter what the cause of the disorder, professional help is almost always needed to help a person recover.

Recovering from an eating disorder can be a long and difficult process. Seeking professional help is an important step.

Review — Lesson 5

Using complete sentences, answer the following questions on a separate sheet of paper.

Reviewing Terms and Facts

1. **Vocabulary**   What is the *Body Mass Index?*

2. **Describe**   List three harmful effects of obesity.

3. **Restate**   What is the relationship between calories and weight gain?

4. **Identify**   What are two types of eating disorders?

Thinking Critically

5. **Explain**   How can exercise be important for both losing and gaining weight?

6. **Recommend**   Suppose that you have a friend who does not have an eating disorder, but who seems to have unrealistic expectations of how thin she should be. What could you say to her to help her avoid future problems?

Applying Health Concepts

7. **Consumer Health**   Choose a weight-loss product or service (such as an exercise machine, diet program, or diet clinic) to research. Find out how much it would cost to use the product or service for a year. Then explain how a person might achieve the same or better results for free with good nutrition and regular exercise. Present your findings to the class.

Chapter 5 Review

Chapter Summary

▶ **Lesson 1** Fitness is the ability to handle the physical work and play of everyday life. A person can become fit by exercising regularly to develop strength, endurance, and flexibility.

▶ **Lesson 2** The circulatory system transports blood throughout the body to carry nutrients, oxygen, and other important materials to body cells. The heart pumps the blood through a system of blood vessels.

▶ **Lesson 3** The skeletal and muscular systems provide a supportive framework for your body and enable it to move. Regular exercise and a balanced diet help maintain a healthy skeleton and muscles.

▶ **Lesson 4** To plan a personal fitness program, you need to set goals, select the right exercises, and think about safety. Your workout should include warming up and cooling down.

▶ **Lesson 5** Achieving and maintaining your ideal weight will help you remain healthy. Weight management principles involve good nutrition and adequate exercise.

Reviewing Key Terms and Concepts

Using complete sentences, answer the following questions on a separate sheet of paper.

Lesson 1

1. What is the meaning of the term *exercise?*
2. Distinguish between *aerobic exercise* and *anaerobic exercise.*

Lesson 2

3. What is another name for the circulatory system?
4. What is *blood pressure?*

Lesson 3

5. In what way does the skeletal system protect the body?

6. What are the three types of muscle tissue?

Lesson 4

7. What are the stages in a typical workout session?
8. Describe how you can determine your target heart rate.

Lesson 5

9. What does the term *obesity* mean?
10. List four tips for people trying to gain weight.

Thinking Critically

Using complete sentences, answer the following questions on a separate sheet of paper.

11. **Predict** How could physical fitness and remaining active help an elderly person remain healthy?
12. **Integrate** Describe how a program of regular exercise designed to improve strength, endurance, and flexibility could help the skeletal and muscular systems.
13. **Analyze** Why might you want to vary your workout over time?
14. **Distinguish** How could you tell the difference between a healthful weight management program and an eating disorder?

Your Action Plan

Making a commitment to fitness involves dedication, not only to exercise, but to maintaining a balanced diet and having a healthful attitude about weight.

Step 1 Look over your journal entries and come up with at least one long-term goal and several short-term goals. For example, if your long-term goal is to exercise for half an hour four times a week, your short-term goals might include walking to school every day or riding your bike every weekend.

Step 2 Think about these goals in terms of your overall health—physical, mental/emotional, and social. Would you add or change any goals in order to increase gains in any of these areas? You might, for example, have a goal of learning a new physical activity. You may also feel, however, that you need more social interaction. You might refine your original goal to include an activity that you can take part in with others.

Decide on dates for reaching your goals. As you reach every short-term goal, check it off and give yourself a reward.

In Your Home and Community

1. **Community Resources** Propose that your school or community hold a fitness fair. Work with interested adults to promote fitness and good nutrition. Fitness and health professionals and local merchants could be invited to share information.

2. **Health of Others** Offer to be an exercise buddy for a younger neighbor or family member. You can encourage your buddy with your support and increase your own fitness program at the same time.

Building Your Portfolio

1. **Personal Fitness Program** Design a personal fitness program. Include a list of long-term and short-term goals, your schedule, and descriptions of your activities in your portfolio.

2. **Editorial** Write an editorial on the subject of body image in American culture. Discuss how both obesity and extreme thinness can be dangerous to health. Suggest actions that might bring about a more realistic view of weight and health. Include the editorial in your portfolio.

3. **Personal Assessment** Look through all the activities and projects you did for this chapter. Choose one or two that you would like to include in your portfolio.

Chapter 6

Sports and Conditioning

Student Expectations

After reading this chapter, you should be able to:

1. Describe the role sports play in a healthful lifestyle.
2. Recognize the importance of good nutrition and prevention of injuries in playing sports.
3. Explain how to use conditioning techniques effectively.
4. Identify ways you can balance school, sports, and home life.

Courtney: Well, I did it. I put my name on the list for field hockey tryouts.

Julie: Go, girl! Just remember, the school team is a lot tougher than our community league was.

Ian: What are you saying—that Courtney shouldn't try out?

Julie: No, it's just that *I'm* scared to. Hardly any seventh graders make the team.

Courtney: I know that already. I talked it over with my dad last night. He said if I didn't make it this year, I could work on my skills and try out again next year.

Ian: Right. And you'll be even better by then.

Julie: I love playing hockey, but I'm not ready for the pressure of trying out. We can still practice together, Courtney, right?

Courtney: Sure—whether I make the team or not!

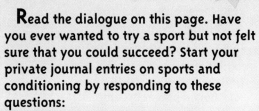

in your journal

Read the dialogue on this page. Have you ever wanted to try a sport but not felt sure that you could succeed? Start your private journal entries on sports and conditioning by responding to these questions:

▶ What would you say to Courtney if you were part of this conversation?

▶ Would you be willing to try out for a team if you weren't sure that you could make it? Why or why not?

▶ What do you consider to be a healthy attitude toward playing sports? Describe your feelings in your journal.

When you reach the end of the chapter, you will use your journal entries to make an action plan.

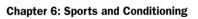

Individual and Team Sports

This lesson will help you find answers to questions that teens often ask about playing sports. For example:

▶ **What role do sports play in a healthy lifestyle?**
▶ **How can I choose which sports to play?**
▶ **What are some benefits of competition?**

Words to Know

commitment
individual sports
team sports
competition

Language Arts Connection

Writing About Sports

ACTIVITY!

If you're interested in your home team, you probably read the sports pages in the newspaper. Even if you're not a big fan, you may enjoy human interest sports stories, such as the kind that tells how a player became successful.

Attend a school or community sports event, and try "covering" it as a sportswriter would. Report on one game, or interview a player or a coach for your article.

Sports and You

One way to achieve fitness is to start and follow a well-thought-out exercise program. One way to remain fit is by playing sports. Some people play sports just for fun. Others make a serious **commitment,** *a pledge or promise,* to one or more sports. Commitment involves dedicating yourself to something over a period of time. If you're committed to a sport, you learn all you can about it, practice regularly, and work to develop the necessary skills.

Becoming involved in sports can result in a lifetime of fitness. Activities such as tennis, golf, and swimming are good lifetime sports. They can be enjoyed by people of almost any age.

Choosing Sports Activities

What do you like about sports? Do you like staying fit, the excitement of a close game, or the satisfaction of mastering a new skill? It is important to think about these questions as you choose a sports activity. You'll be most likely to get the greatest benefit out of a sport if you enjoy it.

Golf can provide excellent exercise for people of varied ages.

Individual Sports

Individual sports are *physical activities you can take part in by yourself or with a friend, without being part of a team.* There are many individual sports to choose from, including the following:

- Biking
- Hiking
- Swimming
- Running
- Horseback riding
- Skateboarding
- Surfing
- Skating

Individual sports have several advantages. For example, you can set your own schedule and determine your own level of commitment. You don't have to be compared to anyone else, and you can set the pace of the activity. On the other hand, you miss some of the social, mental, and emotional benefits of playing on a team.

*inter*NET
CONNECTION
Team up with the World Wide Web to set fitness goals, avoid sports injuries, and focus your concentration.
http://www.glencoe.com/sec/health

| When you are involved in an individual sport, you need self-discipline to follow your regimen.

Team Sports

Team sports are defined as *organized physical activities with specific rules, played by opposing groups of people.* Baseball, basketball, football, soccer, and volleyball are some of the most popular team sports. Team sports have many advantages.

- You have the companionship and encouragement of teammates and coaches.

- Playing against another team may push you to excel.

- Keeping up with regularly scheduled practice can help you become more responsible.

Some teens, however, find team sports too restricting. Individual sports are a better choice for these teens.

| Many teens find that they form close friendships with their teammates.

Sports and Competition

Most sports can be played on several levels: to increase your degree of fitness, to improve your skills, or with the goal of competition. **Competition** is *rivalry between two or more individuals or groups trying to reach the same goal.* When you play team sports competitively, your goal is to help your team win the game. In an individual competitive sport, your goal is to run faster, jump higher, or score more points than another person. You can even compete against yourself by trying to improve on your previous performance.

Some people thrive on competition. They enjoy the challenge of working to be the best. When they don't win, the experience makes them feel even more motivated to win next time. Others don't like competing. They find losing very painful. Still others find it hard to enjoy winning if their friends have to lose.

Competition can be both enjoyable and valuable, however, as **Figure 6.1** shows. Competitive sports can have value far beyond winning one game or even one season. They're a way to have fun, to build skills and fitness, and to work together with others toward a common goal.

Figure 6.1
The Value of Competition
Playing competitive sports can offer you opportunities to grow.

A Competition gives you a reason to work hard, practice, and make your best effort.

B Competition helps you develop mental focus, a skill that will be useful in other areas of your life.

C Competition allows you to learn the value of encouraging others and receiving their encouragement.

D Competition offers you a chance to improve your skills and feel good about your accomplishments.

Using complete sentences, answer the following questions on a separate sheet of paper.

Reviewing Terms and Facts

1. **Vocabulary** Describe what it means to make a *commitment* to a sport.

2. **List** Identify three individual sports and three team sports.

3. **Vocabulary** What is the meaning of *competition*?

Thinking Critically

4. **Recommend** Write a short paragraph that explains how sports can be helpful to people throughout their lives.

5. **Evaluate** Describe your own thoughts and feelings about the benefits of individual sports as compared to the benefits of team sports.

Applying Health Concepts

6. **Personal Health** Intramural sports are team sports that allow different teams from the same school to compete against each other. As a class, hold a brainstorming session about the advantages and difficulties of having such a program. Questions to consider may include how to organize teams, where to hold practices, and how to get a faculty sponsor. If your school does not have an intramural program already, consider presenting a formal plan for such a program to the administration.

LIFE SKILLS
Teamwork

*W*orking as a productive member of a team is a lifetime skill. Teamwork skills can help you get along in school, in your community, and at a job. What skills will help you be a good team player?

▶ **Cooperate.** Use your playing skills to help your team. Don't try to win the game alone. Players need to work together to be successful.

▶ **Communicate.** Let others know when you need help or when you have a good idea. Also, listen to your coach and your teammates.

▶ **Be sensitive.** Instead of criticizing a teammate for making a mistake, offer support. Everybody makes mistakes—even you.

▶ **Be generous.** Pay attention to the game when you're on the bench. Encourage your teammates.

▶ **Be responsible.** Show up for practices on time, and work at home on your skills whenever you can. Come to practice ready to work.

Practice these skills. If you aren't on a team, you can apply similar skills to a team project at school or to interactions within your family.

Follow-up Activity

With a group of four to six people, prepare a skit about teamwork. You may use the setting of a sports team or of some other type of team. Illustrate the benefits of good teamwork or the problems caused by not working together. Perform your skit for the class.

Sports and Physical Wellness

This lesson will help you find answers to questions that teens often ask about sports nutrition and sports injuries. For example:

▶ **How can nutrition affect my level of performance?**

▶ **How can I avoid sports injuries?**

▶ **Why is it harmful to take drugs to improve sports performance?**

Words to Know

dehydration
anabolic steroids

Sports and Energy

You already know that to maintain your weight, you need to use the same number of calories as you put into your body by eating. If you play sports, you will use more energy. Therefore, to maintain your weight, you will need additional calories.

Not all sports require the same amount of energy. Chapter 5 gave information on how many calories are burned during various activities. **Figure 6.2** divides sports into three categories: low-energy, moderate-energy, and high-energy. Knowing the energy requirements of the sports you play can help you plan your diet.

Figure 6.2
Sports and Energy Use
The number of calories burned, as shown in this figure, is calculated for a 100-pound person playing for one hour.

High-energy Sports (over 350)	
Cross-country skiing	Rope jumping
Handball	Running
Racquetball	Soccer

Moderate-energy Sports (250–350)	
Aerobic dancing	Swimming
Badminton	Tennis
In-line and ice-skating	Volleyball

Low-energy Sports (less than 250)	
Baseball and softball	Gymnastics
Basketball (half-court)	Hiking
Bowling	Judo and karate
Golf	

Calorie Furnace

Sports Nutrition

Whether or not you are active in sports, you should have a balanced, nutritious diet. Getting enough complex carbohydrates, proteins, vitamins, and minerals—and not consuming too much fat—is important for anyone. If you play sports, however, you will need to keep your body supplied with additional energy. This may require some changes in what you eat as well as when you eat.

What to Eat

If you play sports, make sure that you get enough of the six major types of nutrients. You can do this most effectively by eating a variety of foods from the five major food groups. Here are a few pointers.

- **Eat plenty of complex carbohydrates.** Fruits and vegetables, pasta, and whole-grain breads will provide your body with carbohydrates, a very efficient source of energy, as well as fiber. If you need to increase your calorie intake because of sports activity, eat larger amounts of foods high in complex carbohydrates.

- **Get enough vitamins and minerals.** A balanced diet should provide the vitamins and minerals that you need. Two minerals that are especially important are iron and calcium. Iron helps to supply your muscles with oxygen while you are exercising. Good sources are red meat and green leafy vegetables. Calcium strengthens bones and helps muscles work properly. Dairy products, salmon, and collard greens are good sources of calcium.

- **Don't load up on protein or fats.** An athlete does not need more protein or fats than a nonathlete. Although protein is used in building muscle tissue, muscles become developed only through exercise and training. Eating two to three servings from the meat, poultry, fish, dry beans, eggs, and nuts group daily will provide all the protein you need. A diet high in fats could put you at risk for several kinds of diseases later in life.

- **Eat breakfast.** If you have a game in the morning, make sure that you eat breakfast. You'll perform better if you've given your body fuel to go on. Eat lightly, however, if your sport requires running.

- **Drink plenty of water.** Make sure that you get enough water. Eight glasses of water are recommended each day for most individuals. If you are playing a sport, raise that to 9–13 glasses of water. While engaging in sports you lose more water because you perspire. **Dehydration** (dee·hy·DRAY·shuhn) is *excessive loss of water from the body.* It can cause muscle cramps and heatstroke, and it is also harmful to other body systems.

Eat Up

Here are some snacks and meals that provide 100 grams of carbohydrates, as well as proteins, vitamins, and minerals. They're good for you and good for your game.

- ► 1 bagel with peanut butter and ²/₃ cup of raisins
- ► 1 cup of low-fat yogurt, 1 banana, and 1 cup of orange juice
- ► 1 turkey sandwich (without mayonnaise) and 1 cup of applesauce
- ► 2 cups of spaghetti with meat sauce and 1 piece of bread

Athletes need access to liquids while participating in any sport.

Q: Do I need to drink sports drinks when I exercise or play sports?

A: Water alone is enough if your workout or game lasts less than an hour, or if you are not playing continuously. Sports drinks do replenish fluids, however, as well as carbohydrates that your body can use for energy. These drinks can be helpful for long, intense games.

When to Eat

Although you may not have to change *what* you eat very much when you begin to play a sport, deciding *when* to eat may require more thought. Important factors include how much energy you will need and when, and how your sport will affect your digestion. **Figure 6.3** provides tips on nutrition before, during, and after playing sports.

Figure 6.3
Knowing When to Eat

If you don't eat enough before or during a strenuous game, you could feel faint. To play your best, follow these tips.

❶ Before You Play
Good foods to eat before a game are those rich in complex carbohydrates. Bananas, bagels, and fruit juices are good choices. Eat about one to two hours before your game. Drink plenty of fluids as well. Some athletes find that they achieve a better energy level by eating a regular meal a couple of hours before a game and then having a light snack about a half hour before they play.

❷ During Your Game
Drink plenty of cool water, at least ½ cup every 20 minutes. Usually it is not necessary to replace carbohydrates, even sugars, unless your game will last more than an hour and you will be playing almost nonstop. Some coaches, however, provide orange or apple slices, rice cakes, or fruit juice on the sidelines, along with water.

❸ After Your Game
After your game you're likely to be hungry. At this point, eat a balanced meal with plenty of carbohydrates but also some protein and fats. Make sure that the meal also replenishes vitamins and minerals. Continue to drink water and other liquids.

Preventing Injuries

When you are playing a sport, you are using your body to run, jump, throw, and kick. You are often thinking and moving fast—and so are the people around you. Here are some tips on how to avoid sports injuries.

- Always warm up, stretch adequately, and cool down.

- Learn the proper techniques for your sport. For example, when you throw a ball, avoid overextending your elbow. When you land from a jump, bend your knees.

- If you get injured during a game, don't return to play until you've been checked out by the coach, a trainer, or a doctor. To be safe, don't return to the game at all unless the injury was a minor one *and* you have been cleared by your coach.

- Control your emotions. Getting angry may cloud your judgment and cause you to get hurt or to hurt someone else.

Having the right equipment and using it properly are the best ways to protect yourself against injury. **Figure 6.4** describes some of the equipment that can help protect you.

Figure 6.4
Protective Equipment
Different sports require different kinds of protective gear.

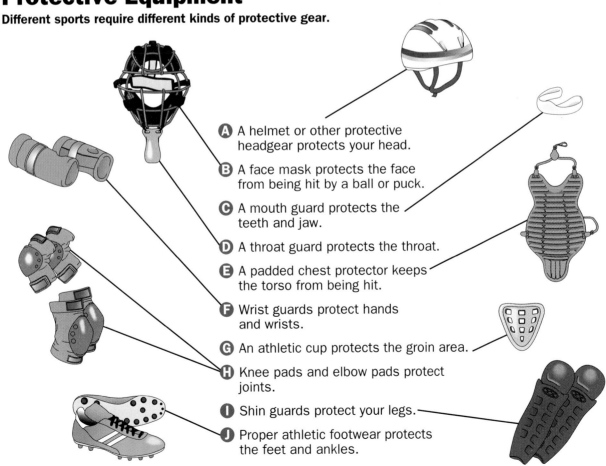

A A helmet or other protective headgear protects your head.

B A face mask protects the face from being hit by a ball or puck.

C A mouth guard protects the teeth and jaw.

D A throat guard protects the throat.

E A padded chest protector keeps the torso from being hit.

F Wrist guards protect hands and wrists.

G An athletic cup protects the groin area.

H Knee pads and elbow pads protect joints.

I Shin guards protect your legs.

J Proper athletic footwear protects the feet and ankles.

Avoiding Harmful Substances

You can build strength and endurance safely with regular workouts and good nutrition. Some people, however, use performance-enhancing drugs such as anabolic steroids. **Anabolic steroids** (a·nuh·BAH·lik STIR·oydz) are *synthetic compounds that cause muscle tissue to develop at an abnormally high rate.*

Anabolic steroids, often referred to as *steroids,* have legitimate medical uses, such as treating some types of cancer. It is illegal, however, to use them to improve athletic performance. They are also very dangerous because of their side effects, which include

- development of acne.

- weakening of tendons, possibly leading to joint or tendon injury.

- damage to the cardiovascular system, affecting heart rate and blood pressure and increasing the risk of heart attack.

- bone damage, since bones can become more brittle.

- harmful effects on sexual characteristics, including growth of facial hair in females and breast development in males.

- mental and emotional effects, such as irritability, anxiety, suspicion, or sudden rage.

- liver and brain cancers.

Avoid anabolic steroids and all other performance-enhancing drugs. They can harm your health and ruin your athletic career.

You don't need performance enhancers to achieve success in a sport.

Lesson 2 Review

Using complete sentences, answer the following questions on a separate sheet of paper.

Reviewing Terms and Facts

1. **List**   Identify three tips for good sports nutrition.
2. **Vocabulary**   What is *dehydration?*
3. **Recall**   List three body areas that might be injured while you are playing sports, and describe a piece of equipment for protecting each one.

Thinking Critically

4. **Recommend**   What advice would you give to a player who begins to feel very angry during a game?

5. **Hypothesize**   Why do you think people take anabolic steroids and other performance-enhancing drugs, despite the dangers of these substances?

Applying Health Concepts

6. **Personal Health**   Create a list of ways to avoid injuries in the sports you enjoy most. You may include information from this lesson as well as from other sources.

7. **Health of Others**   Make a poster to highlight the dangers of anabolic steroids and other performance-enhancing drugs. Describe the serious side effects of various substances.

Conditioning Goals and Techniques

This lesson will help you find answers to questions that teens often ask about conditioning goals and techniques. For example:

▶ **What is conditioning?**

▶ **What techniques will help me get into condition without doing more than I should?**

▶ **How can keeping records help me to reach my goals?**

Conditioning and Your Goals

If you play a sport regularly, you'll need to devote time to getting into shape for it. *Training to get into shape* is called **conditioning.** As in other aspects of life, you'll need to set goals for your conditioning if you expect to accomplish anything. The goals you set, however, will depend on what you want to get out of the sports you play. Ask yourself questions like these.

■ **What are my priorities?** What is most important to me? Fitness? Fun? Friendship? Improving specific skills? Excelling at the sport I have chosen?

■ **What are the demands of this sport?** What do my coach and my teammates expect of me? How serious do I need to be?

■ **What will happen in the future?** What will be expected of me? How might my other responsibilities increase? Do I want to keep on playing this sport?

Did You Know?

Hooray for Hoops

A recent survey of more than 25,000 15- to 18-year-olds in 41 countries asked teens what sports they liked to play and to watch. Basketball was listed by 71 percent of the respondents. Teens in Taiwan, Greece, and Korea showed the most enthusiasm for the game. Soccer came in second with 67 percent of the teens placing it on their lists.

Different sports require different types of conditioning.

Q: Why are my muscles stiff and sore after I've exercised strenuously?

A: Muscles become stiff and sore because of microscopic damage to muscle fibers. The small tears in the muscles fill up with fluids and waste products. As the fibers heal, your muscles feel better. The pain is often at its worst about two days after exercising. For this reason, the pain is known as delayed-onset muscle soreness. If you continue to exercise your muscles regularly, soreness will no longer be a problem.

What kinds of exercises do you think wrestlers might do to condition their bodies?

Getting Good Advice

To set appropriate goals, you may want to ask someone for advice. Your physical education teacher, a coach, or possibly a family physician can give you good advice on how to get into condition for a particular sport.

Different sports demand different levels of strength, endurance, and flexibility. For example:

- A gymnast needs strength, flexibility, and endurance to perform a variety of gymnastic routines.

- A basketball player needs endurance, speed, and agility to handle the ball, as well as strength for shooting.

- A wrestler needs strength, agility, flexibility, and balance.

Cross-Training

Cross-training is *any fitness program that includes a variety of physical activities to promote balanced fitness.* If you play several sports, cross-training is essential. It is also helpful for people who do not play team sports. What are the benefits of cross-training?

Figure 6.5
A Sample Cross-Training Program

Here's a sample weekly program that would promote conditioning for several different sports and be interesting as well. Notice that this teen combines outdoor and indoor activities as well as solitary activities with activities she does with other people.

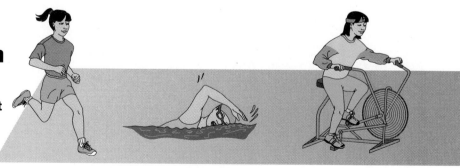

On day 1, run two miles on the school track.

On day 2, take an easy swim in an indoor pool.

On day 3, go for a bicycle ride or ride a stationary bike.

- If you combine a variety of activities you enjoy, you are less likely to become bored or "burned out."

- You avoid injury by strengthening and stretching complementary muscles, such as the hamstrings in the back of the thighs and the quadriceps in the front of the thighs. You also exercise different muscle groups.

- Your total health, including mental/emotional and social health as well as physical health, is improved by achieving overall fitness of your whole body.

Figure 6.5 illustrates the type of variety you might see in a cross-training program.

Avoiding Overtraining

It's great to be enthusiastic about getting into condition, but don't overdo it. Too much exercise without enough rest can be harmful. **Overtraining** is *exercising too hard or too often, without enough rest in between.* What are the signs of overtraining? They include

- an abnormally high heart rate when you are not exercising.

- feeling sore or tired all the time.

- frequent illness.

- disturbed sleeping habits.

- irritability or inability to concentrate.

- frequent muscle strain or injury.

How can you avoid overtraining? First, take at least one day off every week. During the rest of the week, alternate tough workout days with easy workout days. For example, the day before a major event, exercise lightly. (Take another look at Figure 6.5 to see how this might be done.) Finally, every two months, reduce your exercise intensity for a week.

On day 4, take a rest. Don't exercise at all on this day.

On day 5, take a half-hour walk with a friend. Carry light arm weights to strengthen your upper body.

On day 6, spend twenty minutes doing toning exercises.

On day 7, play a game of tennis with a friend.

Set some long-term goals for your exercise or conditioning program. Consider such factors as weather changes and vacations. Will you need to change your routine in the middle of winter or when your family goes on a trip? In your journal, list some of your long-term goals as well as personal circumstances that might affect your ability to reach them.

Keeping Records

Keeping track of your conditioning program helps you to stay aware of your progress. As you improve, you can take pride in your accomplishments. If you experience muscle soreness, you can change activities or seek help before the problem gets worse. **Figure 6.6** shows a useful format for charting your progress.

When you begin your conditioning program, set some short-term and long-term goals. As you reach each short-term goal—for example, riding your bike for 2 miles—record it on your conditioning chart. When you reach a long-term goal, such as finishing in a major race, give yourself a reward.

Figure 6.6
Conditioning Chart

This chart might have been kept by the teen whose cross-training program was presented in Figure 6.5.

Day of the Week	Exercise	Time Spent/ Distance Covered	Comments
Monday (5/16)	Run	3 miles	Good run.
Tuesday (5/17)	Swim	30 minutes	Varied my strokes today.
Wednesday (5/18)	Cycle	3 miles	Had to ride inside—bad weather.
Thursday (5/19)	none	none	———
Friday (5/20)	Walk	1.5 miles	Reached my goal of walking 1.5 miles carrying two 2-pound weights.
Saturday (5/21)	Toning exercises	20 minutes	Next week, work harder on abdominal muscles.
Sunday (5/22)	Tennis	1 hour	I won! Try basketball for a few weeks?

HEALTH LAB
Getting into Condition

Introduction: Fitness testing is one way to find out how fit you are and where you need to improve. Fitness tests can also be a way to measure your progress in a conditioning program.

Objective: With a partner, measure your strength, endurance, and flexibility.

Materials and Method: Perform each of the following tests for strength, endurance, and flexibility. For the strength test you will need a horizontal bar that is anchored firmly enough to support your weight. For the endurance test you will

need a stopwatch as well as a sturdy step about 8 inches high.

▶ **Strength Test: Pull-Ups.** This is a test for upper body strength that requires a horizontal bar. Grasp the bar with your palms facing away. Hang with your arms straight. Pull yourself up until your chin clears the bar. You have completed a pull-up when you have lowered yourself to the starting position. Count the number of pull-ups you can do without resting. (Average rating: females 2; males 6–7)

Using complete sentences, answer the following questions on a separate sheet of paper.

Reviewing Terms and Facts

1. **Vocabulary**   What is *conditioning?*

2. **Recall**   From whom might you obtain advice about a conditioning program?

3. **Identify**   Describe three advantages of a cross-training program.

4. **Explain**   What are typical signs of overtraining?

Thinking Critically

5. **Recommend**   Not all teens have access to gym facilities or swimming pools. List three types of cross-training exercises that could be done with little or no exercise equipment and no special facilities.

6. **Distinguish**   Compare the conditioning that would be important for a long-distance runner with the conditioning that would be important for a wrestler. How might they be similar? How might they be different?

Applying Health Concepts

7. **Health of Others**   With a group of four, plan a booklet or poster that illustrates and describes ways to get into good physical condition for a specific sport. Explain why the activities you recommend are effective.

8. **Consumer Health**   Choose a type of exercise equipment such as a treadmill or a rowing machine. Do research on the Internet, over the telephone, or through magazines to find out about two products of this type. Create a chart that compares the two products in terms of features, price, physical benefits of use, and other qualities.

▶ **Endurance: Step-Ups.** Stand in front of a sturdy step or bench about 8 inches high. When your partner says go, step up with your left foot, bring the right foot up, step down with the right foot, then bring the left foot down. Repeat, alternating legs. After three minutes are up, stop and test your pulse rate. (Average pulse rate: 106–119)

▶ **Flexibility: Shoulder Stretch.** Reach with your left hand over your left shoulder and down your back. At the same time, place your right hand behind your back and reach up. See if you can touch the fingers of one hand to the fingers of the other. Repeat, switching hand positions. (Average rating: fingers touch)

Observations and Analysis: Do you feel the need to improve in any of these elements of physical fitness? If so, what activities could you use to make improvements? (Chapter 5 of this book provides some ideas.) Write an analysis of your own performance on these tests. Then develop a plan for improving your own condition in these or other areas. Perform these tests weekly over the next few months and record the results.

TEEN HEALTH DIGEST

CON$UMER FOCU$

Choose Your Shoes

Perhaps the most important piece of athletic equipment you will ever buy is a good pair of shoes. Well-made shoes can protect you from injury and even improve your performance. The question is, which shoe is right for you?

It's important to find a shoe that's designed for your sport. Even sports as similar as walking and running put different kinds of stress on the feet and legs. If you engage in a variety of sports activi-ties, but don't spend a lot of time on any one sport, cross-trainers may be the best choice.

Whatever your sport, make sure that the shoes you buy fit com-fortably and are well made. If you try to save money by buying a very inexpensive brand, you may end up with a lower-quality shoe. A good pair of shoes will last as long as several seasons, so the money you spend will be a long-term investment in your overall fitness.

Try This: *Ask three people you know how they chose their last pair of sports shoes. Discuss with your classmates what you have learned from this article and your research.*

Sports and Recreation

A "Rhodes" Runner

Runner Nnenna Lynch has been winning track and cross-country titles since high school. However, she didn't use her talent as an excuse to slack off on her studies. Upon graduating from college, she won a Rhodes schol-arship to study at Oxford University in England. She continued to run compet-itively while working to-ward a graduate degree in social anthropology.

In 1997 she attended a month-long training camp in Kenya. She didn't leave her books behind; her activities consisted only of eating, sleeping, running—and reading. Lynch explains: "All my life, I've been juggling things. Now I'm trying to become a full-time ath-lete." She has the focus and drive to make that happen.

People at Work

On the Road to Podiatry

Howard Palamarchuk is a podiatrist (puh·DY·uh·trist)—a foot doctor—who started out as a race walker. He just missed making the 1972 U.S. Olympic team when he was 19. Along the way he's felt a lot of pain—foot pain.

He says that he can treat runners and race walkers because "I've made all the mistakes personally and violated all the rules."

Dr. Palamarchuk is director of sports medicine at the Foot and Ankle Institute of the Pennsylvania College of Podiatric Medicine in Philadelphia. He also tends to the feet of athletes at the Boston Marathon, the Philadelphia Distance Run, and the Marine Corps Marathon in Washington, D.C.

Teens Making a Difference

A Lifesaving Decision

Daniel Huffman used to play football and baseball, but he has given up both. He chose to do something more important: save his grandmother's life.

When Daniel's grandmother was near death because of kidney failure, he decided to donate one of his kidneys to her. The operation was a success.

Daniel can no longer play football or baseball because he cannot risk an injury. Instead he is doing strength training at a gym. He has also been offered scholarships by two state universities. Athletes are valuable to colleges, but so are students as unselfish as Daniel.

Personal Trainer

Back to Basics

If you like to ski or play basketball, you'll want to build strength in the muscles of your hips and lower back. Try this simple exercise.

1. Lie on your back on a pad or rug, arms by your sides, palms down.
2. Bend your knees to a 90-degree angle, keeping your feet flat on the floor.
3. Lift your left foot, and rest your ankle on your right knee.
4. Slowly raise your hips until they are about 6 inches off the floor; hold for a few seconds, and slowly lower them. Repeat for a total of five times.
5. Repeat with your other leg. Gradually build up the number of repetitions to 15.

Try This: Do research to find out more about organ donation. What medical and personal issues are involved?

Balancing School, Sports, and Home Life

This lesson will help you find answers to questions that teens often ask about balancing sports with other parts of their lives. For example:

▶ How can I determine if I have struck a good balance in my life?

▶ What are some of the warning signs that areas of my life are not in balance?

▶ How can I balance sports, school, and my time with my family and friends?

Words to Know

overcommitment
burnout

▶ Did You Know?

B.C. Bowling

Sports have been a part of human life for a very long time. In fact, the oldest sport in the world may be bowling. A bowling ball made of stone was found, along with bowling pins, in the tomb of an Egyptian mummy. The tomb was built about 7,000 years ago.

Deciding What Matters to You

Sports may be a large part of your life right now. Winning a game and being part of a team can make you feel great. However, you are also a student and a family member. Sometimes you may find it difficult to balance sports activities with your other interests and responsibilities.

Balancing your roles does not necessarily mean giving them equal importance. Although each is significant, one area or another may take a leading role at a particular point in your life. If you are a star hurdler on the track team, for example, you may spend much of your time and energy at practice and traveling to and from track meets. You have probably made this choice because of certain values: the desire to excel, to use your talents effectively, and to be a valuable asset to the team. It's always a good idea, however, to be aware of how your commitment to sports is affecting your schoolwork and family life.

Being part of a team can take up a large amount of your time.

Using the Decision-Making Process

The six steps of the decision-making process can be helpful as you consider how to balance areas of your life. After all, balancing your life means choosing among your options; you usually have to give up some goals, at least for a while, in order to achieve others. **Figure 6.7** shows some of the questions you might need to ask yourself as you use the process for this purpose.

Figure 6.7
Balancing Your Life
Does your life need a better balance? Find out by answering these questions.

Decision-Making Steps	Questions to Ask Yourself
State the situation.	How much time am I spending on sports? On schoolwork? With my family and friends? Do I feel that I am shortchanging anyone or failing to meet any of my commitments?
List the options.	Which activities could I spend less time on? Am I continuing any activities merely out of habit? What activities might I give up, at least for now?
Weigh the possible outcomes.	If I miss several practices, will I be cut from the team? If I spend more time studying, will my grades improve? If I spend more time at home doing chores, will my family see me as more responsible?
Consider your values.	How much of my time do I want to devote to sports? What other activities are important in my life? Have I discussed my choices with others?
Make a decision and act.	What have I decided to do?
Evaluate the decision.	Have I taken responsibility for my decision? Has my decision made me feel better about the balance in my life? Do I need to make any further changes?

Warning Signs

One of the purposes of the decision-making process is to help you guard against overcommitment. **Overcommitment** is *obligating yourself to more people or projects than you have time or energy to follow through on.* Being overcommitted can cause you to feel tired and irritable. You may also feel guilty, especially if you believe that you are letting people down.

Overcommitment can also lead to **burnout,** which means *a sense of exhaustion caused by exerting too much energy for too long a time.* Burnout can be physical, mental, or emotional. What are the signs of overcommitment? **Figure 6.8** on the next page describes a few.

Teen Issues

Grounded! ACTIVITY!

When basketball star David Robinson was in eighth grade, he brought home a report card with a C in a subject he usually did well in. Although he had A's and B's in his other subjects, David's parents grounded him for six weeks. How would you feel if this happened to you?

Have a class debate. Should parents ground teens when their grades drop as a result of sports or other activities? What other solutions can you suggest?

Figure 6.8

Warning Signs of Overcommitment

Each of these situations can be a sign of overcommitment to a sport and the beginning of burnout.

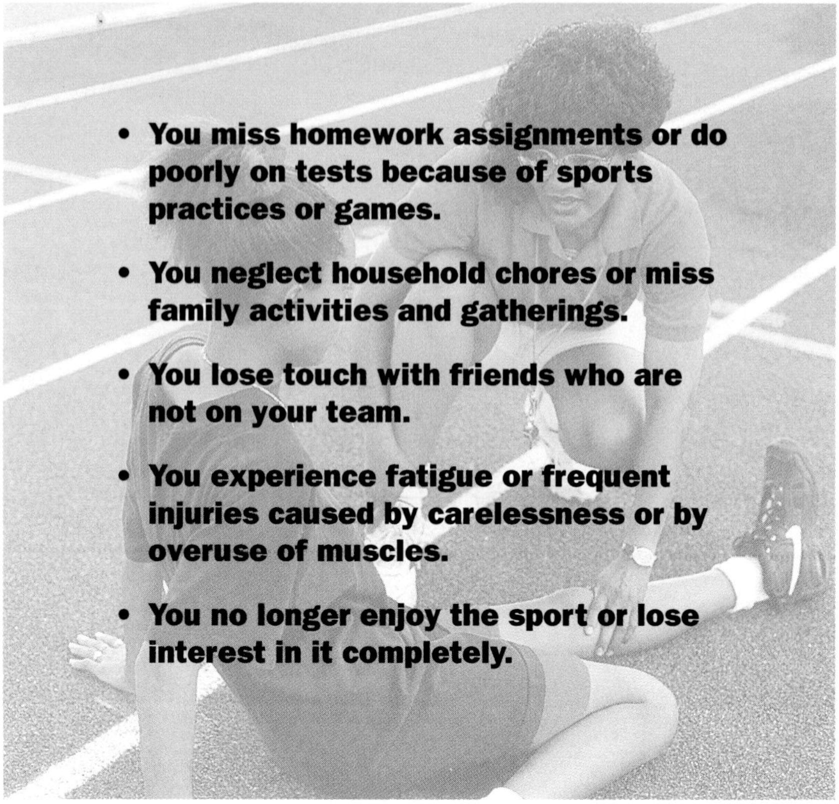

• You miss homework assignments or do poorly on tests because of sports practices or games.
• You neglect household chores or miss family activities and gatherings.
• You lose touch with friends who are not on your team.
• You experience fatigue or frequent injuries caused by carelessness or by overuse of muscles.
• You no longer enjoy the sport or lose interest in it completely.

These signs of overcommitment could be applied to other areas as well. For example, you might lose touch with friends if family commitments make you unavailable to them for long periods.

Skills for Balancing Your Life

If you feel that you need to work on balancing your life, try talking with family members, teachers, or friends. Sometimes someone else can see a solution that you might never consider. The list that follows gives a few practical tips for preventing or fixing an imbalance. Can you think of others?

- If you want to play several sports, choose sports with seasons that don't overlap.
- Eliminate one sport, but continue others. Consider staying with a sport that you might enjoy for a lifetime.
- Look for a different team or league—one that may require less energy and time.
- Play only one season each year in a sport. For example, play soccer in the fall but not in the spring.
- Balance the sports you play by using cross-training techniques. Select those that complement one another in terms of fitness benefits and skill development.

Using complete sentences, answer the following questions on a separate sheet of paper.

Reviewing Terms and Facts

1. **Explain** How can the decision-making process help you make choices about balancing your life?

2. **Vocabulary** What is *overcommitment?*

3. **List** Identify four warning signs of overcommitment.

Thinking Critically

4. **Distinguish** What is the difference between dedication to excellence in a sport and overcommitment?

5. **Describe** Explain how burnout could affect someone physically, mentally, and emotionally.

Applying Health Concepts

6. **Personal Health** Make a circle graph that shows the different roles you have in your life: for example, student, family member, baseball player, chess club member, and so on. Try to make the pie wedges come close to the approximate percentage of time and energy you devote to each role. Color each section. Analyze the graph. Do you like what you see? Is there anything you would like to change?

MAKING HEALTHY DECISIONS
Balancing a Life

*A*nna has always been athletic. She has been in ballet classes since the age of four. She loves softball, and she's a good ice-skater. In seventh grade, Anna fell in love with basketball. She made the school team, and she began to spend four afternoons a week in the gym after school.

Now she has a problem, however. Seventh grade demands more homework time than Anna expected. Her grades are starting to slip. Also, with Anna at basketball most afternoons and ballet class on the weekends, Anna's sister Tori feels as if she is doing more than her share of chores at home. Then there is Katherine, Anna's best friend, who didn't make the team. Anna hardly sees her friend during the basketball season.

Anna knows that she has a problem. She uses the six-step decision-making process to figure out what to do.

① **State the situation**
② **List the options**
③ **Weigh the possible outcomes**
④ **Consider your values**
⑤ **Make a decision and act**
⑥ **Evaluate the decision**

Follow-up Activities

1. Apply the six-step decision-making process to Anna's problem.

2. With a small group, role-play a family discussion on Anna's conflicts or a conversation between Anna and Katherine.

3. After each group's role-play has been performed, discuss how Anna might both solve the problem she has now and prevent such problems from occurring in the future.

Chapter 6 Review

Chapter Summary

▶ **Lesson 1** Playing sports can be an enjoyable way to develop and maintain fitness. You may choose individual sports activities or play as a member of a team.

▶ **Lesson 2** You need to have a nutritious, balanced diet to have enough energy for sports activities. You can avoid injuries by learning appropriate techniques and wearing protective gear. No one should take anabolic steroids or other drugs to improve athletic ability.

▶ **Lesson 3** To set your conditioning goals, evaluate what you want to get out of playing a sport. Ask a sports professional to help you set up a conditioning program. You may choose cross-training to develop whole-body fitness.

▶ **Lesson 4** You will want to achieve a balance among your schoolwork, sports, and your home life. Avoid overcommitment and burnout, which can harm your physical, mental/emotional, and social health.

Reviewing Key Terms and Concepts

Using complete sentences, answer the following questions on a separate sheet of paper.

Lesson 1

1. Use the term *commitment* in an original sentence.

2. List three ways in which competition can be beneficial.

Lesson 2

3. What are *anabolic steroids?*

4. Describe basic principles for eating and drinking before, during, and after a game.

Lesson 3

5. What is *cross-training?*

6. Why should you keep records of your conditioning program?

Lesson 4

7. What is *burnout?*

8. List four ways you might solve the problem of overcommitment to your sports activities.

Thinking Critically

Using complete sentences, answer the following questions on a separate sheet of paper.

9. **Apply** Suppose that you have a friend who has never been on a sports team. You think, however, that he would be a great asset to the community youth softball team. How might you convince him to try out?

10. **Explain** What strong emotions, besides anger, could make a player more likely to be injured in a sport?

11. **Analyze** Why might you want to continue a conditioning program even during your sport's off-season? How might your program change?

12. **Generalize** How can the principles you use to balance sports, schoolwork, and your home life remain useful as you become an independent adult?

Your Action Plan

Many people do not take the time to think about the role that sports play in their lives. This activity will give you a chance to do that.

Step 1 Take a moment to look over your private journal entries for this chapter. Are you satisfied with the role that sports play in your life?

Step 2 Is there anything you would like to change? Do you want to start a new program or increase your amount of activity?

Step 3 Once you have answered these questions, formulate a long-term goal statement. Then create three to five short-term goals to help you reach that long-term goal. For example, if your long-term goal were to jog a mile in 7 minutes, a short-term goal might be to jog half a mile in 3½ minutes and then finish the mile at a comfortable speed.

Keep track of your progress. When you reach a goal, write one or two sentences about how it makes you feel. Share your thoughts with a friend.

In Your Home and Community

1. With family members, discuss the subject of balancing school, sports, and home responsibilities. Ask members to contribute to a list of healthful ways in which young athletes might respond to the demands that sports make on them. Discuss your list in class.

2. Do some research—either at the library or by interviewing preschool teachers—about noncompetitive games for young children. Find out about the value of group games that involve cooperation rather than competition. Write a short report, and present it to your class.

Building Your Portfolio

1. Look in magazines and newspapers for a sports story involving a teen. The story might be about a teen who has overcome obstacles to succeed in a sport or who has used a sport to help others. Write a summary of the article, and place it in your portfolio. Be sure to identify the source of the article.

2. Conduct library research to find out about a sport that you have never played. Write a one-page report about the sport, telling whether you think that you would enjoy it and why. Add the report to your portfolio.

3. Look through all the activities and projects you did for this chapter. Choose one or two that you would like to include in your portfolio.

Unit 3
Understanding Yourself and Others

Chapter 7

Growth and Development

Student Expectations

After reading this chapter, you should be able to:

① Describe the development and changes that occur during adolescence.

② Identify the parts of the endocrine system and explain how the system works.

③ List the parts of the male reproductive system and describe their function.

④ List the parts of the female reproductive system and describe their function.

⑤ Describe human development after fertilization and identify factors that affect development.

⑥ Describe the stages of life from infancy to adulthood.

Dan: I can't believe it! I've been taller than you since second grade. Now you've got 2 inches on me.

Kyle: It's about time.

Dan: It feels weird. I'm not used to reaching up to block your shots.

Kyle: Well, both my parents are tall, so I always figured I'd be tall too.

Dan: How tall is your dad?

Kyle: He's 6 foot 3. My older brother is 6 foot 2. I hope I reach that size.

Dan: I'll *never* block your shots then! Anyway, it's your ball. Let's play.

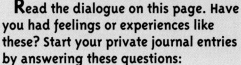

in your journal

Read the dialogue on this page. Have you had feelings or experiences like these? Start your private journal entries by answering these questions:

▶ What would you say to Dan and Kyle if you were part of this discussion?

▶ In what ways have you changed during the past year or two?

▶ Which recent changes in your life have been positive? Which have not?

▶ What have you learned from the changes in your life?

When you reach the end of the chapter, you will use your journal entries to make an action plan.

Adolescence

This lesson will help you find answers to questions that teens often ask about changes that take place during the teen years. For example:

▶ **What physical changes take place during adolescence?**

▶ **What mental and emotional growth occurs during adolescence?**

▶ **How will I grow socially during adolescence?**

Words to Know

adolescence
hormones
puberty

A Time of Change

As you enter your teen years, you'll experience many changes. Some will be physical: your body will grow and develop. Other changes may be less obvious. You'll begin to look at life differently from the way you did when you were younger. You'll also experience new and different thoughts and feelings. Some of these changes will be pleasant. Others, at least at first, may make you feel a little uncomfortable.

This *time of life, between childhood and adulthood,* is **adolescence** (a·duhl·E·suhns). It is a time of growth and change, usually starting somewhere between ages 11 and 15. Some of your friends will begin to develop physically before you do, while others may develop later. This is normal. Each individual goes through the changes of adolescence at his or her own rate. Typically, however, girls experience these changes about two years earlier than boys.

Many of the physical and emotional changes of adolescence are brought about by hormones. **Hormones** (HOR·mohnz) are *chemical substances, produced by glands, which help to regulate the way your body functions.* The changes that hormones cause during adolescence prepare you for adulthood.

Hormones cause physical and emotional changes in adolescents.

Physical Changes

Adolescence begins with the physical changes of puberty. **Puberty** (PYOO·ber·tee) is *the time when you start to develop certain physical characteristics of adults of your own gender.* **Figure 7.1** lists some of these characteristics.

Physical growth during puberty generally occurs at a rapid pace. Many girls grow 3 inches taller between ages 11 and 14. Boys usually begin their growth spurt later than girls. Boys may grow 6 or 7 inches between ages 13 and 16. Both girls and boys often keep growing for several more years after their initial growth spurt.

The rate of physical growth and development varies greatly from person to person and often causes teens to feel uncomfortable or self-conscious. Some teens worry that they are developing too quickly. Others are concerned that they are not developing quickly enough. Such concerns are a normal part of adolescence.

*inter*NET
CONNECTION
Take a journey to self-understanding by exploring adolescent development on the Internet.
http:/www.glencoe. com/ sec/health

Figure 7.1
What Are the Physical Changes of Adolescence?
Many types of physical changes occur during adolescence.

Females
- **Sudden, rapid growth occurs.**
- **All permanent teeth come into place.**
- **Acne may appear.**
- **Underarm hair appears.**
- **Pubic hair appears.**
- **Perspiration increases.**
- **External genitals enlarge.**
- **Breasts develop.**
- **Hips get wider.**
- **Waistline gets narrower.**
- **Ovulation occurs.**
- **Menstruation starts.**
- **Uterus and ovaries enlarge.**

Males
- **Sudden, rapid growth occurs.**
- **All permanent teeth come into place.**
- **Acne may appear.**
- **Underarm hair appears.**
- **Pubic hair appears.**
- **Perspiration increases.**
- **External genitals enlarge.**
- **Breasts may enlarge somewhat.**
- **Shoulders get broader.**
- **Muscles develop.**
- **Sperm production starts.**
- **Facial hair appears.**
- **Larynx gets larger and voice deepens.**
- **Hairline begins to recede.**

in your journal

How do events in your life affect your emotions? In your journal, make two columns. In one column, write down the emotions you remember feeling yesterday. In the other, write what you think was the reason you felt each emotion. If you don't think that there was a reason for a particular emotional change, write "no reason." What conclusions can you draw? For example, what events cause you to feel positive emotions? Do you often experience emotions for what seems to be no reason at all?

Mental and Emotional Growth

During adolescence you develop more complex thinking skills. For example, you learn to analyze and solve more complicated problems. You come to understand that many questions do not have simple right or wrong answers. At the same time you begin to recognize points of view that are different from your own. You will use all of these thinking skills as an adult.

You also realize that you have the power to make choices. You recognize that your actions have consequences, and that you should take responsibility for these consequences. All of these aspects of mental growth may feel overwhelming, but they are a natural part of becoming a mature individual.

Emotional Needs

Adolescence is a time of emotional growth as well. Although people have emotional needs throughout their lives, these needs change over time. Basic emotional needs include the need to care for others and to feel that others care for you. Another basic need is to feel accepted for who you are. You also need to feel that your actions have meaning and value.

As you grow, your emotional needs change. For example, as a child you probably tried hard to win the approval of your parents. As you enter your teen years, parental approval is still important. However, the approval and acceptance of your peers also begins to matter greatly.

Many of the actions people take are ways to meet their own emotional needs. They have to satisfy these needs in order to feel good about themselves and to be content with their lives. Learning to meet your emotional needs in positive and realistic ways is an important task of adolescence.

Doing volunteer work is a way to help others while meeting your own emotional needs.

Emotional Changes

Many teens find that adolescence brings on powerful emotions. Perhaps one day you feel excited and happy. You want to be out having fun with your friends. The next day you may feel gloomy enough to cry. All you want to do is stay in your room alone. In a single day you may experience a confusing up-and-down mix of emotions. Such swings in mood, like the changes in your body, are often caused by hormones. You need to realize that changing moods are a normal part of adolescence.

It is also important to understand, however, that these changes are also signs of emotional growth. During adolescence, your relationships with other people can deepen. You come to recognize that others have needs, just as you do. For example, when you listen to a friend's problems and offer advice, you are helping to meet some of these needs.

During your teen years, you may also have a greater desire to interact with members of the opposite sex. Feelings of attraction may confuse or even scare you, but they are part of growing up, too.

LIFE SKILLS
Dealing with Conflicting Feelings

*H*ave you ever experienced two different feelings at the same time, pulling you in opposite directions? When you start a new year in a new school, for example, part of you may feel excited, while another part feels nervous and uncertain. Here are a few tips for dealing with conflicting feelings.

▶ Keep in mind that you're not alone in feeling this way. Everyone experiences emotional conflicts. Learning to deal with them is part of becoming a mature person.

▶ Remember also that having several opposing emotions is a sign of maturity. After all, few situations are so clear-cut that they could bring forth only a single emotion.

▶ Try to sort out your feelings. Be honest with yourself. Ask yourself: What's the *real* reason behind my feelings?

▶ Take time to *think* before you speak or act. Consider the consequences—short-term and long-term—of what you are about to do.

▶ People often experience conflicting feelings when they have to make decisions. If you face a difficult choice, weigh your options carefully.

Using the six-step decision-making process will help. Seek advice from others, if necessary, but remember that the final decision is yours.

Follow-up Activity

Think about a recent situation in which making a decision caused you to have conflicting feelings. How did it turn out? How might you have made the decision-making process less stressful? Write down one piece of advice that you would give to a friend in a similar situation.

Teen Issues

Social Life

ACTIVITY!

Adolescence is a time of growing independence and more socialization with friends. Make a list of five activities you enjoy with friends now. Then list five activities you and your friends liked when you were in fifth grade. How do the two lists compare? Do you think that your list will change again by the time you reach ninth grade? How?

Emotional Expression

Whatever your feelings may be at a given time—joy, anger, fear—it's important to express them in healthy and appropriate ways. For instance, if you're having a disagreement with a friend or parent, discussing the problem calmly will more quickly lead to a solution than either shouting or keeping silent. Learning how to control and express your feelings is another way that you grow during adolescence.

Social Development

As you move from childhood to adulthood, you're constantly learning about yourself, about others, and about how you fit into the world. Sometimes you may feel confused. You may wonder, "What is the true *me* really like?"

Discovering your "self" will take some time, as **Figure 7.2** shows. At first you may look to your friends to help you figure out your identity. Being part of a group may seem very important. As you get older, however, you'll come to see yourself as a separate individual. You'll still want to be accepted by your friends, of course, but you'll also want to be unique, with your own personal views. In a similar way, you'll still want to be close to your family, but you'll also want to feel independent.

Figure 7.2
Who Am I?

During your teen years, you'll start to get a clearer image of who you are.

Moving Toward the Future

Your growth and development during adolescence will take many paths. You will advance toward adulthood in important, exciting, and challenging ways. In the coming years, you will

- learn to accept your body and its characteristics.

- gain a masculine or feminine image of yourself.

- become more independent in your thoughts and feelings.

- discover who you are and what makes you unique.

- develop your own set of values.

- learn to solve problems and make decisions in a mature way.

- learn to accept responsibility for your own actions.

- establish more mature relationships with people of both sexes.

- develop a greater awareness of, and concern for, your community and the world.

Your teen years open the door to your future. The experiences you have and the knowledge you gain at this time will prepare you for life as an adult.

Your interests and activities tell a great deal about you as an individual and about what is important to you.

Review

Lesson 1

Using complete sentences, answer the following questions on a separate sheet of paper.

Reviewing Terms and Facts

1. **Vocabulary** What is the difference between *adolescence* and *puberty?*

2. **List** Identify six physical changes that occur in females during adolescence and six changes that occur in males during adolescence.

3. **Recall** Give three examples of mental or emotional growth that occur during adolescence.

4. **Recall** Describe two ways in which hormones affect adolescents.

Thinking Critically

5. **Compare** In what ways are you more independent now than you were a few years ago?

6. **Analyze** Which of the many changes of adolescence do you think are most challenging for teens to cope with? Why did you choose these changes?

Applying Health Concepts

7. **Personal Health** Make a montage entitled "The Real Me." Include snapshots, magazine pictures, and other items that highlight various aspects of your life and offer clues to what you are really like.

The Endocrine System

This lesson will help you find answers to questions that teens often ask about the endocrine system. For example:

▶ **What is the endocrine system?**

▶ **How does the endocrine system work?**

▶ **What problems can occur in the endocrine system?**

Words to Know

endocrine system
gland
pituitary gland

Did You Know?

In a Heartbeat

The hormone epinephrine (e•puh•NE•fruhn)—more commonly known as adrenaline—is a powerful heart stimulant. It is so powerful, in fact, that an injection of epinephrine directly into the heart muscle is sometimes used to restart a heart that has stopped beating.

Regulating Body Functions

The hormones that cause physical and emotional changes during adolescence come from your endocrine system. The **endocrine** (EN·duh·krin) **system** consists of *glands throughout your body that regulate body functions.* A **gland** is *a group of cells, or an organ, that produces a chemical substance.*

Hormones produced by the endocrine glands pass directly into your bloodstream. They are then carried to different parts of your body, where they control various functions. For example, some hormones regulate growth. Others aid digestion. Your body produces some hormones continually and others only at certain times. Hormones are involved in some way in nearly every body function.

Excitement or fear can cause your glands to release adrenaline. One effect of this hormone is to make your heart pound.

The Glands of the Endocrine System

Figure 7.3 describes the glands of the endocrine system and the body functions they regulate. Signals from the brain or from other glands keep the endocrine system working. For example, when the brain detects a low level of thyroid hormone in the blood, it sends a signal to the pituitary gland. The pituitary then signals the thyroid, which adds more thyroid hormone to the bloodstream.

Figure 7.3
The Endocrine System

This table describes some of the major glands of the endocrine system.

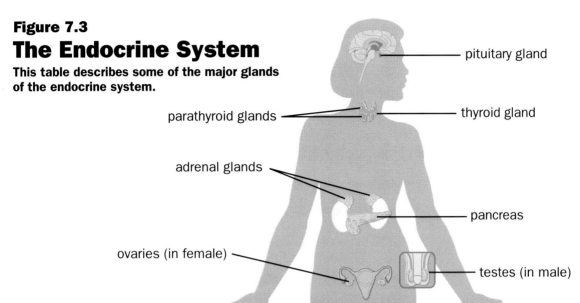

pituitary gland

parathyroid glands

thyroid gland

adrenal glands

pancreas

ovaries (in female)

testes (in male)

Gland	Description
pituitary (pi·TOO·i·tehr·ee) **gland**	Located at the base of the brain, the pituitary gland *produces several hormones that control other glands.* For example, pituitary hormones regulate the thyroid gland, adrenal glands, and kidneys. Pituitary gland hormones also regulate your body's growth and development. The pituitary is sometimes called the "master gland."
thyroid (THY·royd) **gland**	The hormone produced by the thyroid gland regulates body growth and the rate of metabolism. The thyroid is located alongside the trachea (windpipe).
parathyroid (par·uh·THY·royd) **glands**	Located within the thyroid gland, the small parathyroid glands regulate the levels of calcium and phosphorous in the blood.
pancreas	The pancreas, located behind the stomach, is part of both the endocrine system and the digestive system. The pancreas controls the level of sugar in the blood and provides the small intestine with digestive juice.
adrenal (uh·DREE·nuhl) **glands**	Hormones produced by the adrenal glands help regulate the balance of salt and water in the body. They also aid in digestion and control the body's response to emergencies. The adrenal glands are located on the kidneys.
ovaries (OH·vuh·reez)	The ovaries are the female reproductive glands. Hormones produced in the ovaries control sexual development and the production of eggs.
testes (TES·teez)	The testes are the male reproductive glands. The hormone produced in the testes controls sexual development and the production of sperm.

in your journal

List in your private journal some of the physical changes that you have experienced during adolescence. Then explain what role your endocrine system has played in those changes.

How the Endocrine System Works

You may wonder how the body, with so many different glands, keeps track of how much of each hormone to produce and when to produce it. The endocrine system depends on continuous feedback to meet the body's changing needs. That is, the endocrine glands make adjustments based on information that comes back to them from the body. **Figure 7.4** shows how this feedback system works.

Figure 7.4
How the Body Controls Hormone Levels
Hormones are powerful chemicals that regulate body functions.

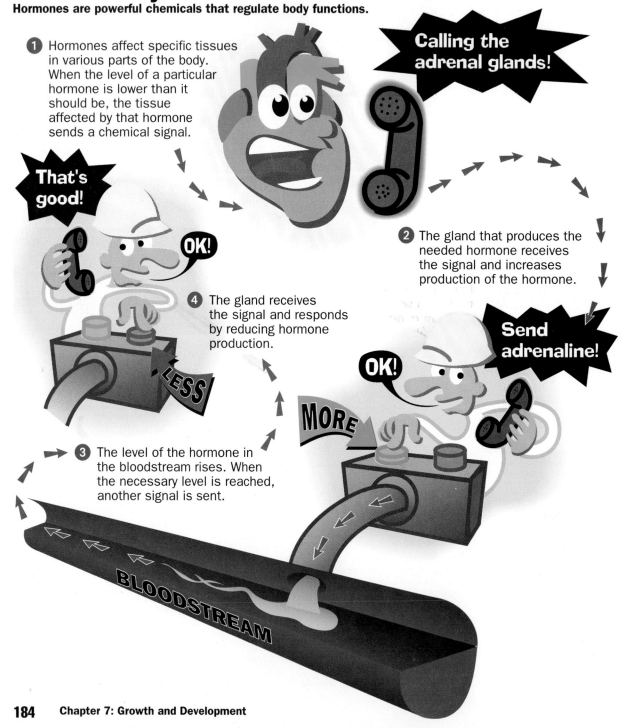

1 Hormones affect specific tissues in various parts of the body. When the level of a particular hormone is lower than it should be, the tissue affected by that hormone sends a chemical signal.

Calling the adrenal glands!

That's good!

OK!

2 The gland that produces the needed hormone receives the signal and increases production of the hormone.

Send adrenaline!

OK!

4 The gland receives the signal and responds by reducing hormone production.

LESS

MORE

3 The level of the hormone in the bloodstream rises. When the necessary level is reached, another signal is sent.

BLOODSTREAM

Problems of the Endocrine System

If the endocrine system produces too little or too much of a hormone, problems will result. Symptoms of endocrine system problems vary greatly because hormones affect so many different body functions. Doctors can usually use a blood test to detect endocrine disorders. For treatment, doctors may prescribe a medication or a synthetic version of a hormone. The following list shows several of the most common endocrine disorders.

■ Diabetes, or diabetes mellitus (dy·uh·BEE·teez ME·luh·tuhs) occurs when the pancreas does not produce enough insulin, a hormone that regulates chemicals in the blood. This lack of insulin keeps the body from using the sugars and starches in food for energy. Chapter 13 discusses this disorder in detail.

■ Growth disorders occur when the endocrine system releases too much or too little of the hormones that regulate growth.

■ Goiter (GOY·ter) is the name for an enlargement of the thyroid gland in the neck. The gland enlarges in an attempt to produce more thyroid hormone.

Specialized summer camps can help children who have diabetes learn to manage their disorder.

Review

Lesson 2

Using complete sentences, answer the following questions on a separate sheet of paper.

Reviewing Terms and Facts

1. **Vocabulary** What is the *endocrine system?*
2. **Vocabulary** What is a *gland?*
3. **Describe** How does the body use feedback to regulate hormone levels?

Thinking Critically

4. **Compare and Contrast** How are the functions of the ovaries and the testes alike? How do they differ?

5. **Analyze** How could knowing about the role of hormones in triggering strong emotions help teens learn to cope with them?

Applying Health Concepts

6. **Growth and Development** Work with a partner to create an illustrated "Guide to the Endocrine System." Include information about the significance of the endocrine system during the teen years.

The Male Reproductive System

This lesson will help you find answers to questions that teens often ask about the male reproductive system. For example:

▶ **What parts make up the male reproductive system?**

▶ **How does the male reproductive system work?**

▶ **What care does the male reproductive system require?**

Words to Know

reproduction
reproductive
   system
sperm
semen

in your journal

Why is it sometimes difficult for teens to ask questions or talk about problems involving the reproductive system? How do you think teens can best obtain valid information about their concerns? Respond to these questions in your private journal.

The Human Reproductive System

Reproduction (ree·pruh·DUHK·shuhn) is the name for *the process by which living organisms produce new individuals of their kind.* Reproduction is essential to all living things. Without reproduction, groups of organisms would disappear over time.

Human life results from the union of two cells: one from the female and one from the male. These cells are produced in the reproductive system. The human **reproductive** (ree·pruh·DUHK·tiv) **system** *consists of body organs and structures that make possible the production of offspring.* Unlike most other human body systems, the parts of the male and female reproductive systems are not alike. Each of the two systems is specially suited to perform its role in reproduction. This lesson will discuss the male reproductive system.

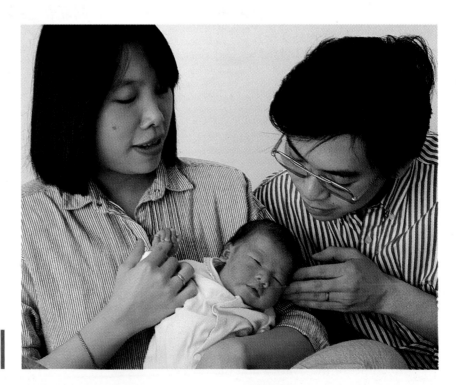

The arrival of a baby is a happy event in a couple's life.

Parts of the Male Reproductive System

Figure 7.5 shows the external and internal parts of the male reproductive system. During puberty, the testes start to produce **sperm,** *the male reproductive cells.* Sperm production usually begins between ages 12 and 15. The creation of new life takes place when male reproductive cells unite with female reproductive cells.

Various organs and structures are responsible for producing, storing, and releasing sperm. After the testes produce sperm, the sperm travel through tubes to the urethra. Along the way, the sperm mix with fluids. This *mixture of sperm and fluids* is called **semen** (SEE·muhn). Semen is released from the urethra through the penis (PEE·nuhs). The muscular action that forces semen through the urethra and out of the penis is called ejaculation (i·ja·kyuh·LAY·shuhn).

Q & A   **?**

How Many?

Q: How many sperm are released during a typical ejaculation?

A: Normally 300 to 500 million sperm are released during one ejaculation.

Figure 7.5
The Male Reproductive System

These illustrations show the internal and external parts of the male reproductive system.

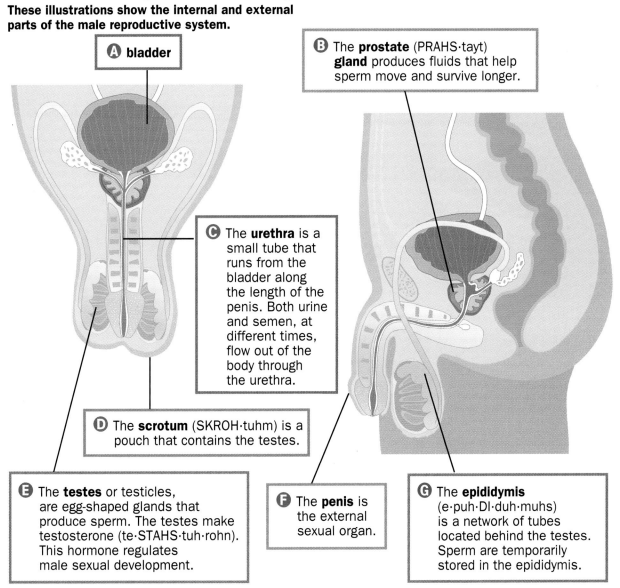

A bladder

B The **prostate** (PRAHS·tayt) **gland** produces fluids that help sperm move and survive longer.

C The **urethra** is a small tube that runs from the bladder along the length of the penis. Both urine and semen, at different times, flow out of the body through the urethra.

D The **scrotum** (SKROH·tuhm) is a pouch that contains the testes.

E The **testes** or testicles, are egg-shaped glands that produce sperm. The testes make testosterone (te·STAHS·tuh·rohn). This hormone regulates male sexual development.

F The **penis** is the external sexual organ.

G The **epididymis** (e·puh·DI·duh·muhs) is a network of tubes located behind the testes. Sperm are temporarily stored in the epididymis.

Caring for the Male Reproductive System

Maintaining a healthy reproductive system requires basic care and common sense. Here are some guidelines for males.

- Take a shower or bath daily to keep your external reproductive organs clean.

- Always wear protective gear when you are participating in contact sports.

- Examine your testes monthly for lumps, swelling, soreness, or other problems. Discuss any concerns with your doctor.

- Have regular physical checkups.

Wearing protective gear can help prevent injuries to the reproductive organs.

Problems of the Male Reproductive System

A number of disorders can affect the male reproductive system. The following are some of the most common:

- **Hernia.** An inguinal hernia (IN·gwuh·nuhl HER·nee·uh) occurs when a part of the intestine pushes into the groin. This occurs because of a weakness in the muscle wall. Hernias can be repaired by surgery.

- **Sterility.** Being unable to produce enough healthy sperm to reproduce is a condition called sterility. Causes of sterility include certain diseases and exposure to certain drugs.

- **Testicular cancer.** Cancer of the testes is rare, but it is most common in males between the ages of 15 and 34. Symptoms may include a lump or swelling in the scrotum, pain or tenderness in one of the testicles, or a heavy feeling in a testicle. Surgery is necessary to prevent the spread of the disease. Regular self-examinations as well as checkups can help males to discover this disease in its early stages.

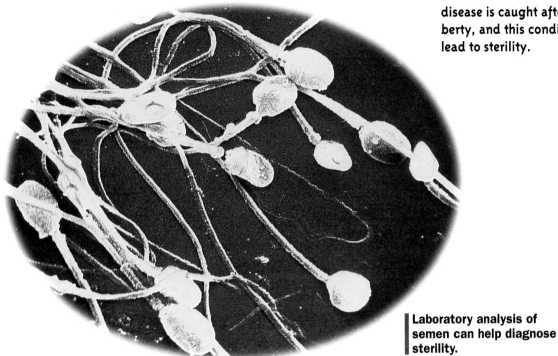

Laboratory analysis of semen can help diagnose sterility.

Review

Using complete sentences, answer the following questions on a separate sheet of paper.

Reviewing Terms and Facts

1. **Vocabulary** Describe the function of the human *reproductive system.*

2. **Vocabulary** What is the difference between *sperm* and *semen?*

3. **Recall** What can males do to keep their reproductive systems healthy?

4. **List** Identify three disorders of the male reproductive system.

Thinking Critically

5. **Explain** Why is regular self-examination of the testes important?

6. **Describe** How are the male reproductive system and the endocrine system related?

Applying Health Concepts

7. **Consumer Health** Urologists treat many diseases and disorders of the male reproductive system. Do research about this medical specialty, and prepare a short brochure that might explain to a male what kinds of problems this doctor treats.

The Female Reproductive System

This lesson will help you find answers to questions that teens often ask about the female reproductive system. For example:

▶ How does the female reproductive system work?
▶ What is menstruation?
▶ What care does the female reproductive system require?

Words to Know

fertilization
ovaries
uterus
menstruation
gynecologist

The Female Reproductive System

The female reproductive system has three main functions. First, it stores and releases female reproductive cells, called egg cells. Second, this system allows fertilization to take place. **Fertilization** (fer·til·i·ZAY·shuhn) is *the joining of a male sperm cell and a female egg cell to form a new human life.* Third, the female reproductive system nourishes and protects the developing child until it is able to survive outside the female's body. **Figure 7.6** shows the female reproductive system.

Figure 7.6
The Female Reproductive System

Fertilization and pregnancy occur in the female reproductive system.

Ⓐ At puberty the two *female reproductive glands*, the **ovaries**, start to release eggs, or ova. The ovaries also produce estrogen (ES·truh·jen), a hormone that regulates female sexual development.

Ⓑ From the ovaries, eggs travel down the **fallopian** (fuh·LOH·pee·uhn) **tubes** to the uterus. Fertilization takes place in the fallopian tube.

Ⓒ A fertilized egg becomes implanted in the **uterus** (YOO·tuh·ruhs), or womb (WOOM). This is a *pear-shaped organ in which a developing child is nourished.*

Ⓓ The lining of the uterus is called the **endometrium** (en·doh·MEE·tree·uhm).

Ⓔ The **cervix** (SER·viks) is the opening at the bottom of the uterus.

Ⓕ The **vagina** (vuh·JY·nuh) is a muscular passageway leading from the uterus to the outside of the body.

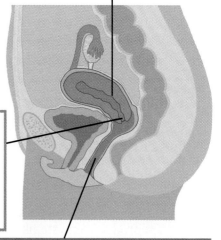

Menstruation

Once puberty begins, the ovaries start to release a single mature egg cell each month. This is the process known as ovulation (ahv·yuh·LAY·shuhn). At the same time, the lining of the uterus thickens. If fertilization occurs, this lining will nourish the fertilized egg. If fertilization does not occur, the egg is shed along with this thickened lining. *The flow of the uterine lining material from the body* is called **menstruation** (men·stroo·WAY·shuhn). For most girls, menstruation starts between ages 9 and 16.

Menstruation usually happens about every 28 days and lasts, on average, from 5 to 7 days. However, the timing of this menstrual (MEN·struhl) cycle may vary widely from one person to another. An adolescent female may find that the length of her menstrual cycle varies from month to month. This variation is normal and should not be a cause for concern unless menstruation stops for months at a time. **Figure 7.7** describes a typical menstrual cycle.

Figure 7.7
The Menstrual Cycle

Menstrual cycles vary. This is a typical cycle of 28 days.

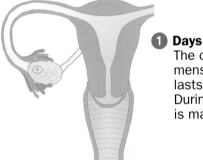

1 Days 1–13:
The cycle begins with the menstrual flow, which usually lasts through day 5 or 7. During this time a new egg cell is maturing inside the ovary.

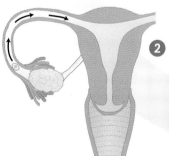

2 Day 14:
Ovulation occurs. The mature egg is released from the ovary into a fallopian tube.

4 Day 21:
The egg enters the uterus. If the egg has not been fertilized, the uterine lining begins to break down. Menstruation begins about 7 days later, on day 28.

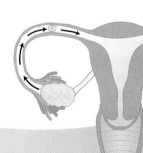

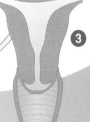

3 Days 15–20:
The egg travels through the fallopian tube.

Fertilization

Sperm entering the vagina travel to the fallopian tubes. Fertilization takes place in the fallopian tube when a male sperm cell and a female egg cell unite. The fertilized egg then moves through the fallopian tube to the uterus. In the uterus, the fertilized egg gradually develops into a baby.

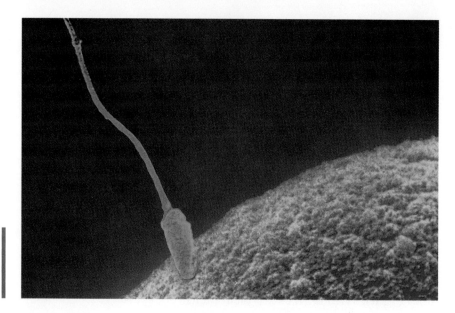

Fertilization occurs when a male sperm cell penetrates a female egg cell. Only one sperm cell can enter an egg cell.

Caring for the Female Reproductive System

For females, just as for males, keeping the reproductive system healthy requires a combination of basic care and common sense. Here are some guidelines for females.

- Shower or bathe daily to keep external reproductive organs clean. Keeping clean is particularly important when menstruation is occurring.

- Be sure to schedule regular physical checkups by a **gynecologist** (gy·nuh·KAH·luh·jist), *a doctor who specializes in the female reproductive system,* beginning at the age recommended by your regular physician.

- Examine your breasts monthly for any unusual lumps, thickening, or discharge. Ask your doctor to explain the self-examination procedure.

- Keep a record of your menstrual cycle. If your cycle becomes irregular, check with a doctor. Check also if you experience severe or unusual pain or excessive bleeding during menstruation.

Problems of the Female Reproductive System

Various disorders can affect the female reproductive system. They include the following:

- **Premenstrual syndrome (PMS).** To different degrees, women may experience physical and emotional changes before menstruation. Symptoms of premenstrual (pree·MEN·struhl) syndrome, such as headache, breast tenderness, and irritability, may range from mild to severe. Regular exercise and dietary changes can often help. If you are troubled by PMS, talk with your doctor, especially if your symptoms make you very uncomfortable.

Q & A

An Important Test

Q: I've heard people refer to something called a "Pap test," but I'm not sure what it is.

A: A Pap test (named after George Papanicolaou, the doctor who developed it) is a test for early detection of uterine cancer. It is quick, easy, and reliable. Gynecologists include a Pap test as part of the routine examination. They use a cotton swab and a small wooden paddle to collect cells from the cervix.

- **Toxic shock syndrome.** This bacterial infection is rare, but it has been linked to tampon use. Symptoms include high fever, a rash, and vomiting. It can be serious and even fatal if not treated. To protect yourself, follow directions for tampon use carefully. Change tampons at least every 4 hours, and avoid using superabsorbent tampons. Check with your doctor if you have questions.

- **Infertility.** Being unable to produce children is called infertility (in·fer·TIL·i·tee). There are a number of possible causes for infertility. Surgery or hormone treatment can overcome some types of infertility.

- **Vaginitis.** Pain, itching, and discharge are symptoms of this infection of the vagina. Doctors treat vaginitis (va·juh·NY·tis) with medication.

- **Cancer.** Cancer can affect the breasts, ovaries, uterus, or cervix. Self-examinations and regular checkups can detect cancer early and increase the likelihood of cure.

in your journal

Do you have any questions about your reproductive system that you would like answered? With whom would you feel comfortable talking about your questions? Write your answers in your private journal.

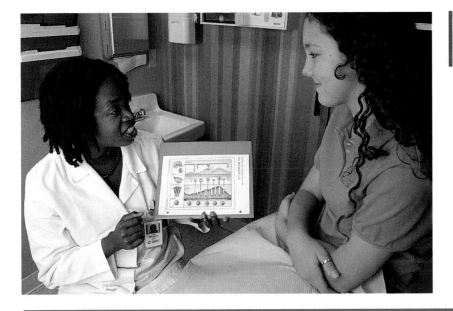

A physician can answer your questions about the female reproductive system.

Review

Lesson 4

Using complete sentences, answer the following questions on a separate sheet of paper.

Reviewing Terms and Facts

1. **Recall**   What are the three most important functions of the female reproductive system?

2. **Vocabulary**   Briefly define the term *fertilization.*

3. **Vocabulary**   What is *menstruation?*

4. **Recall**   What actions can females take to keep their reproductive systems healthy?

Thinking Critically

5. **Analyze**   Why are the fallopian tubes important to reproduction?

6. **Explain**   Provide three sources of valid information about the reproductive system.

Applying Health Concepts

7. **Growth and Development**   Make a chart or poster showing what happens to an egg after it is formed in an ovary. Include what happens if the egg is fertilized and what happens if it is not.

TEEN HEALTH DIGEST

People at Work

Providing Care and Comfort

Job: Hospice worker
Responsibilities: To comfort and care for people who are terminally ill; to help families cope with the loss of a loved one; to administer medication; to help with practical matters
Education and Training: Hospice workers include nurses, doctors, counselors, health aides, and others. Besides training in their specialty area, workers receive special instruction in caring for the terminally ill.
Workplace: Care may be provided at the patient's home or at a residential facility.
Positives: The satisfaction that comes with helping and comforting others
Negatives: The work is emotionally demanding; it may include working nights or weekends and being on call.

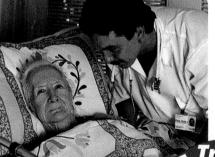

Try This: *Interview a worker at a hospice. Ask the person about the challenges and rewards of the work.*

Teens Making a Difference

Bringing People Together

People have a basic need to care about others and to feel that others care about them. While working at a home for abused children, Connecticut teen Lauren Garsten learned what this need could mean to two very diverse groups of people.

Lauren's idea was to pair up children who desperately needed to feel loved with senior citizens who were seeking ways to make a difference in someone else's life. With the help of other students, Lauren brought the children and the seniors together once a month. The initial purpose was simple: just to have fun. But over time, children who had never trusted an adult before discovered that there were people they could count on. Lauren also discovered that no matter how different people are in age or experience, they can find something to talk about and share.

HEALTH UPDATE

Senior Power

One of the fastest-growing population groups around the world is what demographers (di·MAH·gruh·fuhrz), people who study the characteristics of human populations, call the "oldest old." This group is made up of people over 80 years of age.

Why is the percentage of older people increasing? Throughout the world the birth rate is slowing down, and medical advances allow people to live longer. Adjusting to this aging population will require new kinds of thinking in countries all over the world. The invention and availability of devices to make life easier for an aging population and the extension of the retirement age past the current norm of 65 are two possible adjustments that could be made.

Myths and Realities

Determined at Birth?

Q. Is a baby's brain "wired" at birth—are all the pathways there just waiting to be used?

A. Not at all. Brain research has shown that although the brain at birth has nearly all the nerve cells it will ever have, the way these cells are linked together develops in extraordinary ways after birth. The stimulation a baby receives from its environment can affect greatly the potential that baby will have as a child and as an adult.

Try This:

Find out more about the claims made for antioxidants. Report to your class on your findings.

CON$UMER FOCU$

Eating to Stay Young

Q. I've seen ads for products that are supposed to keep a person young. I know that most of these products really don't do much, but I was wondering if there is anything that *does* keep the body from aging.

A. Although nothing can stop the aging process, certain foods may affect how quickly or slowly you age. For example, substances known as antioxidants (an·tee·AHK·suh·dunhtz) may work to prevent some of the damage done to the body over time by environmental pollutants and harmful foods. Fruits and vegetables high in vitamin C, such as broccoli, cantaloupe, carrots, collard greens, and peppers, are rich in antioxidants. Whole-grain breads and cereals are also good sources.

Human Development

This lesson will help you find answers to questions that teens often ask about the earliest stage of human development. For example:

▶ What is the basic unit of life?

▶ How does a baby develop before birth?

▶ What factors affect a baby's development?

Words to Know

cell
tissue
organ
body system
embryo
fetus
chromosome
gene

Parts of a Whole

Your body is made up of more than 50 trillion microscopic cells. A **cell** is *the basic unit, or building block, of life.* The cells in your body are grouped to form tissues, organs, and body systems (see **Figure 7.8**).

Figure 7.8
From Cell to System
The body is organized from its smallest parts, cells, to complex body systems.

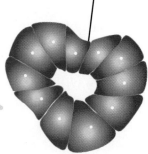

Cells
Cells come in many different forms and shapes. Each type of cell has a particular function. This is a cell from the lining of the stomach.

Tissues
Tissues are *groups of similar cells that do a particular job.* Each kind of tissue is designed to perform one function. These cells from the lining of the stomach protect the stomach from acidic stomach fluids.

Organs
Organs are *body parts made up of different tissues joined together to perform a function.* For example, the stomach is an organ made up of muscle, mucous membranes, and other types of tissue. These tissues work together to store food and prepare it for digestion.

Systems
A group of organs working together to carry out related tasks forms a **body system**. Examples include the digestive system, shown here; the endocrine system; and the reproductive system.

Development After Fertilization

Although the body is made up of countless cells, every human being begins as a single cell. This cell is formed as a result of fertilization. After a sperm cell and an egg cell join, the fertilized egg starts to divide. One cell becomes two, two become four, four become eight, and so on. These cells are referred to as an **embryo** (EM·bree·oh), *the name for the organism from fertilization to about the eighth week.* After the eighth week it is called a **fetus** (FEE·tuhs), *the name for the developing child from about the ninth week until the time of birth.* From fertilization until birth, the growing number of cells develop into the tissues, organs, and systems of the newborn's body (see **Figure 7.9**).

Science Connection

Brain Facts

At six weeks the brain of an embryo is almost as big as the rest of its body. At birth the baby's brain has 100 billion nerve cells, just about the same number of nerve cells as there are stars in the Milky Way.

Figure 7.9

Development Before Birth

It takes only a little over nine months for a baby to develop from two microscopic cells into a child ready to be born.

Time Passed	Approximate Length and Weight	Development
1 month	less than $\frac{1}{3}$ inch long	Major internal organs are forming. Heart starts to beat.
2 months	1 inch long	Organs continue to develop. Tiny arms, legs, fingers, and toes have started to form.
3 months	3 inches; 1 ounce	Fetus starts to move; can open and close mouth; fingers are visible; heartbeat can be heard by using a special instrument.
4 months	5 inches; 6 ounces	Facial features are taking shape; mother can feel movement of fetus.
5 months	almost 10 inches long; 1 pound	Eyes, nose, and mouth are well-developed; movements are stronger.
6 months	12.5 inches; 1.5 pounds	Fetus can kick and cry; footprints appear; fetus can hear sounds.
7 months	14.5 inches; 2 pounds	Eyes open; limbs are able to move freely.
8 months	18 inches long; 4 pounds	Hair grows; skin becomes smoother.
9 months	18-21 inches; 6-9 pounds	Fingers are able to grasp; body organs and systems can function on their own.

Researchers have found that parents in many different cultures all tend to speak to their infants in similar ways. They put their faces close to the baby and speak in a singsong tone. Babies actually seem to respond more quickly and learn language more effectively when it is delivered this way than when parents speak as they would to each other.

Birth

The fertilized egg attaches itself to the lining of the uterus. There it grows and develops into a baby, receiving nourishment and oxygen from its mother through a tube attached to its abdomen. This period of pregnancy lasts a little over nine months. When the baby is ready to be born, muscles in the wall of the uterus begin contracting, causing the baby to be pushed out of the mother's body through the vagina.

Factors that Influence Early Development

In Chapter 1, you read about how heredity and environment shape your development as a unique individual. These factors affect you even before birth and continue to affect your development throughout your life.

HEALTH LAB
Your Unique Fingerprints

Introduction: The ridges and grooves on the pads of your fingers help you grip and feel objects. They also form fingerprints. Each person's fingerprints are different from everyone else's. That's why fingerprints can be used to identify people.

Objective: Identify and compare fingerprint patterns.

Materials and Method: You'll need a washable-ink pad, some white paper, and a magnifying glass. You should also have access to soap and water.

Make clear prints of the five fingers of one hand. You can do this by firmly pressing your finger into the ink pad and then pressing it onto the white paper. Also take prints from two classmates. Wash your hands.

Observations and Analysis: Study your own fingerprints. Look for the three basic fingerprint patterns: *arches, loops,* and *whorls.* How are the patterns of your fingerprints different from one another? How are they alike?

Compare your fingerprints with those of your classmates. What similarities can you find? What differences? How do people use the uniqueness of fingerprints for identification?

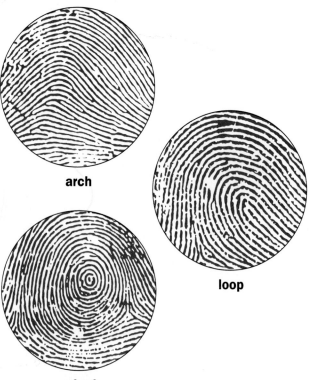

arch

loop

whorl

Heredity

Structures within cells influence heredity. **Chromosomes** (KROH·muh·sohmz) are *threadlike structures that carry the codes for inherited traits.* There are 46 chromosomes—23 pairs—in almost all human cells. Each chromosome is divided into many thousands of small parts called genes. **Genes** are *the basic units of heredity.* They determine the traits that you inherit, such as height, facial features, and the color of skin, hair, and eyes. Children inherit two genes for each trait—one from each parent. Children of the same two parents, however, inherit different combinations of chromosomes and genes.

Only sperm cells and egg cells do not have 46 chromosomes. Each has 23 chromosomes. When the sperm and egg cell join during fertilization, they produce a fertilized cell with 46 chromosomes. Chromosomes determine whether a baby will be a boy or a girl. Each egg cell contains one X (female) chromosome. Each sperm contains either an X (female) or a Y (male) chromosome. An XX chromosome combination will produce a female child; an XY combination will produce a male.

Occasionally, however, genetic problems occur that cause a baby to be born with a disorder. Such disorders may affect the baby's physical or mental development, or both. Some genetic disorders are mild; others are severe. A few rare disorders are fatal.

in your journal

Have you ever known anyone with an inherited disorder? How did it affect the person's life and the life of the rest of the family? Write your answers in your private journal.

Down syndrome is a genetic disorder in which a person's cells have 47 chromosomes instead of the usual 46. A person with Down syndrome has characteristic physical features and some degree of mental retardation, which may be very mild.

Fetal Environment

In addition to heredity, a key factor that affects development is environment. For a developing fetus the environment is the mother's uterus. The health of the baby is directly affected by the actions and health of the mother (see **Figure 7.10**).

Figure 7.10
Healthy Mother, Healthy Baby

During her pregnancy, there are several important ways for a mother to help ensure her baby's good health.

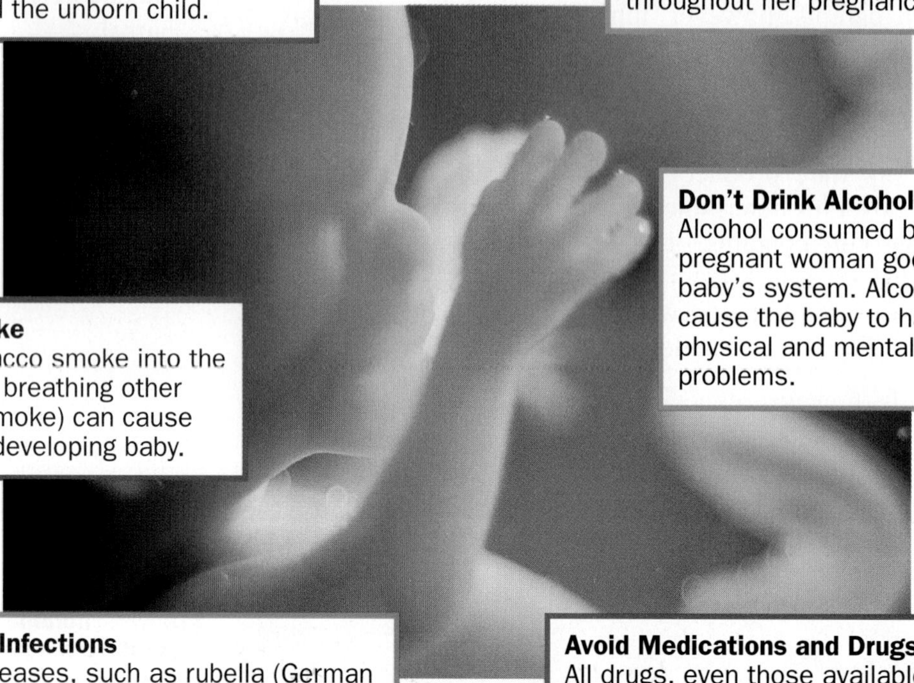

Eat Healthful Foods
The baby's nourishment comes from the mother. Nutritious foods are essential to the health of both the mother and the unborn child.

Get Regular Checkups
A woman should see her doctor as soon as she suspects that she is pregnant. After that, she should keep all regular appointments throughout her pregnancy.

Don't Drink Alcohol
Alcohol consumed by a pregnant woman goes into the baby's system. Alcohol can cause the baby to have both physical and mental problems.

Don't Smoke
Taking tobacco smoke into the body (even breathing other people's smoke) can cause harm to a developing baby.

Beware of Infections
Certain diseases, such as rubella (German measles) and some sexually transmitted diseases, pose severe danger to an unborn baby. A vaccine is available to protect against rubella. A physician can explain how best to avoid other dangerous infections.

Avoid Medications and Drugs
All drugs, even those available without a prescription, can affect a developing baby. A pregnant woman should take medication only if absolutely necessary, and only with a doctor's approval.

Lesson 5 Review

Using complete sentences, answer the following questions on a separate sheet of paper.

Reviewing Terms and Facts

1. **Vocabulary**   What is the difference between an *embryo* and a *fetus?*

2. **Vocabulary**   Describe the relationship between *chromosomes* and *genes.*

3. **Recall**   List five ways in which a pregnant woman can help ensure her unborn baby's good health.

Thinking Critically

4. **Explain**   Describe how cells, tissues, organs, and systems are related.

5. **Infer**   Why would regular checkups during pregnancy be important?

Applying Health Concepts

6. **Growth and Development**   Work with a partner to make a poster showing the relationships among cells, tissues, organs, and systems. Display your poster in the classroom.

Life Stages

This lesson will help you find answers to questions that teens often ask about growing up. For example:

▶ **What are the stages of life?**

▶ **What does it mean to be an adult?**

▶ **How do people deal with death and their feelings about death?**

Birth and Growth

The years between infancy and adulthood are a period of huge change and development. During this time, a child's abilities and confidence grow. As the years pass, the once helpless baby gradually develops into an independent adult.

Infancy

The time of life from birth to the teen years is full of changes. **Infancy** (IN·fuhn·see) *the first year of a baby's life,* is a time of amazing growth. The baby's weight triples, and the baby's size increases by half. Infants learn to sit, crawl, and stand. They reach for objects. They smile and laugh. They start to explore their surroundings. They imitate sounds and may say a few words. During this first year, babies also develop mentally, emotionally, and socially. Their growth and development at this early stage prepares them for the stages of life to come (see **Figure 7.11**).

Words to Know

infancy
toddler
preschooler
grief

in your journal

Talk with a parent or relative about your childhood. In your private journal, write a paragraph explaining how your childhood experiences have helped to shape you as a person.

Figure 7.11
The Stages of Life

Throughout life, people continue to learn, change, and develop. Each period of life prepares you for what follows.

Birth Even before birth, babies begin to sense and react to their surroundings. As they adjust to life outside the uterus, newborns are totally dependent on others for their care.

Be Your Own Person ACTIVITY!

During adolescence, teens try to fit in with their peer group. However, adolescence is also a time to learn to accept responsibility for your own actions. This includes not doing what peers do when you think their actions are wrong. On a sheet of paper, jot down some situations in which you followed your own values. What gave you the strength to do this?

Childhood

Children between the ages of one and three are called **toddlers.** At this early childhood stage, children learn to walk, talk, and use the bathroom. They actively explore their surroundings. They begin to become less dependent on their parents. They take pride in their accomplishments and are eager to master new tasks. Help and encouragement from parents build a toddler's self-confidence.

Children between ages three and five are called **preschoolers.** Physical and mental skills develop rapidly in this period of middle childhood. Preschoolers enjoy singing, sharing stories, and playing make-believe. They like to imitate parents and older siblings. By supporting and encouraging a preschooler's efforts, parents can help develop the child's self-esteem.

Between six and eleven, a period sometimes called late childhood, children continue to develop. At this stage children are going to school and expanding their knowledge and social skills. They can read on their own and perform a growing number of activities independently. Their ability to express themselves increases, as do their problem-solving skills. Games and activities become more challenging. At this age children often like to build or create things. Interaction with friends becomes more and more important.

Adolescence and Adulthood

As you have read in Lesson 1 of this chapter, adolescence is a time of important physical, emotional, mental, and social development. Except for infancy, at no time during your life do you grow and change as much as you do during adolescence. The personal development that occurs during your teen years serves as a bridge from childhood to young adulthood.

Figure 7.11 (continued)

Infancy (to age 1) During this period, infants develop trust.

Early Childhood (ages 1–3) In this toddler period, children learn that they are independent beings.

Middle Childhood (ages 3–5) In this preschool period, children begin to learn about rules and consequences.

The adult years bring responsibility and satisfaction, joy and disappointment, challenge and accomplishment. During adulthood, people develop close and lasting relationships. They raise families, work toward personal goals, and make contributions to society.

Like childhood, adulthood can be seen as a series of stages. **Figure 7.12** shows three stages of adulthood.

Figure 7.12
The Adult Years

During young adulthood, from age 19 to about age 30, people work on developing a career and forming close personal relationships. In middle adulthood, approximately age 31 to 60, people work to achieve goals and to contribute to their families or community. In late adulthood, starting after age 60, individuals reflect on their lives and what they have accomplished.

Late Childhood (ages 6–11)
In this period, children seek the approval of their parents and begin to establish themselves among their peers. They gain mastery over objects and activities.

Adolescence (ages 12–18)
In this period, teens search for their identity and take on greater responsibility.

Adulthood (age 19 and onward)
During adulthood, people work to develop relationships, to achieve goals, and to understand the meaning of their lives.

How Can I Be Angry?

Q: My favorite uncle died in a car accident a few months ago. Sometimes I find myself feeling angry at him for dying. Is that normal?

A: Anger is a very normal response to the death of someone you love. Your anger comes in part because someone important was taken away from you by circumstances beyond your control. Don't feel guilty about these feelings. They will pass in time. If they really bother you, talk with your parents, a counselor, or another trusted adult.

The Life Cycle

The people around us, and we ourselves, move continuously through the cycle of life. Each day people are born and people die. Eventually people we love will die, and we ourselves will die, too. Part of growing up is learning to face this reality and accept it as part of the cycle of life.

Accepting Death

People deal with the reality of death in individual ways. When faced with the prospect of dying, however, most people go through five stages.

- **Stage 1: Denial.** The person refuses to believe that he or she is really going to die.

- **Stage 2: Anger.** The person becomes angry about the unfairness of his or her death.

- **Stage 3: Bargaining.** The person tries to prolong life through bargaining, perhaps promising to live a better life in exchange for escaping death.

- **Stage 4: Depression.** The person feels an intense sadness.

- **Stage 5: Acceptance.** The person accepts the reality of death and makes peace with both self and others.

MAKING HEALTHY DECISIONS
Helping a Friend Deal with Loss

*B*inh and David have been close friends for years. Binh has become worried about David lately. Ever since David's grandmother died two months ago, David has been quiet and withdrawn. He rarely participates in after-school activities anymore. One night David confides to Binh that he's feeling guilty. David wishes that he'd spent more time with his grandmother in the past year instead of hanging out so much with friends. Now, having fun with friends makes him feel somehow disloyal to the memory of his grandmother.

Binh is not sure what to do. Should he just keep quiet and wait for David to work things out on his own? David seems to have become more and more isolated. To make up his mind, Binh uses the decision-making process:

1. **State the situation**
2. **List the options**
3. **Weigh the possible outcomes**
4. **Consider your values**
5. **Make a decision and act**
6. **Evaluate the decision**

Follow-up Activities

1. Apply the six steps of the decision-making process to Binh's concern.

2. With a partner, role-play a conversation between Binh and David, in which Binh offers constructive suggestions to help his friend.

Dealing with Grief

The *sorrow caused by the loss of something precious* is known as **grief.** Grief, whether over the death of a relative, a friend, or a pet, can be intensely painful. People also grieve over other types of loss, including the loss of a job or the end of a marriage.

Everyone experiences grief in his or her own way. Some people feel numb at first, then intensely sad. Others feel anger. Still others are troubled by guilt. They believe that they should have done or said something differently while the person was alive. Most people find that their grief comes in waves—just when they think they are feeling better, they are struck by sadness again.

No matter how deep a person's grief, however, the ache of loss gradually lessens over time. People usually find the grieving process easier if they share their feelings with other people. If you are grieving over a loss or death, don't be afraid to talk about how you feel with a trusted friend or adult.

Funeral services and other ceremonies help people deal with the loss of a loved one.

Review

Using complete sentences, answer the following questions on a separate sheet of paper.

Reviewing Terms and Facts

1. **Recall**   List the stages of life from infancy through adulthood.

2. **List**   What stages do people go through when faced with death?

3. **Vocabulary**   What is *grief?*

Thinking Critically

4. **Analyze**   How can parents help their children move successfully through the stages of childhood?

5. **Explain**   Why is it helpful for people who are grieving to talk about their feelings with others?

Applying Health Concepts

6. **Health of Others**   Find out about support groups in your community for people who have suffered a loss. What kinds of groups are there? Who sponsors these groups? How do they help people cope with their grief? Write a short report about your findings.

Chapter 7 Review

Chapter Summary

▶ **Lesson 1** Adolescence brings physical, mental, emotional, and social changes that prepare teens for adulthood.

▶ **Lesson 2** The endocrine system produces hormones and regulates body functions.

▶ **Lesson 3** The male reproductive system produces, stores, and releases sperm, the male reproductive cells.

▶ **Lesson 4** The female reproductive system stores female reproductive cells (egg cells), allows fertilization to occur, and nourishes the fertilized egg.

▶ **Lesson 5** Humans develop in predictable patterns before birth. Both hereditary and environmental factors have an effect on development.

▶ **Lesson 6** People move through stages of development beginning at birth and continuing through adulthood.

Reviewing Key Terms and Concepts

Using complete sentences, answer the following questions on a separate sheet of paper.

Lesson 1

1. What are *hormones?*

2. What mental and emotional growth takes place during adolescence?

Lesson 2

3. Why is the pituitary gland important to proper body functioning?

4. List three glands other than the pituitary gland, and describe their functions.

Lesson 3

5. What is *reproduction?*

6. List two functions of the testes.

Lesson 4

7. Describe the functions of the ovaries and the uterus in female reproduction.

8. What is a *gynecologist?*

Lesson 5

9. What are *genes?*

10. List two substances that a woman might take into her body that could harm a fetus.

Lesson 6

11. What are the age ranges for infants, toddlers, and preschoolers?

12. What are typical tasks in each of the three stages of adulthood?

Thinking Critically

Using complete sentences, answer the following questions on a separate sheet of paper.

13. **Explain** How do the changes of adolescence prepare you for adulthood?

14. **Summarize** Why is the endocrine system important during adolescence?

15. **Compare and Contrast** Compare and contrast the functions of the male and female reproductive systems.

16. **Select** Choose a particular stage of life, and describe how it prepares a person for a future stage.

Your Action Plan

From the day we are born until the day we die, change is a part of our lives. Some changes are part of the life cycle—happy changes, such as the birth of a child, and sad changes, such as the death of a loved one. Throughout your life, you will want to use these changes to help you grow as a person.

Step 1 Review your journal entries to answer these questions: What changes have you already experienced? Which have you dealt with successfully? Which changes have caused you problems?

Step 2 Set a short-term goal to help you deal with a change that you expect to occur soon. If your family expects to move, you might write: *I will talk with my parents about visiting my new school before the year begins.*

Step 3 Set a long-term goal to help you deal with unexpected changes. For example: *I will work on coping with my emotions so that it is easier to adjust to change.*

Periodically review your goals and check your progress. Evaluate how you have grown as a person, and think about how you would like to continue to grow.

In Your Home and Community

1. **Growth and Development**   Work with classmates to create a guidebook to adolescence entitled *What's Normal?* Include descriptions of the typical changes teens go through. Obtain permission to share the guidebook with other classes.

2. **Health of Others**   Create a poster suggesting ways for pregnant women to help ensure that their babies will be healthy. Ask if you can display your poster in the office of a gynecologist or pediatrician, or at a local hospital.

Building Your Portfolio

1. **Illustrated Chart**   Create an illustrated chart on the stages of life. Use pictures from magazines to show people in various life stages. Add some written information about each stage, or provide quotations from people talking about that stage of life. Place your chart in your portfolio.

2. **Interview**   Interview two senior citizens. Ask them to describe the various stages of their lives. Which events were most memorable? Which experiences did they learn the most from? Summarize the interviews in a few paragraphs. Add the summary to your portfolio.

3. **Personal Assessment**   Look through all the activities and projects you did for this chapter. Choose one or two that you would like to include in your portfolio.

Chapter 8

Mental and Emotional Health

Student Expectations

After reading this chapter, you should be able to:

❶ Identify the traits of good mental health.

❷ Explain the benefits of a positive self-concept and high self-esteem.

❸ Describe ways of dealing with stress.

❹ Identify major mental disorders.

❺ List sources of help to solve problems.

Teen Chat Group

Katie: Try out? Are you kidding? You know I'm shy. I can't try out for the play with you. It'll never work out.

Jerome: Just make yourself do it. It might not be as hard as you think. It could even be fun.

Carmen: Jerome, don't tell her to try out if she's too shy. Anyway, they'll need people to do makeup and build scenery, too. What about doing that, Katie?

Katie: Well, maybe. . . I wish I felt more comfortable up in front of people, though.

Jerome: That's what I mean. If you don't like being shy, you should try to change it. Take a chance. What do you have to lose?

Katie: I could look stupid, for one thing. I'm just not sure of what I really want to do.

in your journal

Read the dialogue on this page. Have you ever been unhappy with some aspect of your personality, yet you are still not sure that you want to change? Start your private journal entries by answering these questions:

► What would you say to Katie if you were part of this conversation?

► Are there aspects of your personality that you would like to change?

► How do you think a person can stay mentally and emotionally healthy?

When you reach the end of the chapter, you will use your journal entries to make an action plan.

Lesson
1
What Is Mental Health?

This lesson will help you find answers to questions that teens often ask about mental health. For example:

► **How can I tell if I am in good mental health?**

► **How can I develop good mental health habits?**

► **What shapes my personality?**

Words to Know

mental health
personality

in your journal

Review the signs of good mental health. For the next three days watch for examples of these signs in the behavior of yourself and others. Write these examples in your journal.

Mental Health

The three important parts of good health rely on one another for total balance and strength. Two sides of your health triangle are physical health and social health. The remaining side is your mental and emotional health. **Mental health** is *your ability to deal in a reasonable way with the stresses and changes of everyday life.* When people are in good mental health, they usually

■ have a positive outlook on life and welcome challenges. (As **Figure 8.1** shows, a positive outlook has many benefits.)

■ accept their limitations and set realistic goals for themselves.

■ feel good about themselves and about others.

Figure 8.1
The Benefits of a Positive Outlook
How can a positive outlook benefit you?

A Having a positive outlook leads to making an effort.

B Making an effort leads to encouragement from others.

- can accept disappointment without overreacting.

- act responsibly at work and in relationships.

- are aware of their feelings and are able to express those feelings in healthful ways.

- accept honest criticism without anger.

interNET
CONNECTION
Discover on the Web how capable you are of managing stress and achieving balance.
http://www.glencoe.com/sec/health

If you showed all of the qualities of mental health all the time, you would have perfect mental health. Of course, no one does. These qualities are goals to work toward. As with physical health, there are many different levels of mental health, and everyone's mental health has its ups and downs. Don't worry if you aren't showing all these qualities at all times. You can, however, improve your overall mental health by practicing good mental health habits. Look at the following tips for achieving good mental health. The first three have to do with the way you view others. The last five have to do with how you view yourself. Which of them do you find the easiest? In which areas do you need to improve?

- Accept other people as they are. It isn't fair to judge everyone by your own background and behavior.

- Focus on other people's strengths, not on their weaknesses.

- Consider other people's feelings.

- Focus on your own strengths.

- Accept the parts of yourself that you cannot change.

- Work to improve what you can change.

- Don't dwell on failures and disappointments.

- Learn from your mistakes.

C Encouragement from others leads to success.

D Success strengthens your positive outlook and leads to efforts in new areas.

We all give and receive impressions of one another at first meetings. Some people rely too much on first impressions in their opinions of others. They make snap judgments from visible personality traits about people they just met. These judgments usually are based on a bias about certain physical or cultural characteristics.

The next time you meet someone new, take the time to get to know the person before you decide if you like him or her. Isn't that the way you want to be judged?

Personality and Mental Health

Just as no two snowflakes are alike, no two people are exactly the same. Each person is an individual with a **personality,** which is a *special mix of traits, feelings, attitudes, and habits.* You may have heard a person described as having no personality. This can never be. Everyone has a personality. Your personality is everything about you that makes you the person you are.

Factors That Shape Your Personality

Many factors influence the development of your personality. The three most important factors are heredity (the passing on of traits from your parents), environment (all of your surroundings), and behavior (the way you act in the many different situations and events in your life). Behavior is the factor over which you have the most control. Study the examples in **Figure 8.2;** then think of one specific example of each factor that describes you.

To some extent, each factor will continue to shape your personality throughout your life. Some factors, such as heredity, are beyond your control. No one gets to choose her or his inherited traits. Much of your environment is also beyond your control. Most young people live where the adults in their family choose to live.

Figure 8.2
What Shapes Your Personality?

Heredity	Environment	Behavior
Height	Community	Caring for yourself
Skin, hair, and eye color	Family and friends	Caring for others
Body type	Experiences	Reflecting your values

Your behavior toward other people is an important factor in shaping your personality.

What you do have control over, however, is how you will deal with your inherited traits and your environment. The final decision about how you act is yours. You decide if you will focus on your strengths or weaknesses. You decide if you will work to improve those situations that can be changed. Your behavior is your choice and your responsibility. A big part of who you are is up to you.

The Factor You Control

Behavior is the way you act in the various situations of your life. It is the factor of your personality over which you have the most control. Your behavior is based on your values, which are beliefs and ideas about what is important in your life. Most of your values are learned from your family, and to a lesser extent from your friends. How you behave reflects those values. If good health is important in your life, then you will behave in a manner that reflects this. You will actively take good care of your mind and your body. You will choose behaviors that promote good health. You will not take risks that endanger your health or the health of others.

Your heredity, environment, and behavior have combined to shape the person you are today. How you handle these factors will define your personality as you grow and mature.

Your family teaches you about values through their actions and behavior.

Review

Lesson 1

Using complete sentences, answer the following questions on a separate sheet of paper.

Reviewing Terms and Facts

1. **Vocabulary**   Define the term *mental health*. Use it in an original sentence.

2. **Recall**   What are the three factors that shape personality?

Thinking Critically

3. **Apply**   List at least five specific examples of good mental health qualities.

4. **Describe**   Give examples of two times in the last week that your personal behavior demonstrated good mental health habits.

Applying Health Concepts

5. **Growth and Development**   Role-play the following situation. A friend on your sports team has seemed unhappy lately. Your friend makes an error that causes the team to lose. You confront your friend angrily. Discuss with your classmates alternative responses to the loss of the game. Replay the situation, using responses that are more healthful.

6. **Personal Health**   Examine an aspect of your physical surroundings, such as your bedroom, the place where you study, or the outside area around your home. How does this place affect your mental well-being? What can you do to improve the space? Share your ideas with your classmates.

Building Positive Self-Esteem

This lesson will help you find answers to questions that teens often ask about liking themselves. For example:

▶ **Why do I feel the way I do about myself?**

▶ **How does self-concept differ from self-esteem?**

▶ **How can I feel better about myself?**

self-concept

in your journal

Write a description of yourself in your journal. How do you think you usually feel, think, look, and act? Mark your calendar to reread what you have written in three weeks. Do you still think it is accurate? Add your answer to your journal.

How Do You See Yourself?

Imagine for a moment that you are about to enter a room to meet some people for the first time. You ready yourself at the doorway, pull open the door, and walk in. Describe the person (you) that these people are about to meet. Are you confident, fun to be with, intelligent, honest, well groomed, happy, healthy, organized, or creative? Are you sincerely interested in other people? Your description paints a word picture of how you view yourself and how you believe others view you. This *view that you have of yourself* is called your **self-concept.**

Your self-concept could be realistic, which means that you have a pretty accurate awareness of the strengths and weaknesses of your personality. Some teens, however, have an unrealistic self-concept. They dismiss their strengths and focus only on their "faults," usually exaggerating them. Think back to the tips for developing good mental health on page 211. Which of the points listed would you associate with having a realistic self-concept?

Focusing only on what you perceive as your "faults" makes them seem greater than they actually are.

How Self-Concept Develops

The self-concept that you have today has been in the making for a long time. It was built gradually from your experiences with other people. In general, people who are given support, encouragement, and love tend to develop a positive self-concept. People who are neglected, discouraged, criticized often, or spoken to harshly tend to develop a negative self-concept.

Your self-concept began in your early years, but it keeps developing as you grow. Remarks that your family, friends, and teachers make and ways in which they act toward you can reinforce, or strengthen, the view you have of yourself. **Figure 8.3** illustrates how various experiences contribute to your self-concept.

Thanks for mowing the lawn, Tom. That was a great help.

Figure 8.3
Shaping Your Self-Concept
What kind of reinforcement—positive or negative—does each of these messages represent?

- Your older sister calls you clumsy when you spill the juice.
- You join two friends at lunch, but they ignore you.
- Your teacher frowns during your oral report.

- The coach gives you a thumbs-up sign.
- Your friends wait for you to catch up and walk with them.
- Your teacher smiles encouragement when you give your report.

HEALTH LAB
The Qualities You Admire

Introduction: "I wish I had Rosa's confidence." "Everyone likes Garrett. I wish I was more like him." Have you ever made statements like these? Most people admire certain qualities in others. Do you look for and admire qualities in others that you also have, or do you most admire qualities that you do not have? You can find out by carrying out the following experiment.

Objective: Look for evidence during the next week that tells you if you have any of the six qualities that you most admire in others.

Materials and Method: List eight to ten qualities that you admire in others. Examples could include being a good listener, keeping secrets, and being reliable.

When you complete your list, circle the six qualities that you most admire. Clip three sheets of notebook paper together, and fold them in half. On each half page, write one of the six qualities. During the next week, look for signs that you have, or don't have, each of the qualities. Every time you have any evidence, either way, write it down under the appropriate quality heading.

Observations and Analysis: At the end of the week, ask a classmate to help you analyze your observations. Remember to weigh the evidence fairly. For example, returning a library book a day late does not mean that you are not reliable. However, breaking your word might. Do you have the qualities that you most admire in others?

Self-Concept and Self-Esteem

Closely tied to your self-concept is your self-esteem. Self-esteem is the confidence and pride you have in yourself. The way you feel about your body, your mind, your emotions, and your interactions with others are all part of your self-esteem. **Figure 8.4** lists the types of behavior that indicate self-esteem.

Figure 8.4
Behaviors That Indicate Self-Esteem
Where do you fall on the self-esteem continuum?

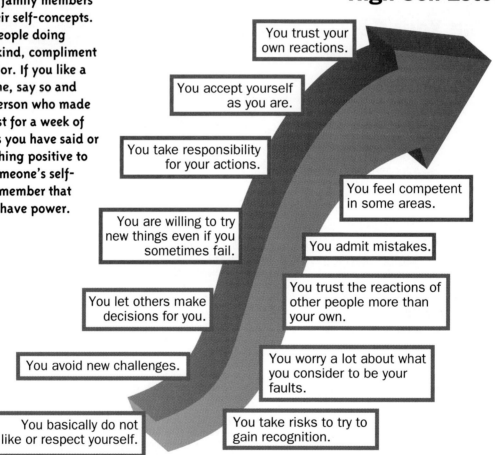

High Self-Esteem

You trust your own reactions.

You accept yourself as you are.

You take responsibility for your actions.

You feel competent in some areas.

You are willing to try new things even if you sometimes fail.

You admit mistakes.

You let others make decisions for you.

You trust the reactions of other people more than your own.

You avoid new challenges.

You worry a lot about what you consider to be your faults.

You basically do not like or respect yourself.

You take risks to try to gain recognition.

Low Self-Esteem

Low self-esteem is often linked to an unrealistic self-concept. For example, people who overlook their strengths and exaggerate their weaknesses in their own minds will probably not feel very good about themselves. In other words, people who do not like or respect themselves have low self-esteem.

Like your self-concept, your self-esteem is formed in part by messages, both positive and negative, that you receive from other people. Your self-esteem is also formed by messages that you send yourself. The messages you give yourself are sometimes powerful enough to change the meaning of messages from others. Have you ever received a compliment that you were unable to accept? Perhaps the more the person praised you, the more you rejected the praise. If you have had this experience, you have let your own negative messages override the positive ones from someone else. What incident can you recall when your own positive messages lessened the sting of negative messages from another person?

Self-Esteem and Your Health

Probably no single factor has a greater impact on your total health than your self-esteem. People with high self-esteem are more likely to practice good health habits than people with low self-esteem. People with high self-esteem are also more likely to avoid harmful behaviors, such as overeating, abusing alcohol and drugs, and refusing to take personal safety measures.

Because people with high self-esteem like themselves, they take good care of themselves. Their health, safety, and appearance are important. They try to accept and learn from fair criticism, and they are able to ignore mean remarks. High self-esteem lets you accept the negative incidents in your life as exceptions, not the rule. People with high self-esteem generally act responsibly toward themselves and others. People with low self-esteem do just the opposite. They tend to believe that all experiences are negative.

Were you ever feeling down when suddenly something really positive happened that made you feel great for the rest of the day? Everyone's level of self-esteem changes from day to day and sometimes from hour to hour. Although your self-esteem goes up and down, it usually falls within a specific range on the self-esteem continuum. Which of the signs of high and low self-esteem in **Figure 8.4** do you think describe you most of the time?

Improving Your Self-Esteem

When your self-esteem is high, you are usually happy with yourself and get along well with others. You are able to bounce back quickly after a loss, and your total health seems to get a boost. For these reasons, having high self-esteem is a worthy goal. There are several actions you can take to help you reach the goal of high self-esteem. **Figure 8.5** on the next page describes some of these actions. What other items would you add to the list?

in Your Journal

Your behavior can sometimes trigger just the response you do not want. For example, if you want more freedom at home, acting irresponsibly will convince your parents that you are not ready for more personal freedom. Think of two recent incidents: one that resulted in the desired response and one that did not. Describe both incidents in your journal.

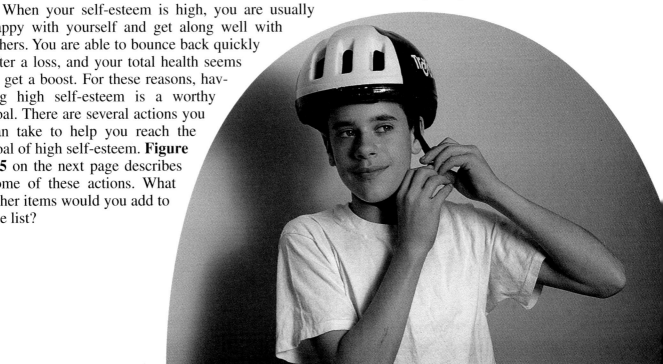

Wearing a helmet when riding a bicycle is an example of a personal safety measure.

Keeping a realistic self-concept and raising your self-esteem takes effort. Although some people always appear confident and happy, everyone has occasional self-doubts and personal concerns. The teen years are usually times of changing self-esteem levels. Temporary periods of unrealistic self-concept and low self-esteem seem to happen frequently, but usually they do not last long. Teens who feel unloved, unimportant, and unworthy most of the time, however, should talk about their feelings with an adult family member, clergy member, school counselor, or coach.

Figure 8.5
Working Toward High Self-Esteem
Here are some suggestions for raising your self-esteem.

Ⓐ Focus on your successes.

Ⓑ Send yourself positive messages.

Ⓒ Set realistic goals for yourself.

Ⓓ Ask people for help when you need it.

Ⓔ Learn from your mistakes.

Lesson 2 Review

Using complete sentences, answer the following questions on a separate sheet of paper.

Reviewing Terms and Facts

1. **Vocabulary** What is the difference between *self-concept* and *self-esteem?*
2. **Give Examples** List three ways to improve self-esteem.

Thinking Critically

3. **Explain** How and when does a person's self-concept develop?
4. **Analyze** Why do people with generally high self-esteem have times when their self-esteem is low?

Applying Health Concepts

5. **Growth and Development** Think of a common problem that affects a teen's self-esteem. Draw a cartoon strip that shows what teens with this problem do to feel better about themselves.

6. **Health of Others** Write down the number of times during the day that you reinforced someone else's self-concept. Perhaps you smiled at someone, complimented a friend on a job well done, or invited someone to join an activity. Include any negative reinforcements you may have given.

Managing Stress

This lesson will help you find answers to questions that teens often ask about stress. For example:

▶ **How does stress affect me?**

▶ **What circumstances in my life might be causing me stress?**

▶ **How can I cope with the stress in my life?**

Stress in Your Life

Stress is a familiar term. You probably hear it mentioned almost every day. Most often stress is mentioned in a negative way, as something to avoid. **Stress,** however, is only *your body's response to changes around you.* Those responses can certainly have a negative effect. Feeling nervous and maybe having an upset stomach because you are worried about an upcoming event are definitely not pleasant experiences. *Stress that keeps you from doing the things you need to do or that causes you discomfort* is called negative stress, or **distress.**

Some stress is considered positive. Positive stress helps you to accomplish and reach goals. The stress that makes you feel excited or challenged by an activity is an example of positive stress.

Like stress, changes in your life may also be labeled either positive or negative. Winning a race is usually considered positive, and losing a race most often seems negative. Your body, however, cannot tell the difference. Because your body responds to every change, any change—positive or negative—causes stress. The Personal Inventory feature on page 223 lists some life changes that cause stress. How many of these events have you experienced lately?

Words to Know

stress
distress
stressor
adrenaline
fatigue
physical fatigue
psychological fatigue
defense mechanism

in your journal

Consider the sources of stress in your life. List them in your journal. Write why you think each one is causing you stress. Write down the signs of stress you notice in yourself.

Positive stress can challenge athletes and motivate them to work hard to meet a goal.

Stress and Stressors

Stress is a natural part of everyday life. The *triggers of stress* are called **stressors.** It isn't just major events that cause stress. Stress is caused by everyday irritations and pleasures.

Your body responds to most stressors by getting ready to act. This response is called the "fight-or-flight" response because your body prepares to fight the stressor or flee from it (see **Figure 8.6**). One part of this response is the release of **adrenaline** (uh·DRE·nuhl·in). This hormone *increases the level of sugar in your blood, which gives your body extra energy.*

Figure 8.6
The Fight-or-Flight Response

When your body responds to a stressor, certain physical reactions occur.

A More blood is directed to your muscles and brain.

D Your senses sharpen. You become more alert.

B Your heart beats faster.

E Your air passages widen so that you can take in more air.

C Your muscles tighten up and are ready for action.

F The level of sugar in your blood increases, which gives you extra energy.

Stress and Fatigue

Once the stressor is gone, your body's response usually stops. However, if the stress is great, or if it lasts long enough, the response may continue. After a time, your body can become exhausted. **Fatigue,** or *extreme tiredness,* then sets in.

There are actually two types of fatigue. **Physical fatigue** is *extreme tiredness of the whole body.* It usually occurs after vigorous activity. Muscles may be overworked and sore, and your body feels tired all over. When this happens, you need rest.

The other type is **psychological** (sy·kuh·LAH·ji·kuhl) **fatigue,** or *extreme tiredness caused by your mental state.* This type is brought on by stress, worry, boredom, or depression. Activity, such as exercise or doing a project, can help relieve this kind of fatigue.

Teen Issues

Reducing Stress ACTIVITY!

Which day of the week is most stressful for you? Try to analyze why you feel more stress on that day. Write your thoughts on a sheet of paper. Examine what you have written to determine if there are ways to reduce the stress of that day.

LIFE SKILLS
Time Management

*P*eople who manage their time well are better able to control this major source of stress in their lives.

To rate your time management skills, answer the following questions with *yes* or *no.*

▶ Are you almost always in a hurry?

▶ Do you leave tasks or chores incomplete?

▶ Do you feel as if you are working hard but not accomplishing much?

▶ Do you not have enough time for rest or for personal relationships?

▶ Are you regularly late with assignments and for appointments?

▶ Are you overwhelmed by demands?

▶ Do you often try to do several things at once?

▶ Do you have trouble deciding what to do next?

If most of your answers are yes, your time management skills need improvement. Try putting the following tips to work in your life.

1. **Set priorities.** Decide which activities are obligations and which are choices. Of the activities that are choices, decide which are most important to you.

2. **Make a schedule** (see **Figure 8.7**). Decide when you will do each activity. Try to be realistic about how much you can do, and leave time for relaxing. If you need to drop some activities, check your priority list.

3. **Learn to say no.** Most important, know your limitations and when to say no.

Follow-up Activity

After three weeks, take the time management quiz again. Have any of your answers changed? What else can you do to manage your time better?

Figure 8.7
Managing Your Time

Sunday	Monday	Tuesday	Wednesday	Thursday	Friday	Saturday
29	30	31	1	2	3	4
Picnic with friends	Photography club after school	Baby-sitting for neighbor from 6:00 to 8:00 p.m.	Marching band tryouts	Trumpet lesson after school	Movie night with Aunt Celia	Grandma's 80th birthday party

Defense Mechanisms

The fight-or-flight response is your body's reaction to stress. Your mind also reacts to stress. These reactions, called **defense mechanisms** (di·FENS MEK·uh·nizms), are *short-term ways of dealing with stress*. Defense mechanisms allow you to set aside a certain amount of stress until you are better able to face the problem and deal with it (see **Figure 8.8**). When used as a temporary solution to problems, defense mechanisms can actually help people. However, if you use them as a permanent substitute for facing the problem, your mental health could be harmed. There are several types of defense mechanisms. Which of the following defense mechanisms are familiar to you?

- **Denial** is a refusal to accept reality. Ted's parents are getting a divorce. Ted refuses to accept that his dad is moving out and acts as if everything is fine with the family.

- **Rationalization** is justifying behavior, ideas, or feelings to avoid guilt or to obtain approval or acceptance. Marlene says she did not finish her homework because she was busy helping her grandmother with her food shopping.

- **Repression** is blocking out unpleasant thoughts. Kahlil has a lot of homework to do tonight, but he does not even think of it when he agrees to go out with his friends.

- **Displacement** is having bad feelings toward someone not really related to the cause of the problem. Wynona had an argument with her friend that left her hurt and angry. Later, at home, Wynona yelled at her sister for no reason.

- **Projection** is blaming someone else for your problem. Will got up late, spilled his juice on his shirt, could not find his homework, and finally missed his bus. While these were his problems, he blamed his mother for everything.

Figure 8.8
Examples of Defense Mechanisms

Identify the defense mechanism or mechanisms that may be at work in each example.

Pete's more popular than I am because you give him everything.

You have to tell Lisa that you were hurt by what she did.

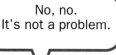

No, no. It's not a problem.

Personal Inventory

Stress and the effect it will have on people is difficult to measure. What causes one person a great deal of stress may hardly affect another person at all. The following chart gives values in "stress points" to certain life changes. Accumulating between 150 and 299 stress points in one year increases a person's chance of getting sick. Whether sickness will actually occur depends on the person. It is not the amount of stress that is important; it is how you respond to it.

Rank	Event	Stress points	Rank	Event	Stress points
1.	Death of a parent	98	17.	Father or mother losing a job	69
2.	Death of a sister or brother	95	18.	Being seriously sick or hurt	64
3.	Death of a friend	92	19.	Arguing with parents	64
4.	Divorce or separation of parents	86	20.	School troubles with teacher or principal	63
5.	Failure in one or more school subjects	86	21.	Discomfort and concern about weight, height, acne	63
6.	Getting arrested	85	22.	Going to a new school	57
7.	Repeating a grade in school	84	23.	Moving to a new home	51
8.	Family member's alcohol or drug problem	79	24.	Change in physical appearance due to braces, glasses	47
9.	Starting to use alcohol or drugs	77	25.	Arguing with sister or brother	46
10.	Loss or death of a pet	77	26.	Beginning to menstruate (girls)	45
11.	Family member's serious illness	77	27.	Making a decision about smoking	45
12.	Making choices about sexual relationships	75	28.	Having someone, such as a grandparent, move in	35
13.	Losing money you've saved	74	29.	Mother's pregnancy	31
14.	Breaking up with girlfriend or boyfriend	74	30.	Beginning to go out on dates	31
15.	Quitting or being suspended from school	73	31.	Making new friends	27
16.	Pregnancy of a close friend	69	32.	Marriage of a sister or brother	26

Serious and long-lasting stress can cause illness. By being ready for changes and planning for them whenever possible, you can reduce both the stress and your chances of becoming sick.

Coping with Stress

Stress can have a strong effect on your total health. Stress can alter your emotions and behavior. You may be so worried about a relative's health that you don't eat or sleep well. Being tired may cause you to snap angrily at a friend or family member.

No matter how you feel pushed and pulled by stress, it's important to keep your head. Defense mechanisms are a temporary way to deal with the effects of stress. They are not, however, a long-term solution to the problem. Coping with stress involves avoiding some stressors entirely by changing your behavior. For those stressors that you cannot avoid, you can use management techniques to keep yourself from suffering negative effects.

Giving yourself plenty of time to complete a project will help you avoid stress.

Avoiding Stress

Fortunately, you can get a head start on coping with stress by keeping certain types of stress out of your life. Think about situations that make you uncomfortable or anxious. Are there ways for you to change your behavior to avoid these sources of stress? For example, you are likely to experience distress if you must stay up late completing an assignment. By using good time management and study skills, however, you could avoid this distress by starting the project in plenty of time to finish it comfortably. Common sense will also help you to avoid certain types of stress. If you know, for example, that there will be alcohol or drugs at a party, you'll save yourself from having to deal with negative peer pressure by making other plans.

High self-esteem and a positive attitude will also help you cope with stress. If you are confident in your abilities, you won't be as likely to feel overwhelmed when things go wrong. Your aim should not be to get rid of stress entirely. That just isn't possible. Changes will always occur in your life, and learning how to adapt effectively to them is an important skill to learn.

Managing Stress Effectively

Stress is a factor in everyone's life. The key to managing it is to identify sources of stress and learn how to handle them in ways that promote good mental and emotional health. **Figure 8.9** lists some tips for handling stress.

Figure 8.9
Tips for Effective Stress Management

Which of these tips do you use?

Stay Healthy During periods of stress, be sure to eat right and get enough sleep. Stress management takes energy.

Redirect Your body reacts to all stress by producing adrenaline, which raises your energy level. Rechannel all that extra energy into something worthwhile.

Relax Try imagining yourself in a quiet, peaceful place, such as under a tree by a lake. As you relax, try to empty your mind of troubling thoughts.

Talk Just talking things out with another person can relieve stress. People who aren't directly involved can often see solutions to your problems that you cannot.

Laugh Spend time with people who enjoy a good laugh. See a funny movie after an especially stressful day. Laughter relieves stress.

Review

Lesson 3

Using complete sentences, answer the following questions on a separate sheet of paper.

Reviewing Terms and Facts

1. **Vocabulary** What is the difference between *stress* and *distress?*

2. **Define** What is a *stressor?* Give three examples.

3. **Recall** What are the two types of *fatigue?*

Thinking Critically

4. **Hypothesize** How could defense mechanisms harm your health? Why do you think people use them?

5. **Analyze** Your friend tells you that she is feeling very tired. She says that she is so worried about some problems at home that she can't think of anything else. What kind of stress is she feeling? What can she do right away to relieve her stress?

Applying Health Concepts

6. **Health of Others** Interview five people about how they handle stress. You can interview family members, teachers, classmates, and friends. Ask each person to suggest at least one tip for coping with stress. Share the tips with your classmates.

TEEN HEALTH DIGEST

Personal Trainer

Take It Easy

Simple breathing exercises can help you deal with stress—right where you are, in ten minutes or less. Here's how.

1. **Choose a quiet place.** Sit in a chair with your feet flat on the floor.
2. **Close your eyes.** Feel how the chair supports you. Let your shoulders relax.
3. **Breathe slowly and deeply.** Count as you breathe, taking twice as long to breathe out as to breathe in. Continue for about five minutes. Stop, however, if you begin to feel dizzy.
4. **As you breathe, clear your mind of all thoughts.** Another method is to think of the most peaceful scene you can imagine.

Do these exercises whenever you feel stressed—or plan to do them twice every day. You'll be surprised how much better you feel.

People at Work

Music Therapist

Interview with Sal Marino, a music therapist.

Q.: What made you choose this job?

A.: Music has always been part of my life. When I started college, I was torn between studying music and psychology. Then a teacher told me how to combine them into a very satisfying career.

Q.: What makes your career such a rewarding one?

A.: I help people to understand that playing music can bring relief from mental and emotional problems. For example, I have several patients who have trouble expressing anger in a healthful way. I often teach people with this problem to play the drums. How good the music sounds isn't really important. How good the patient feels is.

Try This:

Try expressing your own emotions through your voice or a musical instrument. Describe the experience in a paragraph.

Sports and Recreation

Very Special Athletes

In 1963, Eunice Kennedy Shriver started a summer camp for children and adults with mental retardation. She especially encouraged the campers to explore sports and physical activities. Five years later, Shriver's summer camp became the First International Special Olympic Games. One thousand athletes with mental retardation came to Chicago from 26 states and Canada to compete in track and field, floor hockey, and swimming.

Over time the Special Olympics grew, drawing coverage from television networks and gaining support from many different people. In 1995 over 7,000 athletes from 143 countries competed in 21 sports at the Ninth Special Olympics World Games. What had started as a small idea had become a hugely successful and very inspiring international event.

CON$UMER FOCU$

Self-Image Bait

Advertisements aimed at teens imply that if they buy certain products, they will feel good about themselves and be popular.

By encouraging self-doubt, the messages in these ads create a problem and then offer a solution. Many teens have a shaky self-image to start with. Ads like these take advantage of this lack of confidence to undermine the consumer's self-image even more. The ad hints that your looks are in need of improvement and that you do not have enough friends. Don't let ads hurt your self-image or self-confidence.

Teens Making a Difference

Choosing Life

You might say that Tonya Smith's eighth-grade year was both her worst and her best ever. That year several of her friends began talking about suicide. One attempted to end his life. Shaken by the experience, Tonya turned to a program called SAIL—Self Acceptance Is Life.

SAIL helps teens like Tonya get help for troubled friends. SAIL emphasizes that teens cannot become responsible for their friends' lives. SAIL members encourage teens to guide their friends to trusted school or religious counselors, teachers, or parents. That's exactly what has happened with Tonya's friends. Today Tonya speaks at schools, churches, and other community groups so that others can benefit from what she has learned. Tonya emphasizes this message: "With someone to talk to, you can get through troubled times."

Try This: Bring several ads of this type to class and discuss how their messages could be handled by teens.

Mental Disorders

This lesson will help you find answers to questions that teens often ask about mental health problems and mental disorders. For example:

▶ **What is the best way to deal with my problems?**

▶ **How can I tell if my mental problems are serious?**

▶ **What causes mental illness?**

▶ **What should I do if I suspect that a friend is thinking of suicide?**

Words to Know

anxiety disorder
mood disorder
depression
schizophrenia
suicide

Facing Problems

Life is filled with events that create problems and cause stress. Some problems can be solved easily. A misplaced notebook might cause stress for only a few minutes. Other problems, such as a death in the family, have a much more lasting effect on your life.

Regardless of the problem, the healthy way to deal with it is first to face up to it. If you are having trouble dealing with a problem on your own, ask for help. **Figure 8.10** offers information on how to handle problems.

Figure 8.10
How to Handle a Problem
Some problems require professional help.

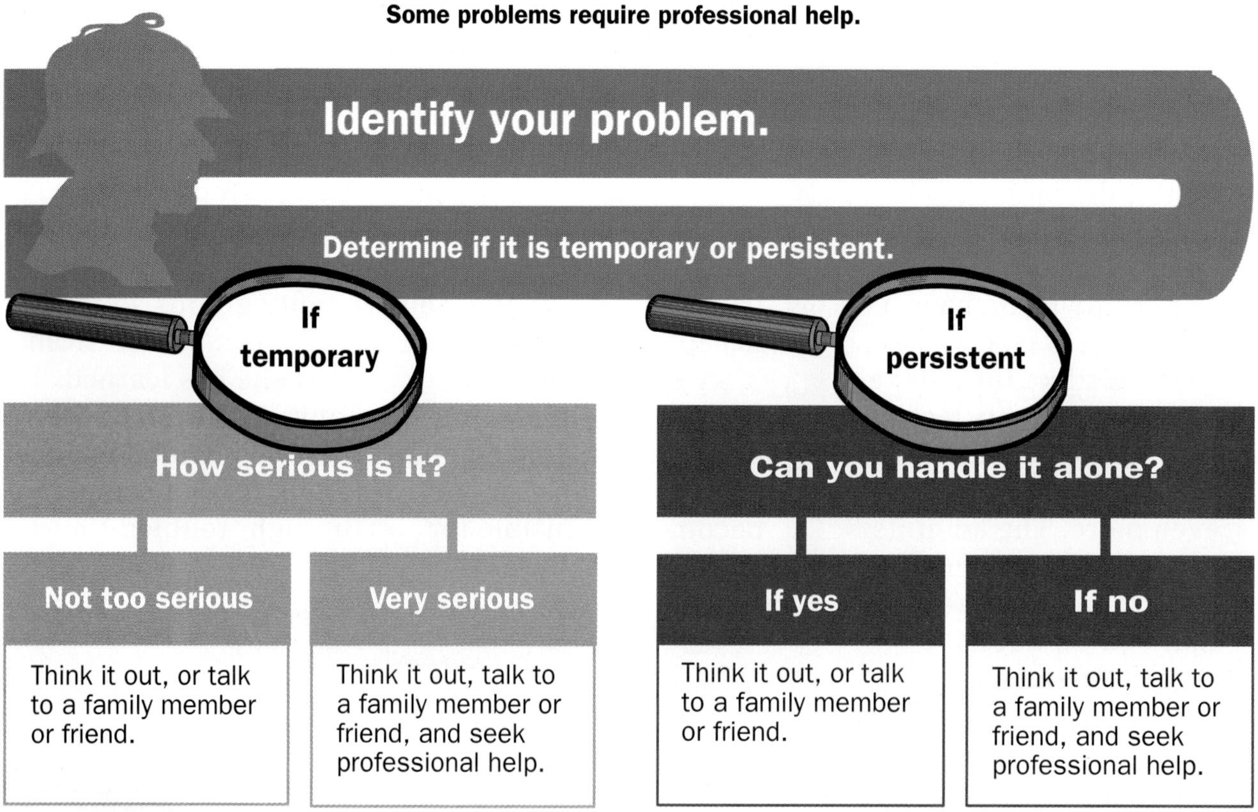

Identify your problem.

Determine if it is temporary or persistent.

If temporary	If persistent
How serious is it?	**Can you handle it alone?**

Not too serious	Very serious	If yes	If no
Think it out, or talk to a family member or friend.	Think it out, talk to a family member or friend, and seek professional help.	Think it out, or talk to a family member or friend.	Think it out, talk to a family member or friend, and seek professional help.

Understanding Mental Disorders

Feeling anxious, fearful, or sad from time to time is natural. When these feelings continue for a long time or make a person feel out of control or unable to deal with life, they could signal a mental disorder. The causes of mental disorders cannot always be identified. Sometimes a mental disorder has a physical cause, such as inherited genetic traits, injury to the brain, or the effects of certain drugs. Emotional causes are harder to pinpoint. A person may, for example, develop a mental disorder in an attempt to avoid a repeated stressor, or in response to a negative experience that is overwhelming.

Types of Disorders

Mental health experts recognize several different groups of mental disorders. They include anxiety disorders, mood disorders, and schizophrenia.

Everyone has, at some time, felt fear or been anxious about something. In some people, however, this nervousness or fear takes the form of an **anxiety disorder,** *a disorder in which real or imagined fears keep a person from functioning normally.* Examples of anxiety disorders follow.

- Phobias are inappropriate or exaggerated fears of something specific. There are many kinds of phobias, including acrophobia (ak·ruh·FOH·bee·uh), or the fear of high places, and social phobia, the fear of group situations.

- Obsessive-compulsive disorder is a condition in which a person cannot keep certain thoughts or images out of his or her mind. The person may then develop repetitive behaviors as a way of relieving the anxiety.

- Various stress disorders may affect people who have been through overwhelming experiences, such as a violent attack, or a conflict, such as a war.

Another category of disorders is made up of mood disorders. A **mood disorder** is *a disorder in which a person undergoes changes in mood that seem inappropriate or extreme.* This is different from the normal mood swings experienced by teens or the emotions that all people go through in response to stressful life events. The mood changes of a person who has a mood disorder are not necessarily related to any event. **Depression** is *a mood disorder involving feelings of hopelessness, helplessness, worthlessness, guilt, and extreme sadness that continue for periods of weeks.* It's common to feel some of these emotions at times, but depression is a very serious condition that may leave a person completely unwilling or unable to function. Severely depressed people may even think about ending their own lives. Another mood disorder is bipolar disorder, in which a person has extreme mood swings for no apparent reason. The person usually veers between periods of hyperactivity and depression, often taking dangerous risks during the hyperactive periods.

Science Connection

The Winter Blues

If you've ever felt sluggish, tired, or irritable on gray winter days, you're not alone. Scientists think that millions of Americans suffer from seasonal affective disorder (SAD). Some researchers theorize that during the short, dark days of winter, people don't get enough sunlight. This lack can affect a hormone called melatonin, which is related to sleep patterns and overall mood. If you feel down in winter, try to get outside for walks and exercise, and sit near windows with the curtains open. Special lamps are available for people who are strongly affected by seasonal affective disorder.

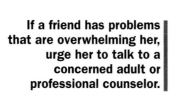

Q & A

Eating Disorders

Q: My friend hates food. She practically never eats. Even when she has food, she seems to just play with it. She is getting thinner and thinner, yet she says she needs to lose weight. What's going on with her? Does she have a mental disorder or an eating disorder?

A: Both. Eating disorders such as anorexia nervosa, in which a person refuses to eat, have long been regarded as emotionally based mental disorders. Eating disorders are dangerous and lead to serious physical illness and even death. Get some help for your friend now. Tell an adult why you are worried about her.

Another category of mental disorder includes **schizophrenia** (skit·zoh·FREE·nee·uh), which is *a serious disorder in which a person's perceptions lose their connection to reality.* A person with schizophrenia may hear voices or see images that are not really there. He or she may suffer from false beliefs—for example, that he or she has unusual powers or is on a special mission. Schizophrenia may be so disruptive that it is often considered the most serious mental disorder.

Treating Mental Disorders

Mental disorders are often very difficult to treat and cure. They are linked to a complex network of causes and effects throughout a person's life. Many mental disorders are treated with a combination of strong medicines and long-term therapy under the care of a psychiatrist. If you believe that you or someone you know may be suffering from a mental disorder, seek professional help as soon as possible.

Seriously Troubled Teens

The teen years are full of changes—in the body, in feelings, in relationships, and in responsibilities. These changes cause stress, which sometimes becomes more than a person can cope with alone. If that happens to you, ask for help. There is nothing wrong with needing help with mental problems. Most people need help sometime. People who do not get help suffer more than they need to.

Suicide

Each year thousands of teenagers attempt suicide. **Suicide,** *intentionally killing oneself,* has been the second-leading cause of death for people between the ages of 15 and 19 since 1986. Suicide is a serious matter, and threats of suicide should never be ignored. The best thing to do is to get help immediately.

Sometimes there are warnings that a person is thinking about suicide. If you notice any of the following signs in someone, try to get the person to talk to someone who can help. If he or she will not, tell an adult why you are worried about that person. It is important to get help before it is too late.

If a friend has problems that are overwhelming her, urge her to talk to a concerned adult or professional counselor.

The Warning Signs of Suicide

- Statements such as "They'll be sorry when I'm gone" or "I wish I could sleep forever"

- Avoiding activities involving friends or family

- Low level of energy

- Taking greater risks than usual

- Loss of interest in hobbies, sports, job, or school

- Giving away prized personal possessions

- A past history of suicide attempts—80 percent of suicides have attempted suicide before

What the Numbers Mean

Every year, more than 5,000 teens and young adults commit suicide, and many more make an attempt. Most teens who talk about suicide or attempt it are really pleading for help. They do not really want to die—they just want their troubles to go away. When anyone attempts suicide, he or she is choosing a permanent solution to a temporary problem.

Although most teens who attempt suicide do not really want to die, many do want to end their lives. That is why it is important to seek help for yourself or a friend when problems seem overwhelming. Remember that you are never alone. With the help of a concerned adult or a professional counselor, you can find solutions to your problems. You can prevent suicide.

in your journal

Imagine that you write an advice column for teens. You receive a letter from a teen who says he is beginning to think that suicide is the only solution to the stress he feels. In your journal, write an answer to that person.

Review

Lesson **4**

Using complete sentences, answer the following questions on a separate sheet of paper.

Reviewing Terms and Facts

1. **Vocabulary** What are some major characteristics of *anxiety disorders?* How are they different from *mood disorders?*

2. **Explain** What is *depression?*

3. **Define** Explain the meaning of the term *schizophrenia.*

Thinking Critically

4. **Explain** Why do you think some people avoid seeking help for a mental or emotional problem?

5. **Compare** Explain how the behavior of someone with normal anxiety is similar to and different from that of someone who has an anxiety disorder.

Applying Health Concepts

6. **Health of Others** Imagine that you have a friend who is having mental/emotional problems, but who does not want to seek help. Write a note explaining to that person why he or she should seek help.

Sources of Help

This lesson will help you find answers to questions that teens often ask about where to get help for mental health problems. For example:

▶ **How do I know when the situation is serious enough to ask for help?**

▶ **Who can really help?**

▶ **What responsibility do I have for friends in trouble?**

Words to Know

support system
teen hot line

in Your Journal

Is it easy for you to ask for help with problems? Why or why not? Write your answer in your private journal.

Knowing When to Go for Help

Everyone needs help in solving problems at one time or another. Being able to ask for help is a sign that you are growing up. It shows that you are capable of deciding which problems or parts of a problem you need help with and which you can solve yourself.

Figure 8.11

Warning Signs

The following signs may signal a serious problem.

■ Suspecting that everyone is against you	■ Aches and pains that seem to have no medical cause
■ Continually feeling sad	■ Feelings of hopelessness
■ Sudden or extreme changes in mood	■ Trouble sleeping or frequent nightmares
■ Trouble concentrating or making decisions	■ Taking extreme or unusual risks
■ Not taking care of yourself	■ Loss of appetite

Teens who are mature are not afraid to ask for help in solving problems.

With mental and emotional health problems, knowing when to seek help is largely a matter of paying attention to warning signs. Paying attention to these signs could actually save a life. **Figure 8.11** shows some warning signs that often signal serious problems. Naturally, no one warning signal is a sure sign of a serious problem. On the other hand, any one signal may be a symptom of an unhealthy buildup of stress. If you experience—or see in another person—any of the warning signs over a period of days or weeks, something may be seriously wrong. It is time to go for help, just to be on the safe side.

Knowing Who Can Help

Talking out your problems with someone will not make them vanish instantly. It will, however, reassure you that you are not alone. This is often the first step in solving the problem. There are a number of people you can turn to when you or someone you know has a serious emotional problem (see **Figure 8.12**).

Figure 8.12
Sources of Help

All of these can be good sources of help for mental and emotional problems.

Language Arts Connection

Help in Any Language ACTIVITY!

Needing help from time to time is a universal need. There are dozens of ways to say "help me" both with and without words. In Spanish, the word is "ayúdame." Work with a partner to compile a list of different ways to ask for help. Ask people from different cultural backgrounds to tell you how to ask for help in their native language. Don't forget sign language.

Identify your problem.

Decision to get help

Parent or Other Family Member. Families are built-in support systems. A **support system** is *a network of people available to help when needed.* A parent, older brother or sister, or grandparent can be a great source of help. These people care about you the most.

Mental Health Professional. These people are specially trained to deal with mental and emotional problems. Your family doctor or school counselor can help you find the program for you.

School Nurse. Nurses are specially trained to understand and deal with the problems of teenagers. They can give you real help and will respect your privacy.

Priest, Minister, Rabbi, or Other Clergy Member. The leader of your church, synagogue, or mosque may be a good person to talk to. Members of the clergy are educated in counseling people with emotional problems.

Teacher or School Counselor. A teacher or guidance counselor that you like and trust could be a friend when you are in need.

Hot Line. Teen hot lines are *special telephone services that teens can call when feeling stressed.* Some hot lines are answered by teens; others are answered by adults. Both groups are trained to listen to and help teens who are experiencing a crisis.

Figure 8.13
If Someone Talks About Suicide

You can help your friend by both listening and speaking.

Listen. Let the person talk. This lets your friend know that you are there for him or her. Your calmness can also be a source of comfort to your friend. Do not, however, promise to keep the discussion secret.

Talk. Never challenge the person to carry out the suicide threat. Tell your friend that his or her life is very important to you. Point out that this bad time will pass. Urge your friend to come with you now to get some help. Tell your friend that you will stick by him or her.

Troubled Friends

Figure 8.13 explains what to do if someone you know talks about suicide. However, there may be times when you feel that it takes all of your time and energy to keep your own stress under control. What is your obligation to your friends or sisters and brothers? Are you supposed to get involved with their problems, too? Are you responsible for their health and safety? These are questions that everyone must answer for himself or herself. Consider the following points when answering them.

MAKING HEALTHY DECISIONS
Deciding Whether to Tell

Mason and Steve have known each other since second grade. From the start, they got along well and have always run with the same crowd. For years each has considered the other to be among his closest friends.

Somehow, this year things have begun to change. For one reason or another Mason hasn't seen as much of Steve as before. Lately, Mason has made a special effort to invite Steve to join in some activities. Steve always seems to have a reason not to go. When they do run into each other, Steve seems different to Mason. Once a generally happy, easygoing guy, Steve now always appears sad.

As Mason becomes more and more aware of the changes in Steve, he decides to talk to him. Steve confides that he just can't shake his sadness. He says he started feeling sad a few months ago because of some problems at home, but now he does not even know why he feels sad.

Mason suggests that Steve talk to a counselor at school or to a teacher, but Steve refuses. "There's no point. I can't be helped. It's just hopeless," says Steve. When Mason offers to talk to someone for Steve, Steve gets angry. "Mind your own business," shouts Steve. "If you want to stay my friend, you'd better not tell anyone about how I feel."

Everyone who is mentally and physically capable must take responsibility for his or her own behavior. Even if you help a friend, the final outcome is your friend's responsibility.

Another consideration is how you feel when you need help. The golden rule to treat others as you would have them treat you still makes a lot of sense. Perhaps no one needs immediate help more than people who are thinking of suicide.

Review

Using complete sentences, answer the following questions on a separate sheet of paper.

Reviewing Terms and Facts

1. **Recall** When may a warning sign signal that a person has a serious problem?

2. **Vocabulary** Define the term *support system*. Use it in an original sentence.

Thinking Critically

3. **Interpret** One of your friends has been acting irritable for a couple of weeks. You have noticed that he hasn't been eating much and that he seems suspicious of you. Should you get involved? If so, what should you do?

4. **Summarize** Describe what you would do, and not do, if a friend threatened suicide.

Applying Health Concepts

5. **Consumer Health** **Figure 8.12** on page 233 lists possible sources of help. For as many sources as possible, list the names of people you know whom you would recommend as people to go to with problems.

Now Mason does not know what to do. He is worried about Steve and thinks Steve might need help, but he is not sure. He is sure that he does not want to lose Steve's friendship. He decides to use the six-step decision-making process to make up his mind:

1. **State the situation**
2. **List the options**
3. **Weigh the possible outcomes**
4. **Consider your values**
5. **Make a decision and act**
6. **Evaluate the decision**

Follow-up Activities

1. Compare Steve's behavior with the warning signs in **Figure 8.11** on page 232. Could this information help Mason make a decision?

2. Apply the six steps of the decision-making process to Mason's story.

Chapter Summary

▶ **Lesson 1** A positive outlook helps you to maintain good mental health. Personality is shaped by heredity, environment, and behavior.

▶ **Lesson 2** The view that you have of yourself is your self-concept. You can increase your confidence in yourself by focusing on your successes and learning from your mistakes.

▶ **Lesson 3** Every change in your life causes some stress. You can develop skills to help you control the stress you will experience.

▶ **Lesson 4** There are many types of mental disorders. People who are very deeply troubled may attempt to commit suicide.

▶ **Lesson 5** Knowing where to go for help in solving problems is an important health skill. People should not be afraid to seek help when they need it.

Reviewing Key Terms and Concepts

Using complete sentences, answer the following questions on a separate sheet of paper.

Lesson 1

1. Describe how a positive outlook can help you maintain good mental health.

2. List two examples of ways to develop good mental health habits.

Lesson 2

3. Give an example of a realistic self-concept and an unrealistic self-concept.

4. Why do people with high self-esteem usually take better care of themselves than do people with low self-esteem?

Lesson 3

5. Describe what happens during the fight-or-flight response.

6. List five tips for effectively managing your stress.

Lesson 4

7. Describe how you might handle a persistent problem that you cannot handle alone.

8. Identify three warning signs that a person is thinking about suicide.

Lesson 5

9. What is a support system?

10. What are five good sources of help for mental and emotional problems?

Thinking Critically

Using complete sentences, answer the following questions on a separate sheet of paper.

11. **Synthesize** Compare the signs of good mental health with signs of high self-esteem. How are they related?

12. **Analyze** How could working together with your friends and family help you cope with stress?

13. **Distinguish** Describe the difference between a phobia and depression.

14. **Hypothesize** What might be signs that a person wants help, even if he or she does not say so directly?

Your Action Plan

Most teens experience periods of stress and low self-esteem. Perhaps there are aspects of your mental and emotional health that you would like to improve. An action plan can help you do this.

Step 1 Review your private journal entries for this chapter to decide on a long-term goal. Once you've established what your long-term goal is, write it down. Perhaps, for example, you want to be more assertive in your behavior.

Step 2 Now think of a series of short-term goals—actions you can take to reach your long-term goal. If your goal is to be more assertive, possible short-term goals could involve behaving more assertively with particular people. You will have reached a short-term goal when you are comfortable with the way you relate to that person.

Plan a schedule for checking your progress. You might ask a family member or friend to help you evaluate how you are doing.

In Your Home and Community

1. **Health of Others** Choose a family member and give him or her a specific day to be special. On that day, go out of your way to build up that family member's self-esteem just by being nice to him or her. Spend time with the person, listen, and show that you care. Choose a different family member each week.

2. **Community Resources** Helping other people is one way to build self-confidence and self-esteem. Talk to a person who does volunteer work in your community. Ask the person about how this volunteer work affects his or her self-concept and self-esteem. Write a short account of your interview.

Building Your Portfolio

1. **Interview** Interview other students about how they manage stress. Ask about situations that produce stress and how the students deal with them. Take notes and write a short summary of any of the ideas that you could use to help you manage stress. Keep these ideas in your portfolio.

2. **Script** Write a script involving a conversation between two teens, one of whom is very depressed. Show how the other teen can help his or her friend to find help. Put the finished script in your portfolio.

3. **Personal Assessment** Look through all the activities and projects you did for this chapter. Choose one or two that you would like to include in your portfolio.

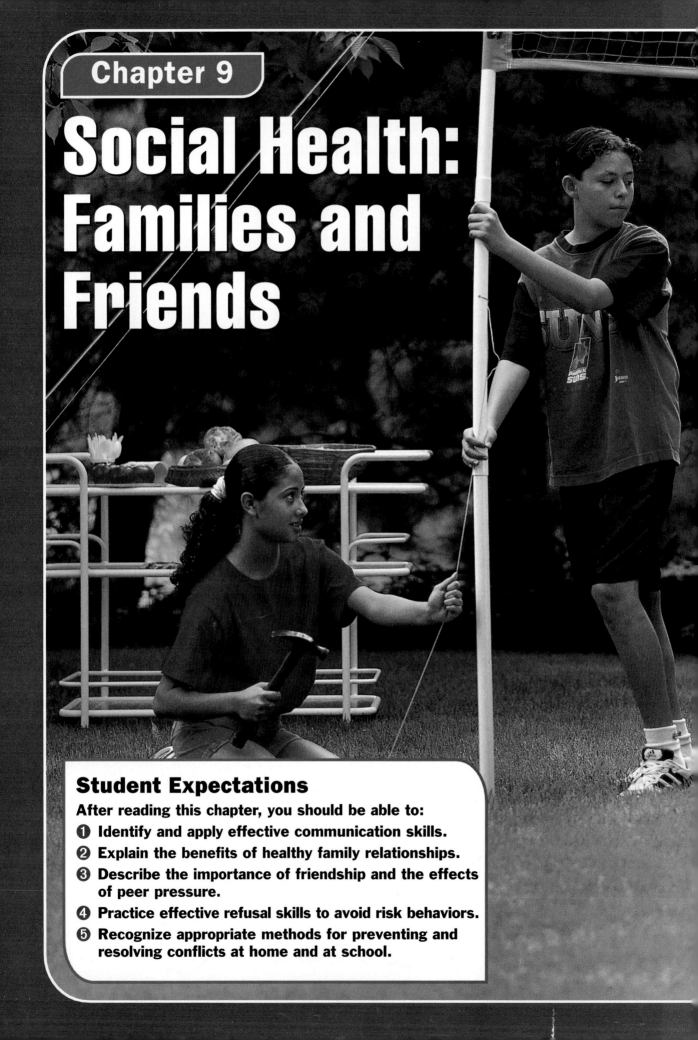

Social Health: Families and Friends

Student Expectations

After reading this chapter, you should be able to:

❶ Identify and apply effective communication skills.

❷ Explain the benefits of healthy family relationships.

❸ Describe the importance of friendship and the effects of peer pressure.

❹ Practice effective refusal skills to avoid risk behaviors.

❺ Recognize appropriate methods for preventing and resolving conflicts at home and at school.

Teen Chat Group

Lisa: Before anybody else gets here, I want to talk to you two.

Sharon: What's up?

Lisa: I wanted to tell you that I invited Miyoko to the cookout. You know her—she was in my pre-algebra class this year.

Andy: She's the girl who moved from Japan this year, right?

Lisa: Right. The problem is, Carl is coming, too. Sharon, you remember how he kept making fun of her accent and getting other people to laugh at her, too.

Sharon: Carl never seems to think about other people's feelings. He's really popular, though, and people go along with him.

Lisa: Well, I just don't want that to happen today. If you hear Carl getting started, find a way to change the subject. I'm depending on you guys!

in your journal

Read the dialogue on this page. Have you ever been in a situation like this one? Start your private journal entries about your own relationships with friends and other classmates by responding to these questions:

▶ If you were at this cookout and Carl began making fun of Miyoko, what would you do?

▶ Why is it hard to speak up when someone is encouraging others to do wrong, even if you strongly disagree?

▶ How can good communication skills help you in your relationships with friends and family?

When you reach the end of the chapter, you will use your journal entries to make an action plan.

1 Communication Skills

This lesson will help you find answers to questions that teens often ask about communication. For example:

▶ **How do people communicate?**

▶ **What are the advantages of expressing myself clearly?**

▶ **How can I improve my speaking skills?**

▶ **What can I do to become a better listener?**

Words to Know

communication
verbal
    communication
nonverbal
    communication
body language
tact
empathy
compromise

in your journal

Think about the communication habits of people you know. Which people do you think are especially good communicators? What types of skills do they use effectively? How might you work to improve your own communication skills? Respond to these questions in your journal.

What Is Communication?

Communication is *the exchange of thoughts, feelings, and beliefs among people.* Communication has three basic components:

■ Sender

■ Receiver

■ Message

Communication is not always simple, however. The sender must express the message clearly, and the receiver or receivers need to listen attentively and thoughtfully. In many cases, people don't say what they really intend to say, and listeners often hear only what they want to hear. The result may be a failure to communicate.

When sender and receiver do communicate effectively, everyone benefits. Effective communication builds positive relationships between people. It creates a healthy social environment in which people can not only be themselves but also understand and appreciate each other.

Effective communication leads to positive and fulfilling relationships.

Types of Communication

Communication can be verbal (using words) and nonverbal (without words). Most communication is a mixture of both types. **Figure 9.1** shows several types of communication.

Communicating Effectively

Speaking and listening skills play an important role in a healthy life. Expressing your thoughts and feelings clearly allows you to make your experiences and opinions known to others. In order to maintain relationships, you must also understand the messages that are sent to you. When conflicts arise, your speaking and listening skills go into action to allow you to reach the best possible solutions.

Figure 9.1

Types of Communication

How many types of communication can you find in this scene?

Verbal Communication means *using words to express yourself, either in speaking or in writing.*

Nonverbal Communication includes *all the ways in which you can get a message across without using words.* The most common form of nonverbal communication is body language. **Body Language** includes *posture, gestures, and facial expressions.*

Communicating Through Colors

ACTIVITY!

Russian artist Wassily Kandinsky (1866-1944) assigned feelings to certain colors in his paintings. To Kandinsky, orange meant health, green meant happiness, red meant the presence of strong feelings, and gray meant sadness. Use paints or markers in colors of your own choice to make a drawing that nonverbally communicates a thought or feeling.

Expressing Yourself Clearly

With the words you speak, you can share your likes and dislikes, your interests, and your hopes for the future. In addition, you can express the care and consideration you feel for the people in your life. Here are a few tips for expressing yourself clearly.

■ Think before you speak. A few seconds of thought can make it much easier to find the right words.

■ Be direct, but avoid being rude or insulting.

■ Control your tone of voice. In most cases, a friendly and polite tone will encourage a listener to pay attention.

■ Avoid speaking too quickly or too slowly.

■ Make eye contact, and use gestures as needed to clarify your meaning.

■ Let your listener respond. Then you will see what you need to make clearer.

■ Use "I" messages. An "I" message keeps the focus on your own thoughts and feelings instead of blaming or criticizing someone else. For example, saying "You're wrong!" may make your listener feel defensive and can lead to an argument. Saying "I disagree because. . ." makes your opinions clear without starting an argument.

Although honesty is important, expressing your exact feelings may at times hurt other people. Therefore, it is crucial to use **tact**—*the quality of knowing what to say to avoid offending others.* Tact is essential in developing mature relationships. Ask yourself: *Would I be hurt if someone said this to me?* If the answer is yes, find another way to make your point.

LIFE SKILLS

Giving and Taking Criticism

*C*riticism—both receiving it and giving it—is a part of daily life. Criticism can be helpful, revealing weaknesses in a plan or a way of behaving. However, criticism can also make a person feel foolish. Whether criticism has a positive or a negative effect depends on how it is given and how it is received. Follow these tips when you give and take criticism.

When Giving Criticism

► **Choose the right time and place.** Be considerate of the other person's feelings. Don't criticize anyone in front of other people.

► **Don't criticize actions that can't be changed.** Saying "You should never have said that about Elise" doesn't change what has been done. It would be more helpful to say "Elise is pretty upset. Do you think you should call her and explain what you meant when you said . . . ?"

► **Be as positive as possible.** Praise the good before pointing out problems. For example, "I like your plan for getting a sponsor for the team. A couple of us have some ideas, too. In future meetings, we'd also like the chance to present other plans and discuss them."

► **Be specific and helpful.** Saying to a teammate "You let us down" provides only negative information. Instead, you might say "I know it's tough to shoot free throws. Do you want me to show you how I learned to do it?"

Listening to Others

You are an essential part of a conversation even when you are not speaking. Listening should be an active process in which your thoughts and feelings become involved in what someone else is saying. In fact, skilled listening can actually help you to express your own thoughts and feelings more clearly.

Effective listeners try to understand not only what people are saying but also what they are feeling. **Empathy,** *the ability to identify and share another person's feelings,* is a crucial part of effective communication. You will need to pay attention both to what a speaker says and to the way he or she says it. A speaker's facial expression, gestures, and tone of voice will help you identify the feelings behind the message. Effective listeners also let the speaker know they are listening with techniques like these.

- Look at the speaker when he or she is talking.

- Use appropriate facial expressions or gestures, or nod your head to show that you are listening.

- Avoid interrupting the speaker, but ask questions when they are appropriate.

- Don't jump to conclusions. Keep an open mind about what the speaker is saying.

What is this teen doing to show that he is actively listening?

When Receiving Criticism

▶ **Consider why the person is criticizing you.** Someone who risks criticizing you is often someone who also cares about you. Use this knowledge to keep the criticism in perspective.

▶ **Focus on the message.** Your critic is trying to help you improve. Remember that it is your performance on a task or your behavior, not you as a person, that is being criticized.

▶ **Don't let someone else's poor communication skills cause conflict.** Even helpful messages can be delivered badly. When people are nervous or upset, they may communicate poorly. If you don't understand what the person is trying to tell you, ask for clarification.

▶ **Evaluate the message.** Listen carefully to the message and be as objective as possible. Is the criticism helpful? Is some part of it helpful? If the criticism is not helpful, ignore it—then try to forget about it.

Follow-up Activity

Perform a skit with several other students. The skit should show how criticism could be given or received for a positive result. In your skit, describe a scene in which someone is criticizing a friend's health habit, such as smoking or skipping meals. The skit should show both helpful criticism and its positive results.

in Your Journal

Write a summary of a situation in which you and a friend, or you and a sibling, compromised to solve a disagreement. Do you feel that the compromise was successful? Explain your answer.

Knowing When to Compromise

People put speaking and listening skills to work every day in solving disagreements. Some disagreements, however, can be solved only by **compromise,** *a method in which each person gives up something in order to reach a solution that satisfies everyone.* Compromise is the give-and-take at the heart of healthy and mature relationships.

It is important to know the difference between situations that require compromise and those in which you should stand your ground and say no. Never compromise your deepest values; your sense of right and wrong; or the rules of your parents, school, and community. You will, however, need to make compromises in everyday situations in which you and a family member or friend disagree on common, nonthreatening matters. For example, you can easily compromise on which movie to see or who plays a game first.

Compromise can solve many everyday conflicts. What do you think these teens are disagreeing about? What compromise would you suggest to them?

Lesson 1

Review

Using complete sentences, answer the following questions on a separate sheet of paper.

Reviewing Terms and Facts

1. **Vocabulary** Define *tact,* and give an example of how a person might display this quality.
2. **List** Identify five tips for communicating effectively.
3. **Restate** Define *empathy,* and use the word in an original sentence.

Thinking Critically

4. **Apply** Give at least three examples of body language, and explain the message each might send.

5. **Compare and Contrast** Give three examples of situations in which a person could safely compromise and three in which a person should stand her or his ground.

Applying Health Concepts

6. **Personal Health** With a small group of classmates, write and perform a skit that illustrates effective or ineffective communication skills. Make the situation as realistic as possible, involving a familiar issue that might arise between friends or family members.

Friendships and Peer Pressure

This lesson will help you find answers to questions that teens often ask about their relationships with friends. For example:

► **What are the qualities of a good friend?**
► **What is peer pressure?**
► **How can I deal with negative peer pressure?**

The Importance of Friends

Everyone forms relationships with people beyond her or his own family. As social experience grows, people form **friendships,** *relationships between people who like each other and who have similar interests and values.* Friends become especially important during the teen years. A circle of friends adds to the enjoyment of life and plays a major role in physical, mental/emotional, and social health.

Friendships usually develop over time, based on shared experiences, values, and goals. The old saying, "To have a friend you must be a friend," still holds true. Friendship grows out of each person's willingness to reach out to the other person, to listen, support, and care, in order to create a healthy, growing relationship.

Good friends are a reliable source of companionship, shared fun, and mutual support.

Words to Know

friendship
peers
peer pressure

Did You Know?

Something to Say

A friend who needs you to listen may not know how to begin. Watch for clues that a person is having a problem, such as

► questions like "Are you busy right now?"
► being unusually quiet.
► a drop in grades.
► irritation or a quick temper.
► any behavior that is abnormal for this person.

With a partner, role-play a scene in which someone discovers that a friend needs to talk about a problem. Make the dialogue as natural as possible, and have the friends display an honest desire to communicate and to listen.

What Is a Good Friend?

A friend is much more than an acquaintance, someone you see occasionally or know casually. Your relationship with a friend is deeper and means more to you. Although there is no accepted test for friendship, most people you call friends will have the following qualities:

■ **Sympathy and empathy.** True friends understand how you feel. In fact, close friends even identify with strong feelings such as joy, sadness, or disappointment. They appreciate your talents and strengths and help you overcome your weaknesses.

■ **Loyalty.** True friends remain on your side and don't desert you, even when the going gets tough. They are available to you when you need support.

■ **Reliability.** A true friend is someone you can depend on to keep promises and to live up to realistic expectations. You feel confident that your true friends will make sacrifices for you.

■ **Shared values.** True friends will not ask you to do things that are wrong or dangerous. They respect your beliefs and help you hold true to your values.

Personal Inventory

ARE YOU A GOOD FRIEND?

To have good friends, you must be willing to be a good friend. Use this self-assessment form to examine the qualities that make you a true friend. On a separate sheet of paper, write yes or no to tell whether each statement describes you.

1. I do what I can to be a positive influence and help my friends to make healthy decisions.

2. I listen carefully when my friends want to talk about serious issues or problems.

3. My friends know that they can trust me to keep promises and secrets.

4. I respect my friends' right to have opinions that are opposed to mine.

5. I am willing to compromise if my friends and I disagree, but my friends know that I won't compromise my values.

6. I recognize my friends' strengths and talents and tell my friends about them.

7. I accept my friends' feelings, even if they are different from mine.

8. My friends know that I will accept their weaknesses, but that I will also try to help them overcome them.

9. I am honest with my friends.

10. I am loyal to my friends.

Give yourself 1 point for each yes. A score of 9–10 is very good, 7–8 is good, and 5–6 is fair. If you scored 0–4, you need to brush up on your friendship skills.

Recognizing Peer Pressure

As you move through the teen years, your relationships with your **peers**—*people close to your age who are similar to you in many ways*—become more and more important. What your peers think of you, how they react to you, and how they accept you can affect your decisions about how you should act and think. This *influence that your friends have on you to believe and act like them* is called **peer pressure.** Peer pressure can be either positive or negative, as **Figure 9.5** shows.

in your journal

List at least two examples of positive peer pressure that you have experienced. Then select one example and describe how the peer pressure helped you grow as an individual.

Figure 9.5
Positive and Negative Peer Pressure

There are two types of peer pressure: positive and negative.

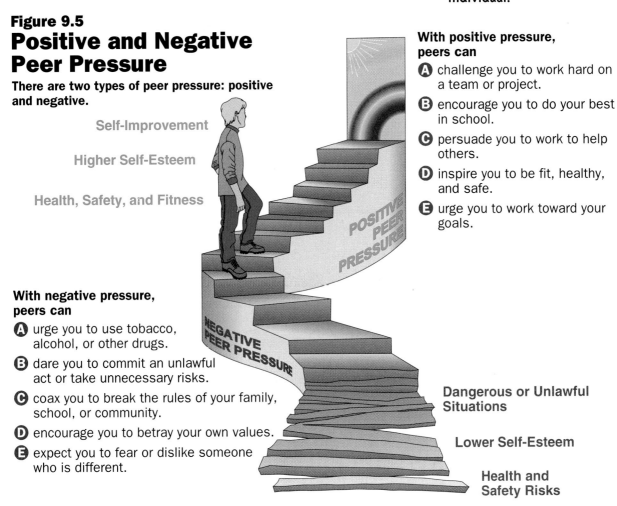

Self-Improvement

Higher Self-Esteem

Health, Safety, and Fitness

POSITIVE PEER PRESSURE

NEGATIVE PEER PRESSURE

With positive pressure, peers can

A challenge you to work hard on a team or project.

B encourage you to do your best in school.

C persuade you to work to help others.

D inspire you to be fit, healthy, and safe.

E urge you to work toward your goals.

With negative pressure, peers can

A urge you to use tobacco, alcohol, or other drugs.

B dare you to commit an unlawful act or take unnecessary risks.

C coax you to break the rules of your family, school, or community.

D encourage you to betray your own values.

E expect you to fear or dislike someone who is different.

Dangerous or Unlawful Situations

Lower Self-Esteem

Health and Safety Risks

Handling Negative Peer Pressure

Standing up for what you know is right can be difficult, particularly when friends are very persuasive. After all, everyone wants to be liked and accepted. You may worry that if you don't go along with your peers, you will be unpopular, or people will laugh at you.

As a teen, however, you have developed the ability to think for yourself. Unlike a small child, you make many of your own decisions. As you become more independent, you gain more strength as an individual. You can use that strength to resist negative peer pressure. **Figure 9.6** on the following page provides some practical tips for handling negative peer pressure.

Figure 9.6
Standing Up to Negative Peer Pressure
Here are some ways to handle several types of negative peer pressure situations.

Types of Situations	What to Do
Situations that have a strong potential for danger. For example, a friend asks you to go to an unsupervised party, or someone who has been drinking alcohol offers to drive you home.	**Say no.** You don't have to defend your position. If, however, you *want* to say more, state your reasons clearly. If possible, suggest an alternative plan that is safer, or join forces with another peer who agrees with you.
Situations that are clearly unsafe or illegal. For example, a peer urges you to play a dangerous practical joke on someone or to shoplift.	**Rely on your values.** If the situation is dangerous, point out what might happen. If the situation involves breaking the law, say that you don't want to do something illegal.
Situations in which compromise is clearly inappropriate. For example, someone offers you a cigarette. When you refuse, he or she says, "Oh, come on. Just take one little puff. It won't hurt you."	**Stand your ground.** Be firm, and don't compromise. If the person won't take no for an answer, make up an excuse, change the subject, or simply walk away.
Situations in which your refusal leads a peer to make fun of you. For example, you refuse to go swimming in an unsafe place, and a peer says, "What are you, a baby?"	**Focus on the issue.** Tell the other person why you are saying no. Don't exchange insults, however.
Situations in which your refusal causes a peer to get angry or abusive. For example, you refuse to go along with a peer's hurtful verbal abuse of someone. The peer then turns on you and begins insulting you, too.	**Walk away.** The most dangerous kind of negative peer pressure involves threats or other forms of abuse. Don't let yourself be hurt by a bully. Report abuse to a parent, teacher, counselor, or other trusted adult. Then avoid contact with the abusive peer.

MAKING HEALTHY DECISIONS
Facing Peer Pressure

*J*ulie is looking at the items displayed in a downtown store window when she notices Marcie and Tina, two of her friends, at the counter inside. Marcie and Tina don't see Julie. In fact, they think that no one is watching them as they slip several pairs of earrings into their pockets. As they turn to leave the store, they spot Julie. They realize from the look on her face that she has seen them shoplifting.

Marcie and Tina continue out of the store and walk over to Julie. After greeting her, they whisper: "Want some free earrings? It's easy to take the ones on

that counter. They never watch at this store. Take a few. They'll never miss them."

Julie feels very uncomfortable. When she doesn't respond, Marcie and Tina just look at each other, laughing, and walk away.

Later that night, Julie is thinking about the incident. She knows that she would never shoplift, but she has to think about what to do the next time she sees her friends. She tries the six-step decision-making process.

Using complete sentences, answer the following questions on a separate sheet of paper.

Reviewing Terms and Facts

1. **Vocabulary** Define the terms *friendship* and *peers*.

2. **List** Identify three qualities of a true friend, and provide an example of each quality.

3. **Describe** Explain the difference between the two types of peer pressure. Support your description by providing one example of each.

Thinking Critically

4. **Compare and Contrast** Explain what makes some people your friends and some just acquaintances. How are they alike? How are they different?

5. **Hypothesize** How might one teen who resists negative peer pressure be helpful to other teens? Support your response with a specific example.

Applying Health Concepts

6. **Health of Others** Make a poster explaining to young children the qualities to look for in a true friend and how to *be* a true friend. Be sure to use language and examples that younger children will be able to understand.

① **State the situation**
② **List the options**
③ **Weigh the possible outcomes**
④ **Consider your values**
⑤ **Make a decision and act**
⑥ **Evaluate the decision**

Follow-up Activities

1. Apply the six steps of the decision-making process to Julie's situation.

2. Role-play the scene that takes place as Julie meets her friends the next time.

3. In small groups, discuss options that Julie might choose. What would you have done in her situation? Do you think that she has a responsibility to talk with the store owner? Explain your answer.

Abstinence and Refusal Skills

This lesson will help you find answers to questions that teens often ask about protecting themselves from dangerous situations. For example:

▶ Why should I avoid high-risk activities and situations?

▶ How can I make good choices?

▶ What should I say and do if someone pressures me to engage in risk behaviors?

Word to Know

abstinence

Acting Responsibly

Parents establish rules in order to protect and guide their children. As you grow up, an important part of becoming responsible is to accept the task of protecting and guiding yourself. You can make wise choices and decisions right now that will protect your health and happiness in the years ahead.

The teen years are very challenging. You and your peers are no longer young children—you are adolescents. You may feel like travelers crossing an ocean to a new country. You are naturally eager to get to that new country, adulthood, as quickly as possible. You feel that you are becoming ready to make your own decisions, set your own rules, and be responsible for your own actions.

Avoiding Risk Behaviors

When you were a small child, you learned to avoid certain risk behaviors—not to run out into the street and not to accept rides from strangers, for example. Now your world has become larger and more complex than it was when you were younger. Teens make decisions about many issues, including the use of alcohol and tobacco and whether they will engage in sexual activity.

It is important to keep a balanced outlook—positive but cautious, confident but careful. Be honest with yourself. Consider the consequences of your actions, and protect yourself. Why take chances with all that you have going for you?

In your teen years you have more freedom and more responsibility.

What Is Abstinence?

In today's world, the pressures on teens to engage in risk behaviors can come from peers, from adult role models, from advertising, from movies and television, and from many other sources. In obvious ways and not-so-obvious ways, teens are urged to take risks, to experiment, to engage in activities that make them seem more mature. Many of these activities are very dangerous.

Refusing to participate in unsafe behaviors or activities is called **abstinence.** To abstain means to say no to sexual activity before marriage, to the use of tobacco, alcohol, and drugs, and to other risk behaviors. Abstinence is the only sure way to protect yourself against the potentially dangerous consequences of risk behaviors.

Figure 9.7 lists some of the ways in which abstinence can help you stay physically, emotionally, and socially healthy.

Figure 9.7
Practicing Abstinence
Abstaining from certain behaviors can save your life.

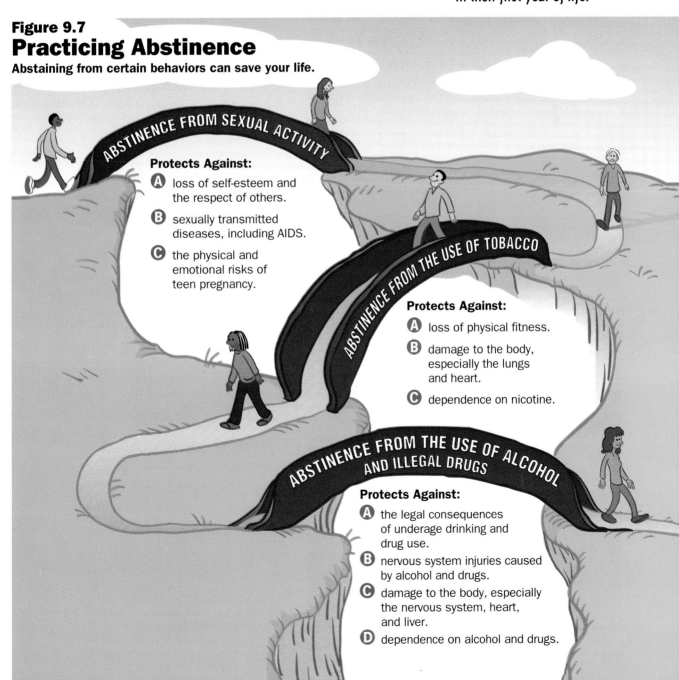

ABSTINENCE FROM SEXUAL ACTIVITY

Protects Against:

Ⓐ loss of self-esteem and the respect of others.

Ⓑ sexually transmitted diseases, including AIDS.

Ⓒ the physical and emotional risks of teen pregnancy.

ABSTINENCE FROM THE USE OF TOBACCO

Protects Against:

Ⓐ loss of physical fitness.

Ⓑ damage to the body, especially the lungs and heart.

Ⓒ dependence on nicotine.

ABSTINENCE FROM THE USE OF ALCOHOL AND ILLEGAL DRUGS

Protects Against:

Ⓐ the legal consequences of underage drinking and drug use.

Ⓑ nervous system injuries caused by alcohol and drugs.

Ⓒ damage to the body, especially the nervous system, heart, and liver.

Ⓓ dependence on alcohol and drugs.

Effective Refusal Skills

Standing up to negative peer pressure requires the confidence and strength to say no. You learned how to use some specific refusal skills—ways to say no effectively—in Lesson 3 as you looked at negative peer pressure situations. Like other skills, refusal skills take time and commitment to develop. Refusal skills involve being honest and polite, but also being firm. The tips below will help you develop and use refusal skills effectively.

■ **Choose your friends carefully.** Sometimes teens take dangerous risks in order to be accepted by a group or to become popular. True friends, however, won't pressure you to put your health or your life at risk. Instead, they'll look out for your welfare, and they'll rely on you to help keep them safe, too.

■ **Choose your situations carefully.** Avoid situations in which you might be pressured to engage in risk behaviors. A party at which you know there will not be adult supervision is an example of a dangerous situation. Evaluate every situation carefully. Does it sound dangerous? Suspicious? Just plain wrong? Say no.

■ **Talk to adults you trust.** Parents, teachers, and other trusted adults *want* you to be happy. They also want you to be healthy and safe. They understand that you are no longer a small child, and that you have developed many decision-making skills. They also know, however, that their knowledge and experience can be helpful. If you're under pressure and don't know what to do, get some good advice.

■ **Look to the future.** Always try to focus on what you want and need to do to fulfill your goals. Don't jeopardize your future freedom, independence, and success by taking a dangerous action today.

■ **Be prepared to leave a situation—or end a relationship—if the pressure becomes too strong.** If someone threatens you or urges you to do something that makes you uncomfortable, walk away. Walking away may be difficult, but getting into a high-risk situation could be far worse. Protect your pride and self-esteem by giving reasons for your refusal. The tips in **Figure 9.8** on the following page may help.

It takes courage to refuse pressure from friends to engage in a risk behavior.

Figure 9.8
Pressure Statements and Possible Responses

On the left are some common statements peers may use to persuade you to engage in risk behaviors. On the right are possible responses you might make. Can you think of others?

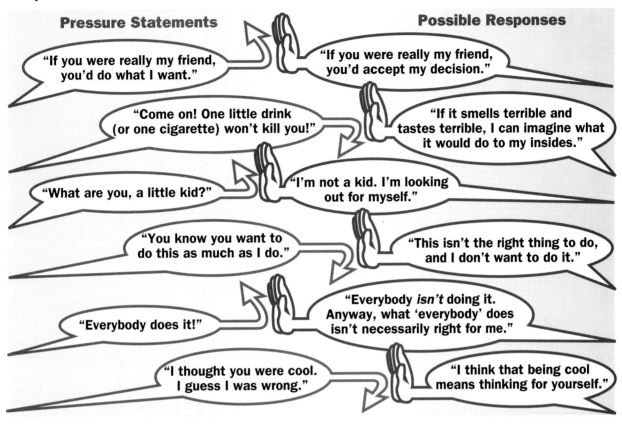

Pressure Statements

"If you were really my friend, you'd do what I want."

"Come on! One little drink (or one cigarette) won't kill you!"

"What are you, a little kid?"

"You know you want to do this as much as I do."

"Everybody does it!"

"I thought you were cool. I guess I was wrong."

Possible Responses

"If you were really my friend, you'd accept my decision."

"If it smells terrible and tastes terrible, I can imagine what it would do to my insides."

"I'm not a kid. I'm looking out for myself."

"This isn't the right thing to do, and I don't want to do it."

"Everybody *isn't* doing it. Anyway, what 'everybody' does isn't necessarily right for me."

"I think that being cool means thinking for yourself."

Review

Lesson
4

Using complete sentences, answer the following questions on a separate sheet of paper.

Reviewing Terms and Facts

1. **Vocabulary**   Define *abstinence,* and explain why it is the most effective way to avoid risk behaviors.

2. **List**   What serious problems can a teen avoid by abstaining from drugs and alcohol?

3. **Identify**   List five tips that will help teens avoid risk behaviors.

Thinking Critically

4. **Infer**   How can choosing your friends carefully help you avoid risk behaviors? Explain your answer.

5. **Apply**   Give an example of a risk behavior that a teen might engage in that could have long-term negative effects.

Applying Health Concepts

6. **Health of Others**   With a small group, present a panel discussion about the effectiveness of refusal skills in avoiding risk behaviors or unsafe activities. You might open the discussion with the question: "How well do refusal skills work?"

TEEN HEALTH DIGEST

Sports and Recreation
Big-Time Players, Lifetime Friends

Hockey stars Mark Messier and Wayne Gretzky have known each other since childhood and have been best friends for 20 years. They have also been able to play as teammates for some of that time.

From 1980 to 1987, Mess and Gretz, as they are called by their teammates, played for the Edmonton Oilers and led the team to four Stanley Cup victories. Then Messier moved to the New York Rangers and Gretzky to the Los Angeles Kings. In 1996, when Gretzky had the chance to play for the Rangers, both men were pleased. Unfortunately, they were able to play together for only one year. In 1997 Messier joined the Vancouver Canucks. Trying to see the bright side, Messier pointed out that at least he would be in a different conference—not in danger of opposing his friend on the ice.

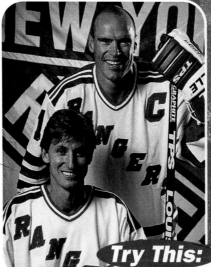

HEALTH UPDATE
New Phones for the Hearing Impaired

Technology can have a great impact on the ways in which people communicate. In the 1970s, scientists developed special phones called TDDs—telecommunication devices for the deaf. Each TDD displayed conversations line by line, much like today's Internet conversations. TDDs were not portable, however, and they could transmit messages only from one TDD to another.

In 1996 a marketing manager named Mark Elderkin developed a device that makes communication easier—a cellular phone for the deaf. Consisting of a tiny modem and a portable computer the size of a small book, the phone is easy to carry and can transmit calls to and from anyone with a computer and modem. A battery allows the computer to stay switched on at all times—just like a regular telephone.

Try This: What are the advantages of teammates being friends? What challenges might friends face as teammates? Write a short paragraph explaining your ideas.

People at Work

A Therapist for Children

Psychologist Becky Talmadge is a therapist for foster children at Foster Care Connection, an agency in Colorado. Becky's clients, who range in age from 4 to 17, have all been separated from their parents because of severe abuse or neglect.

Talmadge explains that the goal of therapy is to make children feel listened to and safe. "It's impossible to undo what abused or neglected children have been through," Becky says, "but we can help them to learn to cope and to develop skills that will help them protect themselves."

Becky first became interested in this type of work as a teen. In high school she worked as a peer mediator. After four years of college, she went on to get a master's degree in psychology.

To be a therapist, Becky says, "You must have empathy. You must be patient, too. These kids have been through such crises that their progress is often in baby steps."

Try This: *Make a list of activities or volunteer jobs a teen might get involved in to prepare for a career like Talmadge's.*

Teens Making a Difference

A Friend in Need

While working on her paper route, 15-year-old Rachael Nadeau of Connecticut made friends with a 92-year-old customer. Upon reaching her friend's house one day, however, Rachael noticed that newspapers had begun to pile up out front. When she knocked on the door and got no response, Rachael went home and tried to reach the woman by phone. When that failed, Rachael went back to the house. Peering through a window, she saw her friend lying on the floor. Rachael called 911. The woman had fallen two days earlier and had not been able to get up by herself. Rachael's friendly concern probably saved the woman's life.

Myths and Realities

The Family Balancing Act

Teens are old enough to share in family responsibilities. Parents who are both bringing in paychecks need to stay flexible and keep lines of communication open. Here are some tips for success offered by families in this situation.

- **Communicate.** Everybody needs to know what needs to be done during a particular day or week and who is available to help.

- **Do your share.** Helping your family with household chores will make the day run more smoothly. For example, you could prepare part of the evening meal, sort laundry, or vacuum your bedroom.
- **Make time for the family.** Some families select one or two nights each week to spend together. This aids communication and also strengthens relationships.

Resolving Conflicts at Home and at School

This lesson will help you find answers to questions that teens often ask about conflict resolution. For example:

▶ How can I recognize when a situation may be building toward a conflict?

▶ How can I stop a conflict before it gets serious?

▶ How can I help others avoid conflicts?

Words to Know

conflict
prejudice
nonviolent
    confrontation
neutrality
mediation
negotiation

Teen Issues

Fight Stoppers

If one approach fails to stop a disagreement, try another.

▶ Do something creative and unexpected. For example, write a friendly note on a lunch bag.

▶ Offer the other person a way out of the conflict by proposing a truce or a compromise.

▶ Apologize for your part in the conflict.

Conflicts are a natural part of life. The way you handle them, however, determines whether or not you learn from them.

How Conflicts Begin

A **conflict** is *a disagreement between people with opposing viewpoints.* Conflicts occur for all kinds of reasons. For example, your brother borrows your baseball mitt without asking first. A teen accuses a classmate of stealing her athletic shoes.

Sometimes the reason for a conflict may seem unimportant. Even so, a small quarrel may result in a nasty, even deadly, fight. When fights occur, it is usually because the people involved do not know healthy ways to settle their differences. Disagreements do not have to end in violence. In this lesson, we will examine causes of fights and nonviolent ways to deal with conflicts.

This is my sweater. I told you not to go in my closet!

I didn't have anything to wear!

Arguments

Arguments occur when people are not communicating well or when they are disrespectful of one another. When arguments get out of hand, fights may result. Here are some of the most common reasons for teen arguments:

- **Property.** Teens may not respect one another's property. They may use items that belong to someone else without getting permission ahead of time.

- **Jealousy.** Young people may feel jealous when they are not included in certain activities, or when a boyfriend or girlfriend pays attention to someone else.

- **Territory.** Teens may not want others to cross the boundaries that make up their neighborhood.

- **Values.** Teens may refuse to do something that goes against their values, such as lying, cheating, or stealing.

Hurt Pride

Sometimes fights begin because someone's pride has been hurt. A teen may do something hurtful such as insult a member of someone else's family, spread a rumor, or ridicule another in public. Often the injured party feels hurt or angry and responds by fighting back.

Peer Pressure

Fights also begin when teens encourage others to "fight it out." They may stand on the sidelines, heckling and cheering the fighters. This behavior only worsens the situation. Once a crowd has gathered, the chances for settling the problem peacefully decrease greatly.

Revenge

One mean act or insult can start a chain of events in which the victim wants to get even. He or she may recruit family or friends to get involved in the conflict. As the need for revenge grows, the fighting may become more intense and more dangerous.

Acts of revenge are common among rival gangs when one of their own members has been harmed. Because gangs frequently use weapons, a minor misunderstanding can result in violence, such as a stabbing or a shoot-out.

Prejudice

Sometimes people refuse to accept others who are different from them. Their feelings may be based on **prejudice** (PRE·juh·dis), *a negative and unjustly formed opinion, usually against people of a different racial, religious, or cultural group.*

People who are prejudiced may single out a person and harass, intimidate, or threaten him or her. That person, in turn, may strike back, either alone or with supporters. As a result, fights or even gang warfare may occur.

Art Connection

Peace Mural

 ACTIVITY!

A mural is a scene painted on a very large space such as the side of a building. Get a large roll of paper and some friends to help. Work together to create a mural of peace, showing many different kinds of people cooperating or having fun. Ask for permission to display your mural at school.

Teen Issues

An Eye for an Eye

In ancient times, the law often required revenge—"an eye for an eye." Today revenge is discouraged. Instead, a show of respect to someone during a nonviolent confrontation increases the chances that a resolution will be reached and that no one will be injured. Remember to choose your words carefully, and look the other person in the eye. This will let him or her know that you are paying attention and showing respect.

Preventing Conflicts

It is not always easy to avoid conflicts, but it is possible. Like a balloon that is inflated too much, anger can build up inside you until the pressure makes it explode. However, you can learn healthy ways to keep conflicts from reaching the explosion stage. The best way to prevent problems is to recognize conflict early, control your anger, and ignore some conflicts. When you are unable to avoid a conflict, nonviolent methods can help you resolve the problem in a peaceful way.

Recognize Conflict Early

There are usually signs that a problem exists. For example, there may be name-calling, insults, threats, or shoves. The key to preventing fights is to recognize the signs early and deal with them before they reach the danger stage. It is easier to resolve a conflict peacefully when you are still in control of your emotions.

HEALTH LAB

Mediating a Conflict

*I*ntroduction: In some schools, when students have a conflict they cannot resolve on their own, they sign up to meet with a student mediator, or a neutral third person. Usually adults are not present at this meeting. The mediator takes the students through the following steps to resolve the conflict.

1. Emphasize neutrality, and assure the participants that everyone will cooperate to reach a satisfactory solution.

2. Set guidelines for the meeting. For example, there should be no name-calling, insults, swearing, or interrupting.

3. Allow each person to give her or his side of the situation without interruptions. A mediator should listen carefully but does not react. Ask people to repeat or clarify their points when necessary.

4. Help the participants brainstorm solutions that will feel right to both sides.

5. Have both sides promise to abide by the agreement.

Objective: During the next week, observe conflicts around you that would benefit from mediation. Consider examples of these conflicts in your own family, among your friends, or in the news.

Control Your Anger

The first step in managing your anger is recognizing its early signs so you can stay in control. The body usually reacts to anger with physical changes such as increased heart rate and breathing, sweaty palms, flushed face, stuttering, or a high-pitched voice. By being alert for these signs, you can try to resolve the conflict peacefully or ignore it altogether.

To manage your anger, find a way to relieve pent-up feelings that works for you. Some suggestions follow.

- Walk, jog, swim, or shoot some baskets.
- Listen to quiet music.
- Take a long bath or shower.
- Pound a pillow.
- Talk it out with a good friend.
- Have a good cry.
- Sit quietly for half an hour or so.

If, however, you feel really angry, find someone such as a school counselor or health care professional who can help you sort it out.

Ignore Some Conflicts

Some issues are not worth your time and effort. For instance, if the other person is a stranger or someone you will never see again, it is probably best just to walk away. If the other person is someone you care about, you need to communicate your feelings in a calm and reasonable manner.

Materials and Method: You will need one 3-by-5-inch card for each conflict you are observing and a long strip of paper. On each card, write *Observations* on one side and *Analysis* on the other. On the *Observations* side, write the facts—the words, gestures, facial expressions, and actions of the people you are observing. On the *Analysis* side, write how these behaviors make it more or less likely that the conflict will be resolved. Select one of the cards, and imagine that you are the mediator in that conflict. Divide the strip of paper into frames, and create a mediation cartoon for this conflict. In a series of drawings with dialogue in cartoon balloons, take the argument through the mediation process.

Observations and Analysis: At the end of the week, share your observations, analyses, and cartoon with your classmates. Find out what other solutions they might suggest.

Q: My brother is having a big feud with another guy at school. They always fight in the locker room. Things are really heating up. Now my brother wants me to back him up when they meet after school to fight it out. What should I do?

A: Don't get caught in the middle of someone else's battle, even your brother's. Tell him that fighting will only make it worse. Urge him to talk with a peer counselor or mediator at school. Suggest that he use some of the skills you've learned for nonviolent confrontation.

Use Nonviolent Confrontation

Nonviolent confrontation means *resolving your conflict by peaceful methods*. In nonviolent confrontation, you settle matters without angry words or looks, threats, punches, or weapons. The benefit of nonviolent confrontation is that the argument is likely to be settled so that both parties are satisfied. See **Figure 9.9** and try some of the following guidelines.

- Carefully plan what to say, stay calm, and stick to the subject.
- Pick the right time and place.
- Talk to the other person when he or she is alone.
- Be a good listener; do not interrupt.
- Be sensitive to body language, or any nonverbal communication.
- Be positive; avoid insults, blame, sarcasm, accusations, and threats.
- Be willing to compromise.
- Leave the area if there is a weapon present.

Helping Others Avoid Fights

Friends can help one another to avoid fights by showing disapproval of fighting. For instance, they can refuse to spread rumors, and they can ignore people who talk badly about others. Advising your friends to act in these ways can help them stay safe.

When people you know and care about are starting to argue, you can help without getting hurt. You can assist by sharing what you know about neutrality, mediation, and negotiation.

Figure 9.9
Two Approaches to Conflict

Look at the pictures on this page and the next one. The teens are reacting differently in each picture. Why does one response promote settling the conflict while the other makes it worse?

- **Neutrality** (noo·TRA·luh·tee) is *not taking sides when others are arguing.* Avoid fights and urge others to do the same.

- **Mediation** (mee·dee·AY·shuhn) is *resolving conflicts by using a neutral person to help reach a solution that is acceptable to both sides.* Many people use mediation to resolve disagreements.

- **Negotiation** (ni·goh·shee·AY·shuhn) is *the process of discussing problems face-to-face in order to reach a solution.* Negotiation involves talking, listening, considering the other point of view, and compromising.

Toward a Win-Win World

People often think of situations in terms of winning and losing. In relationships, win-lose thinking can leave people feeling angry or cheated.

Mediation is a way to turn a win-lose situation into a win-win situation. Many families, schools, and communities are using mediation as a way to prevent violence. When people resolve their differences peacefully, both sides, as well as society, benefit.

in your journal

Think of a recent argument you had at home or at school. Take the conflict through the mediation steps presented in this lesson. How might the conflict have been resolved? Write your answer in your private journal.

Review   Lesson 5

Using complete sentences, answer the following questions on a separate sheet of paper.

Reviewing Terms and Facts

1. **Give Examples**   List three causes of conflicts.

2. **Vocabulary**   Compare and contrast the following terms: *neutrality, negotiation.*

Thinking Critically

3. **Suggest**   How can you manage your anger before it gets out of control?

4. **Recall**   How does *mediation* result in a positive outcome for all people involved in a conflict?

Applying Health Concepts

5. **Health of Others**   Do some research on Mohandas Gandhi and Martin Luther King, Jr., and their commitment to non-violence. Share your findings in class.

6. **Personal Health**   List your own signs and symptoms of anger, and decide at what point you are likely to use poor judgment. What do you need to do before you reach this point of anger?

In a hurry? Sure, you can go ahead of me.

Chapter 9 Review

Chapter Summary

▶ **Lesson 1** Communication is the exchange of thoughts, feelings, and beliefs. Effective verbal and nonverbal communication skills help people express themselves clearly and listen actively to others.

▶ **Lesson 2** Families nurture their members by meeting physical, emotional, mental/intellectual, and social needs, and by sharing values.

▶ **Lesson 3** Friends become especially important in the teen years. True friends display sympathy, empathy, loyalty, and reliability, and usually share similar values. Peers can exert both positive and negative peer pressure.

▶ **Lesson 4** Abstinence is the only sure way to protect yourself from the results of risk behaviors, such as engaging in sexual activity and using tobacco, alcohol, or other drugs.

▶ **Lesson 5** Conflicts can be resolved through neutrality, mediation, or negotiation.

Reviewing Key Terms and Concepts

Using complete sentences, answer the following questions on a separate sheet of paper.

Lesson 1

1. Define *communication,* and identify the two basic types.

2. What does it mean to *compromise?*

Lesson 2

3. Define the term *family.* Then describe a blended family and an extended family.

4. Explain how a family can meet its members' physical and emotional needs.

Lesson 3

5. Define *peer pressure.* Then explain how it can be either negative or positive.

6. Why is compromise a poor way to handle negative peer pressure?

Lesson 4

7. List three sources of pressure for teens to engage in risk behaviors.

8. What problems can a teen avoid by abstaining from tobacco?

Lesson 5

9. Define the term *prejudice,* and explain how prejudice can cause a conflict.

10. What is the benefit of nonviolent confrontation?

Thinking Critically

Using complete sentences, answer the following questions on a separate sheet of paper.

11. **Explain** How might a person use good communication to strengthen relationships?

12. **Compare** How are your relationships with family members like your relationships with your friends? In what ways are they different?

13. **Compose** Create a list of three pressure statements (in addition to those provided in the text) and an effective response to each.

14. **Predict** How might poor communication skills lead to conflict?

Your Action Plan

Throughout this chapter you have reflected on your relationships with family members and friends. You have also examined ways to resolve conflicts. You can apply what you have learned in your everyday life.

Step 1 Review your journal entries from this chapter. Think about the communication skills that are your strongest. Then think about the areas in which you might want to strengthen your skills.

Step 2 Summarize your thinking in a two-column chart. Use the chart to set a long-term goal. For example, you might want to get into fewer conflicts.

Step 3 Having decided on a long-term goal, set some short-term goals that will help you reach it. Examples of short-term goals might be finding ways to relieve stress and walking away when a situation is getting out of hand.

Write a contract with yourself in which you commit to reaching your long-term goal in a specific length of time. Decide which of your skills will help you in reaching your long-term goal. Your reward for reaching your goal will be closer, happier relationships with family and friends.

In Your Home and Community

1. **Personal Health** For one week, concentrate on communicating effectively with each member of your family. After the week has passed, write a paragraph that describes the positive results of your improved communication.

2. **Community Resources** Search out groups in your community that work to strengthen families and family relationships. What techniques do they use to help and encourage families? Write a short report on what you have found out.

Building Your Portfolio

1. **News Analysis** Find one or more articles in newspapers and magazines about a conflict between political opponents, workers and managers, or athletes and team owners. Report on how negotiation was used in resolving the conflict. If negotiations did not resolve the conflict, suggest a possible solution.

2. **Short Story** Write a short story in which a teen effectively uses refusal skills to stand up to negative pressure. Remember that pressure can come from anyone. Make the situation and dialogue as realistic as possible.

3. **Personal Assessment** Look through all the activities and projects you did for this chapter. Choose one or two that you would like to include in your portfolio.

Unit 4
Protecting Your Health

Tobacco

Student Expectations

After reading this chapter, you should be able to:

1. Identify the harmful effects of tobacco on the body.
2. Describe how your respiratory system works and how it may be affected by tobacco.
3. Discuss how tobacco addiction develops.
4. Identify ways to say no to tobacco and to learn skills that can help break the tobacco habit.

Carlos: What's wrong, Rob?

Rob: My mom caught my brother smoking last night. They had a big fight.

Carlos: I thought you said he was quitting.

Rob: He tried to, but it was really hard. My mom said he just wasn't trying hard enough. But my brother says she doesn't realize how hard it is to quit.

Carlos: Well, think about how she feels. I don't like it when he smokes around me either. The smoke makes my clothes stink.

Rob: I know. It's so bad for him. I'm scared he might get cancer or something. I wish he'd never started.

in your journal

Read the dialogue on this page. Do you know about people who have experienced problems in their lives because of a tobacco habit? Start your private journal entries on tobacco use by answering these questions:

▶ If you were Rob's brother, how would you solve the problems caused by your cigarette habit?

▶ Why do you think teens start smoking?

▶ How does the decision to use tobacco affect a person's physical, mental/emotional, and social health?

▶ How does a person's use of tobacco affect the lives of other people?

When you reach the end of the chapter, you will use your journal entries to make an action plan.

What Tobacco Does to Your Body

This lesson will help you find answers to questions that teens often ask about using tobacco. For example:

▶ **What is in tobacco that causes health problems?**

▶ **Is tobacco harmful in all of its forms?**

▶ **What parts of my body would be affected by tobacco?**

Words to Know

nicotine
tar
carbon monoxide

In your journal, write some questions you have about smoking. If any of the questions have not been answered by the end of this chapter, ask a parent, teacher, or health care provider to answer them. Then write the answers in your journal.

The Facts About Tobacco

A single puff of tobacco smoke exposes the body to more than 4,000 chemicals. Almost all of these make the body unable to work as it should. At least 43 of the chemicals in tobacco smoke are known to cause cancer in smokers. Smoke also harms the health of nonsmokers. Even smokeless tobacco causes health problems, including cancer, in its users.

What Is in Tobacco?

Three substances in tobacco smoke are especially harmful to your health. **Nicotine** (NIK·uh·teen) is *an addictive drug found in tobacco.* This drug makes tobacco users crave more nicotine. **Tar** is *a thick, dark liquid that forms when tobacco burns.* This liquid covers the lining of the lungs, causing disease. **Carbon monoxide** (KAR·buhn muh·NAHK·syd) is *a colorless, odorless, poisonous gas produced when tobacco burns.* All of these dangerous substances are in tobacco smoke whether the user is smoking a cigarette, a cigar, or a pipe (see **Figure 10.1** on the next page).

Tobacco in Many Forms

Tobacco products come in several forms, which are smoked or chewed. The most commonly used form is cigarettes.

In this smoker's lung, chemicals from tobacco smoke have coated the inner structures. This makes the lungs work less efficiently and can cause serious diseases, such as cancer and emphysema.

Cigarettes

Cigarettes are made from shredded tobacco leaves. Although filters can reduce the amount of nicotine and tar in cigarette smoke, they do not help to decrease the amount of carbon monoxide and other disease-causing chemicals. Some kinds of cigarettes contain other ingredients, such as spices, that make the cigarettes taste and smell sweet.

Smokeless Tobacco

Two forms of tobacco are placed in the mouth instead of being smoked. Chewing tobacco is made from compressed, coarsely ground leaves. A wad is placed between the cheek and gum, where it is sucked or chewed. Snuff is a finely ground, powdery substance. It is placed between the lower lip and gum, where it mixes with saliva and is absorbed.

Smokeless tobacco is not a safe alternative to smoking tobacco. The nicotine in smokeless tobacco is just as harmful and addictive as that in cigarette smoke. In addition, smokeless tobacco is linked to an increased incidence of mouth cancer and cancers of the esophagus, larynx, and pancreas. It also causes inflamed gums, bad breath, yellowed teeth, and stomach ulcers.

interNET
CONNECTION
Learn on-line how to keep your lungs healthy, including tips on how to resist peer pressure and stay tobacco free.
http://www.glencoe.com/sec/health

Figure 10.1
Some Harmful Substances in Tobacco Smoke

Tobacco smoke contains many dangerous chemicals.

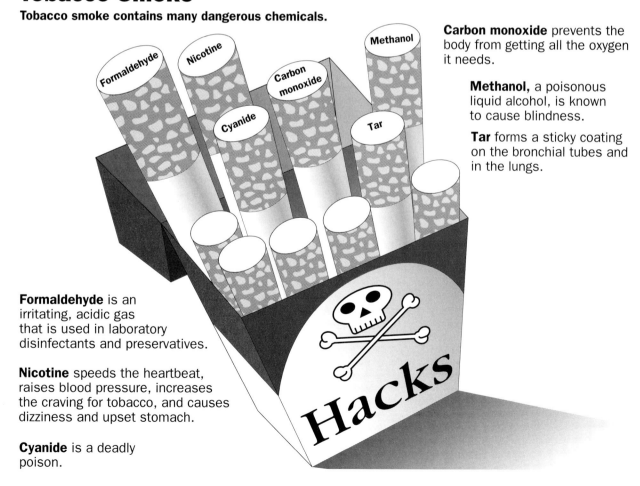

Carbon monoxide prevents the body from getting all the oxygen it needs.

Methanol, a poisonous liquid alcohol, is known to cause blindness.

Tar forms a sticky coating on the bronchial tubes and in the lungs.

Formaldehyde is an irritating, acidic gas that is used in laboratory disinfectants and preservatives.

Nicotine speeds the heartbeat, raises blood pressure, increases the craving for tobacco, and causes dizziness and upset stomach.

Cyanide is a deadly poison.

Math Connection

The Price of Smoking ACTIVITY!

Smokers not only damage their bodies; they spend money on the products that hurt them. Calculate the cost of cigarettes over the course of one year, two years, five years, and ten years, at $2.50 per pack. Assume that a smoker buys one pack of cigarettes a day.

Pipes and Cigars

Pipes and cigars also use shredded tobacco leaves, some of which may be flavored. Pipe and cigar smokers develop lung cancer less often than cigarette smokers because they usually inhale less smoke. However, pipe and cigar smokers are more likely to develop cancers of the lip, mouth, tongue, and throat.

Tobacco and Your Body

Tobacco damages the body in many ways. **Figure 10.2** illustrates tobacco's effect on five body systems.

Figure 10.2

What Tobacco Does to the Body

Tobacco has harmful effects on nearly every body system.

Body System	Effects of Tobacco Use
Nervous system	Smoking reduces the flow of oxygen to the brain, possibly leading to a stroke.
Respiratory system	Tar and other chemicals leave a sticky residue that destroys structures in the lungs. Smoking also damages the alveoli (al·VEE·uh·ly), the tiny air sacs in the lungs. This damage causes difficulty in breathing and prevents oxygen from getting to the rest of the body. Smokers are ten times more likely than nonsmokers to develop lung cancer.
Circulatory system	Smoking weakens the blood vessels. Smoking also causes a fatty buildup that clogs the blood vessels, increasing the risk of heart attack or a stroke.
Digestive system	Tobacco causes bad breath. It stains the teeth and makes them susceptible to cavities. Tobacco dulls the taste buds and can cause cancer of the mouth and throat. It is also a cause of stomach ulcers.
Excretory system	Smoking increases the danger of bladder cancer. Smokers have twice the risk of bladder cancer that nonsmokers have.

The Costs to Society

Smokers pay a high price for their tobacco habit, including the price of tobacco products and the cost of health care. Nonsmokers who are exposed to the tobacco smoke of others also pay a price. They are at increased risk for lung cancer and other respiratory diseases. The developing babies of pregnant women who smoke can also suffer serious effects. To help reduce all these costs to society, the government has regulated the tobacco industry. In 1965 health warnings began to appear on cigarette packs. In 1971 cigarette advertisements were banned from radio and television. New regulations, approved in 1996, limit the access persons under 18 have to tobacco. Store owners must verify the age of a person who is purchasing tobacco products, and cigarette vending machines are allowed only in places where people under 18 are not admitted.

Using complete sentences, answer the following questions on a separate sheet of paper.

Reviewing Terms and Facts

1. **Vocabulary**   Describe the following substances in tobacco smoke: *nicotine, tar,* and *carbon monoxide.*

2. **List**   Name three forms of tobacco.

3. **Give Examples**   List four ways in which smoking or chewing tobacco harms the body.

Thinking Critically

4. **Explain**   If you had a friend who chewed tobacco, how could you persuade him to quit using it?

5. **Hypothesize**   Why do you think it is difficult to quit smoking?

Applying Health Concepts

6. **Health of Others**   Collect newspaper and magazine articles about the harmful effects of using tobacco. Use the articles and draw illustrations to make a bulletin board display.

HEALTH LAB
Smoking and Breathing

Introduction: For people who smoke, breathing deeply can be difficult. Tar covers their airways and lungs, paralyzing or destroying the hairs that trap dirt from air. Without these hairs, smoke that is inhaled into the lungs deposits harmful gases and particles in the bronchi and alveoli. Taking deep breaths of fresh air causes irritation, causing "smoker's cough."

Objective: Work with a partner to recognize that chemicals produced by cigarette smoke stay inside the smoker's body.

Materials and Method: You will need the following materials: a squeezable rubber bulb, rubber or glass tubing, a clean white handkerchief, cigarettes, and matches. You will also need a sheet of paper to record your results. Divide the sheet into two columns: *Observations* and *Analysis.* In the observations column, write what occurred during the experiment. In the analysis column, write your interpretation of the experiment.

Attach the bulb to the tubing, placing a handkerchief between the bulb and the tubing. Compress the bulb, and hold a lighted cigarette at the other end of the tube. Release the bulb, drawing the smoke through the tube and handkerchief. Repeat this procedure three or four times, until tar accumulates on the handkerchief. Put out the cigarette safely.

Observations and Analysis: Do you think that what happened to the handkerchief happens to the smoker's body, too? Where do you think the chemicals are deposited in the body? What harm might that do? Share your analysis of the experiment with your classmates. Discuss the effects of smoking on breathing.

The Respiratory System

This lesson will help you find answers to questions that teens often ask about the respiratory system. For example:

▶ **What are the parts of the respiratory system?**

▶ **What is my body doing when I breathe?**

▶ **How can I take care of my lungs?**

Words to Know

respiratory system
trachea
bronchi
diaphragm
alveoli

in your journal

Most of the time, you breathe without even thinking about it. Sit down and concentrate on your breathing for one minute. Then write a description in your journal of how breathing makes your body feel. Do you think that someone who smokes tobacco breathes differently? How and why?

Oxygen for Life

Take a deep breath. Now let the air out. These two motions, inhaling and exhaling, are the basic actions of your **respiratory system,** *the set of organs that supply your body with oxygen and rid your body of carbon dioxide.* This process is crucial because you can only survive for a few minutes without oxygen.

Parts of the Respiratory System

Many body parts work together to help you breathe. Air goes in and out through your nose and mouth. The lungs exchange oxygen and carbon dioxide. Muscles in the chest allow the lungs to expand. The table in **Figure 10.3** lists and describes many of the body parts that make breathing possible.

Figure 10.3
Parts of the Respiratory System

All of these structures work together to help you breathe. Damage to any one of them can make breathing difficult.

Body Part	Description
Nose/Mouth	Passages for air; nose lined with cilia (SIH·lee·uh), fine hairs that trap dirt from air
Trachea (TRAY·kee·uh)	*Tube in throat that takes air to and from lungs (also called the windpipe)*
Epiglottis	Flap of tissue in back of mouth that covers the trachea to prevent food from entering
Bronchi (BRAHNG·ky)	*Two tubes that branch from the trachea, one to each lung*
Lungs	Two large organs that exchange oxygen and carbon dioxide
Diaphragm	*Large dome-shaped muscle below the lungs that draws air in and pushes air out*

How Breathing Works

Breathing consists of three main stages. When you inhale, you take air and oxygen into your lungs. There oxygen enters the bloodstream, replacing the carbon dioxide that must leave the body. Then you exhale, breathing out the carbon dioxide. These three stages repeat in a cycle. Look again at the parts of the respiratory system listed on the previous page. Now find them in **Figure 10.4,** which shows the steps in the breathing cycle.

Figure 10.4
The Breathing Process
Every day you take about 25,000 breaths of air.

1 Inhaling
Your diaphragm (DY·uh·fram) moves down, and your rib cage expands, creating more room in your chest. This expansion causes air to rush in. The air enters the nose and mouth, then moves past the epiglottis into the trachea and bronchi.

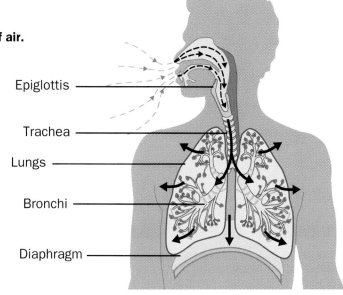

Epiglottis

Trachea

Lungs

Bronchi

Diaphragm

Alveoli

Pulmonary vein

2 Inside the Lungs
The bronchi divide into smaller passages called bronchioles (BRAHN·kee·ohlz). Air passes through to the **alveoli** (al·VEE·uh·ly), *microscopic air sacs in the lungs where gases are exchanged.* Tiny blood vessels called capillaries surround the alveoli. Here the oxygen in the air moves into your bloodstream, and carbon dioxide enters the alveoli.

Capillaries

Pulmonary artery

Bronchiole

3 Exhaling
Your diaphragm pushes up, and your ribs move in and down, forcing air out of your lungs. The air, now containing carbon dioxide, moves back through the bronchioles and bronchi, up the trachea, and out through the nose and mouth.

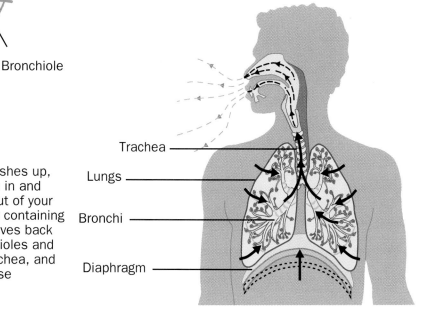

Trachea

Lungs

Bronchi

Diaphragm

Problems of the Respiratory System

As **Figure 10.4** shows, the respiratory system is made up of many complex and delicate parts. Damage to the system may occur in several ways. For example, germs may enter through the nose and mouth. Tobacco smoking, inhaled chemicals, or environmental pollution may also cause damage. Look at **Figure 10.5** at the bottom of this page. It describes some of the illnesses that can harm your respiratory system. Which ones can be most easily avoided?

Caring for Your Respiratory System

If you've ever held your breath too long in the swimming pool or gagged on fumes from a passing truck, then you know what it's like when you can't breathe freely. Your whole body depends on your respiratory system and on the air you breathe. **Figure 10.6** on the next page shows several ways to take good care of your respiratory system.

Figure 10.5
Problems of the Respiratory System

Some respiratory problems are common; others are rare. All of them can be dangerous if they are not treated properly and at an early stage.

Disease or Disorder	Description	Treatment
Colds/Flu	Infection caused by virus; symptoms include runny nose, cough, fever, aches	Bed rest and fluids; flu vaccine can prevent some types
Pneumonia	Infection of lungs by virus or bacteria; symptoms include fever, chest pain, breathing difficulty	Antibiotics for bacterial type; bed rest for viral type
Asthma	Disease in which airways narrow; symptoms include wheezing, shortness of breath, coughing	Medication can relieve symptoms; individual can also avoid substances that trigger the attacks
Tuberculosis	Communicable disease in which lungs become infected by bacteria; symptoms include cough, fatigue; can be fatal	Antibiotics
Emphysema	Disease in which alveoli are destroyed; symptoms include extreme difficulty in breathing; often caused by smoking	No known cure; pure oxygen can make breathing easier
Lung cancer	Uncontrolled growth of tumors in lungs; often caused by smoking	Surgery, radiation, and medications; survival rates are very low

Figure 10.6
Keeping Your Respiratory System Healthy

These teens are taking action to keep their breathing strong and healthy. How can you make these tips work for you?

Ⓐ Exercise and breathe deeply. Giving your lungs a good workout makes them stronger and more efficient.

Ⓑ Stay away from smoke and air pollution. Don't start smoking, and stay away from people who do. Avoid heavily polluted air whenever possible. For example, don't jog on streets where there is heavy traffic. If you know that you are allergic to a substance, such as pollen, do all you can to avoid it.

Ⓒ Take care of illnesses. See a doctor right away if you have any problems with breathing. Preventing serious illness will keep your lungs healthy for life.

Review

Lesson
2

Using complete sentences, answer the following questions on a separate sheet of paper.

Reviewing Terms and Facts

1. **Vocabulary**   List the parts of the respiratory system through which air passes when you inhale.

2. **Recall**   What is the name of the large muscle below your lungs? How does it help you breathe?

3. **Identify**   What two gases are exchanged in your lungs when you breathe?

Thinking Critically

4. **Explain**   Why are the alveoli important? What happens if they are damaged by smoking?

5. **Describe**   List some ways in which the respiratory system protects itself from damage and infection.

Applying Health Concepts

6. **Growth and Development**   Read at least two recent articles on the effects of smoking on an unborn baby. Write a letter from the baby to its mother, asking her to stop smoking. Use facts from the articles in your letter.

TEEN HEALTH DIGEST

It's Smart to Be a (Cold) Turkey

Myth: I want to quit smoking, but I'm worried about the withdrawal symptoms. I've heard that if I taper off gradually, I'll have an easier time adjusting.

Reality: In fact, this method can actually make withdrawal symptoms worse. If you are in the habit of smoking many cigarettes each day, your body is used to a constant high level of nicotine. Any time your nicotine level drops below that point, you experience withdrawal symptoms. When you gradually reduce the number of cigarettes smoked, your body is in a constant state of withdrawal. On the other hand, if you quit suddenly—go "cold turkey"—your body rids itself of nicotine much more quickly. After that, your body adjusts to being free of nicotine.

Personal Trainer

The Recovery Workout

When smokers quit, they can experience unpleasant withdrawal symptoms, such as fatigue, stomach problems, and nervousness. Many of these symptoms can be relieved by doing the following.

- Exercise, or just take a brisk walk.
- Avoid sweets, spicy foods, and foods that are high in fat. Add more fiber to your diet gradually. Drink plenty of water and other fluids.
- Relax. Take slow, deep breaths.
- Think positively. Withdrawal symptoms are temporary, but the benefits of quitting smoking last a lifetime.

Try This:

Ask several people who successfully quit smoking or using other tobacco products how they did it. Make a list of their suggestions.

Smoking Out the Beauty Myths

Have you ever seen an unattractive person in a cigarette advertisement? Tobacco companies appeal to young people's insecurities about their bodies with images of physically appealing smokers. Cigarettes that are marketed with women in mind include a special emphasis. Often these brands of cigarettes are called "slims" or "lights" to give the impression that smoking them will make you slender.

In fact, smoking is likely to damage a person's appearance. Nicotine reduces the amount of oxygen in the skin, and so causes wrinkles. Cigarette smoke also stains the teeth and fingers and causes bad breath. These unattractive qualities are never shown in the advertisements.

Try This: *Look through a magazine that prints cigarette ads. Compare the people in these ads with the people in ads for other products. Are they noticeably different? What messages are these companies sending, and why?*

HEALTH UPDATE

Smoke Less, See More

Smoking is known to harm the lungs, heart, and stomach. Now scientists are finding that it can also damage the eyes. Macular degeneration (MA·kyuh·ler di·je·nuh·RAY·shuhn), the most common cause of blindness in people over the age of 65, is more than twice as common among smokers. It occurs when membranes in the eye break down, causing damage to the macula, the center of the retina. More than one and a half million Americans have lost their vision due to macular degeneration.

Sports and Recreation
Getting Tobacco Off the Field

In the past, tobacco companies often attempted to promote their brands by sponsoring sports events. Seeing the brand name posted everywhere led sports fans to have positive feelings about that brand of tobacco product. Many of these fans were teens.

In the future, tobacco companies may not have this opportunity. Tobacco companies and some anti-smoking groups are engaged in a legal battle over regulation of tobacco advertising. Antismoking groups want to make it illegal for tobacco brands to be sponsors of sports events. Once these brand names have been removed from the sports arena, antismoking groups hope that teens may get the message that sports and tobacco don't mix.

Tobacco Addiction

This lesson will help you find answers to questions that teens often ask about tobacco dependency. For example:

▶ Why do teens begin using tobacco?

▶ How do people become addicted to tobacco?

Words to Know

addiction
withdrawal
physiological
   dependence
psychological
   dependence

Did You Know?

Serious Stuff

▶ Nicotine addiction is the most common form of drug addiction. It causes more death and disease than all other addictions combined.

▶ Nicotine is as addictive as alcohol, cocaine, or heroin.

▶ The earlier in life people start smoking cigarettes, the more likely they are to become strongly addicted to nicotine.

Why Teens Begin Using Tobacco

Why do teens start to use tobacco? One of the main reasons is that their friends smoke, although nationally only about one in four teens does smoke. Many teens think smoking will give them confidence in social situations or will make them appear sophisticated and cool. Some teens use tobacco because their parents and other adults smoke. They become curious and want to experiment. Unfortunately, before they know it, they are hooked.

Other teens smoke because tobacco advertising on billboards and in magazines makes smoking look attractive. Teens also may think that the bad effects of smoking happen only after many years of smoking or when people are older. They do not realize that the negative effects on their health begin with the first cigarette.

Most young smokers believe they can quit at any time. Some do not realize how addictive smoking is. Others know about the addictive effects of nicotine but believe that they can avoid this problem.

Parents can serve as positive role models for their children by avoiding all tobacco products.

Reasons for Tobacco Use Among Teens

Every day about 3,000 American teens begin using tobacco. Even though schools and the media send messages to warn them about the health hazards of tobacco use, teens continue to smoke and chew tobacco. Why? Here are some of the reasons.

- Teens smoke because of peer pressure. As one teen put it, "All my friends smoke, so I smoke, too."

- Some teens blame their smoking on their parents' habit. "Both my mom and dad smoke. I wanted to find out what it was like," explains a teen smoker.

- "I tried cigarettes because I thought it would make me be more grown up and in control of my life," explained another teen.

- "I wanted to look cool like the models I see in the cigarette advertisements," admitted still another teen.

- One teen explained how his chewing tobacco habit began: "I wanted to be just like my favorite pro baseball player."

- After just a few cigarettes, teens may find it difficult to quit. "It wasn't hard to get hooked," said one.

Tobacco Addiction

Teens often wonder why people get hooked on tobacco products. The answer is nicotine. Nicotine has a powerful effect on the brain and nervous system. The tobacco user forms an **addiction** (uh·DIK·shuhn), *a physical or psychological need for a drug or other substance.* For a person addicted to nicotine, it is extremely difficult to stop using tobacco. When tobacco users try to quit or reduce their use of tobacco, they go through what is known as **withdrawal**—*unpleasant symptoms that occur when someone stops using an addictive substance.* People experiencing withdrawal usually become anxious, depressed, irritable, and tired. As an addictive drug, nicotine causes two kinds of dependence: physiological (fi·zee·uh·LAH·ji·kuhl) and psychological.

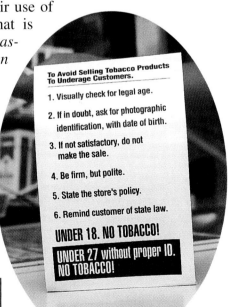

To Avoid Selling Tobacco Products To Underage Customers.

1. Visually check for legal age.
2. If in doubt, ask for photographic identification, with date of birth.
3. If not satisfactory, do not make the sale.
4. Be firm, but polite.
5. State the store's policy.
6. Remind customer of state law.

UNDER 18. NO TOBACCO!

UNDER 27 without proper ID. NO TOBACCO!

All stores that sell tobacco products are required to ask any customer who looks younger than 27 for a photo ID. If customers cannot prove that they are 18 or older, they cannot buy tobacco products.

Did You Know?

An Early Decision

The decision to smoke is nearly always made during the teen years. Studies have shown that if people do not begin to smoke as children or teens, it is unlikely that they ever will. Therefore, saying no to tobacco now could save your life many years down the road.

Cultural Connections

Making a Difference

Thailand has some of the strongest antismoking laws in the world. Its leadership has played an important role in encouraging the antismoking movements that have taken root in many parts of Asia, including China, Japan, Mongolia, and South Korea.

Q: How can you tell if someone is addicted to tobacco?

A: If a person experiences a craving for tobacco or cannot stop using it without becoming anxious and irritable, then he or she is probably addicted.

Physiological Dependence

Physiological (fi·zee·uh·LAH·ji·kuhl) **dependence** is *a type of addiction in which the body itself feels a direct need for a drug.* In tobacco, the drug to which a person becomes addicted is nicotine. Nicotine affects many parts of the body, as shown in **Figure 10.7.**

Nicotine addiction is very strong. The tobacco user does not feel normal until he or she has another dose of the drug. Only by chewing tobacco or smoking is this need met. The smoker feels better after smoking, but the feeling does not last long. Soon the smoker feels a need to smoke again. As the smoker's body becomes more accustomed to the drug, he or she needs it more often to feel its effect. This same dependence is caused by the nicotine in other forms of tobacco, such as chewing tobacco.

Figure 10.7
Nicotine's Negative Effects on the Body

Nicotine causes serious problems for many of the body's important organs.

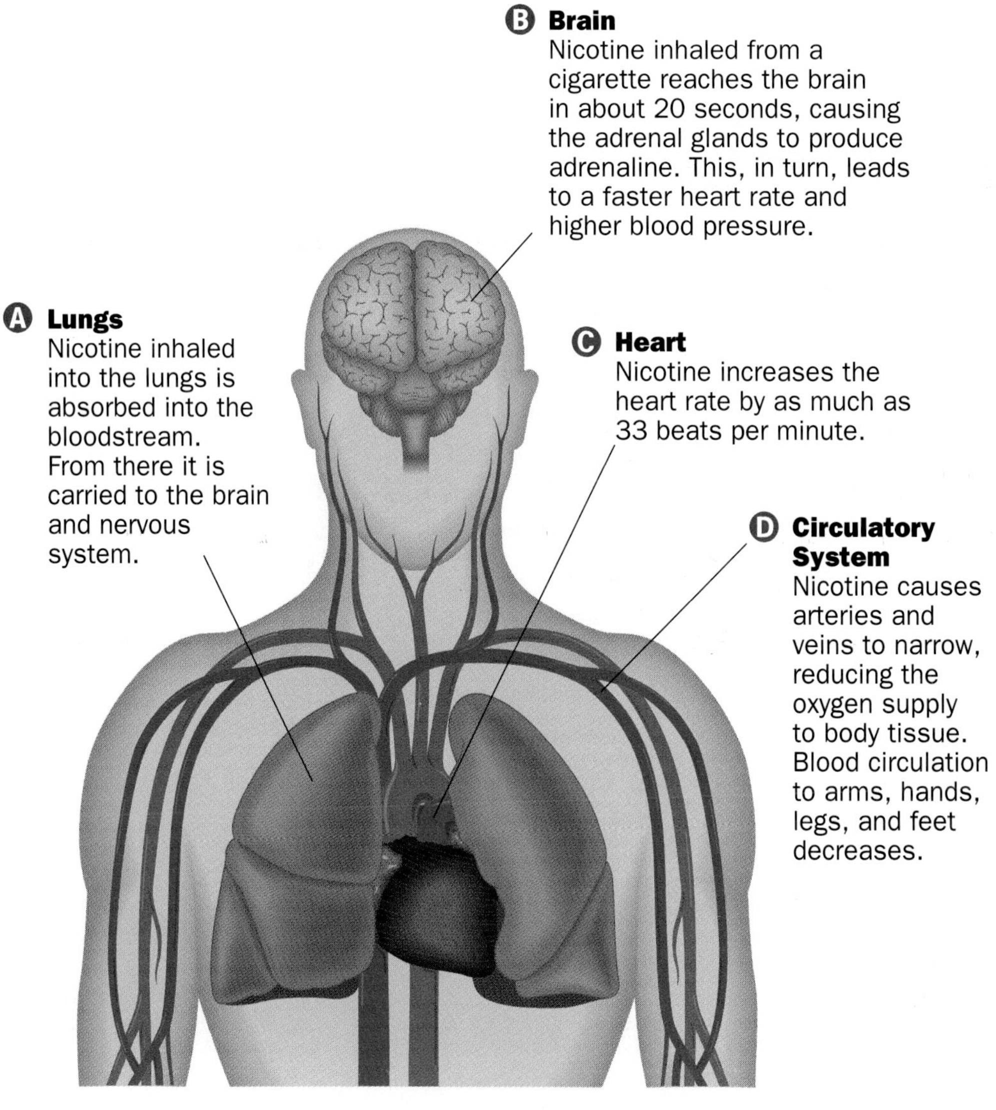

B Brain
Nicotine inhaled from a cigarette reaches the brain in about 20 seconds, causing the adrenal glands to produce adrenaline. This, in turn, leads to a faster heart rate and higher blood pressure.

A Lungs
Nicotine inhaled into the lungs is absorbed into the bloodstream. From there it is carried to the brain and nervous system.

C Heart
Nicotine increases the heart rate by as much as 33 beats per minute.

D Circulatory System
Nicotine causes arteries and veins to narrow, reducing the oxygen supply to body tissue. Blood circulation to arms, hands, legs, and feet decreases.

Psychological Dependence

Psychological (sy·kuh·LAH·ji·kuhl) **dependence** is *an addiction in which the mind sends the body the message that it needs more of a substance.* This kind of dependence can be caused by physiological dependence—the effect of nicotine, for example—as well as by other factors. Psychological dependence can be created by the pleasurable experiences or rewards that smokers may associate with smoking. Tobacco use is often linked with daily routines. A smoker may develop the habit of always smoking a cigarette after a meal, while reading the newspaper, or during a work break. Some people reward themselves with a cigarette after they have completed a difficult task. These habits, along with the physiological dependence on nicotine, make it harder for a person to quit using tobacco.

Psychological dependence may form as a result of tobacco's perceived effects. Some smokers believe that cigarettes provide them with extra energy. Others think that cigarettes help calm them down when they are tense. Still others feel that they need tobacco to keep their weight under control because smoking reduces their appetites. Although these benefits are imaginary, smokers may become convinced that they're real.

in your journal

For a week, take note of every tobacco ad you see. In your journal, record where the ads appeared, and include descriptions of them. What are the messages in the ads? Why do you think the ads were placed where they were? Write your answers in your journal.

LIFE SKILLS
Analyzing a Media Message

What flashes through your mind when you see a cigarette ad that shows smokers having fun? Do you believe that smoking is a way to make friends and share a good time? This is the hidden message that the cigarette makers want you to receive. They send this message to influence your decision about smoking. They show appealing pictures to make you feel good about the idea of smoking. They try to persuade you to smoke. The ad is concerned with image, or the way people or objects appear. This image is the ad's message, but it does not tell the truth about smoking.

You can avoid being confused by this false advertising message. Just analyze any ad to see the hidden messages in its pictures and words. Look carefully at the ad on this page. Then, to analyze its message, ask yourself the following questions:

1. What is the hidden message in the ad's picture? What is the hidden message in the ad's words?

2. After analyzing this ad, what decision about smoking would you make? Explain your choice.

**Be Cool
Have Fun
Smoke *Flavor***

SURGEON GENERAL'S WARNING:
Quitting Smoking Now Greatly Reduces
Serious Risks to Your Health.

Your Total Health

Bad Habits Multiply   ACTIVITY!

A person who has one bad habit is likely to have others. A survey conducted by a fitness research center found that people who smoke are more likely to have other unhealthful habits. Examine your own habits. List them on a separate sheet of paper. If there are any habits on your list that you think are unhealthful, make a plan to change them. Predict what might happen to the status of your health if you choose not to change them.

Replacing smoking with a different ritual is one way to break the cigarette habit. For example, if a person smokes after a meal, he or she could try chewing sugarless gum instead.

Smokers also may develop rituals that create psychological dependence. For example, some smokers reach for a cigarette when they begin certain activities. Others talk with an unlit cigarette in their mouths before they light it. These rituals can become as difficult to stop as the actual habit of smoking. One key to breaking the habit is to change the ritual. Instead of reaching for a cigarette, think of something else to do—take a walk, call a friend, play on the computer, or work on a hobby.

Lesson 3

Review

Using complete sentences, answer the following questions on a separate sheet of paper.

Reviewing Terms and Facts

1. **Give Examples**   List five factors that have an influence on teens' decisions to use tobacco.

2. **Vocabulary**   Define the terms *addiction* and *withdrawal*. Use each word in an original sentence.

3. **Recall**   How does nicotine affect the circulatory system?

Thinking Critically

4. **Apply**   Select a magazine advertisement for cigarettes. Describe how the picture and the words of the advertisement encourage tobacco use.

5. **Analyze**   Which part of tobacco addiction do you think is more powerful—the physiological dependence or the psychological dependence? Give reasons for your answer.

Applying Health Concepts

6. **Consumer Health**   Create an advertisement to discourage teens from smoking. Use the same kinds of hidden messages in your advertisement that the media use to encourage teens to smoke.

7. **Personal Health**   With a classmate, write a short play about breaking a psychological dependence on tobacco.

Choosing to Be Tobacco Free

This lesson will help you find answers to questions that teens often ask about remaining tobacco free or giving up tobacco use. For example:

▶ **How can I remain tobacco free?**
▶ **What are some ways of breaking the tobacco habit?**
▶ **How can I defend my rights as a nonsmoker?**

Words to Know

secondhand smoke
sidestream smoke
mainstream smoke
passive smoker

Saying No to Tobacco

Saying no when friends pressure you to use tobacco can be difficult. There are ways to resist, however. The first line of defense is to be prepared for the pressure. Practice your refusal skills. Know ahead of time what you can say to respond to the pressure to use tobacco.

If the pressure is light, you can simply refuse. Say that you're not interested or that you don't like the taste or smell of cigarettes. If you think you will need more help, refer to **Figure 10.8.** It will provide you with 12 very good reasons to remain tobacco free.

Sometimes the pressure to use tobacco can be very strong. If you are an athlete, you can say that you want to keep your breathing healthy for your sport. You can simply say no and ask people to respect your right to make your own decisions. If the pressure continues, leave the scene. One way to resist the pressure to use tobacco is to choose friends who do not use it.

in your journal

Look at the reasons for quitting tobacco use. Review the list again. Are there any reasons you can think of that are not included in the list? If so, write them down in your journal.

Figure 10.8
The Top 12 Reasons to Be Tobacco Free
There are plenty of good reasons not to smoke.

1 You will be healthier.
2 Your breath will smell better.
3 You can save money.
4 Your senses of taste and smell will be sharper.
5 You will have fewer allergies.
6 You will not be confined to smoking areas.
7 You will have more energy and stamina for sports.
8 Your skin will be healthier and look better.
9 Your hair and clothes will not smell like smoke.
10 You will not be forcing others to breathe smoke.
11 You will not have to lie to parents, teachers, or friends.
12 You will not be breaking the law.

Kicking the Habit

Many people who used tobacco in the past are kicking the habit. It is not easy to do. However, there are many ways to stop. There are also people and places to go to for help in breaking the habit.

Since the nicotine in tobacco is addictive, people who quit using it experience withdrawal symptoms. These symptoms do not last long, but they include nervousness, moodiness, and difficulty in sleeping. If you or someone you know is trying to quit smoking, here are some tips that can help.

Friends who do not smoke can provide support and encouragement for people who are trying to quit.

- Make a list of reasons why you want to quit smoking. Read the list whenever you get the urge to smoke.

- Set small goals. Try quitting one day at a time. Every year the American Cancer Society sponsors the "Great American Smokeout," a campaign that calls for all smokers to avoid smoking for one day.

- If possible, avoid being with people who smoke. Stay away from places where lots of smokers hang out.

- Change any habits you have that are linked to smoking. For example, if you smoke after a meal, take a short walk instead. Learn other methods of relaxing and relieving stress.

- Exercise when you feel the urge to reach for tobacco. Stretch, take deep breaths, go for a walk, or take a ride on your bike.

- Think positively. Seek encouragement from your nonsmoking friends.

- Eat healthful snacks instead of reaching for tobacco.

MAKING HEALTHY DECISIONS
Overcoming the Pressure to Smoke

All the science classes in seventh grade made a trip to Cape Henry every spring for four days. Tracy was looking forward to being with her friends away from home and at the beach.

Every evening after dinner, the students had half an hour of free time. The first evening, Tracy was returning to her cabin when a friend called her to come around back. Tracy was surprised to find two of her friends and two girls she didn't know smoking cigarettes. After Jill introduced Tracy to Sally and Liz, she offered Tracy a cigarette and said,

"Have a few puffs. It's a great way to unwind after following teachers' orders all day."

Tracy declined Jill's offer and said that she had to leave to help set up for that night's special program. The next evening she noticed that the four girls were behind the cabin again. Tracy could hear them laughing and thought about joining in.

The next morning, one of the girls, Sally, confronted Tracy. "Why don't you have a smoke with us after dinner? Do you think you're too good for us?"

Programs That Help

The "cold turkey" method of quitting tobacco is popular, and it is recommended by many experts. In this method, the smoker simply stops using all forms of tobacco. Some people need support or assistance to quit. They should contact a group that offers a program to help people quit. The American Lung Association, the American Heart Association, and the American Cancer Society are just a few of the many groups that offer such programs. You can contact these groups by telephone or by mail to get more information about quitting.

Books and recordings can help people quit smoking on their own. Many can be borrowed from local libraries. There are also several products available to help lessen withdrawal symptoms. They include over-the-counter drugs (such as chewing gum that contains nicotine and the nicotine patch) and sets of graduated filters designed to reduce tar.

People who are trying to quit need support and encouragement from family and friends. If you are close to someone who wants to kick the habit, do what you can to help. Praise the person for each day that he or she avoids smoking.

The support of friends is a powerful tool in fighting nicotine addiction.

Teen Issues

Tips for Supporters

Helping someone quit using tobacco is not an easy task. You must be patient, caring, and supportive. Help the ex-tobacco user avoid situations in which he or she might be tempted to reach for tobacco. Offer to join him or her in healthy activities such as walking or bike riding. Reassure the person that his or her irritability, lack of energy, or other withdrawal symptoms will pass in time, and that the health benefits will make the effort of quitting worthwhile.

Tracy was embarrassed by Sally's comments. She was torn between her unwillingness to smoke and her desire to be part of the group. Tracy decided to use the six-step decision-making process to make up her mind about smoking:

① **State the situation**
② **List the options**
③ **Weigh the possible outcomes**
④ **Consider your values**
⑤ **Make a decision and act**
⑥ **Evaluate the decision**

Follow-up Activities

1. Apply the six steps of the decision-making process to Tracy's story.
2. With a classmate, role-play a scene in which Tracy resists the peer pressure to use tobacco.

How Tobacco Affects Nonsmokers

Even if you are not lighting up and smoking, you may be breathing *air that has been contaminated by tobacco smoke,* or **secondhand smoke.** Each time a smoker lights a cigarette, smoke fills the air from two sources. *The smoke coming from the burning tip of the cigarette is* called **sidestream smoke.** It contains twice as much tar and nicotine as *the smoke that the smoker exhales,* or **mainstream smoke.** This is because sidestream smoke has not passed through the cigarette filter or the smoker's lungs.

Nonsmokers who breathe secondhand smoke become **passive smokers.** Passive smoking is harmful to your health because it contributes to respiratory problems. Passive smoking irritates your nose and throat, and it also causes itchy and watery eyes, headaches, and coughing. Some people are much more sensitive to secondhand smoke than others.

A smoke-filled room has high levels of nicotine, carbon monoxide, and other pollutants. In such a room, a nonsmoker can inhale as much nicotine and carbon monoxide in one hour as if he or she had smoked a whole cigarette. Long-term exposure to secondhand smoke poses the same risk of serious illness for passive smokers as smoking does for active smokers. These risks include heart and lung diseases and respiratory problems. According to the U.S. Environmental Protection Agency, secondhand smoke is a human carcinogen, or cancer-causing substance, that is responsible for 3,000 lung cancer deaths each year.

Most restaurants provide separate nonsmoking sections for their customers.

Unborn Babies and Children

A woman who smokes during pregnancy seriously endangers the health of her unborn child. Cigarette smoking during pregnancy is associated with increased chances of miscarriage, stillbirth, and low birth weight. The lower a baby's birth weight, the higher the risk of complications in the baby's development. The effects of tobacco may affect the growth, mental development, and behavior of children for up to 11 years after their birth. In addition, infants whose mothers smoke during and after pregnancy are three times more likely to die from Sudden Infant Death Syndrome (SIDS) than infants whose mothers do not smoke. If their mothers stop smoking during pregnancy but resume immediately after the birth, infants are twice as likely to die from SIDS as those born to non-smoking mothers.

Rights of Nonsmokers

The fact is clear that inhaling secondhand smoke is as dangerous as smoking. Laws continue to be passed to restrict smoking in public places. In 1989 smoking was banned on all domestic airplane flights. In 1994 more than 600 state and local ordinances restricted smoking. Employers now have a legal right to restrict smoking in the workplace, and some have banned smoking.

What does all of this mean to you? As a nonsmoker, you have the right to breathe air that is free of harmful tobacco smoke. You have the right to express your preference that people not smoke around you. You also have the right to work for the passage of laws that prevent nonsmokers from being exposed to tobacco smoke in public places.

Because of the potential damage to children, both before birth and during their later development, women should not smoke while they are pregnant.

Review

Lesson 4

Using complete sentences, answer the following questions on a separate sheet of paper.

Reviewing Terms and Facts

1. **Recall** List four of the top 12 reasons to be tobacco free.

2. **List** Name three methods that can help smokers to quit.

3. **Vocabulary** How are *secondhand smoke, sidestream smoke,* and *mainstream smoke* different from each other?

Thinking Critically

4. **Suggest** Miguel is at a party with his friend Sam. Another friend offers them cigarettes, but Miguel does not want to smoke. How can Miguel say no to tobacco and still keep his friends?

5. **Apply** A friend of yours has asked you to help her to quit smoking. What could you do?

6. **Analyze** Although you enjoy bowling, the local bowling alley has no restrictions on smoking. You would like to exercise your rights as a nonsmoker. What could you do in this situation?

Applying Health Concepts

7. **Health of Others** Organize a support group for students who want to stop using tobacco. Ask the school nurse to train some students as peer supporters. Have the students who are former smokers keep a record of the days they have been tobacco free.

Chapter 10 Review

Chapter Summary

▶ **Lesson 1** There are many harmful substances in tobacco. Tobacco comes in several forms, which are either placed in the mouth or smoked.

▶ **Lesson 2** Your respiratory system supplies your body with oxygen and gets rid of carbon dioxide. Breathing is a cycle that includes inhaling, an exchange of oxygen for carbon dioxide, and exhaling.

▶ **Lesson 3** Many teens start smoking because they are influenced by friends, advertisements, or other factors. Smokers can easily become addicted because nicotine causes physiological dependence. Smokers can also develop a psychological dependence on tobacco.

▶ **Lesson 4** Resisting the pressure to smoke is an important decision for your health. There are many ways to kick the tobacco habit and many individuals and groups who are willing to help a user quit.

Reviewing Key Terms and Concepts

Using complete sentences, answer the following questions on a separate sheet of paper.

Lesson 1

1. List three harmful substances found in tobacco smoke.

2. How is using smokeless tobacco harmful to the body?

Lesson 2

3. Identify three problems that can affect your respiratory system.

4. Name three actions you can take to keep your respiratory system healthy.

Lesson 3

5. List two parts of the body that are negatively affected by nicotine, and tell how they are affected.

6. How does psychological dependence develop?

Lesson 4

7. What are some of the effects of nicotine withdrawal?

8. Describe how secondhand smoke affects passive smokers.

Thinking Critically

Using complete sentences, answer the following questions on a separate sheet of paper.

9. **Assess** Some brands of cigarettes contain very little tar. Do you think these brands are safe to smoke? Why or why not?

10. **Hypothesize** If your respiratory system were damaged by smoking or disease, how might the rest of your body be affected?

11. **Compare and Contrast** Do you think that adults who start smoking do so for the same reasons as teens? What reasons do they have in common, and how might their reasons differ? For which group do you think that it is harder to quit?

12. **Recommend** You are in a restaurant, enjoying your dinner, when a person at the next table lights a cigarette. You cannot stand the smell of smoke, especially while you are eating. How could you handle this situation?

Your Action Plan

Tobacco can have a negative impact on your life whether you use it or not. Protecting yourself from the health risks of tobacco is very important.

Step 1 Look back through your journal entries. What do they tell you about your feelings toward tobacco? What changes would you like to make to improve your health or the health of others?

Step 2 Decide on a long-term goal for yourself, and write it down. Your long-term goal might be to help a friend kick the tobacco habit.

Step 3 Next, write down a series of short-term goals to help you achieve your long-term goal. For example, you might try to persuade your friend to join a support group.

Plan a schedule for accomplishing each short-term goal. When you reach your long-term goal, reward yourself. If your goal involves a friend, include her or him in the reward.

In Your Home and Community

1. **Community Resources** Action on Smoking and Health (ASH) is a national organization working for a smoke-free America. Find out whether your community has a local chapter of ASH. If not, write to: Action on Smoking and Health, 2013 H Street NW, Washington, DC 20006. Ask how you can start a chapter in your community.

2. **Health of Others** Write or call the American Lung Association or the American Cancer Society, and ask if they have any training programs in which you might learn how to help your peers stop smoking. Once you are trained, ask an adult who does such work to help you begin a program in your school or through your community recreation department.

Building Your Portfolio

1. **Poster** Interview an administrator in your school to find out what the penalties are for teens who buy or use tobacco. Use this information to create a "Wanted" poster for an underage tobacco user. Include the person's "crimes" and the penalties he or she can expect to pay. Put the poster in your portfolio.

2. **Script** Write a script about teens being pressured to use tobacco. Have some of your friends or classmates act out the script. Place a copy of the script in your portfolio.

3. **Personal Assessment** Look through all the activities and projects you did for this chapter. Choose one or two that you would like to include in your portfolio.

Chapter 11

Alcohol and Drugs

Student Expectations

After reading this chapter, you should be able to:

❶ Describe the effects of the use and abuse of alcohol on the body.

❷ Identify how misuse and abuse of drugs can affect health.

❸ Explain how to keep the nervous system healthy.

❹ Recognize the risks of alcohol and drug use to physical, mental/emotional, and social health.

❺ Identify ways to avoid substance abuse.

❻ Describe the process of addiction to and withdrawal from alcohol or drugs.

Teen Chat Group

Robert: I'm having a party at my house on Saturday night. Do you guys want to come?

Eduardo: Are your parents going to be home?

Robert: Yeah, they'll be there. Why?

Eduardo: Last weekend I went to a party at Heather's house. I didn't know that her parents were away for the weekend. Some of her brother's friends started drinking, and they wanted me to drink, too.

Erin: What did you do?

Eduardo: At first I just said no, but they kept pressuring me, so I left the party.

Erin: That was a good idea. You could get into a lot of trouble just being around people who are drinking.

Robert: Well, you won't have to worry about that on Saturday. Just get there around eight.

in your journal

Read the dialogue on this page. Have you ever felt pressured to try illegal substances? Start your private journal entries on alcohol and drugs by answering these questions:

► Do you think that Eduardo's decision to leave the party was a wise one? Explain your answer.

► How might knowing the effects of alcohol and drugs on your body help you make healthful choices?

► What are some risks involved in alcohol and drug use?

► What are some ways in which you could resist pressure to try alcohol or drugs?

When you reach the end of the chapter, you will use your journal entries to make an action plan.

Lesson 1

Use and Abuse of Alcohol

This lesson will help you find answers to questions that teens often ask about alcohol. For example:

▶ **How does alcohol affect the body?**

▶ **Why do different people react differently to alcohol?**

▶ **What is alcoholism, and what can be done about it?**

Words to Know

alcohol
cirrhosis
alcoholism

Science Connection

Deadly Alcohol

The word alcohol actually refers to several related chemicals. The type found in alcoholic drinks is ethanol (E•thuh•nawl), also called ethyl (E•thuhl) alcohol and grain alcohol. Other types of alcohol include methanol (ME•thuh•nawl), also called wood alcohol, and isopropyl (eye•suh•PROH•puhl) alcohol, the main ingredient in rubbing alcohol. Both methanol and isopropyl alcohol are highly poisonous.

What Is Alcohol?

Alcohol is found in beer, wine, whiskey, and other beverages. **Alcohol** is *a drug created by a chemical reaction in some foods, especially fruits and grains.* This drug can have strong physical and mental effects on the drinker.

Alcohol is the most commonly abused drug in this country. It is illegal for people under the age of 21 to drink alcohol. Even so, the average age for taking a first drink is 13. Nearly 90 percent of older teens feel that alcohol abuse is a critical problem in their schools.

Why do some teens begin drinking alcohol? Some are trying to escape from their problems or relieve stress. Others may feel peer pressure to drink at parties and on other social occasions. Learning about the effects of alcohol on the body, however, will help you make the decision not to drink.

Staying away from alcohol helps keep you physically and mentally healthy. What healthy activities do you enjoy doing with your friends?

How Alcohol Affects the Body

Alcohol has both short-term and long-term effects on the body. Even one drink can impair judgment; large quantities of alcohol can cause death. **Figure 11.1** shows how alcohol affects various parts of the body.

*inter*NET
CONNECTION
Control your own destiny by knowing how to avoid substance abuse. You have the power!

http://www.glencoe.com/sec/health

Figure 11.1
Effects of Alcohol on the Body

The short-term effects of alcohol occur within a few minutes of drinking. The long-term effects may develop in a person who drinks heavily over an extended length of time.

Brain

A *Short-term effects*: Alcohol reaches the brain soon after it is swallowed. It impairs such functions as judgment, reasoning, memory, and concentration. Reaction time is slowed, coordination decreases, and speech becomes slurred. Vision and hearing are distorted. Alcohol also reduces people's inhibitions—the ability or desire to control their behavior—sometimes leading them to engage in dangerous activities. Too much alcohol can lead to unconsciousness and death.

B *Long-term effects*: Over time, alcohol use can cause brain cell destruction, nervous disorders, and memory loss.

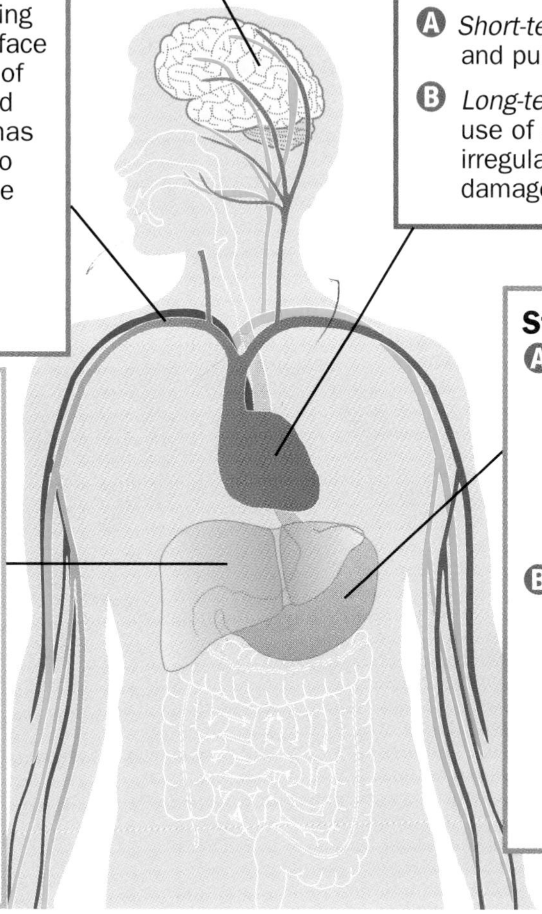

Blood Vessels

A *Short-term effects*: Blood vessels are enlarged, bringing blood closer to the skin surface and creating a false sense of warmth. This effect can lead a person whose judgment has been impaired by drinking to go outside without adequate clothing in cold weather.

B *Long-term effects*: Drinking alcohol can lead to high blood pressure and stroke.

Liver

A *Short-term effects*: Too much alcohol overloads the liver, which filters alcohol from the bloodstream and removes it from the body. Liver poisoning can result.

B *Long-term effects*: Heavy drinking can lead to **cirrhosis** (suh·ROH·sis), or *scarring and destruction of liver tissue*, which can cause death. Heavy alcohol consumption is also linked to liver cancer.

Heart

A *Short-term effects*: Heart and pulse rate are increased.

B *Long-term effects*: Extended use of alcohol can cause irregular heartbeat and damage to the heart muscle.

Stomach

A *Short-term effects*: Too much alcohol in the stomach can cause vomiting. If a person vomits while unconscious, choking may result.

B *Long-term effects*: Drinking alcohol can lead to ulcers, or open sores, in the stomach lining. Heavy use of alcohol is also linked to stomach cancer.

Differing Effects

Figure 11.2 shows the amount of alcohol in three typical alcoholic drinks. The level of alcohol in the blood is the primary factor in determining how a person is affected. The impact varies, however, for different people and in different situations. Factors to consider include the following:

- **Size and gender.** In general, females can tolerate a smaller amount of alcohol than males. Females usually weigh less than males, and their bodies may carry more fat, in which alcohol will not dissolve.

- **Food in the stomach.** Food in the stomach slows down the body's absorption of alcohol.

- **How fast a person drinks.** Gulping down a drink raises the alcohol level in the blood because the body has less time to process it.

- **Other substances in the body.** Drinking alcohol while taking prescription drugs or illegal drugs may have dangerous effects and may even be fatal.

Figure 11.2
Alcohol Content of Three Types of Drinks

A typical drink of each of the three most common types of alcoholic beverages contains about the same amount of alcohol.

12 oz. beer

4 oz. wine

1.5 oz. of 80-proof liquor

Alcoholism

Alcoholism is *an illness caused by a physical and mental need for alcohol.* Alcoholics differ from moderate or social drinkers in that they are not able to limit the amount of alcohol they drink. In addition, alcoholics need to drink more alcohol in order to experience the same effects from drinking. A person may be an alcoholic if he or she

- drinks increasing amounts of alcohol and becomes drunk often.

- places drinking alcohol ahead of other activities.

- drinks alone.

- experiences blackouts and cannot remember what he or she said or did while drinking.

- shows personality changes when drinking alcohol.

- makes excuses for drinking, promises to quit but does not, or refuses to admit how much he or she is drinking.

If you suspect that a friend or relative is an alcoholic, you should seek help from a trusted adult.

LIFE SKILLS

Helping Someone with a Drinking Problem

*Y*ou may suspect that someone close to you has a problem with alcohol. How can you be sure? Check for some of the signs of alcoholism listed in this lesson. A person who has even a few of these symptoms may have a drinking problem. You may or may not be able to do anything for this person. However, you can be supportive by

- learning about both alcoholism and sources of treatment.

- guiding the person to treatment, if possible.

- acting to encourage the person during and after treatment.

Remember that alcoholism is an illness. You are not to blame for the person's alcoholism. You are also not responsible for the alcoholic's actions. Although you may want to help, it is important not to put yourself in danger. Here are some strategies for helping someone with a drinking problem.

- Do not confront the person when he or she is drunk.

- Communicate with the person, when he or she is sober, about the damage that is being done.

- Encourage the person to seek help from a health care professional or a support group.

- Show concern and sympathy.

- Join a support group for people who have friends or relatives who are alcoholics.

- Discuss your problem with a counselor or health care worker.

- Do not cover up or make excuses for the person.

- If the person won't get help, consider seeking help for the person. The person may be angry with you at first, but your action could save his or her life.

Follow-up Activity

With a partner, role-play a conversation between two teens about problems with alcohol. One teen should be talking with the other teen (both are sober), expressing concern about the other's use of alcohol.

After reading this lesson, how do you feel about alcohol? In your journal, discuss your feelings. What problems could alcohol cause in your life? How might you avoid these problems? Make a list of health reasons not to drink alcohol.

Peer support can help teens deal with the challenges of living with someone who has a problem with alcohol.

Help for Alcoholism

Although there is no medical cure for alcoholism, the illness can be treated. An alcoholic must go through a treatment process involving several steps to begin the process of recovery from alcoholism. An alcoholic must

- admit that he or she has a problem and decide to seek help.

- go through detoxification, a process of removing all alcohol from the body.

- get counseling and support to learn to avoid alcohol.

Lesson 6 of this chapter discusses in more detail the process of recovery from both alcohol and drug addiction.

Some alcoholics may need to be hospitalized to stop drinking and get the alcohol out of their bodies. After alcoholics stop drinking, they must never touch alcohol again. They may need support for a long time—even for life—to continue to avoid alcohol. Several groups help recovering alcoholics and their friends and family members.

- Alcoholics Anonymous is an organization of people who help each other avoid alcohol. The group promotes a 12-step program.

- Alateen is an organization for teens who have friends or relatives who are alcoholics. At Alateen meetings, teens get peer support to help them cope.

- Al-Anon is a peer support organization of adult friends and relatives of alcoholics.

Lesson 1 Review

Using complete sentences, answer the following questions on a separate sheet of paper.

Reviewing Terms and Facts

1. **Vocabulary** Define the term *alcohol.* Give two examples of beverages that contain alcohol.

2. **Recall** Name and describe a long-term effect of alcohol on the liver.

3. **List** Identify three of the signs of alcoholism.

Thinking Critically

4. **Infer** Why is it easier to avoid alcohol now than to stop drinking later?

5. **Analyze** Why are support groups helpful to recovering alcoholics?

Applying Health Concepts

6. **Consumer Health** Do research to find support organizations for alcoholics and their friends and relatives. Make a pamphlet listing this information, and post it in the classroom.

7. **Growth and Development** With a partner, make a poster listing reasons not to drink alcohol. Include some of the short-term and long-term effects of alcohol on the body. Display your poster in school.

Use and Abuse of Drugs

This lesson will help you find answers to questions that teens often ask about drugs. For example:

► **How should medicines be used?**

► **In what ways do some people misuse and abuse drugs?**

► **How do various kinds of drugs affect the body?**

Using Drugs Properly

You sometimes hear people refer to newly discovered drugs as "miracle drugs." On the other hand, drugs are blamed for causing serious problems in our society. How can these substances be both helpful and harmful? Their effects depend on the types of drugs and how they are used. A **drug** is a *nonfood substance taken into the body that can change the structure or function of the body or mind.* When people talk about drugs that are beneficial, they often call them medications or medicines. A **medicine** is a *drug that is used to treat an illness or relieve pain.*

When you are sick, you might take either prescription or over-the-counter medicine. Prescription medicine is medicine that you can get only with a doctor's written order. You can buy over-the-counter (OTC) medicine without a prescription at pharmacies and other types of stores. Both kinds of medicine can have side effects and should be used with caution.

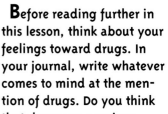

Words to Know

drug
medicine
stimulant
amphetamine
depressant
inhalant
narcotic
hallucinogen

in your journal

Before reading further in this lesson, think about your feelings toward drugs. In your journal, write whatever comes to mind at the mention of drugs. Do you think that drugs are a serious problem for teens? Why or why not?

When you buy an OTC medicine, read the label carefully to be aware of possible side effects.

Simpler Labels

In February 1997 the Food and Drug Administration (FDA) proposed the simplification of labels on over-the-counter drugs. The FDA's recommendations are designed to make medicine labels easier to read and understand. Crucial information, for example, will be listed at the top of the label, not buried in small print near the end. In addition, language will be simplified. The word "pulmonary," for example, will be replaced with the word "lung," and the phrase "consult a physician" will be replaced by "ask a doctor." The FDA hopes that the changes will take effect by mid-1999.

Reading package labels carefully is important, no matter what kind of medicine you plan to use. The labels on over-the-counter medicines include the following information:

- Directions that explain the medicine's purpose and how to use it

- Warnings about any side effects and when to ask a doctor before using the medicine

- A list of active ingredients

- The expiration date, which is the date after which the medicine should not be used

Figure 11.3 at the bottom of this page identifies the information that appears on a typical prescription medicine label.

Misusing and Abusing Drugs

Medicines can cause harm if misused or abused. Drug misuse means using a legal drug in an improper way. A person is misusing drugs if he or she

- takes more than the recommended or prescribed dosage of a medicine or mixes medicines without asking a doctor.

- continues to take medicine after it is no longer needed.

- stops taking a prescribed medicine sooner than the doctor's instructions indicate.

- uses medicine that was prescribed for someone else (even if he or she has the same symptoms).

Drug abuse is a different and more serious problem in our society. It means using substances that are illegal (such as marijuana, cocaine, or LSD) or that are not intended to be taken into the body. Drug abuse may also involve using a legal drug, such as a painkiller, in an illegal or harmful way.

Figure 11.3
Prescription Medicine Label

If you don't understand the information on a prescription label, ask your doctor or pharmacist to explain it to you.

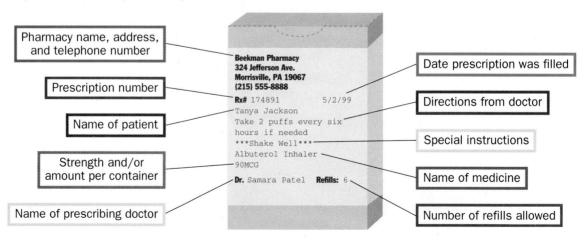

Marijuana

Marijuana (mar·uh·WAH·nuh) is a mood-altering drug made from the leaves, stems, and flowering tops of the hemp plant. It is usually smoked in hand-rolled cigarettes or in pipes. Occasionally it is mixed with food. The effects of marijuana vary and often depend on the user's surroundings and feelings at the time. Some users feel relaxed and unusually sensitive to sights and sounds, while others may feel sad, fearful, and suspicious. **Figure 11.4** shows some short-term and long-term effects of marijuana.

Figure 11.4
Effects of Marijuana Use
Some effects of marijuana are obvious right away, while others occur after repeated use.

The immediate effects of marijuana use may include	Long-term regular marijuana users may experience
• inability to think or speak clearly.	• problems with normal body development (if use begins in adolescence or earlier).
• inability to concentrate.	• damage to lung tissue and the immune cells that fight cancer.
• loss of short-term memory.	• feelings of anxiety and panic.
• lack of coordination and slowed reaction time.	• possible psychological dependence.
• increased heart rate and appetite.	• infertility.

Healthy teens stay away from drugs and other harmful substances.

Stimulants

Stimulants (STIM·yuh·luhnts) are a type of *drugs that speed up the body's functions.* Amphetamines (am·FE·tuh·meenz), cocaine (koh·KAYN), and crack cocaine are stimulants. Stimulants cause increases in heart rate, breathing rate, and blood pressure. They give users a false sense of energy and power. Abuse of stimulants eventually leaves the user feeling exhausted.

Although stimulants are prescribed for some conditions, the use of most stimulants is illegal. These drugs can affect the body in unpredictable ways, even causing death. Users can also become addicted to them.

Amphetamines

Amphetamines are *strong stimulant drugs that speed up the nervous system.* They come in many forms and can be swallowed, inhaled, smoked, or injected. People may abuse amphetamines to stay awake and to get a temporary feeling of energy. Abuse of amphetamines has serious side effects, however. Some of these are shown in **Figure 11.5.**

Figure 11.5
Effects of Amphetamine Abuse

Amphetamine abuse can cause many serious problems, including death.

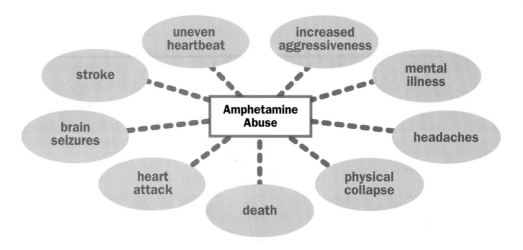

Cocaine and Crack Cocaine

Cocaine is an illegal stimulant drug. It is a white powder made from the leaves of the coca plant. Cocaine can be inhaled, smoked, or injected. Entering the bloodstream quickly, it gives the user a brief, powerful feeling of well-being. That feeling, however, is quickly replaced by anxiety and depression. In a matter of days, a cocaine user can become addicted to the drug.

The use of cocaine can cause loss of appetite, nausea, sleeplessness, seizures, and stroke. Because of its effect on the heart rate, even a first-time user of cocaine runs the risk of a fatal heart attack. Cocaine can also damage the nasal membranes and lungs. A user may have trouble concentrating, become aggressive, or deny responsibility for his or her actions. In addition, a person who injects cocaine with a shared needle risks becoming infected with the human immunodeficiency virus (HIV) or with hepatitis B.

Crack cocaine, or crack, is a concentrated form of cocaine. When smoked, it reaches the brain within 10 seconds. Crack produces a feeling of energy and excitement, but the feeling lasts only about 15 minutes. Then the user feels depressed and craves more of the drug. The side effects of crack are similar to those of cocaine, including possible heart attack and death. In addition, crack users become dependent on the drug even faster than cocaine users.

Depressants

Depressants (di·PRE·suhnts) are *drugs that slow down the body's functions and reactions, including heart and breathing rates.* They come in tablet or capsule form and are swallowed. Doctors sometimes prescribe depressants to treat patients who suffer from anxiety and sleeplessness. Types of depressants include tranquilizers (TRANG·kwuh·ly·zuhrz), hypnotics (hip·NAH·tiks), and barbiturates (bar·BI·chuh·ruhts). Alcohol is also a depressant.

Depressants may make users feel relaxed and less anxious. However, depressants can also cause poor coordination and impaired judgment. People who abuse depressants may experience mood swings or depression. In addition, people can become addicted to depressants. If combined with alcohol, depressants can cause coma and death.

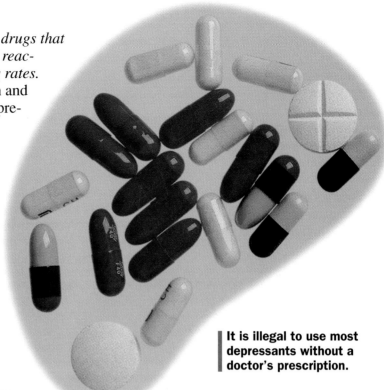

It is illegal to use most depressants without a doctor's prescription.

Other Illegal Drugs

Marijuana, stimulants, and depressants are some of the best-known drugs that people abuse. However, many other illegal and dangerous drugs are also abused. **Inhalants** (in·HAY·luhnts) are *substances whose fumes are breathed in to produce mind-altering sensations.* Most inhalants are substances that were not intended to be taken into the body, such as glue, gasoline, and spray paint. Inhaling these substances can cause nausea or vomiting, dizziness, mental confusion, and loss of motor skills. Inhalant use—even a single use—can lead to permanent brain damage, coma, or death.

Narcotics (nar·KAH·tiks) are *drugs that relieve pain and dull the senses.* Many narcotics, including heroin (HER·uh·wuhn), are very powerful and also illegal. Other narcotics, such as morphine (MAWR·feen) and codeine (KOH·deen), are legal for a person who is under a doctor's care and has a prescription. Narcotics are very carefully controlled because their effects are so strong, and because users can easily become addicted.

Hallucinogens (huh·LOO·suhn·uh·jenz) are *drugs that distort moods, thoughts, and senses.* Two hallucinogens are lysergic (luh·SER·jik) acid diethylamide (dy·e·thuh·LA·myd), or LSD, and phencyclidine (fen·SY·kluh·deen), or PCP. These drugs sometimes cause the user to experience imaginary images and sounds or distortions of real objects. Users may lose control of their actions and behave strangely or violently, possibly endangering their own lives or the lives of others.

Q & A

"Roofies"

Q: I overheard a couple of kids talking about "roofies." What are they?

A: "Roofies" is the street name for Rohypnol, a very powerful sleeping pill. It is not legal in the United States. Roofies are often used with alcohol and other drugs. Recently, roofies have become associated with date rape. A victim is given roofies without her knowledge. She then passes out and may not remember that sexual contact has occurred.

The Dangers of Drug Abuse

All mood-altering drugs have powerful effects on the nervous system. This is why some people turn to drugs when they are anxious, bored, or feeling hopeless. They see drugs as a way to change their feelings and even to escape from them.

Drugs of these kinds are very dangerous, however. Some drugs, such as heroin, LSD, and cocaine, may actually alter the way the nervous system works. Because the nervous system controls the way people receive, process, and transmit information, drug abuse causes individuals to lose control over their own lives. Drugs that are injected can also expose people to deadly infections from viruses such as HIV and hepatitis. Drug addiction destroys many lives. In addition, many of the drugs discussed in this lesson can cause permanent brain damage, coma, and death.

Read your journal entry from the beginning of the lesson. Have your feelings about drugs changed now that you have read the text? In your private journal, describe your thoughts about the need for discussions on drugs among friends, family members, and the school population.

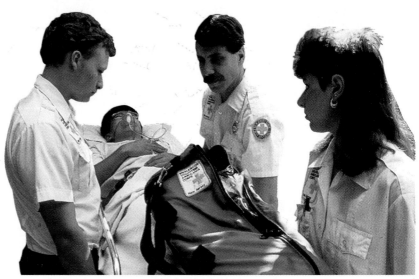

Those who use alcohol and drugs risk their own health and safety and the health and safety of those around them.

Lesson 2 Review

Using complete sentences, answer the following questions on a separate sheet of paper.

Reviewing Terms and Facts

1. **Define**   Explain the terms *drug* and *medicine.*
2. **Explain**   What is the difference between misuse and abuse of drugs?
3. **Give Examples**   Describe the effects of narcotics, and give two examples.

Thinking Critically

4. **Analyze**   In what ways are inhalants different from many of the other drugs discussed in this lesson?

5. **Suggest**   What advice would you give to a friend who was thinking about taking amphetamines so that she could stay awake to study for a test?

Applying Health Concepts

6. **Health of Others**   Make a list of rules telling how to use prescription and over-the-counter medicines correctly. For each rule, explain why it is important. Post your list at home or at school.

The Nervous System

This lesson will help you find answers to questions that teens often ask about the brain and the nervous system. For example:

▶ **What are neurons, and what is their function?**

▶ **What are the parts of the nervous system?**

▶ **How can I keep my nervous system healthy?**

The Body's Control System

As you have learned, the use of drugs and alcohol can produce harmful effects throughout the body. The nervous system, however, is most directly affected by these substances. Abuse of drugs and alcohol can permanently damage the nervous system.

The nervous system is the control center of your body. It responds to changes from inside or outside the body and sends messages to the brain. It also relays instructions from the brain to other parts of the body. The nervous system controls thought processes, senses, movement, and such functions as heartbeat, breathing, and digestion. Therefore, it is essential to keep your nervous system healthy by protecting it from disease, injury, and the effects of alcohol and drugs.

Neurons

The cells that make up the nervous system are called **neurons** (NOO·rahnz). They are also known as nerve cells. Neurons send and receive information in the form of tiny electrical charges. These charges carry messages throughout the body. **Figure 11.6** shows the path that the messages follow to cause the body to react.

Words to Know

neuron
central nervous
 system (CNS)
peripheral nervous
 system (PNS)
brain
spinal cord

Figure 11.6
How Neurons Work

The three types of neurons work like a relay team to carry messages throughout the body.

1 A receptor—the ear—responds to sound waves. **Sensory neurons** in the ear receive information and send impulses to the brain via the auditory nerve.

2 **Connecting neurons,** found in both the brain and the spinal cord, relay information about the sound to motor neurons.

3 The **motor neurons** deliver the message to the muscles. Lauren turns her head toward the sound.

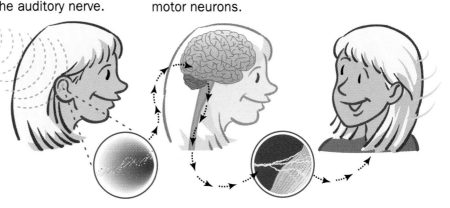

Lauren!

The Nervous System

The nervous system has two main parts, as shown in **Figure 11.7.** The **central nervous system (CNS)** consists of *the brain and the spinal cord.* It coordinates the body's activities. The **peripheral (puh·RIF·uh·ruhl) nervous system (PNS)** is made up of *all the nerves outside the central nervous system.* It connects the brain and the spinal cord to the rest of the body.

The **brain** is the *information center of the nervous system.* It receives and screens information and sends messages to other parts of the body. **Figure 11.7** shows the three main parts of the brain. The **spinal cord** is *a long bundle of neurons that relays messages to and from the brain and all parts of the body.*

Figure 11.7
Parts of the Nervous System

The brain is the largest organ of the central nervous system, which is shown in yellow. The peripheral nervous system, which is shown in blue, links the CNS to the skeletal muscles. It also controls heart rate, breathing, and digestion.

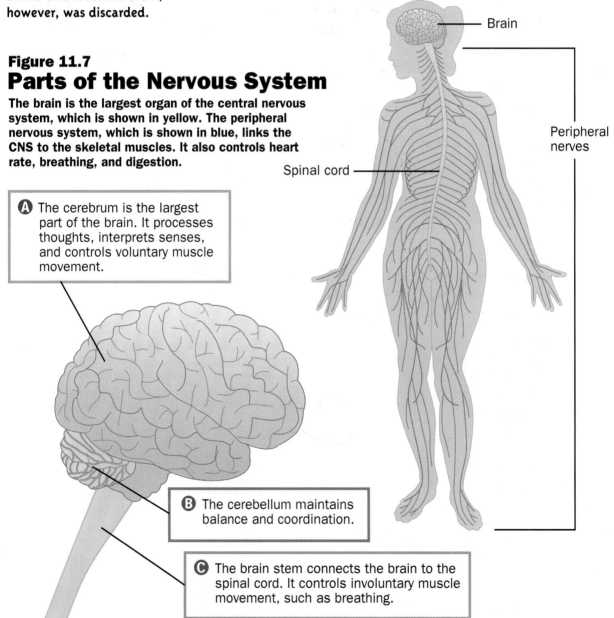

A The cerebrum is the largest part of the brain. It processes thoughts, interprets senses, and controls voluntary muscle movement.

B The cerebellum maintains balance and coordination.

C The brain stem connects the brain to the spinal cord. It controls involuntary muscle movement, such as breathing.

Brain

Peripheral nerves

Spinal cord

Problems of the Nervous System

Several diseases and disorders may affect the nervous system. Healthy lifestyle decisions can prevent many of these problems. The following factors may lead to nervous system disorders:

- **Infections.** Illnesses such as polio, rabies, and meningitis (me·nuhn·JY·tuhs) are caused by viruses that affect the nervous system. Fortunately, vaccines are available for some of these diseases. Others can be treated successfully with medicines.

- **Degenerative disorders.** Some disorders are caused by damage to the nervous system, but they cannot be prevented or cured. These disorders include multiple sclerosis (skluh·ROH·suhs) and cerebral palsy (suh·REE·bruhl PAWL·zee).

- **Injuries.** The most common cause of nervous system damage is physical injury. The results of head, neck, and back injuries can be very severe. A spinal cord injury, for example, can cause paralysis—the loss of feeling and movement in part of the body. Many of these injuries to the nervous system can be prevented by taking safety precautions.

- **Drug abuse.** The misuse and abuse of drugs can cause damage to the nervous system. Drugs act directly on the brain stem, which helps control heart rate, breathing, appetite, and sleeping. Some drugs also create problems with the way messages are sent, received, and responded to by the nervous system.

- **Alcohol abuse.** Drinking alcohol has an immediate effect on the brain. It can impair memory, thought processes, perception, judgment, and attention. Over time, abuse of alcohol can destroy millions of brain cells. Once destroyed, these cells can never be repaired or replaced.

Women who are pregnant should avoid consuming alcohol. Drinking during pregnancy may damage the baby's central nervous system, leading to a condition known as fetal alcohol syndrome (FAS).

Caring for Your Nervous System

You can take care of your nervous system by practicing good health habits, such as eating properly and getting enough sleep. In addition, the following safety measures will help prevent nervous system damage.

- **Protect yourself from disease.** Most likely, you have already been vaccinated against some diseases, such as polio. To protect yourself from rabies, avoid contact with strange or wild animals. Good hygiene will help protect you from infections such as meningitis.

- **Wear a helmet.** When you are riding a bike, skateboarding, in-line skating, or playing a contact sport, wear a helmet. It will help to protect your head from injury.

- **Wear a seat belt.** Always fasten your seat belt when you are riding in a car.

- **Play it safe.** Be careful when playing sports. For example, never dive into shallow water. If you use gymnastics equipment, such as a trampoline, have spotters watch you.

- **Lift properly.** When lifting heavy objects, use the proper techniques to prevent back injuries. If the object is too heavy, ask someone for help.

- **Observe safety rules.** When walking or riding a bicycle, follow all traffic safety rules.

- **Avoid alcohol and drugs.** By not using alcohol and drugs, you will prevent many disorders of the nervous system.

HEALTH LAB

Nervous System Tricks

Introduction: Your perception of the world is based partly on your senses and partly on past experience. Your perception can be faulty, however, if your nervous system is being fooled—for example, by an optical illusion. Your eyes can play tricks on you because of the way the nerves in your eyes normally react to light and color.

Your retina, the network of nerves that absorbs the light rays that enter your eye, has two kinds of receptors. Cone cells are sensitive to bright light and colors. Rod cells help you see in dim light. The way these cells work together can make the contrast between dark and light confusing.

Objective: View optical illusions, and examine how they occur.

Materials and Method: Look at the picture of the two circles within squares. Which circle looks larger—the white or the black?

Next, look at the picture of black squares. Focus your eyes on one of the squares. What do you perceive in the intersections of the white bars? Now focus closely on one intersection. What happens?

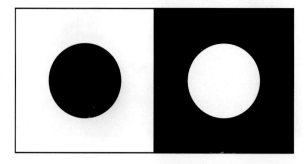

Using complete sentences, answer the following questions on a separate sheet of paper.

Reviewing Terms and Facts

1. **Vocabulary**   Define the term *neuron.* What is the function of neurons?

2. **Compare**   What is the difference between the *central nervous system* and the *peripheral nervous system?*

3. **Identify**   Name the three main parts of the brain and explain the function of each part.

4. **List**   What are four causes of problems in the nervous system?

5. **Recall**   Identify five safety measures you can take to protect your nervous system.

Thinking Critically

6. **Describe**   Think of any movement that a person might make during a volleyball game. Explain how neurons would enable this action to occur.

7. **Hypothesize**   What attitudes might lead to the types of accidents that damage the nervous system?

Applying Health Concepts

8. **Growth and Development**   With a small group of classmates, create a skit to show how neurons carry messages and cause a reaction. Decide on an action to portray, choose roles, and act it out for the class. One person can act as the narrator to explain the steps. Your group may need to do some research to create the skit.

9. **Health of Others**   With a partner, make a poster showing safety rules to follow to prevent damage to the nervous system. Include drawings that illustrate the dangers, and write brief explanations of how to prevent each problem. Display your poster in the classroom.

Observations and Analysis:

Measure the diameters of the two circles in the first picture. Did your perception fool you? The way cone cells and rod cells work can make bright objects seem larger than dark ones.

In the second picture, did you perceive dark spots in the intersections when you were looking at a black square? Why do you think the spots seemed to disappear when you looked directly at an intersection? The explanation is that the color white appears whiter when it is next to something black. The white bars appear whiter than the intersections because the bars are right next to black squares, while the intersections are seen as the color white meeting the color white. When, however, you look at the intersection area by itself, you perceive the white as white. Your eye is not comparing it to any other white area.

What other optical illusions have you experienced? Why might they occur? Find another example of an optical illusion in a book or magazine. Write a paragraph about this illusion and how it tricks the eye. Share your observations with your classmates.

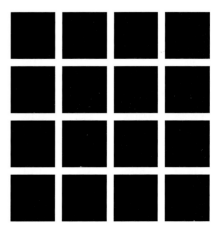

TEEN HEALTH DIGEST

People at Work

Country Counselor

From her office window, Maria Rodriguez can see farmland and just a few houses. Inside, however, the scene is less peaceful. Maria is a counselor at an alcohol and drug treatment clinic. Her clients are people who have abuse and addiction problems.

Maria sometimes helps on a practical level. For example, she may assist a recovering addict in finding a job or a place to live. She also holds counseling sessions for her clients.

"Many people think that alcohol and drugs are found only in the cities," Maria says. "But people in the country face these kinds of problems, too."

Maria grew up in a nearby small town. She decided to become a counselor after helping a friend who had been abusing drugs. After finishing high school, Maria got an associate degree in counseling and began working at the clinic.

CON$UMER FOCU$

On-Line Targets?

It sounds great—a Web site that includes the latest music, interviews with rock stars, and reviews of CDs. The problem is that the site is sponsored by a well-known beer company. Mixed in with the music are numerous promotions for the beer.

Web sites sponsored by other beer and liquor companies include interactive games. Some feature chat rooms and interactive stories. Are these sites designed to appeal to the underage consumer?

Industry representatives claim that the Web sites are geared to adults. Some sites run messages warning that they are for people aged 21 or older. Many people are concerned, however, and feel that these sites are designed to appeal to minors as they promote alcohol products.

Try This:

Do you think that a warning message saying that a Web site is for adults only would be effective at keeping teens out? Write a paragraph explaining your opinion.

Tough Guy?

Q.: I heard some people saying that a guy they know can really "hold his liquor." What does that mean?

A.: They probably think that the person can drink a lot of alcohol without getting drunk. They may assume that because they do not see any change in his behavior, the alcohol is not affecting him. In fact, it is the amount of *alcohol consumed* that causes health risks, not how much a person's *behavior* appears to be affected by alcohol. Over time, heavy drinkers get used to alcohol and need greater amounts to produce the same feelings. This heavy drinking causes damage to the liver, heart, and brain. Unfortunately, these people may not realize that they are abusing alcohol and risking their health until it is too late.

Teens Making a Difference

Tricks and Talks

The Shooting Stars are a group of 12- to 15-year-olds who perform basketball tricks. They put on exhibitions during half-time at high school and college games. Their routines include dribbling in unison, spinning balls on the ends of their fingers, and dribbling three balls at once.

Once they have the audience's attention, the Stars talk about the dangers of drugs. They encourage kids to get involved in activities they enjoy instead of using harmful substances. With their talent and such an important message, the Shooting Stars are invited to perform at many schools.

HEALTH UPDATE

Danger to the Unborn

When a pregnant woman is addicted to alcohol or drugs, her baby can be severely damaged. During the early stages of pregnancy, each system in a baby's body is at an important stage of development. Harmful substances used by the mother can cause birth defects, such as low birth weight and heart problems. During the later stages of pregnancy, drug use by the mother can result in slowed growth and brain defects.

A baby born to a drug-addicted mother is sometimes born addicted and can suffer severe and long-lasting withdrawal symptoms. Even if the baby survives the withdrawal process, in later life the child may experience behavioral and psychological disturbances.

Try This:

Do research about alcohol, drugs, and fetal development. Report on your findings to the class.

4 Risks Involved with Alcohol and Drug Use

This lesson will help you find answers to questions that teens often ask about the risks and consequences of using alcohol and drugs. For example:

▶ What are the physical risks of alcohol and drug use?

▶ How can alcohol and drug use affect my thoughts and emotions?

▶ How can alcohol and drug use harm my relationships with others?

Word to Know

intoxicated

in your journal

How do you feel about taking risks? In your journal, describe your attitude on this subject. You may have ideas that contradict one another. For example, you may not want to put yourself in danger. However, you may also feel that taking risks is exciting. What are some ways in which you can experience fun and excitement but not harm yourself or others?

Knowing the Risks

Drinking alcohol and taking drugs are risk behaviors. As you learned in Chapter 1, a risk behavior is an action or choice that may cause injury or harm to you or to others. Alcohol and drug abuse involve many risks. Most are quite serious, and some are even deadly.

These risks affect every part of a person's life and health. Alcohol and drugs can be especially dangerous to teens, who are still growing and developing. These substances cause physical, mental, and social harm.

■ Alcohol and drug use may slow down the time it takes a teen's body to mature physically. Height, weight, and sexual development may be affected.

■ Alcohol and drug use may shorten a person's attention span. Users may have less interest in pursuing their goals.

■ Alcohol and drug use may cause people to lose control and act in ways they later regret. Relationships with family and friends may become strained.

Being aware of the consequences of alcohol and drug use can help you stay away from risky situations. If you do find yourself in such a situation, knowing the dangers will help you make the right decision. You'll feel confident about choosing not to use alcohol or drugs.

Staying away from alcohol and drugs will help you maintain a good relationship with your family.

Physical Consequences

You have already read about ways in which using alcohol and drugs can affect a person's short-term and long-term physical health. The intensity of effects produced by these substances varies and may be unpredictable. Short-term effects may include headaches, fever, dizziness, and vomiting. Long-term effects may include serious damage to organs and body systems. Alcohol and drug use can also affect physical fitness by causing

■ loss of physical coordination, including difficulty in walking, running, dancing, and playing sports.

■ muscle twitches and cramps.

■ decreased endurance.

■ reduced strength.

■ lowered energy level.

■ slowed reflexes.

In addition to these health problems, a person may face other physical consequences from alcohol and drug use. Under the influence of alcohol or drugs, people sometimes cause physical harm to themselves or others. An alcohol or drug user may take risks that he or she would normally avoid, such as starting a fight.

Drinking and Driving

Why is it so dangerous to drink and drive? It's because even one alcoholic drink can slow a person's reaction time, impair judgment, and interfere with decision making. The more alcohol a person drinks, the more dangerous he or she is behind the wheel. When a driver has been drinking, the chances that he or she will be involved in an accident are very high. About half of all fatal automobile accidents involve alcohol. In 1995 alcohol-related automobile accidents were the leading cause of death for 15- to 24-year-olds.

Drivers who have been drinking endanger not only themselves but many other people as well. Their passengers face great risk of injury or death. The lives of pedestrians and people in other cars are also threatened. For these reasons, it is illegal for a person to drive while **intoxicated** (in·TAHK·suh·kay·tuhd), also called *drunk*.

Never accept a ride with a driver who has been drinking. Be firm in refusing to get into the car.

The Effects on Others

The physical consequences of alcohol and drug abuse extend beyond the user. If a pregnant woman uses these substances, for example, she can cause disease and birth defects in her unborn child. Children whose mothers abused drugs during pregnancy often have delayed development and learning disabilities. Women who drink alcohol while pregnant may have babies with fetal alcohol syndrome (FAS). This condition causes delays in development and psychological and behavioral problems throughout life.

Mental/Emotional Consequences

As a teen, you are developing your self-concept and trying to find your place in the world. This is an exciting time, but it is also stressful. To try to relieve this stress, some teens turn to alcohol or drugs. These substances actually have the opposite effect, however, making life even more confusing and difficult.

The psychological consequences of alcohol and drug abuse are very serious. A person's ability to think and learn are negatively affected. Alcohol and drug abuse also has many serious emotional consequences. **Figure 11.8** shows some of the mental and emotional consequences of alcohol and drug abuse.

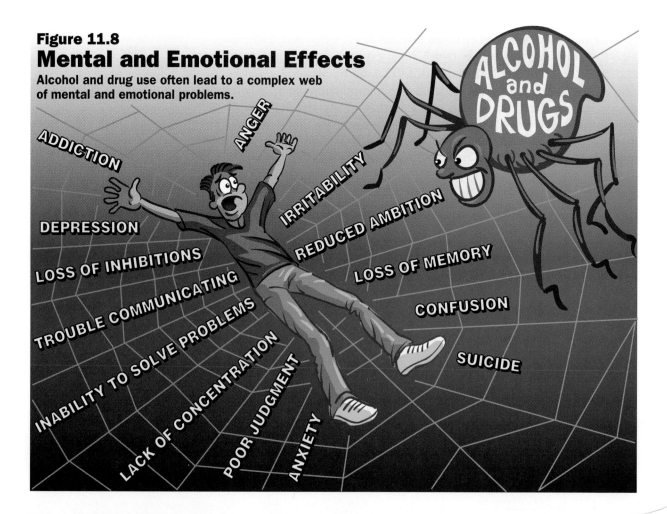

Figure 11.8
Mental and Emotional Effects
Alcohol and drug use often lead to a complex web of mental and emotional problems.

Social Consequences

Involvement with alcohol and drugs also leads to problems in social relationships. The use of these substances may cause personality changes. The user may lose control of his or her behavior and do things that he or she later regrets. These actions often cause relationships with others to become strained or even to break apart.

Abusers may become obsessed with alcohol and drugs. This obsession usually causes them to lose interest in family, friends, and even personal hygiene. To avoid being caught, users may lie to loved ones. Some stop seeing their friends and become involved with other people who are also obsessed with alcohol or drugs. Lacking true friendships and honest relationships, drug abusers may feel very lonely.

Risks in School

Teens who use alcohol and drugs also cause problems for themselves in school. They may

- be late or miss school often.

- get bad grades.

- lose the chance to play sports because of missed practices.

- let down classmates or teammates because of poor performance.

- lose opportunities to learn new skills and develop their abilities.

Risks to the Family

When any member of a family abuses alcohol or drugs, the rest of the family is affected. Alcohol and drug abuse cause great disruption in the home.

- A person who uses alcohol or drugs may become violent and hurt other family members.

- Someone who abuses alcohol or drugs may spend more time away from home, lie to other family members, and be moody and unpredictable.

- If parents abuse drugs, they cannot fulfill their obligations to their children or provide emotional support. They may lose their jobs, creating serious financial problems for the family.

- Teens who abuse drugs may disappoint their parents. They usually fail to meet their family responsibilities.

- Alcohol or drug abuse may even cause a family to break up.

Did You Know?

Legal Responsibilities [ACTIVITY!]

The host of a party can be held responsible for guests' drinking. If someone leaves a party and drives while intoxicated, causing an accident, the host may face legal action. Write a paragraph explaining the reasoning behind this law.

A drug-related arrest has many serious long-term consequences.

Risks with the Law

Teens who use alcohol and drugs often get into serious trouble with the law. It is a crime to buy, sell, or possess marijuana, cocaine, and other illegal substances. The penalties vary from state to state. Breaking the law can lead to arrest, fines, or time spent in a detention center.

It is also illegal for a person under 21 to buy or possess alcohol. An underage person who is caught driving while intoxicated will lose his or her license. Adults who sell liquor to underage individuals are also breaking the law. Tragically, involvement with alcohol and drugs often leads teens to commit other crimes. A person under the influence of alcohol or drugs has an increased chance of becoming violent. For these reasons, even a single use of alcohol or drugs may lead to years in prison.

In addition, people who abuse alcohol or drugs are at risk of becoming crime victims themselves. They may encounter dangerous situations when buying or seeking drugs. Under the influence of alcohol or drugs, people often make unwise decisions. These choices may cause them physical injury and may even result in death.

Lesson 4 Review

Using complete sentences, answer the following questions on a separate sheet of paper.

Reviewing Terms and Facts

1. **Vocabulary**   Write a definition of the term *intoxicated.*
2. **List**   Name five mental and emotional consequences of alcohol and drug use.
3. **Identify**   List three problems teen alcohol or drug users may have at school.

Thinking Critically

4. **Hypothesize**   How might a teen's use of alcohol or drugs create tension within his or her family?

5. **Analyze**   Penalties for selling drugs are usually more severe than those for possessing drugs. Why do you think this is so?

Applying Health Concepts

6. **Personal Health**   With a partner, role-play a scene in which a teen refuses to ride in a car with someone who has been drinking. Then role-play a scene in which the teen tries to convince the driver not to drive while under the influence of alcohol.

Avoiding Substance Abuse

This lesson will help you find answers to questions that teens often ask about ways to avoid alcohol and drugs. For example:

▶ **What are some reasons to avoid substance abuse?**

▶ **How can I say no to alcohol and drugs?**

▶ **What alternatives are there to alcohol and drug use?**

Making Responsible Decisions

When you care about yourself, you take responsibility for your actions. You also feel confident in making your own decisions based on your values. If you value your health, you will protect it by avoiding the risks associated with alcohol and drugs. Making responsible decisions involves an effort on your part. One way to make that effort is to think ahead of time about how you will handle difficult situations.

Using alcohol or drugs will not help you feel good about yourself. In fact, people who use these substances often have a poor self-concept. People with a negative self-concept may think that using alcohol or drugs will make them feel more confident.

Alcohol and drugs, however, are not necessary to give a person self-confidence. In fact, your sense of your own value as an individual is a powerful tool that can help you to choose an alcohol- and drug-free life. When you are in control, you can take pride in the choices you have made.

Words to Know

invulnerable
assertive
alternatives

Q & A ?

Helping Others

Q: I don't use drugs, and I don't want my friends to, either. How can I help other people avoid drugs?

A: By not using drugs, you show other teens that it's okay to avoid substance abuse. You can encourage your friends to stay away from situations where drugs are used, support one another, and participate in healthful activities. If you feel that a friend needs help, ask a school counselor or a trusted adult about organizations that offer support to troubled teens.

Teens who feel good about themselves and have a sense of purpose can more easily avoid alcohol and drugs.

Reasons to Avoid Substance Abuse

Although most teens are aware that alcohol and drugs are dangerous, some are still tempted to try them. Some teens may want to do something risky; others may just want to satisfy their curiosity. Some teens think that using alcohol or drugs will make them seem more mature. Others begin using these substances because of peer pressure. Still others believe that they are **invulnerable,** or *not able to be hurt.*

In reality, however, there are no good reasons to try alcohol or drugs. As you have learned, substance abuse can have negative consequences in all areas of a person's life. There are many good reasons—even beyond protecting your health—to avoid abusing alcohol or drugs. **Figure 11.9** identifies some of them.

Figure 11.9
Reasons to Avoid Substance Abuse
You should have a ready supply of reasons to avoid abusing alcohol and drugs.

Saying No to Substance Abuse

For many teens, peer pressure is the main reason given for using alcohol or drugs. One of the keys to avoiding substance abuse is to avoid social situations where such abuse might take place. These situations often involve peer pressure. If you think that there will be alcohol or drugs at a party, for example, it's smarter not to go.

It is not always possible, however, to avoid situations involving peer pressure. For this reason, you should prepare yourself ahead of time to say no to alcohol and drugs. You can do this by recognizing possible situations in which you might encounter peer pressure and deciding how you will handle them. **Figure 11.10** describes a few situations and suggests ways to deal with them.

The first step is to decide that you are not going to drink alcohol or take drugs. Sticking to this decision takes determination. You need to be **assertive,** which means *having the determination to stand up for yourself in a firm but positive way.* You also need effective refusal skills. If someone tries to pressure you into trying alcohol or drugs, follow these tips for saying no:

■ Use humor to make the situation less tense. Make a joke or give a funny reason for not wanting to use the substance.

■ Use "I" messages. Don't accuse or blame the person.

■ Take your time. Collect your thoughts if necessary.

■ Stand up straight and look the person in the eye.

■ Speak in a firm but polite voice.

■ Don't apologize for saying no.

■ Walk away from the situation.

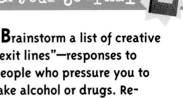
in your journal

Brainstorm a list of creative "exit lines"—responses to people who pressure you to take alcohol or drugs. Remember that you don't owe anyone an explanation for refusing to use these substances. You just want to get your message across— that you're not interested.

Figure 11.10
Facing Peer Pressure
Being prepared for peer pressure situations will help you make the right choices.

Situations	Solutions
• Some of your friends have started smoking marijuana after school. They are pressuring you to join them.	• Tell them that you aren't interested, and find a substitute activity. Join an after-school club, or find volunteer work that you can do during that time.
• At a park near your home, some older teens have offered you drugs.	• Tell them that you need to leave. Avoid the park in the future when these teens are present.
• You go to a friend's house, and no adults are home. Your friend offers you a drink containing alcohol.	• You don't have to explain why you don't want to drink. Leave the house, but don't get into a car with anyone who has been drinking. Next time, check first to make sure that adults will be present.

Some teens say that family or personal problems lead them to drink or take drugs. How could you respond to a friend who gave those reasons as an excuse for using drugs? You might tell your friend that substance abuse only causes more trouble and doesn't solve the original problem.

Make a poster that gives reasons not to use alcohol and drugs. Use illustrations and words to encourage teens to find more constructive solutions to their problems. Be positive!

Reaching Your Potential

What are your plans for the future? You may want to travel to other countries, go to college, become an auto mechanic, or work with computers. Making your dreams come true means not letting yourself be sidetracked by alcohol or drugs.

There are many alternatives to alcohol and drug use. **Alternatives** are *other ways of thinking or acting*. The following list suggests some positive alternatives. What others can you think of?

- Improve your skills in a sport you enjoy, or try a new sport.
- Join a school club or other extracurricular activity.
- Take art classes, or learn to play a musical instrument.
- Study a new language.
- Volunteer in a hospital, homeless shelter, or soup kitchen.

Using your skills and talents, such as musical ability, is a healthy alternative to substance abuse.

MAKING HEALTHY DECISIONS
Offering Alternatives

*E*mma and Samantha have been friends since second grade. For a long time, they did everything together. Since starting middle school, however, Emma has noticed that Samantha is changing. When Emma speaks with her mother about this, her mother says that maybe it's just time for both of them to develop other friendships. Emma decides to join the school newspaper and begins making new friends. Samantha seems to be finding new friends, too.

One day, Emma and Samantha meet up with each other while walking home from school. Emma is happy to be with her old friend. She asks Samantha to come over to her parents' apartment to listen to a new CD. Samantha has a different idea, though. She suggests that they stop off at the park, where some of Samantha's new friends are smoking marijuana.

Emma knows that she doesn't want to use marijuana or be around people who are using it. She is also concerned about Samantha. She still has some time to think before she and Samantha will reach the park entrance. She uses the time to go through the six-step decision-making process.

Using complete sentences, answer the following questions on a separate sheet of paper.

Reviewing Terms and Facts

1. **Vocabulary** What is the meaning of *invulnerable*?

2. **Restate** Why is it a good idea to avoid situations where substance abuse might take place?

3. **Vocabulary** Define *assertive*. Then use the term in an original sentence.

4. **List** Suggest five tips for saying no to alcohol and drugs.

5. **Identify** List four positive alternatives to alcohol and drug use.

Thinking Critically

6. **Analyze** How does a positive self-concept help teens avoid using illegal substances?

7. **Suggest** What advice would you give to a friend who was being pressured to try alcohol or drugs?

Applying Health Concepts

8. **Personal Health** Make a list of all the reasons why you do not want to try alcohol or drugs. Keep the list with you, and look at it when you need encouragement. Add to the list when you think of other good reasons.

9. **Health of Others** With a small group, make up a skit in which teens face peer pressure to use alcohol or drugs. Create a realistic setting for the skit, such as a party or school event, and think of ways for the teens to say no. Present your skit to the class.

① **State the situation**
② **List the options**
③ **Weigh the possible outcomes**
④ **Consider your values**
⑤ **Make a decision and act**
⑥ **Evaluate the decision**

Follow-up Activities

1. Apply the steps in the decision-making process to Emma's situation.

2. With a partner, role-play a scene in which Emma says no to Samantha. Include several alternative activities that Emma might suggest.

3. As a class, discuss what Emma could do to maintain her friendship with Samantha without using drugs.

Addiction and Recovery

This lesson will help you find answers to questions that teens often ask about addiction and recovery. For example:

▶ **How do people become addicted to alcohol and drugs?**

▶ **Why is withdrawal from a drug so difficult?**

▶ **Where can an addicted person get help?**

Words to Know

tolerance
recovery

Addiction

As you have learned, addiction is a physical or psychological need for a drug or other substance. With a physical addiction, the body feels a direct need for the drug. With a psychological, or mental, addiction, the mind tells the body that it needs more of the substance.

Addiction starts with alcohol or drug use and then continues with abuse. It then progresses through increased tolerance into total dependency. **Tolerance** (TAHL·er·ens) occurs when *the body becomes used to a drug and needs greater amounts to get the desired effect.* Addiction cannot be cured, but it can be controlled. The only way for a person to control a drug addiction, however, is never to use the substance again.

When people are addicted to a drug, they may put it ahead of everything else in their lives. Many drugs are addictive, including the following.

■ Nicotine is considered one of the most addictive substances.

■ Marijuana can cause psychological dependence.

■ Amphetamines are addictive. Crack and cocaine can be addictive after just one use.

■ Alcohol can be addictive. Other types of depressants, such as barbiturates, are also addictive.

■ Heroin and other narcotics are highly addictive.

The best way to avoid becoming addicted to alcohol or drugs is never to start using them.

Substance addiction is like a slide downward, and **recovery,** or *the process of becoming well again,* is a steep climb back up. A recovering addict must continually resist the desire to use the substance again. **Figure 11.11** shows the process.

Figure 11.11
Stages of Addiction and Recovery

A person who is addicted to alcohol or drugs must make an extraordinary effort to become free of the substance.

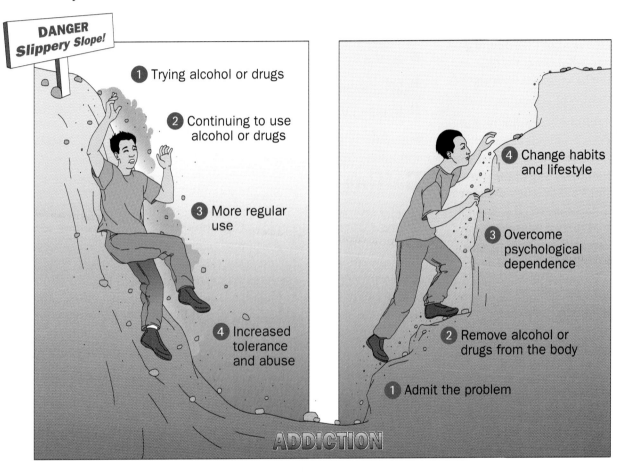

DANGER Slippery Slope!

1. Trying alcohol or drugs
2. Continuing to use alcohol or drugs
3. More regular use
4. Increased tolerance and abuse

4. Change habits and lifestyle
3. Overcome psychological dependence
2. Remove alcohol or drugs from the body
1. Admit the problem

ADDICTION

The Pain of Withdrawal

Ending an alcohol or drug habit is much harder than resisting the use of the substance in the first place. The addict must remove all traces of the substance from the body. This process causes withdrawal, a series of painful physical and mental symptoms that occur when a person stops using an addictive substance.

A person going through withdrawal often needs professional help. The withdrawal process strongly affects the nervous system. It can cause very unpleasant symptoms, including

■ severe anxiety.

■ confusion, memory loss, or hallucinations.

■ nausea, vomiting, and diarrhea.

■ headaches and chills.

Teen Issues

Danger Zone

Young teens who try alcohol or drugs are at greater risk of addiction than older teens or adults. They are often more vulnerable to the influences of alcohol and drugs because of their physical size and stage of development.

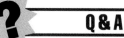
Is My Friend in Trouble?

Q: A friend of mine has started spending a lot of time with some older kids who have a bad reputation. She doesn't include me anymore. She has also been secretive about where she goes and what she is doing. Could she be involved with alcohol or drugs?

A: It is a possibility, but you should not assume that it is true. Check to see if your friend has any of the warning signs of addiction described in this chapter. If you think that there is cause for concern, talk honestly to your friend about your feelings.

Language Arts Connection

Stories of Addiction **ACTIVITY**

Many novels and short stories for young adults deal with the subject of addiction. Ask your teacher or librarian to recommend an appropriate book for your age group. Read it and write a short review. Describe how the book addresses the problems of alcohol addiction or drug addiction.

Parents and other trusted adults can help you get treatment for an addiction. They can also give you good advice about where to get help for a friend.

Knowing When to Get Help

How can you tell if a friend or family member is addicted to drugs? It can be hard to determine because most people try to hide the problem or deny that one exists. The signs of addiction to drugs are similar to the signs of alcoholism mentioned earlier, such as

- using drugs on a regular basis.

- lying about the amount or frequency of drug use.

- thinking that drugs are a necessary part of having fun.

- avoiding other people in order to use substances.

- giving up activities that the person used to enjoy.

- pressuring others to use substances.

- frequent moods of depression and hopelessness.

- regularly missing school or work.

Getting Help

You can get help for yourself, a friend, or a family member who has an alcohol or drug addiction. First, try going to people who are close at hand, such as parents; teachers, clergy members, and school counselors; trusted friends; or peer counselors. If you do not know anyone who can help you, you can turn to organizations and agencies that offer counseling and treatment. The phone numbers and addresses for these groups are in the Yellow Pages of your telephone directory. They are listed under headings such as "Drug Abuse" or "Alcoholism Treatment." Places to go for help include

- toll-free drug hot line counselors.

- support groups.

- alcohol or drug treatment centers.

The Challenge of Recovery

As you learned in Lesson 2, recovery from addiction begins with admitting that there is a problem. If you have a friend or family member who has an addiction, he or she may be reluctant to seek help. In that case, join a support group for friends or relatives of addicts. Although you want to help the person, you must remember that you are not responsible for the addiction.

Once an addict has admitted the problem, he or she must receive treatment to stop alcohol or drug use. The person might check into a substance abuse clinic, go to a clinic as an outpatient, or join a long-term support program. The goal is for the person to learn to live without alcohol or drugs.

When teens become addicts, their recovery may include catching up on skills they have missed. They may have dropped out of school, for example, and need to receive tutoring to finish their education. They also need to learn new ways to handle their problems so that they don't return to alcohol or drug use.

in your journal

What would you say to a friend who appeared to have an alcohol or drug problem? Make a list of ways to convince the person to get help. In your journal, write a letter asking the friend to seek counseling.

With help, teens can recover from addiction and achieve their long-term goals.

Review

Lesson 6

Using complete sentences, answer the following questions on a separate sheet of paper.

Reviewing Terms and Facts

1. **Vocabulary**   Define *tolerance*. Then use it in an original sentence.

2. **Recall**   List four of the symptoms of withdrawal.

3. **List**   Name four people or places you might contact to get help for someone with a substance abuse problem.

Thinking Critically

4. **Infer**   Why might an addict not seek treatment on his or her own?

5. **Describe**   Why is recovery so much more difficult than avoiding drugs in the first place?

Applying Health Concepts

6. **Health of Others**   Make a pamphlet about sources of help for people who abuse drugs. Find agencies and organizations in your area where teens can go for help with substance abuse problems. Identify which organizations help teens with their own problems and which ones give support to friends and family members of addicts. If possible, make copies of your pamphlet, and distribute them in the school library, the public library, and other public places in your community.

Chapter 11 Review

Chapter Summary

▶ **Lesson 1** Alcohol has many unhealthful effects on the body. Alcoholism is a disease in which a person cannot control his or her drinking.

▶ **Lesson 2** When used properly, medicines are valuable drugs. However, illegal drugs should be avoided.

▶ **Lesson 3** The nervous system sends messages to the brain and from the brain to the rest of the body. Alcohol and drug use can damage this system.

▶ **Lesson 4** The use of alcohol and drugs can damage a person's physical, mental/emotional, and social health. Teens who understand the risks of using these substances will be more likely to avoid them.

▶ **Lesson 5** Having a positive self-concept, staying away from risky situations, and resisting peer pressure are ways to avoid substance abuse.

▶ **Lesson 6** Recovery from alcohol or drug addiction is much more difficult than resisting these substances in the first place. Help is needed.

Reviewing Key Terms and Concepts

Using complete sentences, answer the following questions on a separate sheet of paper.

Lesson 1

1. What is *cirrhosis?*

2. Name three groups that help recovering alcoholics and their families and friends.

Lesson 2

3. Contrast *stimulants* and *depressants.*

4. What are *hallucinogens?*

Lesson 3

5. What is the function of the spinal cord?

6. How can drug abuse cause problems with the nervous system?

Lesson 4

7. How can alcohol and drug use affect physical fitness?

8. Explain why it is so dangerous to drink and drive.

Lesson 5

9. How can teens prepare themselves to say no to alcohol and drugs?

10. What are *alternatives?*

Lesson 6

11. What are the four steps involved in recovery from addiction?

12. What is withdrawal?

Thinking Critically

Using complete sentences, answer the following questions on a separate sheet of paper.

13. **Suggest** How would you help someone who began abusing painkillers?

14. **Analyze** Why is alcohol and drug abuse considered a preventable cause of nervous system disorders?

15. **Hypothesize** Why might someone who knows the risks associated with alcohol and drugs continue to use them?

16. **Invent** Imagine and describe a social situation in which you say no to alcohol.

17. **Apply** What could you do if you felt that you had an alcohol or drug problem?

Your Action Plan

In this chapter you have learned how drinking alcohol and using drugs can harm your health. You can set a long-term goal of avoiding alcohol and drugs. Short-term goals can help you keep on track. For example, a short-term goal could be to get involved in a healthful activity with people you like.

Step 1 Review your private journal entries for this chapter. Highlight the journal entries that seem most useful in achieving your long- or short-term goals.

Step 2 Divide a sheet of paper into two columns. List aids to short-term goals in one column and aids to long-term goals in the other. One aid to a short-term goal might be to find out about clubs or sports teams at your school.

Step 3 In your journal, write a letter to your family and friends explaining your goals and how you plan to accomplish them.

Your reward for working toward your goals will be freedom from dependence on alcohol or drugs. You will know that you are managing your own life, not allowing yourself to be controlled by a dangerous substance.

In Your Home and Community

1. **Personal Health** Arrange a time to sit down and talk with members of your family. Tell them that you want to write and sign a contract in which you agree not to use alcohol or drugs. Ask the adults in your family to sign an agreement to support you in keeping to your contract.

2. **Growth and Development** With your classmates, organize a panel discussion on alcohol and drugs. Invite community professionals to take part. Choose an individual to guide the discussion and request questions from audience members.

Building Your Portfolio

1. **Diagram of the Nervous System** Create an illustration that explains how the nervous system works. You will need to include both drawings and text. If necessary, do more research about the nervous system in health and science books. Add the illustration to your portfolio.

2. **Health Care Interview** Interview a professional who helps people overcome addictions. Before conducting the interview, prepare a list of questions to ask. Tape-record or videotape the interview, and add the tape to your portfolio.

3. **Personal Assessment** Look through all the activities and projects you did for this chapter. Choose one or two that you would like to include in your portfolio.

Chapter 12

Understanding Communicable Diseases

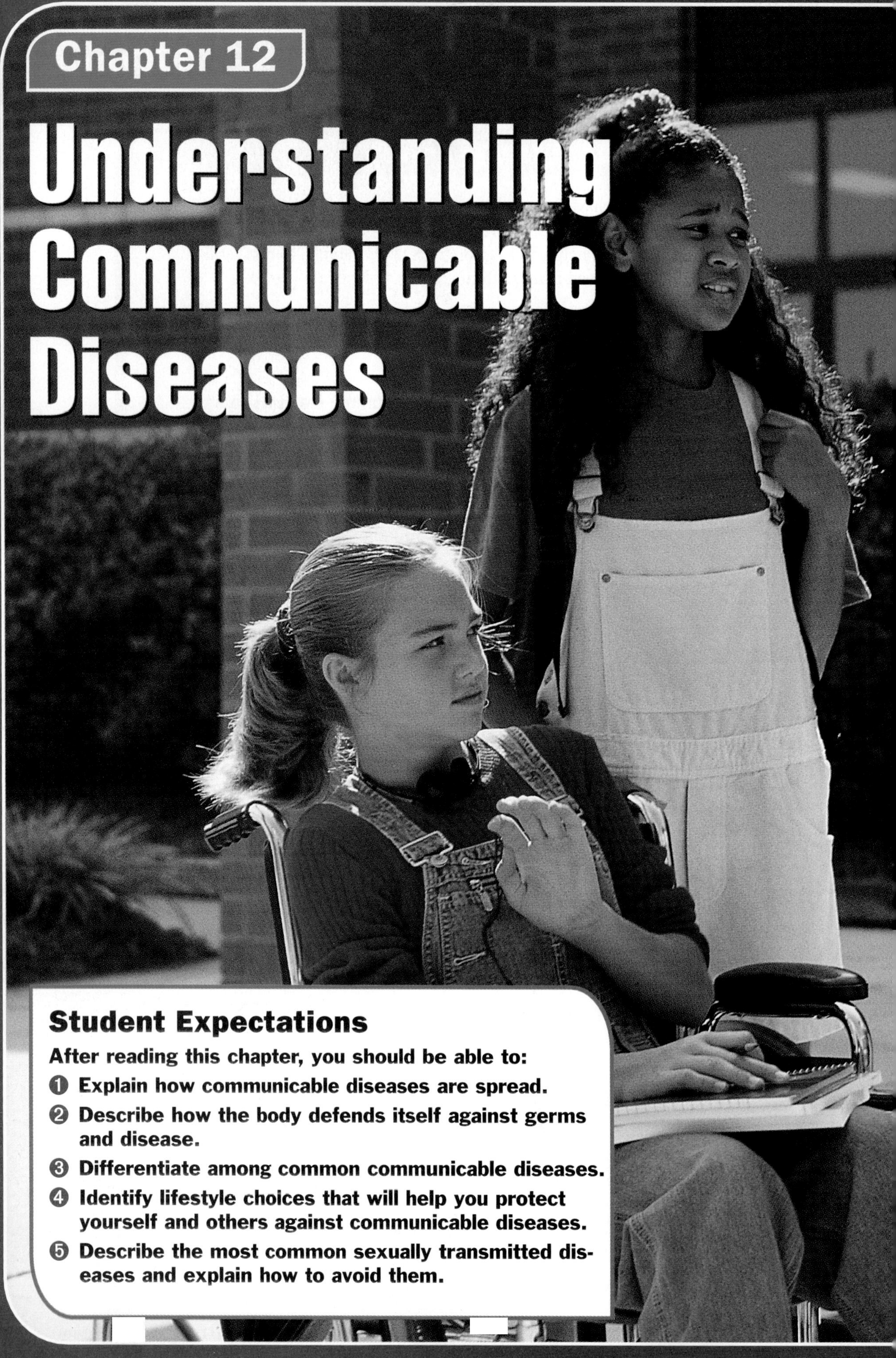

Student Expectations

After reading this chapter, you should be able to:

1. Explain how communicable diseases are spread.
2. Describe how the body defends itself against germs and disease.
3. Differentiate among common communicable diseases.
4. Identify lifestyle choices that will help you protect yourself and others against communicable diseases.
5. Describe the most common sexually transmitted diseases and explain how to avoid them.

Teen Chat Group

Lisa: You look awful, Adam!

Adam: Thanks a lot.

Lisa: No, I mean you look sick.

Adam: I *am* sick. My head's totally stuffed, and I'm hot one minute and cold the next.

Jen: So what are you doing in school?

Adam: I have a math test today. I can't miss it.

Lisa: So you figured you'd just share your germs with all your friends?

Jen: Yeah. You're coughing and sneezing all over the place!

Adam: What is this, the health police? What's the big deal?

Lisa: I've already had a bad cold this month. I don't need another one.

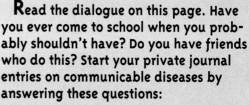

in your journal

Read the dialogue on this page. Have you ever come to school when you probably shouldn't have? Do you have friends who do this? Start your private journal entries on communicable diseases by answering these questions:

▶ What would you say to Adam if you were part of this conversation?

▶ What actions can you take to reduce your chances of getting sick?

▶ If you do get sick, what can you do to keep from spreading your germs to other people?

When you reach the end of the chapter, you will use your journal entries to make an action plan.

Causes of Communicable Diseases

This lesson will help you find answers to questions that teens often ask about the causes of communicable diseases. For example:

▶ **What causes disease?**

▶ **What is an infection?**

▶ **What types of germs are there?**

▶ **How are germs spread?**

Germs and Disease

Just about everyone has had some experience with disease. A **disease** is *a condition that interferes with the proper functioning of the body or mind.* Diseases are sometimes broken down into two categories. A **communicable** (kuh·MYOO·ni·kuh·buhl) **disease** is *a disease that can be passed from one person to another.* **Noncommunicable diseases** are *diseases such as asthma and cancer, that cannot be spread from one person to another.* You'll read about noncommunicable diseases in Chapter 13.

Communicable diseases are caused by microorganisms (mi·kroh·OR·guh·ni·zuhmz)—organisms so small that they can be seen only through a microscope. **Germs** are *the microorganisms that cause disease.* An **infection** results when *germs get inside the body, multiply, and damage body cells.* If the body is not able to fight off the infection, a disease occurs.

 **Did You Know?**

From One to Many

Bacteria are tiny, but they reproduce amazingly fast. In several hours, just one bacterium can multiply to 250,000!

Even though germs can be seen only through a micro-scope, they are present almost everywhere. The average person's mouth contains more than 600 different kinds of germs.

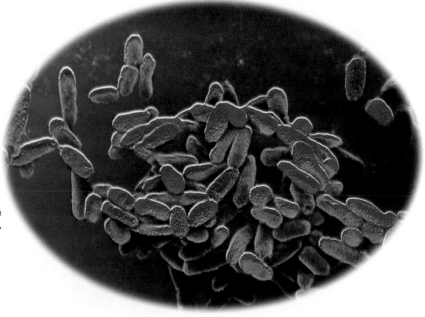

Viruses, Bacteria, and Other Germs

Not all germs are the same. The types of germs that cause disease include viruses, bacteria, fungi, and protozoa. Most diseases that occur in the United States are caused by viruses or bacteria. **Figure 12.1** shows the most common disease-causing germs.

interNET
CONNECTION
Discover on-line how to steer clear of behaviors that put your future at risk of disease.

http://www.glencoe.com/sec/health

Figure 12.1
Causes of Disease

Viruses cause most communicable diseases. Bacteria are another primary cause of illness.

Ⓐ Viruses (VY·ruh·suhz) *are the smallest and simplest life form.* They cause a wide range of diseases, including the following:

colds	flu	herpes
chicken pox	measles	rabies
AIDS	smallpox	polio
viral pneumonia	mumps	mononucleosis

Vaccination can prevent many of the diseases caused by viruses.

Ⓑ Bacteria (bak·TIR·ee·uh) *are tiny one-celled organisms that live nearly everywhere.* Many bacteria are harmless. Some are even helpful. Bacteria in your intestines, for example, help with digestion. Harmful bacteria, however, can cause such diseases as these:

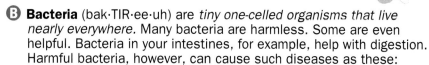

strep throat	food poisoning	diphtheria
tuberculosis	typhoid fever	Lyme disease
pinkeye	gonorrhea	bacterial pneumonia

Ⓒ Fungi (FUHN·jy) *are primitive life forms that cannot make their own food.* Athlete's foot and ringworm are examples of diseases caused by fungi.

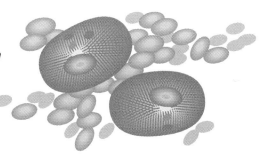

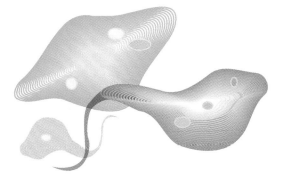

Ⓓ Protozoa (proh·tuh·ZOH·uh) *are one-celled, animal-like organisms.* Many are harmless. However, harmful protozoa cause such diseases as malaria and amebic dysentery.

Figure 12.2 describes the principal ways in which germs are spread. What actions can you take to protect yourself against germs? How can you protect others from your germs? Write your answers in your journal.

How Germs Are Spread

Germs can be spread in several ways. Staying healthy involves both knowing the ways germs can be spread and knowing how you can best protect yourself. **Figure 12.2** describes some of them.

Figure 12.2
Spreading Germs

Germs that invade the body come from a variety of sources. A good way to reduce the chances of picking up other people's germs is to wash your hands frequently and thoroughly, especially before eating.

Direct Contact
You can get germs on your hands and skin through direct contact with another person. Germs that cause skin infections and rashes may be spread in this way. Germs are also spread through sexual contact. Diseases such as AIDS, gonorrhea, and herpes are transmitted through direct contact.

Indirect Contact
Someone coughs or sneezes, expelling germs into the air. Other people then breathe in these germs. Diseases such as colds, flu, and tuberculosis are spread in this way. People "share" germs when they share drinking glasses, eating utensils, or other personal items. Germs are also spread when someone touches a surface—a doorknob or a telephone receiver, for example—that is contaminated with another person's germs.

Contact with Animals or Insects
Germs may be spread through animal and insect bites. For example, the bite of a rabid animal spreads rabies. Lyme disease is transmitted through tick bites.

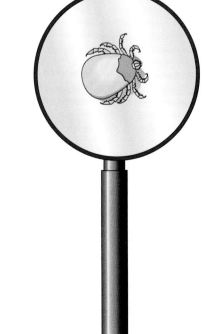

Other Contacts
Germs can be spread through contaminated food or water. For example, a type of food poisoning called salmonellosis is caused by salmonella bacteria in certain foods, such as chicken.

Using complete sentences, answer the following questions on a separate sheet of paper.

Reviewing Terms and Facts

1. **Vocabulary**   What is the difference between a *communicable disease* and a *noncommunicable disease?*

2. **List**   Name four kinds of germs.

3. **Identify**   List three ways in which germs can be spread.

Thinking Critically

4. **Analyze**   How can washing your hands carefully help prevent the spread of germs?

5. **Explain**   What is the relationship between germs and infection?

Applying Health Concepts

6. **Health of Others**   Find out how to protect yourself against Lyme disease. Create a poster to educate others about this disease. Ask permission to display your poster at a doctor's office or nature center.

HEALTH LAB
Observing Bacteria

Introduction: Bacteria are microscopic in size. However, given the right nutrients, bacteria will increase in number until they form a group (known as a colony) that can be seen with the unaided eye. In this experiment you will take samples of bacteria from various places and watch them grow.

Objective: Determine where the greatest concentrations of bacteria can be found around your school.

Materials and Method: You will need three petri dishes, or other small glass containers with lids, filled with agar or another culture medium—a substance in which bacteria can grow and multiply. You will also need disinfectant soap and paper towels.

Choose two places to collect samples of bacteria. You might use your unwashed hands for one sample. Other areas to collect bacteria could include water fountains, doorknobs, floors, and furniture. Touch the object to the agar in the dish, or wipe the object with a clean paper towel and then wipe the towel on the agar. Immediately after depositing the

sample, cover the dish and label it with the specific location where the sample was collected. Wash and dry your hands between collections.

For the third sample, wash your hands carefully with disinfectant soap, and dry them on a paper towel. Then press your fingers against the agar in the third dish. Cover the dish and label it "clean hands." Put the dishes in a warm, dark place for five days.

Observations and Analysis:
Study the contents of the three dishes. What do you observe? Which jar shows the greatest growth of bacteria? Which shows the least? What conclusions can you draw from your observations?

The Immune System

This lesson will help you find answers to questions that teens often ask about how the body fights germs. For example:

▶ **How does the immune system work?**

▶ **What are antibodies, and how do they protect me?**

▶ **How do I become immune to a disease?**

Words to Know

immune system
lymphatic system
lymphocytes
antigens
antibodies
immunity
vaccine

 in Your journal

Do you usually have some warning when you are getting sick? What signs tell you that you are coming down with something? Write these in your private journal, and describe what you could do to protect your own health and the health of others when you know you are getting sick.

Defending Against Invaders

Each day your body is exposed to countless germs. To protect itself against these germs, your body takes action to repel, trap, or destroy them. The body has natural barriers that keep germs out or destroy them before they can do any damage. The five major barriers, or "first lines of defense," are listed below:

■ **Skin.** The skin covering your body acts as a protective barrier.

■ **Mucous** (MYOO·kuhs) **membranes.** These tissues line your mouth, nose, throat, eyes, and other body parts. They trap germs. Actions such as coughing and sneezing get rid of the germs trapped by these membranes.

■ **Saliva.** Saliva in your mouth destroys many harmful organisms.

■ **Tears.** Tears wash away germs. They also contain chemicals that kill some harmful organisms.

■ **Stomach acid.** The acid in your stomach kills many germs.

As effective as these defenses are, viruses, bacteria, and other germs do sometimes get through. That's when your immune system springs into action. Your **immune** (i·MYOON) **system** is a *combination of body defenses made up of cells, tissues, and organs that fight off germs and disease.*

Millions of helpful bacteria live on your skin and are part of the skin's defense against germs.

The Immune System's General Reactions

When germs get inside your body, your immune system launches an attack. Three general reactions may occur, no matter what kind of microorganism has invaded.

■ Special white blood cells called phagocytes (FA·guh·syts) attack the invading germs. These cells actually surround the germs and destroy them.

■ The cells may release a chemical substance called interferon (in·ter·FIR·ahn) that stops viruses from reproducing.

■ Rising body temperature, commonly called a fever, makes it difficult for some microorganisms to reproduce.

The Immune System's Specific Reactions

If invading germs survive the immune system's general reactions, the body responds with more specific defenses. These are responses to certain microorganisms and the toxins, or poisons, that they produce. Often these specific reactions both defend the body when the microorganisms enter and allow the immune system to remember the particular germ. That way it can be destroyed if it enters the body again.

To fight against specific germs, the body calls upon the lymphatic system. The **lymphatic** (lim·FA·tik) **system** is a *secondary circulatory system that helps the body fight germs and maintain its fluid balance.* The lymphatic system carries a watery fluid known as lymph (LIMF). *Special white blood cells in the lymph* are called **lymphocytes** (LIM·fuh·syts). There are two types of lymphocytes: B-cells and T-cells. Both are important in fighting off germs and disease. The lymph also contains phagocytes known as macrophages (MA·kruh·fay·juhz), which help the lymphocytes identify invading germs.

Antigens and Antibodies

Antigens (AN·ti·jenz) are *substances that send your immune system into action when your body is invaded by germs.* The body recognizes antigens as invaders. For example, the toxins produced by bacteria are antigens. Blood cells from a blood type different from yours, as you learned in Chapter 5, are also sensed by the body as antigens. Your body reacts to antigens by producing antibodies. **Antibodies** are *proteins that attach to antigens, keeping them from harming the body.* Your immune system produces specific antibodies to fight each antigen. **Figure 12.3,** on the next page, shows the immune system in action.

Your Total Health

Help Your Immune System

To boost your body's immune system, exercise regularly and maintain a healthy diet. Eat plenty of fruits and vegetables, and limit fats. Also, do what you can to minimize stress, which can weaken the immune system.

Look for magazine and newspaper articles on how your diet can benefit your immune system. What nutrients are especially important to immune system function? How can you make sure that you get enough of these nutrients in your diet?

Unfortunately, some people's bodies react to certain pollens as antigens. The body's immune system reacts to the pollen as if it were an invader, producing symptoms such as sneezing or swelling of mucous membranes.

Figure 12.3
How the Immune System Responds to Germs

Notice how the different cells in the immune system work together to respond to an invading virus.

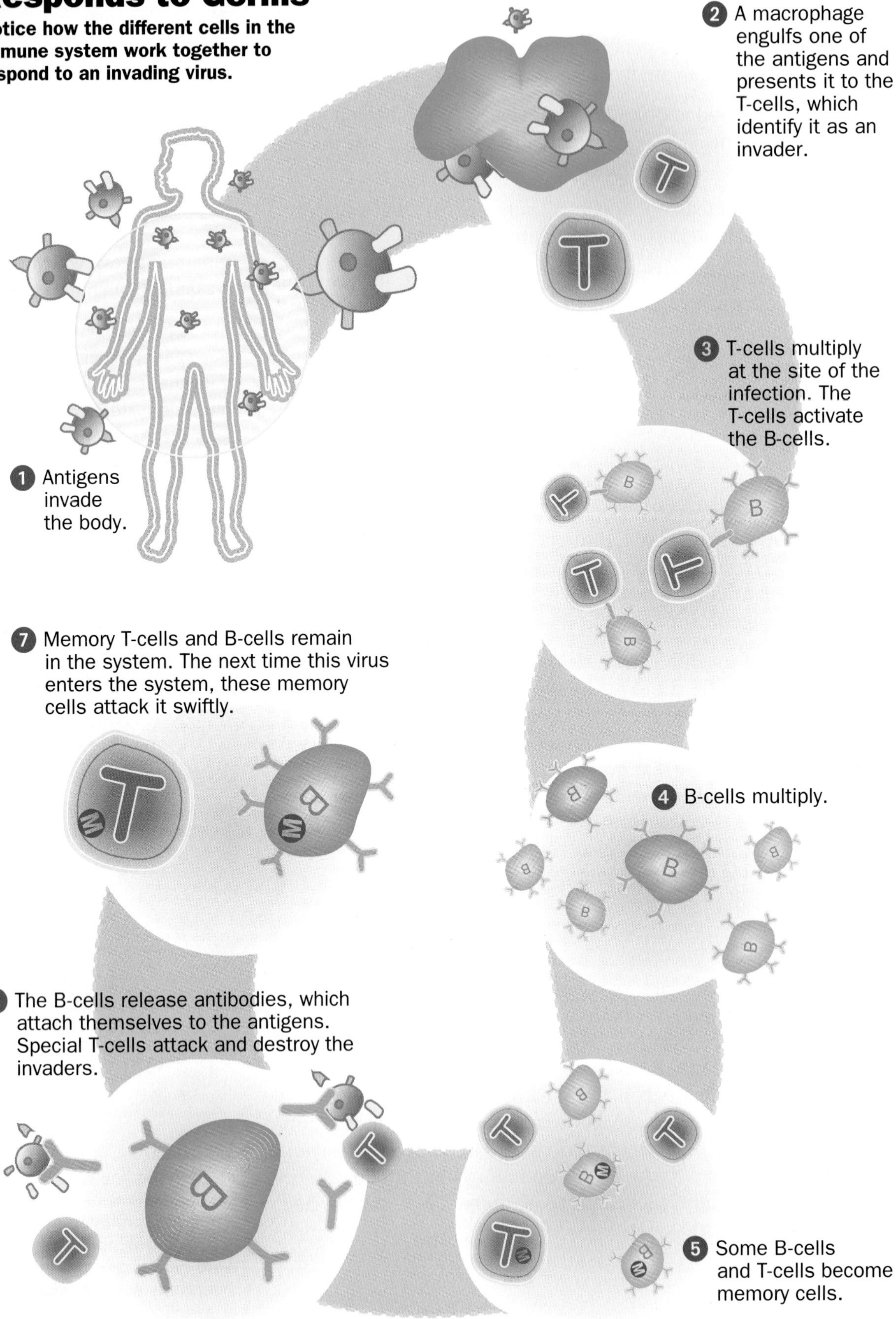

1 Antigens invade the body.

2 A macrophage engulfs one of the antigens and presents it to the T-cells, which identify it as an invader.

3 T-cells multiply at the site of the infection. The T-cells activate the B-cells.

4 B-cells multiply.

5 Some B-cells and T-cells become memory cells.

6 The B-cells release antibodies, which attach themselves to the antigens. Special T-cells attack and destroy the invaders.

7 Memory T-cells and B-cells remain in the system. The next time this virus enters the system, these memory cells attack it swiftly.

Immunity

Your *body's ability to resist the germs that cause a particular disease* is called **immunity.** You develop immunity in two ways:

- **Natural exposure to germs.** Throughout your life you are exposed to many different germs. As **Figure 12.3** showed, your body produces memory B-cells and T-cells. Often these memory cells stay in your blood. If the same germs return, memory cells allow your body to fight the germs off more quickly.

- **Immunization.** Health care workers administer vaccines to make people immune to certain diseases. A **vaccine** (vak·SEEN) is a *preparation of dead or weakened germs that is injected into the body to cause the immune system to produce antibodies.* Vaccines exist for many diseases, including polio, measles, and mumps. Being vaccinated won't make you ill because the germs used are dead or weak. However, the antibodies your body produces in response to the vaccine will build your immunity.

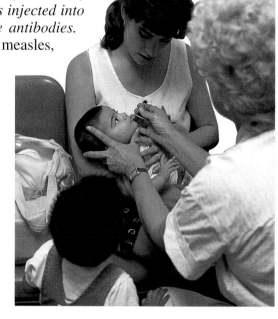

Many vaccines are given by injection, but the polio vaccine is often given orally.

Review

Lesson 2

Using complete sentences, answer the following questions on a separate sheet of paper.

Reviewing Terms and Facts

1. **Explain**   What are the body's five barriers against disease?

2. **Identify**   List three general reactions of the immune system.

3. **Vocabulary**   Define the terms *antigen* and *antibody.*

4. **Recall**   List two ways in which people can develop immunity to a disease.

Thinking Critically

5. **Explain**   Why are diseases that damage the immune system so dangerous to the body?

6. **Analyze**   Vaccines have all but eliminated certain communicable diseases. How is this possible?

Applying Health Concepts

7. **Health of Others**   Like people, animals can be vaccinated against certain diseases. Find out what vaccines cats and dogs generally receive. Which of these vaccines indirectly protect the health of people? Share your findings with the class.

Common Communicable Diseases

This lesson will help you find answers to questions that teens often ask about familiar communicable diseases. For example:

▶ **What is the most common communicable disease?**

▶ **How is a cold different from the flu?**

▶ **What are some other common communicable diseases?**

Words to Know

influenza
mononucleosis
hepatitis
tuberculosis

in your journal

How many colds have you had in the last 12 months? In your private journal, describe what factors you think make you more likely to get a cold (lack of sleep, stress, being indoors, and so on). Which of these factors are ones you can control?

Facts About the Common Cold

Of all communicable diseases, the cold is the most common. Consider the following facts.

■ Children miss school more often because of colds than for any other medical reason. Colds are also the most common reason for workers to miss days on the job.

■ On the average, adults get at least two or three colds a year. Children and young adults get about two to three times as many colds as adults.

Why are colds so common? One reason is that they are spread in several ways. Indirect contact is a common means of spreading cold germs—touching objects or surfaces that someone with a cold has previously handled, and then touching your mouth, nose, or eyes. You can also get cold germs through direct contact—shaking hands, for example. When a cold sufferer coughs or sneezes, germs are expelled into the air. Other people inhale these germs.

People often catch colds by handling objects that someone with a cold has touched. Viruses can live on surfaces for hours, or even days. Washing your hands often can help you avoid picking up someone else's germs.

Another reason why colds are so common is that colds may be caused by hundreds of different viruses. This is why no cold vaccine has been developed. A vaccine that would give you immunity to one cold virus would not protect you against all the other viruses. You would need a different vaccine for each one!

Facts About the Flu

Although some of their symptoms are the same, influenza—"flu"—and colds are caused by different viruses. **Influenza** (in·floo·EN·zuh) is *a communicable disease characterized by fever, chills, fatigue, headache, muscle aches, and respiratory symptoms.*

The flu usually begins more abruptly than a cold and lasts longer. The flu is spread by airborne germs as well as through direct and indirect contact. Each year different strains of flu arise. (December through early March are the peak flu months.) Vaccines are generally available in October and November for the strain of flu that doctors expect to be present for the following months. Anyone can get a flu vaccine, but vaccination is particularly recommended for certain groups of people, including

- people who are 65 years of age or older and people who live in nursing homes or other long-term care facilities.

- adults and children with lung or cardiovascular disorders.

Other Communicable Diseases

Several communicable diseases are discussed in **Figure 12.4** on the next page. The three diseases listed below are caused by viruses and can be spread by direct or indirect contact. People who have these diseases should stay at home during the time when they are able to infect others. Vaccines are available for all three:

- **Chicken pox.** This illness involves an itchy rash, fever, headache, and body aches. This disease can be passed to others from two days before the rash appears until about six days after.

- **Measles.** Measles is characterized by a rash with fever, runny nose, and coughing. People with measles can infect others from several days before the rash appears until about five days after.

- **Mumps.** This disease causes a fever, headache, and swollen salivary glands. It is most easily passed to others around the time when the symptoms appear, but may be passed on from as much as seven days before the symptoms appear until nine days after.

Residents of nursing homes should have flu shots yearly. Flu is easily passed from one person to another in any residential facility.

Q & A

No Sure Shortcuts

Q: If I start taking cold medicines when I feel as if I'm getting a cold, will that keep me from getting sick?

A: There's an old saying that a cold will last about a week if you treat it and seven days if you don't. That's because cold medicines can't cure the illness or kill the germs that cause it. All they can do is treat the symptoms. To treat a cold, get plenty of rest and let your immune system do its job.

Figure 12.4
Some Communicable Diseases

Many communicable diseases require a doctor's diagnosis and treatment. For some, a doctor may prescribe antibiotics or other medication.

Disease	Symptoms	Transmission Method	Treatment
Mononucleosis	Known as "mono" or "the kissing disease," **mononucleosis** (MAH·noh·noo·klee·OH·sis) is *a virus-caused disease characterized by swelling of the lymph nodes in the neck and throat.* It is most common in teens and young adults. Other symptoms may include fatigue, appetite loss, fever, headache, and sore throat.	Mononucleosis is usually spread through kissing or by sharing drinking glasses, eating utensils, or toothbrushes.	Mononucleosis is treated with rest and pain relievers. Recovery may take 3 to 12 weeks. Fatigue may linger much longer.
Hepatitis	**Hepatitis** (he·puh·TY·tis) is *a virus-caused liver inflammation characterized by yellowing of the skin and the whites of the eyes.* There are several types. The two main ones are hepatitis A and hepatitis B, caused by different viruses. Hepatitis B may permanently damage the liver. Hepatitis symptoms may include weakness, nausea, fever, headache, sore throat, and appetite loss. A vaccine is available for both types.	Hepatitis A is transmitted through contaminated food or water. Hepatitis B is usually spread through direct contact with the body fluids of an infected person. Both types can also be spread through sexual contact.	Hepatitis is treated with rest and a healthful diet. Although most people recover completely, those infected with hepatitis B can remain contagious for the rest of their lives.
Tuberculosis	**Tuberculosis** (too·ber·kyuh·LOH·sis), or TB, is *a bacteria-caused disease that usually affects the lungs.* Symptoms may include cough, fatigue, night sweats, fever, and weight loss. Although a TB vaccine is available, as many as 3 million people around the world die from the disease each year.	Tuberculosis is spread by water droplets in the air from coughs and sneezes.	Tuberculosis is treated with antibiotics for a period of several months.

Vaccination Schedules

Some communicable diseases, such as measles and mumps, used to be much more common than they are now. The vaccination of infants and children is making such diseases increasingly rare. **Figure 12.5** shows a typical vaccination schedule.

Figure 12.5
Vaccination Schedule

These are the vaccinations recommended by the American Academy of Pediatrics.

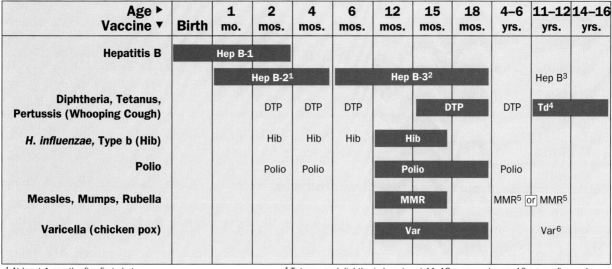

Age ▶ Vaccine ▼	Birth	1 mo.	2 mos.	4 mos.	6 mos.	12 mos.	15 mos.	18 mos.	4–6 yrs.	11–12 yrs.	14–16 yrs.
Hepatitis B	Hep B-1	Hep B-1	Hep B-2[1]			Hep B-3[2]				Hep B[3]	
Diphtheria, Tetanus, Pertussis (Whooping Cough)		DTP	DTP	DTP		DTP			DTP	Td[4]	Td[4]
H. influenzae, Type b (Hib)		Hib	Hib	Hib	Hib	Hib					
Polio		Polio	Polio		Polio	Polio			Polio		
Measles, Mumps, Rubella					MMR	MMR			MMR[5] or MMR[5]	MMR[5] or MMR[5]	
Varicella (chicken pox)					Var	Var				Var[6]	

[1] At least 1 month after first shot
[2] At least 4 months after first shot and 2 months after second shot
[3] Children who were not vaccinated in infancy should begin series of shots at 11–12 years

[4] Tetanus and diphtheria booster at 11–12 years and every 10 years afterwards
[5] Second dose of MMR at either 4–6 years or 11–12 years
[6] For children who were not vaccinated in infancy and who have not had the disease

Review

Lesson 3

Using complete sentences, answer the following questions on a separate sheet of paper.

Reviewing Terms and Facts

1. **Recall**   How can you tell the difference between a cold and influenza?

2. **Vocabulary**   What is *mononucleosis?* How is it spread?

3. **Vocabulary**   What is *tuberculosis?* How is it treated?

Thinking Critically

4. **Explain**   Why do you think children get more colds than adults?

5. **Infer**   Why would it be important to know when a disease can be passed on to others?

Applying Health Concepts

6. **Consumer Health**   Go to a pharmacy, and compare over-the-counter medicines that are meant to relieve cold and flu symptoms. Read the labels carefully. How do the various medicines differ? How are they alike? Which would you consider buying? Make a chart that compares at least three different brands in terms of their ingredients and claims.

Avoiding Common Communicable Diseases

This lesson will help you find answers to questions that teens often ask about staying healthy. For example:

▶ **How can I avoid communicable diseases?**

▶ **How can I protect other people against diseases?**

Cultural Connections

Blocking Germs

In Japan, people who have a cold or the flu may wear a mask to keep germs from spreading. While this measure is not always effective against colds—which are more often spread by hands—it may help to prevent the spread of airborne flu viruses.

Preventing the Spread of Disease

Anyone who's suffered through a cold, flu, or other disease would certainly agree that it's far better to avoid an illness than to treat one. In this chapter you have read about many communicable diseases. This lesson will help you make decisions that will protect you against disease and protect those around you as well.

Protecting Yourself

The first rule in staying healthy is to use your common sense. Be smart. Don't take risks with your health. Here are some tips.

■ Avoid close contact with people who are ill, especially during the contagious period of a disease. The **contagious period** is *the length of time when a particular disease can spread from person to person.* Avoid even shaking hands with someone who you know has a contagious disease.

■ Do not share eating utensils, dishes, or glasses with others.

■ Wash your hands often, especially when you have been around people who are ill. **Figure 12.6**, on the next page, presents some handwashing tips.

■ Keep your hands away from your mouth, nose, and eyes.

■ Encourage cold and flu sufferers to cover their mouths and noses when they cough or sneeze.

■ Take proper precautions against known dangers, such as exposure to ticks that may carry disease.

■ To avoid food poisoning and other diseases, follow safe practices in handling, preparing, and storing food.

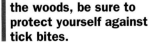

When you walk or hike in the woods, be sure to protect yourself against tick bites.

Figure 12.6
Washing Away Germs

Washing your hands is an important way to protect yourself against germs.

Always wash with soap. Consider buying liquid soap for home use. Bar soaps may accumulate germs. Special germicidal or antibacterial soaps are also available.

To do a thorough job, spend at least 20 seconds washing your hands. One to three minutes would be even better.

Use a brush to scrub under nails.

Always wash your hands before handling or eating food. Also, wash your hands after using the bathroom, handling garbage, or touching any other obvious germ source.

Protecting Others

Part of behaving responsibly involves doing whatever you can to avoid spreading germs to other people. The following are some examples of ways to protect others.

- Seek medical treatment if you need it. Delaying a visit to the doctor can allow your condition to worsen while increasing the chances that you'll spread germs to others.

- Cover your mouth and nose when you cough or sneeze. Use disposable tissues—and dispose of them properly.

- If you are ill, stay home from school during the contagious period of the disease, and avoid close contact with other people. Wash your hands frequently.

- When taking a prescribed medication, follow the directions carefully. Take all of the medication—don't stop taking it just because you feel better.

- Encourage other people to follow wise health practices.

Make a list in your journal of positive habits that you have that contribute to a healthy lifestyle. Then make a mental list of habits that you have that work against a healthy lifestyle. How can you change your negatives to positives? You might want to discuss your ideas for change with an encouraging adult whom you respect and admire.

Developing a Healthy Lifestyle

To feel well and keep your body in top condition, practice good health habits. Having a healthy body increases your ability to resist germs and disease. The following health habits are part of a healthy lifestyle.

■ Eat a well-balanced, nutritious diet.

■ Exercise regularly.

■ Get an adequate amount of sleep.

■ Take a shower or bath daily.

■ Don't use alcohol or other drugs.

■ Don't smoke.

■ Be sure that you are vaccinated against diseases for which a vaccine exists. If you're not sure which vaccinations you need, ask your doctor.

■ Learn to manage stress.

LIFE SKILLS
Being a Reliable Information Source

People share information constantly. They ask one another questions and try to give helpful answers. One topic about which people seek a great deal of information is health. You can make a valuable contribution to your community if you are a source of accurate health-related information. Here are some guidelines.

▶ You've learned about a wide range of health topics and concerns, from nutrition to communicable diseases, from sports and conditioning to

drug abuse. Share your knowledge with others when the opportunity arises.

▶ Give sound advice based on your knowledge. For example, explain the benefits of remaining tobacco-free to a friend who is thinking of taking up smoking.

▶ Substitute information for misinformation. For example, if you hear someone repeat myths about how to treat a cold, provide facts.

▶ Know where to go for additional information. You can find up-to-date health information at the library, in magazines and newspapers, at doctors' offices, and from other reliable sources. Identify resources in your community.

▶ If you don't know, don't guess. Instead, find out the facts. Too often people mistake myths and half-truths for reliable information. If you need the answer to a medical question, look it up, or ask a health care worker.

Follow-up Activity
Recall a time when someone you know needed health-related information. Were you able to help? What other useful suggestions could you have made?

Personal Inventory

GOOD HEALTH HABITS

You can protect yourself and others from germs and disease by developing good health habits. Keeping your body healthy helps you feel your best and enables you to recover quickly if you do get sick. Have you developed good health habits? To find out, write yes or no for each statement below. Use a separate sheet of paper.

1. I always wash my hands after using the bathroom and before handling food.

2. I take a shower or bath daily.

3. I cover my mouth and nose when I cough or sneeze.

4. I avoid contact with anyone who has a contagious disease.

5. When I am sick, I take precautions to avoid spreading germs.

6. I generally eat a well-balanced, nutritious diet.

7. I get an adequate amount of rest.

8. I exercise regularly.

9. I don't use alcohol or other drugs.

10. I don't smoke.

Give yourself 1 point for each yes. A score of 9–10 is very good. A score of 7–8 is good. If you score below 7, you need to improve your health habits.

Review  Lesson 4

Using complete sentences, answer the following questions on a separate sheet of paper.

Reviewing Terms and Facts

1. **Vocabulary**   Use your own words to define the term *contagious period*.

2. **State**   List five ways to protect yourself against germs and disease.

3. **Recall**   Identify three ways to protect others from disease.

Thinking Critically

4. **Explain**   Many people do not recognize the importance of frequent handwashing. Why do you think this is true?

5. **Evaluate**   A friend tells you that he's planning to go to school, even though he's running a fever and thinks he may have the flu. What would you say?

Applying Health Concepts

6. **Personal Health**   With a partner, choose one of the guidelines for healthy living mentioned in this chapter. Write a short story depicting two characters: one who regularly follows this guideline and one who does not. Show how their different habits affect their overall health and the health of others.

TEEN HEALTH DIGEST

CON$UMER FOCU$

Health Hype

Q. Ads for cold remedies toss around phrases like "extra strength," "new and improved," and "special formula." Do such phrases mean anything?

A. Catchy phrases aren't much help to comparison shoppers because there are no standards regarding their meaning. For example, "extra strength" or "maximum strength" may just mean that a product contains more medication than similar products made by the same company. Suppose that the product is a multisymptom cold remedy. How can the buyer know which of the many ingredients has been increased to provide the "extra strength"? The smart way to shop for cold remedies is to compare ingredients and amounts. Then buy the simplest medications for your particular symptoms.

"Extra-strength!"   "New and improved!"   "Special formula!"   "Extended relief!"

Sneeze BAN   COLD COMFORT

Try This: *Examine the various over-the-counter cold remedies sold at the pharmacy. Which phrases do you see repeated most often on the product packaging?*

Teens Making a Difference

Hoping to Save a Life

Although she's only 12, Hydeia Broadbent is one of the nation's best-known AIDS activists. She's spread her message about the dangers of AIDS to thousands of people. Hydeia has appeared in a National Institutes of Health video about AIDS, spoken with the president, and even addressed the Republican National Convention.

Hydeia knows about AIDS from personal experience. Her mother, who abandoned her shortly after Hydeia was born, was infected with HIV. Hydeia, too, is infected with the virus.

Hydeia looks forward to speaking to many more groups of people. Her reason is simple: "It might save someone's life."

Try This: *Find out about some other ways in which individuals are fighting the spread of AIDS. Report this information to your class.*

HEALTH UPDATE

Fleeing the Flu

Flu vaccines are given every year because flu viruses change from one year to the next. Some people resist getting annual vaccinations because they hate shots. However, studies suggest that flu vaccines—which work about 90 percent of the time—may, for many people, be worth a twinge of discomfort.

About one in five people gets the flu each year. Studies have shown that workers who get flu shots have 25 percent fewer cases of upper respiratory illness than those who don't. In addition, they lose 43 percent fewer days from work for illness.

Already used by millions of people in the United States each year, flu vaccines may soon become even more common. Within three years, the vaccines may be available in nasal sprays—a great relief for those who hate needles!

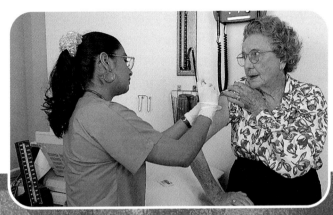

Myths and Realities

Feed a Cold? Not Too Much

Q: How much truth is there to the old saying, "Feed a cold, starve a fever"?

A: This idea shouldn't be taken too seriously. However, it's probably best to eat easily digestible foods when you're sick. Liquids are especially good choices, because they will prevent dehydration. Liquids also loosen nasal secretions, so that you'll feel better and may even get better sooner.

People at Work

Disease Detective

Alex Wong is a disease detective. His job is to study diseases to figure out what causes them and how they can be prevented. Alex is an epidemiologist (e·puh·dee·mee·AH·luh·jist).

Alex first became interested in studying diseases when he was in high school. He studied biology in college and then went on to get a master's degree in public health. Now he works for his state's health department, gathering information about how often different diseases occur in the state.

Asked what he likes about his job, Alex says, "You get to see the whole picture. When a doctor treats an individual for tuberculosis, he or she is interested in just that one person—what the patient's symptoms are, how the patient is responding to the treatment, and so on. An epidemiologist can look at *all* the cases of tuberculosis and see that more and more cases are not responding to the drugs used to treat it. That's important information that can help doctors with their specific cases."

Sexually Transmitted Diseases and HIV/AIDS

This lesson will help you find answers to questions that teens often ask about sexually transmitted diseases and AIDS. For example:

► **What is a sexually transmitted disease?**
► **What treatments are there for sexually transmitted diseases?**
► **What is the difference between HIV infection and AIDS?**
► **How is AIDS transmitted?**
► **What are the benefits of practicing abstinence before marriage?**

Words to Know

STD (sexually
    transmitted
    disease)
chlamydia
gonorrhea
genital herpes
syphilis
AIDS (acquired im-
    munodeficiency
    syndrome)
HIV (human immu-
    nodeficiency
    virus)

What You Should Know About STDs

STD stands for **sexually transmitted disease**—that is, *a disease spread from person to person through sexual contact.* Talking about sexually transmitted diseases makes many people feel uncomfortable or embarrassed. However, knowing about STDs gives you the power to avoid them. **Figure 12.7** shows some common misconceptions about STDs as well as the facts.

Figure 12.7
Get the Facts!

A lot of people have an "It can't happen to me" attitude about sexually transmitted diseases. In fact, STDs can happen to anyone who doesn't practice abstinence.

Myth: Young teens don't get STDs.

Fact: Some 12 million new cases of STDs are reported annually in the United States. About 3 million occur in teens.

Myth: Getting an STD is no big deal.

Fact: STDs can have serious health consequences, including sterility and even death.

Myth: You can always just take medicine to get rid of an STD.

Fact: Some STDs are curable, while others are not. All STDs, however, are preventable.

Myth: If you're careful, you won't get STDs.

Fact: The only sure protection against STDs is sexual abstinence—avoidance of sexual contact.

Common STDs

Sexually transmitted diseases differ from most other communicable diseases in a number of ways.

- Most STDs can be spread only through sexual contact, especially sexual intercourse.

- Someone who has an STD may not have visible symptoms, or may have symptoms that come and go.

- Having an STD once does not make you immune to the disease in the future.

- There are no vaccines available against STDs.

- STDs can make a person sterile or infertile.

- STDs can be prevented by avoiding sexual activity.

Many people who think that they may have an STD delay seeking medical attention. Some are embarrassed. Others hope that the symptoms will somehow just go away. Postponing medical treatment, however, is dangerous. Prompt diagnosis and treatment is the first step toward curing or controlling an STD *and* preventing its spread to others.

Chlamydia

Chlamydia (kluh·MI·dee·uh) is *a bacteria-caused STD that may affect the reproductive organs, urethra, and anus.* In 1995 chlamydia was the most frequently reported infectious disease in the United States. Nearly 4 million cases of the disease are reported each year, the majority of them in women.

About half of the people who have chlamydia do not even know that they have it. Symptoms, when they are present, may include a genital discharge and burning during urination. If it is not treated, chlamydia can cause pelvic pain, infertility, and various additional infections. Antibiotics can cure chlamydia.

Language Arts Connection

Infectious = Contagious? ACTIVITY!

Many people think that the terms "infectious" and "contagious" have the same meaning. Actually, an infectious disease is one that can be spread by any means, such as by infected animals or through contaminated food. A contagious disease, however, is one that can be directly transmitted from one person to another.

Find out which infectious diseases pose a danger to people. Share your findings with the class.

Abstaining from sexual activity before marriage is the only healthy choice for teens.

Gonorrhea

Gonorrhea (gah·nuh·REE·uh) is *a bacteria-caused STD that affects the genital mucous membrane and sometimes other body parts, such as the heart or joints.* Symptoms include a thick, yellow genital discharge and burning during urination. People often catch chlamydia and gonorrhea at the same time. If left untreated, gonorrhea can cause serious damage, including sterility in men and infertility in women. Doctors can treat gonorrhea with antibiotics.

Genital Herpes

Genital herpes (jen·i·tuhl HER·peez) is *an STD caused by a virus that produces painful blisters in the genital area.* An estimated 30 million Americans have this disease, although many may not realize that they do. While the signs of herpes may temporarily go away, the disease has no cure, and symptoms often recur. Herpes can be passed on to others when symptoms are present. It may also be contagious for some time before symptoms appear and after they are gone. Medications can relieve herpes symptoms.

Syphilis

Syphilis (SI·fuh·lis) is *a bacteria-caused STD that can affect many parts of the body.* Symptoms vary as the disease progresses. Early symptoms may include only a painless sore at the site where the disease entered the body and swollen lymph glands in the genital area. However, syphilis is a very dangerous disease. Over time, untreated syphilis may spread to the central nervous system and the heart, causing heart disease, insanity, and eventually death. If treated early, syphilis can be cured by antibiotics.

Your parents, doctor, and school nurse are good sources of health care information.

HIV and AIDS

AIDS, or **acquired immunodeficiency syndrome,** is *a deadly disease that interferes with the body's ability to fight infection. The virus that causes AIDS* is called **HIV,** which stands for **human immunodeficiency virus.** In 1996 more than 1.5 million people around the world died of AIDS.

A person who is infected by HIV may not show any signs of illness for a long time. In fact, an average of 10 years may pass before HIV infection leads to AIDS. Nevertheless, during this time the virus is doing serious damage to the infected person's immune system. When the system's defenses are critically weakened, AIDS develops. The body becomes unable to fight off other infections and diseases, which eventually prove fatal. **Figure 12.8** shows how HIV attacks the body.

Figure 12.8
How HIV Attacks the Body

AIDS is a progressive disease. Early symptoms of HIV infection may include fatigue, rash, fever, swollen lymph nodes, and diarrhea. Over time, the immune system of the HIV–infected person weakens. The person becomes vulnerable to other infections.

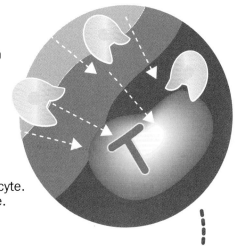

1 After the virus enters the body through the mucous membranes or through a break in the skin, HIV invades a "host" cell—a T-cell lymphocyte. The virus uses the cell's resources to reproduce. Eventually the host cell is destroyed.

KEY

 HIV

 Lymphocytes

 Germs

2 The virus multiplies within the body. More and more lymphocytes are destroyed. These cells are a key part of the immune system.

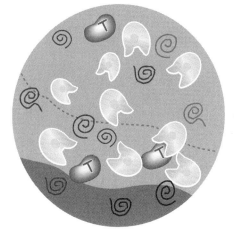

3 As the number of T-cells drops, the immune system gets weaker and weaker. The body loses its ability to resist infections and diseases that a healthy immune system could fight off.

Infection with HIV nearly always occurs in one of the following four ways:

- **Having sexual relations with an infected person.** This is the most common way of getting AIDS. HIV circulates in the bloodstream and in body fluids. Therefore, an infected person can pass on the disease even if he or she has no symptoms. People who have sex with multiple partners are at highest risk. *Avoiding sexual contact is the only sure way to protect yourself against this kind of transmission.*

- **Using a contaminated needle.** A tiny amount of blood left in the needle can pass the virus from person to person. To protect yourself, avoid illegal drugs, and be sure that any procedure involving needles or blood is performed by a health professional.

- **Getting blood from an infected person.** Most people who were infected through blood transfusions were infected before 1986. In 1985 the Red Cross began routinely testing all donated blood for HIV.

- **Passing HIV from infected mother to fetus.** About one third of HIV-infected mothers transmit the infection to their children. The child usually dies within a few years.

How HIV Is *Not* Spread

People are afraid of getting AIDS—and they should be. However, don't let fear cause you to mistake myth for truth. HIV is *not* spread in the following ways:

- Through the air, by coughing or sneezing, for example

- By casual contact with an HIV-infected person—for example, by shaking hands or hugging

- By using the same sports equipment, clothing, towel, comb, or furniture as an infected person

- By using the same telephone, shower, bathtub, or toilet as an infected person

  - By sharing eating utensils or dishes with an infected person (although other kinds of germs are capable of being spread this way)

  - Through the bites of mosquitos, ticks, or other insects

    - By swimming in the same pool as an infected person

      - By donating blood

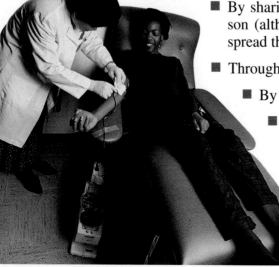

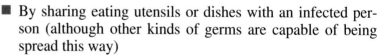

People do not risk getting HIV when they donate blood. A fresh, sterile needle is used for each donor.

Did You Know?

Stopping the Virus

Some of the most promising new drugs used to treat AIDS are drugs called protease inhibitors (PRO•tee•ays in•HI•buh•terz). These are drugs that prevent the virus from reproducing itself. Protease inhibitors, taken along with other AIDS-fighting drugs, have made it impossible to detect the virus in the blood of a large number of the patients treated. Unfortunately, these drugs are much too expensive for most AIDS patients to afford.

The Continuing Battle Against AIDS

Scientists, health workers, educators, and many other people around the world are fighting against the AIDS epidemic. AIDS is a fierce enemy, but much progress has been made:

■ **Drug therapy.** Combinations of powerful new drugs can dramatically reduce HIV levels in the blood and prolong the life expectancy of many HIV-infected people. Medical researchers have also reported some success in improving the immune systems of some HIV-infected people. However, many of the drugs now in use have serious side effects, and they do not work for all patients. The drugs are also much too expensive for everyone to afford. Research continues, with well over a hundred drugs currently under development.

■ **Vaccine research.** Scientists are working intensively to develop an AIDS vaccine. However, the virus that causes the disease occurs in many forms. A vaccine that works against one form of HIV may not work against another form. Most researchers feel that the development of an effective vaccine for AIDS is still many years away.

■ **AIDS education.** With neither a cure for AIDS nor a vaccine, educating people about AIDS is crucial. Health professionals, educators, and workers in federal, state, and local governments are making an all-out effort to teach the public how AIDS is spread and how the disease can be prevented.

Q & A **?**

Testing for AIDS

Q: My cousin was tested for AIDS. The test was negative. Does that mean that he's okay?

A: That depends on the timing. A blood test searches for antibodies to HIV to determine whether you are infected. However, it may take three to six months after infection before antibodies can show up on the test.

Government and community programs are available to help people with HIV and AIDS.

Across the country, more and more teens are practicing abstinence. The 1995 Survey of Family Growth—a government survey conducted every five years—found that the number of teen girls who had had sexual intercourse had dropped nearly 10 percent since the 1990 survey. Researchers believe that education about AIDS may be responsible for the decline.

Abstinence Before Marriage

STDs are extremely dangerous. They can even be deadly. The only sure way to protect yourself from STDs is to practice sexual abstinence. Because most STDs can be transmitted only through sexual contact, by avoiding sexual activity you will be able to avoid the dangers of STDs.

Although the pressure to engage in sexual activity can be very strong, abstinence is the only healthy decision. Every day you are exposed to messages in the media that give the impression that everyone is having sex. Sex is often portrayed as an activity that is fun, exciting, safe, and very important. Sex, however, is the wrong choice for teens. It can lead to unintended pregnancy as well as STDs. It can also cause emotional problems for people who decide to have sex before marriage.

It is important to recognize the many benefits of choosing sexual abstinence before marriage. Some of these include:

- You will avoid the risk of unplanned pregnancy.

- You will avoid the risk of getting a sexually transmitted disease.

- You will be respecting the wishes of your parents.

- You will be focused and committed to long-term goals such as education, career, and family.

Physical attraction to another person is a normal part of life. However, it is important not to let these feelings control your decisions. You can acknowledge your feelings without acting irresponsibly on them. You can also express affection for another person in ways that don't risk your health or compromise your values. By practicing abstinence, you can be sure that your relationships with others are built on shared interests and mutual trust, rather than on sex. When you are an adult, you may choose to marry. By choosing abstinence now, you will know that you can safely enjoy sexual activity within a mutually faithful relationship with your husband or wife.

Teens can express their feelings in many healthy ways.

Using complete sentences, answer the following questions on a separate sheet of paper.

Reviewing Terms and Facts

1. **Vocabulary** What is *chlamydia?* How is it treated?

2. **Compare** What is the difference between *HIV* and *AIDS?*

3. **Recall** Identify four ways in which HIV is spread.

Thinking Critically

4. **Analyze** What factors do you think make STDs especially dangerous?

5. **Explain** Why should teens abstain from sexual activity?

Applying Health Concepts

6. **Growth and Development** Chlamydia, AIDS, herpes, and many other STDs can spread from a pregnant woman to her baby. Do some research to find out what kinds of effects these STDs have on a child during its development. Write a report summarizing your findings.

MAKING HEALTHY DECISIONS
Deciding Whether to Speak Up

*A*t school, Michael eats lunch at a table with four other students. His friends have recently been talking about AIDS and how the disease is spread. Michael's neighbor has AIDS, so Michael knows that much of what his friends are saying is wrong. They think that AIDS can be spread in all sorts of ways that are actually impossible. One student even said that anyone who is infected with HIV should not be allowed in school because "then everyone would catch it." No one at the table disagreed—or at least, no one said anything.

Michael wants to explain to his friends that they are mistaken. However, he's afraid that they will all tell him that *he's* wrong. They might even reject him as a know-it-all. Still, Michael feels that speaking up would be the right thing to do. To figure out what to do, Michael uses the six-step decision-making process:

❶ **State the situation**
❷ **List the options**
❸ **Weigh the possible outcomes**
❹ **Consider your values**
❺ **Make a decision and act**
❻ **Evaluate the decision**

Follow-up Activities

1. Apply the six steps of the decision-making process to Michael's dilemma.

2. As a class, discuss the best ways to go about correcting myths about AIDS when you hear people spreading them.

Chapter Summary

▶ **Lesson 1** Communicable diseases are caused by germs. These germs can be spread in several ways, including direct and indirect contact with other people and contact with animals or insects.

▶ **Lesson 2** The body's immune system protects against disease. People develop immunity through exposure to germs and through vaccination.

▶ **Lesson 3** The cold is the most common communicable disease. Other common communicable diseases include the flu, mononucleosis, hepatitis, and tuberculosis.

▶ **Lesson 4** Good health habits can help protect you and other people against infection and disease.

▶ **Lesson 5** STDs are sexually transmitted diseases, which include chlamydia, gonorrhea, and AIDS. HIV, the virus that causes AIDS, weakens and eventually destroys the immune system.

Reviewing Key Terms and Concepts

Using complete sentences, answer the following questions on a separate sheet of paper.

Lesson 1

1. Define the word *disease.* Use it in an original sentence.

2. List three diseases that are caused by viruses.

Lesson 2

3. What are *lymphocytes?*

4. How does the lymphatic system protect the body against disease?

Lesson 3

5. Describe the disease referred to as *influenza.*

6. What is *hepatitis?*

Lesson 4

7. List three of the procedures you should follow to wash your hands thoroughly.

8. Give four examples of healthy lifestyle choices you can make to keep your body resistant to disease.

Lesson 5

9. List four sexually transmitted diseases besides AIDS.

10. Identify four ways in which AIDS is *not* spread.

Thinking Critically

Using complete sentences, answer the following questions on a separate sheet of paper.

11. **Analyze** How can understanding the ways in which germs are spread help people stay healthy?

12. **Explain** How does exposure to germs enable the body to develop immunity?

13. **Describe** Explain how HIV damages the immune system and causes this system to stop functioning.

Your Action Plan

Protecting yourself against communicable diseases is an important part of your total health. Are you doing all you can to prevent disease?

Step 1 Review your journal entries for this chapter. Make a list of ways in which you can help yourself remain healthy.

Step 2 Prioritize the elements of the list. Give each one a rating of 1 for "very important," 2 for "fairly important," and 3 for "less important."

Step 3 Set a long-term goal that will help you address all the points that you have rated with a 1. Set several short-term goals that will help you gauge your progress toward that goal.

As you achieve your goals, you will be rewarded by getting sick less often and feeling healthy and strong. Next, try setting a new long-term goal—one that will cover the other points on your list.

In Your Home and Community

1. **Personal Health** Are you and your family members doing all you can to protect yourselves and others against germs and disease? Which behaviors need to be changed? What additional actions might be taken? Work with family members to develop a checklist of health habits to follow in your home.

2. **Health of Others** Create an illustrated poster entitled "AIDS: Fact and Fiction." Include basic information about the disease, explaining how it is—and is not—spread. List at least two reliable sources of additional information. Discuss with your teacher where you might display your poster.

Building Your Portfolio

1. **Vaccine Research** Do research to learn more about vaccines that scientists are working to develop. For example, what progress have researchers made in developing a vaccine against Lyme disease? Against the different strains of flu? Summarize your findings in a report. Include the report in your portfolio.

2. **True or False Test** Create a true-false test asking ten basic questions about STDs. Give the test to at least six peers (not in your class) or adults. Evaluate the results. Make a chart summarizing your findings. At the bottom, write a paragraph suggesting ways to communicate information about STDs to teens. Add your chart to your portfolio.

3. **Personal Assessment** Look through all the activities and projects you did for this chapter. Choose one or two that you would like to include in your portfolio.

Chapter 13

Understanding Noncommunicable Diseases

Student Expectations

After reading this chapter, you should be able to:

❶ Describe how heart disease harms the body and how it may be treated and prevented.

❷ Explain what cancer is, how it is treated, and behaviors that may help to prevent it.

❸ Describe allergies and asthma and how people handle these conditions.

❹ Identify arthritis, diabetes, and Alzheimer's disease and treatment options for each.

Teen Chat Group

Tia: What's the matter, Zach?

Zach: I'm worried about my sister. We just found out that she has arthritis.

Troy: But she's only eight. I thought only older people got arthritis.

Zach: The doctor told my parents that people of any age can get arthritis—even kids.

Tia: That's not something you can catch, right?

Zach: No, you can't catch it from someone else.

Troy: Will your sister be okay?

Zach: I think so. My parents and I have to make sure that she takes her medicine, does her exercises, and gets plenty of rest.

Tia: Will she be able to play sports?

Zach: I don't know. Her doctor said we'll have to see how her disease responds to the medication.

in your journal

Read the dialogue on this page. How much do you know about conditions such as arthritis, heart disease, and cancer? Start your private journal entries on non-communicable diseases by responding to these questions:

▶ Have you ever known someone young who had arthritis?

▶ Do you know anyone who has any other noncommunicable disease? How does he or she manage the condition?

▶ Which noncommunicable diseases do you think that people can prevent with a healthy lifestyle?

When you reach the end of the chapter, you will use your journal entries to make an action plan.

Understanding Heart Disease

Lesson 1

This lesson will help you find answers to questions that teens often ask about heart disease. For example:

▶ How does heart disease harm the body?

▶ How is heart disease treated?

▶ What can I do to avoid heart disease?

Words to Know

chronic
stroke
heart attack
hypertension
atherosclerosis
arteriosclerosis
angioplasty

Cultural Connections

Inherited Conditions

Some diseases are found almost only among people of a particular origin. Tay-Sachs disease, a disorder that destroys brain cells, generally affects only Jewish people whose families came from a particular area of Eastern Europe. Sickle-cell anemia is a blood disorder that affects mainly people whose families come from Africa, India, and Middle Eastern and Mediterranean countries.

Some noncommunicable diseases are caused by environmental factors, such as leaks of hazardous chemicals.

Noncommunicable Disease

A noncommunicable disease is a disease that cannot be spread from person to person. Common noncommunicable diseases include heart disease, cancer, asthma, and Alzheimer's disease. These diseases are *not* caused by germs that can be spread by contact. Instead, they are caused by changes within the body.

Most noncommunicable diseases are **chronic** (KRAH·nik), or *present continuously or on and off over a long time.* These diseases generally fall into one of the following three categories:

■ Diseases present from birth

■ Diseases resulting from lifestyle behaviors

■ Diseases caused by the person's environment

Many noncommunicable diseases involve one or more of these factors. Some conditions, however, do not fit into any of these categories because their causes have not been determined. **Figure 13.1** on the following page provides more information about noncommunicable diseases.

Heart Disease

Heart disease is any condition that reduces the strength or functioning of the heart and blood vessels. Heart disease kills more American adults than any other cause of death. In addition to those who die from it, more than 60 million Americans are living with some form of heart disease.

How Heart Disease Kills

Heart disease is responsible for more than 42 percent of all deaths each year. In the United States, someone dies from heart disease every 33 seconds. **Figure 13.2** on the following page shows the types of heart disease and their causes.

*inter*NET
CONNECTION
Good health habits are key to preventing many diseases. Unlock a treasure chest of health tips on the Internet.
http://www.glencoe.com/sec/health

Figure 13.1
Types of Noncommunicable Disease

Noncommunicable diseases can be organized into several different categories, based on their causes.

Type	Description	Examples
Present at birth	Diseases that are caused by hereditary factors or that occur because of problems during a baby's development or birth.	• Cerebral palsy • Cystic fibrosis • Muscular dystrophy • Sickle-cell anemia • Tay-Sachs disease
Lifestyle behaviors	Diseases that occur more often in people with unhealthful habits or lifestyles, including poor food choices, obesity, lack of exercise, smoking, drinking alcohol, and poor stress management.	• Heart disease • Many types of cancer • High blood pressure
Environmental causes	Diseases that are caused by exposure to the hazards around us, including air pollution, toxic wastes, asbestos, and secondhand smoke.	• Allergies • Asthma • Many types of cancer
Unknown causes	Diseases whose causes remain unknown.	• Alzheimer's disease • Arthritis • Chronic fatigue syndrome • Multiple sclerosis

Figure 13.2
Problems of the Cardiovascular System
Heart disease affects more than just the heart itself.

Ⓐ Stroke

A **stroke** occurs when *part of the brain is damaged because the blood supply to the brain is cut off.* Damage occurs because blood normally carries oxygen to the brain, and when the blood supply is cut off, the brain does not receive enough oxygen. Some strokes are caused by a blood clot that blocks an artery leading to the brain. Other strokes are caused when an artery in the brain breaks. Depending on what part of the brain is affected, a person who has a stroke may have trouble moving or speaking. A stroke can also cause death.

Ⓑ Heart Attack

In healthy arteries, blood flows to the heart muscle and supplies it with oxygen. Sometimes, however, an artery becomes blocked. This blockage is often caused by a buildup of fatty substances on the artery walls. A **heart attack** occurs when *the blood supply to the heart slows or stops and the heart muscle is damaged.* A heart attack is a sign of coronary (KOR·uh·nehr·ee) heart disease.

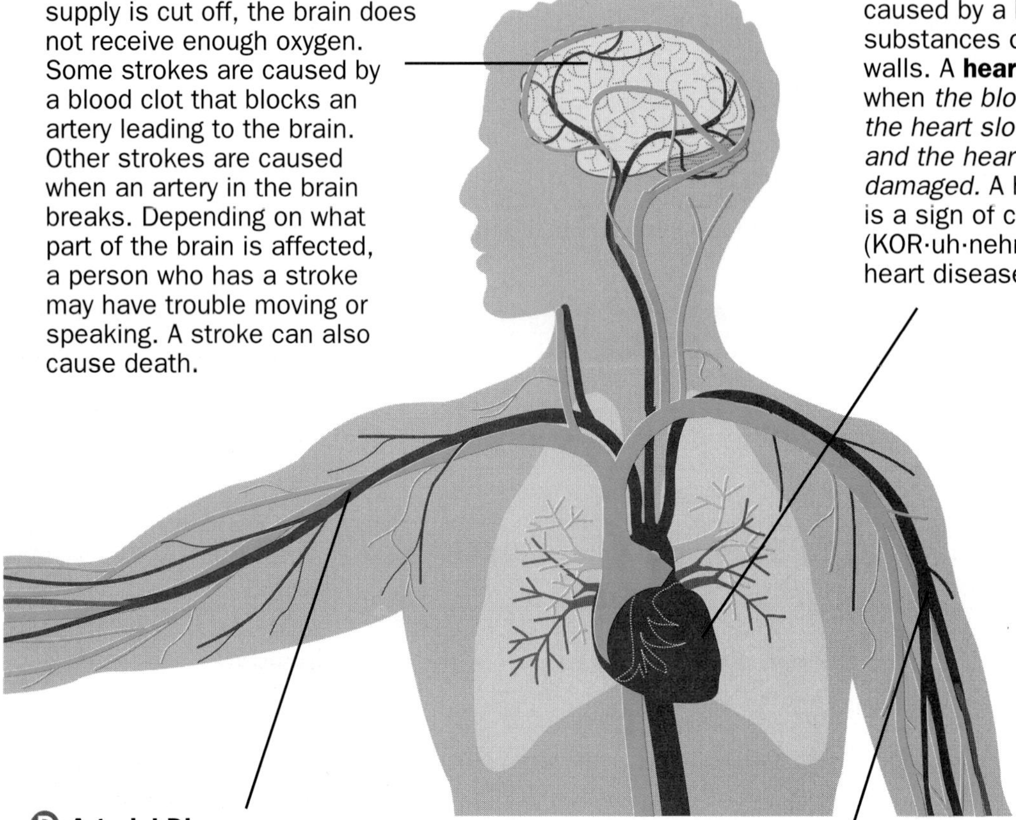

Ⓓ Arterial Diseases

For the heart to function normally, blood must be able to flow through the arteries freely. A slowing or stopping of the blood flow can cause serious problems. *A condition in which fatty substances build up on the inner lining of arteries* is called **atherosclerosis** (a·thuh·roh·skluh·ROH·sis). High levels of cholesterol are associated with atherosclerosis.

Another arterial disease is **arteriosclerosis** (ar·tir·ee·oh·skluh·ROH·sis), or *hardening of the arteries.* Some hardening of the arteries is a natural part of the aging process. Arteriosclerosis causes the blood flow through the arteries to slow down. If atherosclerosis is also present, it worsens the problems caused by arteriosclerosis. These arterial diseases can lead to a heart attack or stroke.

Ⓒ Hypertension

As the heart beats, it is pumping blood throughout the body. The force of the blood on the inside walls of the blood vessels is called blood pressure. Your blood pressure varies with certain factors. For example, it may go down when you are sleeping, and will increase when you are exercising. If, however, *a person's blood pressure stays at a level that is higher than normal,* he or she has **hypertension** (hy·per·TEN·shuhn). Another term for hypertension is *high blood pressure.* This condition can lead to serious health problems, including heart attack and stroke.

Combating Heart Disease

Medical science has made great strides in the treatment of heart disease. Today, medications are used to treat some heart problems and to help prevent others. In addition, surgical procedures have been developed to correct some of the more severe types of heart disease.

What Doctors Can Do

When treating heart disease, doctors have several options. The choice depends on many factors, such as the person's age, the type of heart disease, and the extent of the problem. Possible treatments include the following:

- **Angioplasty.** Sometimes used to treat severe atherosclerosis, **angioplasty** (AN·jee·uh·plas·tee) is *a surgical procedure in which an instrument with a tiny balloon attached is inserted into the artery to clear a blockage.* When the balloon is inflated, it crushes the deposit that was blocking the artery. At the end of the procedure, doctors deflate and remove the balloon.

- **Medication.** In some people, blood vessels become blocked, and blood clots form. Doctors may use medication to dissolve these clots and to stop new clots from forming. Medication is also prescribed for people with hypertension. Regular exercise and a reduction in stress are usually suggested as well.

- **Pacemaker.** Some people have an irregular or weak heartbeat. A pacemaker (PAYS·may·ker) is an electrical device that can be surgically inserted in the body. It sends pulses to the heart to make it beat regularly.

- **Bypass surgery.** When an artery is blocked, doctors can perform bypass surgery to create new paths for the blood to flow around the blockage. During this procedure, surgeons take a vein from the person's leg. They reattach it in the area around the heart so that it takes the blood on a detour around the blocked area.

- **Heart transplant.** If a person's heart has been severely damaged by heart disease, he or she may need a new heart. Surgeons can replace a diseased heart with a healthy one that has been donated.

High blood pressure (hypertension) can usually be kept under control with medication.

in your journal

Are you "heart smart"? Do you practice healthful behaviors—such as exercise and stress management—that can help prevent heart disease? In your journal, make a list of your "heart smart" habits. Then list any risk behaviors that you would like to change. Describe how you might make those changes.

What You Can Do

You may think that you are too young to be concerned about heart disease. Children and teens with certain risk behaviors, however, increase their chances of developing heart disease as adults. Following these tips will help you maintain a healthy heart.

- **Eat healthful foods.** Choose foods that are low in fat and cholesterol and high in fiber. Be sure to include plenty of fruits, vegetables, and grains in your diet.

- **Get plenty of exercise.** Regular exercise strengthens your heart. It also helps build muscle tone and keep you trim.

- **Maintain a healthy weight.** By keeping your weight within a healthy range, you put less strain on your heart. If you are overweight, talk to your doctor about a weight-loss program.

- **Manage stress.** Learn to cope with stressful situations. Good stress management will help you keep your blood pressure and cholesterol level down, which is good for your heart.

- **Don't smoke.** Smokers greatly increase their risk of heart disease and stroke. Almost 20 percent of deaths from heart disease are directly related to smoking.

Healthy relationships with others help teens reduce stress.

Lesson 1 Review

Using complete sentences, answer the following questions on a separate sheet of paper.

Reviewing Terms and Facts

1. **Vocabulary** What is a *chronic* disease?
2. **Relate** In what way is blood pressure related to *hypertension?*
3. **Compare** What is the difference between the following conditions: *atherosclerosis* and *arteriosclerosis?*
4. **Identify** List five treatment options that doctors can use to combat heart disease.

Thinking Critically

5. **Hypothesize** Why might some people continue to practice unhealthy lifestyle behaviors after these behaviors have been linked to diseases?
6. **Analyze** What lifestyle behaviors help to prevent both communicable and noncommunicable diseases?

Applying Health Concepts

7. **Growth and Development** Create a poster to teach children about healthful behaviors that protect the heart. Use colorful drawings or magazine clippings to illustrate each of the positive behaviors mentioned in this lesson. Ask permission to display your poster in a public area in your community where children gather.

Understanding Cancer

This lesson will help you find answers to questions that teens often ask about cancer. For example:

▶ **What is cancer?**

▶ **What are some of the causes of cancer?**

▶ **How can cancer be treated?**

▶ **What can I do to avoid cancer?**

Cancer

Cancer is the second leading cause of death in the United States, just behind heart disease. What exactly is cancer? **Cancer** occurs when *abnormal cells grow out of control.* It is not just one disease, however. Cancer is actually a group of over 200 different diseases that affect many different parts of the body.

The human body is made up of many trillions of cells. These cells are continually growing and reproducing themselves. Although the majority of cells are normal, some are abnormal. The body's natural defenses usually destroy these abnormal cells. Sometimes, however, an abnormal cell survives and starts to reproduce itself.

A **tumor** (TOO·mer) is *a group of abnormal cells that forms a mass.* Tumors can be either benign (bi·NYN) or malignant (muh·LIG·nuhnt). A **benign** tumor is *not cancerous* and does not spread. A **malignant** tumor is *cancerous* and may spread to other parts of the body.

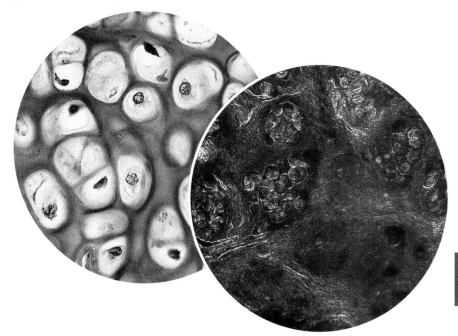

The photo on the left shows normal cells, while the photo on the right shows cancer cells.

Types of Cancer

Cancer can affect many different parts of the body. Sometimes it begins in one area and then spreads to other areas. **Figure 13.3** shows the number of new cases in 1997 of some common types of cancer. It also provides information about these forms of cancer, including their risk factors.

Figure 13.3

Estimated Number of New Cancer Cases, 1997

By understanding risk factors, you can take steps to lower your chances of developing some types of cancer.

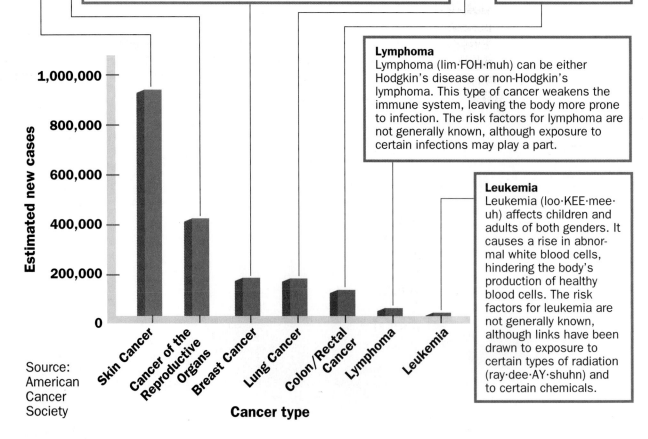

Skin Cancer
This is the most common form of cancer in the United States. It occurs most often in people with light skin, hair, and eyes. The most important risk factor is exposure to the sun. There are several different types of skin cancer, some of which are easier to treat than others.

Lung Cancer
Cigarette smoking is clearly the biggest risk factor in the development of lung cancer, which is the largest cause of cancer death in men and women. Nearly 90 percent of lung cancer cases in men and 79 percent in women are related to smoking.

Cancer of the Reproductive Organs
In females, this type of cancer can affect the ovaries, cervix, and uterus. In males, it can affect the testicles and prostate. The risk factors are varied but include age, family history of cancer, obesity, and cigarette smoking.

Colon/Rectal Cancer
This type of cancer has declined somewhat in recent years, probably because of increased cancer screening. Risk factors include a high-fat, low-fiber diet and lack of exercise.

Breast Cancer
This is the second major cause of cancer death in women. Age is a risk factor for breast cancer. It is more commonly found in women over 50 years old, but it also occurs in younger women and men. A family history of breast cancer is another risk factor.

Lymphoma
Lymphoma (lim·FOH·muh) can be either Hodgkin's disease or non-Hodgkin's lymphoma. This type of cancer weakens the immune system, leaving the body more prone to infection. The risk factors for lymphoma are not generally known, although exposure to certain infections may play a part.

Leukemia
Leukemia (loo·KEE·mee·uh) affects children and adults of both genders. It causes a rise in abnormal white blood cells, hindering the body's production of healthy blood cells. The risk factors for leukemia are not generally known, although links have been drawn to exposure to certain types of radiation (ray·dee·AY·shuhn) and to certain chemicals.

Estimated new cases

1,000,000
800,000
600,000
400,000
200,000
0

Skin Cancer · Cancer of the Reproductive Organs · Breast Cancer · Lung Cancer · Colon/Rectal Cancer · Lymphoma · Leukemia

Cancer type

Source: American Cancer Society

Causes of Cancer

Like other noncommunicable diseases, cancer can be linked to inherited traits, lifestyle behaviors, and environmental factors. **Carcinogens** (kar·SI·nuh·juhnz) are *substances in the environment that cause cancer.* Usually a person must be exposed to a carcinogen over a long period in order for cancer to develop. The following is a list of substances and conditions that have been linked to the development of cancers:

- Tobacco in any form
- Ultraviolet rays from the sun
- Certain types of radiation
- Certain minerals and chemicals used in construction and manufacturing, including asbestos and benzene
- Air and water pollution
- A diet high in fat and low in fiber

Some carcinogens may be difficult to avoid, such as those found in air and water pollution. Other carcinogens, however, can be avoided by choosing a healthful lifestyle.

You Are Entering A *Smoke - Free* Environment. Extinguish All Smoking Materials.

Teen Issues

Check Your ABCD's

Early detection of skin cancer is essential, even for teens. Check your skin for new growths or changes in growths. The American Cancer Society has devised the following ABCD rule that outlines the warning signs of skin cancer in moles.

A Asymmetry: One side of a mole looks different from the other side.

B Border irregularity: The edges are jagged or blurred.

C Color: The color is not uniform or the same throughout.

D Diameter: The diameter is greater than six millimeters (about the size of a pencil eraser). A growth that has grown to this size over time should be checked.

Smoke from other people's cigarettes is one environmental factor that you should avoid as much as possible.

Combating Cancer

The best weapon in the fight against an existing cancer is early detection. To find cancer early, you need to have regular physical checkups. Doctors look for warning signs of cancer during a routine examination.

You also play a role in early detection of cancer. Train yourself to become aware of any unusual changes in your body. One way to do this is to perform regular self-examinations. If you notice something abnormal, be sure to tell your doctor.

A recent scientific study found that a mineral called selenium helps fight cancer. This mineral seems to help stop some types of tumors from growing and cause cancerous cells to die. Most Americans do not need to take selenium supplements, however, because they get enough of the mineral in their diet. Good sources of selenium include fish, meats, and poultry.

What Doctors Can Do

Doctors treat cancer in several ways. The most common cancer treatments are surgery, radiation therapy, and chemotherapy (kee·moh·THEHR·uh·pee). Often a combination of these methods is used.

■ **Surgery** is the primary treatment for many types of cancer. These types include breast, skin, lung, and colon cancer. During surgery, doctors remove tumors and other cancerous cells. Surgery is most effective when the cancer is limited to just one part of the body.

■ **Radiation therapy** is *a treatment for some types of cancer that uses X-rays or other forms of radioactivity.* These rays can be used to destroy cancer cells. Radiation is often used to kill any cancer cells that may remain after surgery.

■ **Chemotherapy** is *the use of chemicals to destroy cancer cells.* This treatment is used to stop cancers that have spread throughout the body.

All three of these treatments have side effects, including the destruction of some healthy cells along with cancerous ones. Both radiation and chemotherapy often cause temporary nausea, fatigue, and hair loss.

What You Can Do

Although there are no guaranteed ways to avoid cancer, there are many precautions you can take. You can, for example, make lifestyle decisions that will lower your risk of developing the disease. You can also take action to find cancer early, thereby improving your chances of recovering from it. By following the guidelines on the next pages, you will be helping to protect yourself from cancer.

LIFE SKILLS
Dietary Guidelines to Lower Cancer Risk

*F*or several decades, scientists have known about the relationship between diet and heart disease. In recent years they have also found a link between diet and cancer. Experts estimate that 35 percent of all deaths from cancer can be linked with food choices. Improving your eating habits can improve your chances of preventing cancer and other diseases.

The American Institute for Cancer Research has created four dietary guidelines. By following them, you can help reduce your risk of getting cancer.

1. **Limit the amount of fat in your diet.** Your total intake of fat should be no more than 30

- **Avoid tobacco.** In the United States, tobacco use is the single most preventable cause of disease and death. Avoiding tobacco is the easiest way to lower your risk of cancer. If you never start using tobacco, you will never have to break the habit.

- **Eat healthful foods.** A diet low in fat and rich in fruits, vegetables, and whole grains can help prevent cancer. The Life Skills feature in this lesson provides more information about dietary guidelines that will lower cancer risk.

- **Limit sun exposure.** Skin cancer is the most common form of cancer in the United States. To reduce your risk, it is best to avoid being outdoors when the sun's rays are at their strongest—between 10:00 a.m. and 3:00 p.m. If you must be in the sun, wear a hat and use a sunscreen with a sun protection factor (SPF) of at least 15.

If you plan an outdoor activity during the day, take precautions to protect your skin from the sun's rays. Use a sunscreen with an SPF of at least 15.

- **Perform self-examinations.** Once a month, females should perform a breast self-examination. Males should perform a testicular self-examination. Ask your doctor how to check for lumps that may be cancerous. In addition, both males and females should check their skin for changes in moles or other growths.

- **Know the seven warning signs.** The American Cancer Society has identified seven warning signs that may signal cancer. The first letters of these warning signs spell the word *caution,* as shown in **Figure 13.4** on the following page. If you notice one of these signs, check with your doctor.

percent of total calories. Specifically, limit the amount of saturated fat to less than 10 percent of total calories. A large amount of fat in the diet has been shown to increase a person's chances of developing cancer.

2. **Eat fruits, vegetables, and whole grains.** Including more fruits, vegetables, and whole grains in your diet can lower your risk of developing cancer. The nutrients in these foods can assist your body in getting rid of carcinogens before they cause cancer. A healthy diet should include at least five servings of fruits and vegetables per day.

3. **Be moderate in your consumption of salt-cured, salt-pickled, smoked, and grilled foods.** Curing, pickling, and smoking are methods of preserving foods. Food preserved in these ways, however, often contain

substances that turn into carcinogens in the body. The charred surface of some grilled foods also contains a large number of carcinogens.

4. **Avoid alcoholic beverages.** For teens, of course, drinking alcoholic beverages is illegal. Adults, however, should keep in mind that consumption of alcohol seems to increase the likelihood of getting certain types of cancer. For this reason and many others, it is best not to start drinking alcohol at all.

Follow-up Activity

Think about the four dietary guidelines to lower cancer risk. Which ones do you follow? Which ones do you need to work on? Make an action plan to improve your eating habits and improve your health.

Think about the lifestyle behaviors you have learned about that can help you prevent cancer. In your journal, describe the actions you already take to reduce your risk of cancer. Then write down any behaviors you would like to improve, and describe ways in which you can make those changes.

Figure 13.4
The Seven Warning Signs of Cancer

If you notice any of the following signs, speak with a physician. Although these signs could be connected to a condition that is not cancer, it is safest to check with a doctor.

C hange in bowel or bladder habits

A sore that does not heal

U nusual bleeding or discharge

T hickening or lump in breast or elsewhere

I ndigestion or difficulty swallowing

O bvious change in a wart or mole

N agging cough or hoarseness

Lesson 2 Review

Using complete sentences, answer the following questions on a separate sheet of paper.

Reviewing Terms and Facts

1. **Vocabulary** Define the term *cancer*. Use it in an original sentence.
2. **Compare** Explain the difference between a *benign* tumor and a *malignant* tumor.
3. **Recall** What is the main risk factor for lung cancer? What are the risk factors for colon/rectal cancer?
4. **Give Examples** Identify four examples of carcinogens.
5. **Identify** What are the three main ways to treat cancer?

Thinking Critically

6. **Hypothesize** Why do you think skin cancer is the most common form of cancer in the United States?
7. **Analyze** How might knowing the seven warning signs of cancer help people protect themselves from the disease?

Applying Health Concepts

8. **Health of Others** Write a script for a public service announcement for radio or television. Your goal is to convince people of the importance of practicing healthy lifestyle behaviors, such as avoiding sun exposure, to reduce the risk of cancer.

Allergies and Asthma

This lesson will help you find answers to questions that teens often ask about allergies and asthma. For example:

▶ **What are allergies?**

▶ **How are allergies treated?**

▶ **What is asthma?**

▶ **How do people who have asthma manage their condition?**

Allergies

In the United States, between 40 and 50 million people suffer from allergies. An **allergy** is *an extreme sensitivity to a substance.* As you have learned, the human body's immune system fights and destroys germs. In a person with allergies, however, the immune system is overly sensitive to certain substances that would normally be harmless. *The substances that cause an allergic reaction are called* **allergens** (AL·er·juhnz). Some common allergens are shown in **Figure 13.5.**

Words to Know

allergy
allergen
pollen
histamines
antihistamine
asthma
bronchodilator

Figure 13.5
Common Allergens

Allergens can be found both indoors and outdoors and in any season.

A Pollen
Allergy to **pollen,** *a powdery substance released by certain plants,* is very common. Pollen is released by flowers, grasses, and weeds.

B Dust
Household dust contains several types of allergens.

C Pets
A number of animals, from various birds to rabbits and cats, can cause an allergic reaction.

D Plants
Many people are allergic to plants such as poison ivy and poison oak. Recognizing these plants can help avoid an allergic reaction.

E Insects
The venom of some insects, such as yellow jackets and wasps, can cause an allergic reaction.

F Food
Almost any food can be an allergen. Common food allergies include milk, eggs, wheat, seafood, and nuts.

Allergic Reactions

When an allergen enters the body, the body releases histamines. **Histamines** (HIS·tuh·meenz) are *chemicals in the body that cause the symptoms of an allergic reaction.* **Figure 13.6** illustrates how the body reacts to allergens. Allergic reactions may involve the following parts of the body:

■ **Eyes.** Allergies can make the eyes red, watery, and itchy.

■ **Nose.** Common allergy symptoms include a runny nose and sneezing.

■ **Throat.** Some food allergies cause difficulty in swallowing. In extreme reactions, the throat can close up.

■ **Skin.** An allergic reaction can cause the skin to break out in a rash. It can also cause hives, which are raised, itchy welts.

■ **Respiratory system.** Allergies can cause coughing and difficulty in breathing.

■ **Digestive system.** An allergic reaction to food may cause stomach pain, cramps, and diarrhea.

Treating Allergies

How do you know what you are allergic to? Sometimes the answer is obvious. Perhaps you develop a rash if you touch poison ivy. Sometimes, however, the source of the allergy is not obvious. In these cases, doctors can perform tests. One test involves injecting small amounts of possible allergens into the skin. In another test, patches are soaked with possible allergens and taped to the skin. With either test, the skin becomes red and itchy if the person is allergic to the substance.

Once the specific allergy is known, there are several possible ways to cope with it.

■ **Avoid the allergen.** If you are allergic to peanuts, for example, you can easily prevent a reaction by not eating them (or any foods that contain them). Some allergens, such as dust and pollen, are more difficult to avoid.

■ **Take medication.** If you can't avoid the allergen, antihistamines may provide relief of symptoms. **Antihistamines** are *medications that relieve the symptoms of allergic reactions.*

■ **Get injections.** For people with severe allergies, doctors may recommend a stronger treatment plan. This involves getting shots of tiny amounts of the allergen to help the individual overcome his or her sensitivity to it.

Figure 13.6
The Body's Response to Allergens

Allergens can enter the body in three ways: through breathing, touching, or swallowing.

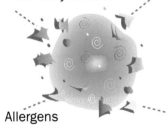

① When a person who has an allergy comes in contact with an allergen, the allergen locks onto the body's cells.

Allergens

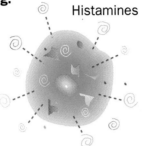

Histamines

② These cells then release histamines, the chemicals that cause the symptoms of an allergic reaction.

in your journal

Do you have any allergies? In your journal, make a list of any known allergies and describe your body's reactions. Maybe you think that you have allergies but aren't sure what substances you are allergic to. If so, keep a record of any suspected allergic reactions in your journal. Note when and where the reactions occurred and what you were doing at the time.

If you can pinpoint your allergens, you will be better able to avoid future reactions. Discuss any severe symptoms with your doctor.

Asthma

The number of people with asthma (AZ·muh), especially children, has risen in the past two decades. About 5 million children and 10 million adults in the United States are affected by this disorder. **Asthma** is *a chronic respiratory disease that causes air passages to become narrow or blocked,* making breathing difficult.

What causes asthma? Many of the same substances that cause allergies also cause asthma. These substances, along with several specific conditions, are called asthma triggers. Common asthma triggers include

- certain allergens, such as pollen, dust, pets, and mold.

- strenuous exercise, especially in cold weather.

- infections of the respiratory system, such as colds and flu.

- irritants, such as cigarette smoke, and fumes, such as those from paint and gasoline.

- situations in which the breathing rate increases, such as stressful events and hard laughing or crying.

- changes in the weather and cold air.

A Typical Asthma Attack

The signs of an asthma attack may include wheezing, shortness of breath, a high-pitched whistling noise in breathing, a feeling of gagging or choking, and chest tightness. **Figure 13.7** shows how an asthma attack affects the airways to the lungs.

Figure 13.7
Effects of an Asthma Attack

The changes caused by an asthma attack make the airways more narrow. This narrowing makes breathing difficult.

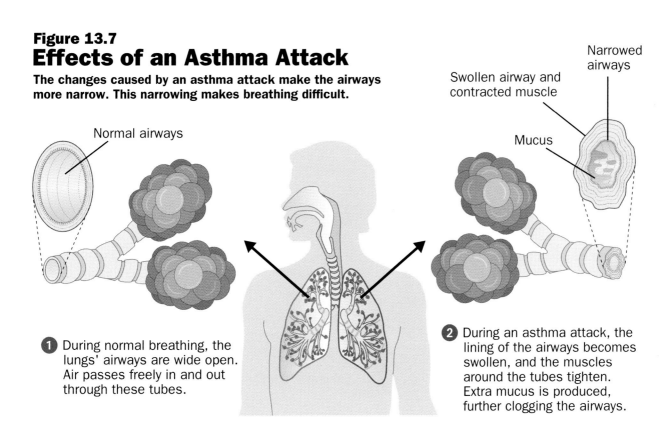

Normal airways

Swollen airway and contracted muscle

Narrowed airways

Mucus

1 During normal breathing, the lungs' airways are wide open. Air passes freely in and out through these tubes.

2 During an asthma attack, the lining of the airways becomes swollen, and the muscles around the tubes tighten. Extra mucus is produced, further clogging the airways.

The Real Culprits **ACTIVITY!**

Contrary to popular belief, dust itself is not the main problem for allergy sufferers. The real culprits are dust mites, microscopic insects that live in beds, linens, and carpets. Find out some ways to cope with dust mites and other allergens. Share your findings with the class.

Asthma did not keep swimmer Tom Dolan from winning a gold medal in the 1996 Olympics.

Coping with Asthma

Most people who have asthma can take part in normal activities, including sports. Under the direction of a doctor, individuals with asthma can develop a treatment plan that will keep the condition under control. The following coping strategies are common:

- **Monitoring the condition.** Because asthma is a chronic disease, people who have asthma should always remain aware of their condition. Many doctors suggest using an instrument called a peak flow meter to monitor lung capacity. By breathing into this device, a person can detect when airways are becoming narrower—even before there are any symptoms. In addition, people who have asthma learn to recognize the warning signs of a severe attack.

- **Managing the environment.** This involves avoiding or getting rid of asthma triggers. In the home, floors and carpeting should be vacuumed regularly. If necessary, carpeting can be removed to reduce the amount of dust. Bed linens should be washed frequently in hot water. Feather pillows may be replaced with ones stuffed with cotton or synthetic fibers.

- **Managing stress.** Stress can sometimes trigger an asthma attack or make the condition worse. It is therefore important for people with asthma to control their stress levels. Relaxation techniques and special breathing exercises may also be helpful.

- **Taking medication.** Two main types of medication are used to treat asthma. One type helps prevent asthma attacks by making the airways less sensitive to triggers. The other type is a **bronchodilator** (brahng·koh·dy·LAY·ter), or *medication that relaxes the muscles around the bronchial air passages.* Bronchodilators help relieve asthma symptoms.

HEALTH LAB
Determining Lung Capacity

*I**ntroduction:*** During an asthma attack, a person's airways become blocked. This blockage reduces the air capacity of the lungs and makes breathing difficult.

Objective: With a partner, measure the air capacity of your lungs.

Materials and Method: You will need a clean 1-gallon plastic milk jug with a cap, masking tape, a two-foot length of plastic tubing, a plastic dishpan, two plastic drinking straws, and two pens in different colors. Tape a long strip of masking tape up the side of the plastic milk jug. Completely fill the jug with water, and put the cap on. Then fill a dishpan about halfway with water. Turn the jug upside down, put it in the dishpan, and remove the cap (keeping the top underwater).

Have your partner hold the jug, being careful not to let in air bubbles. Take the two-foot length of tubing,

Using complete sentences, answer the following questions on a separate sheet of paper.

Reviewing Terms and Facts

1. **Vocabulary**   Define the term *allergy.*

2. **Give Examples**   Name four common *allergens.*

3. **Compare**   Explain the difference between *histamines* and *antihistamines.*

4. **List**   What three methods are used for treating allergies?

5. **Identify**   List four ways to cope with asthma.

Thinking Critically

6. **Hypothesize**   Why do you think allergies often become worse over time?

7. **Synthesize**   How would you help a friend who was undergoing an asthma attack?

Applying Health Concepts

8. **Personal Health**   Many people think that they have a cold when they actually have allergies. Find out how to recognize the difference between a cold and an allergy. Then create a chart that compares the two.

9. **Consumer Health**   In magazines and newspapers and on television, find advertisements of products for people who have allergies or asthma. Discuss the ads with a classmate. What techniques did the advertisers use? What claims did they make? Do you think that the ads are effective?

and put one end into the jug opening. In the other end of the tubing, insert a drinking straw. (Put your hand around the top of the tubing to seal it and to keep the straw from sliding down the tubing.) Take a normal breath of air, and then exhale it into the straw. The air from your lungs will displace some of the water in the jug. Take time to note the water level, and mark it on the tape.

Refill the jug with water, and put it back into the dishpan. Then take a deep breath, and try to exhale all of the air from your lungs into the straw. Mark this water level on the tape.

Using a clean drinking straw, let your partner follow the same procedures. In a different color of ink, mark his or her water levels on the tape.

Observations and Analysis:

After you and your partner have completed this experiment, discuss your findings. Did the water level drop more when you exhaled a deep breath than when you exhaled a normal breath? Which partner's lung capacity was greater? Imagine that you were having an asthma attack and could not get a deep breath. What does this experiment suggest to you about lung capacity during an asthma attack?

TEEN HEALTH DIGEST

Teens Making a Difference

Cancer Crusader

When Robert Abramson was only ten years old, doctors discovered that he had a cancerous brain tumor. After more than 25 hospital stays and five operations, doctors removed the tumor and got rid of the cancer. Today, Abramson is a healthy young man in his twenties.

Grateful to be alive, Abramson is eager to help in the fight against cancer. He is one of the top youth fund-raisers for the American Cancer Society. Each year he takes part in the walka-thon called Making Strides.

Abramson also volunteers as a peer counselor. He visits a children's hospital to talk to children who have cancer. He encourages them to have a positive attitude.

Sports and Recreation

Super Mario

His fans call him Super Mario. Mario Lemieux is an ice hockey player who lives up to his nickname. Lemieux led his team to two championships in a row.

Winning these championships wasn't Lemieux's biggest challenge, however. In 1993 he faced a more personal one. After Lemieux noticed a lump in his neck, doctors found that he had Hodgkin's disease, a type of cancer.

Lemieux had radiation treatments every day for five weeks. These treatments make people feel weak and tired. Even so, on the day of his final treatment, Lemieux rejoined his teammates on the ice. He even scored a goal!

Now Lemieux wants to help other people who have cancer. He started the Mario Lemieux Foundation to support cancer research. Each year he hosts a golf tournament that raises thousands of dollars.

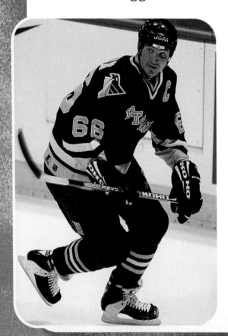

Try This: *Find out about another sports star who overcame a noncommunicable disease. Write a brief report, and share it with the class.*

People at Work

Physical Therapist

Michelle Huarez is a physical therapist at Oakcrest Rehabilitation Center.

Q. What is your main responsibility?

A. I help people improve their physical mobility, or ability to move around, after an illness or injury.

Q. What types of problems do your patients typically have?

A. Some people have had an illness, such as a stroke. Other people have had surgery, such as a knee replacement. Still others have had an injury, such as a broken leg or a dislocated shoulder.

Q. How do you help these people?

A. I teach them exercises and show them how to apply heat and cold to relieve pain. I also teach them how to use aids, such as crutches, and exercise equipment, such as a stationary bicycle.

Q. What type of education does a person need for this job?

A. You need a bachelor's degree. It usually takes about 18 months after that to complete your certification. But different states have different rules, so you have to check with the state you expect to practice in.

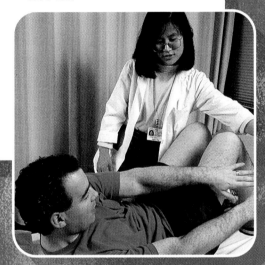

Myths and Realities

A Mysterious Illness

Q. My neighbor has chronic fatigue syndrome. What is it? I've heard people say that it's not really a disease.

A. Chronic fatigue syndrome, or CFS, is a real illness. People who have CFS feel extremely tired all the time. They also suffer from muscle pain and depression. CFS is often misunderstood because many people feel tired and depressed at times. CFS, however, is a chronic, or long-lasting, illness. With CFS, people have trouble working or leading normal lives.

HEALTH UPDATE

No More Shots?

Diabetes is a disease in which the body has problems with the production and function of insulin, a hormone. Many people who have diabetes must get a shot of insulin every day.

Now, however, some people with diabetes have another option. The Federal Drug Administration (FDA) recently approved a drug called troglitazone. It is taken in pill form. For some diabetics, the drug reduces or eliminates the need for insulin shots.

Try This:

Learn more about the FDA. What is its function? How does it protect consumers? Discuss your findings with the class.

Other Noncommunicable Diseases

This lesson will help you find answers to questions that teens often ask about other noncommunicable diseases. For example:

▶ **What is arthritis, and how is it treated?**

▶ **What is diabetes, and how is it treated?**

▶ **What is Alzheimer's disease, and how do people cope with it?**

Words to Know

arthritis
rheumatoid
   arthritis
osteoarthritis
diabetes
insulin
Alzheimer's
   disease

in your journal

Do you know anyone who has arthritis? What common, everyday tasks might be difficult for someone with this condition? In your journal, describe these potential problems. Then think of at least one possible solution for each.

Arthritis

Arthritis (ar·THRY·tuhs) affects about 40 million people in the United States. The term *arthritis* actually refers not just to one disease but to a group of more than 100 conditions. **Arthritis** is *a disease of the joints marked by painful swelling and stiffness.* Although arthritis is more common among older people, anyone can be affected by it, including children.

Types of Arthritis

Although the term *arthritis* refers to many different diseases, there are two main types. **Rheumatoid** (ROO·muh·toyd) **arthritis** is *a chronic disease characterized by pain, inflammation, swelling, and stiffness of the joints.* It is the most serious and disabling form of arthritis. **Osteoarthritis** (ahs·tee·oh·ar·THRY·tuhs) is *a chronic disease, common in elderly people, that results from the breakdown of cartilage in the joints.* It is the more common type of arthritis. **Figure 13.8** shows the causes, characteristics, symptoms, and diagnoses for both types.

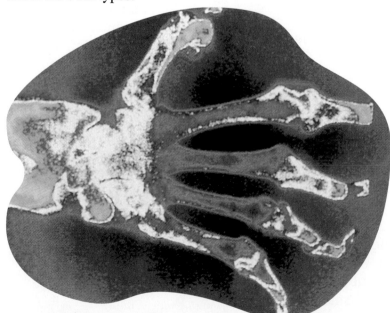

Arthritis can affect any joints, making them stiff and painful.

Figure 13.8

A Comparison of Rheumatoid Arthritis and Osteoarthritis

Although they have similarities, rheumatoid arthritis and osteoarthritis also have many differences.

Rheumatoid Arthritis	Osteoarthritis
Cause: The cause of rheumatoid arthritis is not known. This disease causes the immune system to attack healthy joint tissue, causing swelling and damage to the joints. Children with arthritis usually have this type.	*Cause:* The cause of osteoarthritis is not known. Because it is more common among older people, age is considered a major risk factor. Obesity and joint injuries are also risk factors.
Characteristics: Rheumatoid arthritis can affect any joints, including those of the hands, elbows, knees, hips, and feet. The disease usually progresses symmetrically—when one knee shows symptoms, the other knee will soon also show symptoms. Joints feel stiff and painful and may become deformed.	*Characteristics:* Osteoarthritis most often affects weight-bearing joints, such as the knees and hips. With this disease, the cartilage surrounding the joints breaks down. Because cartilage normally cushions the end of the bones, a breakdown causes bone to rub against bone. This causes pain and may limit movement.
Symptoms: The symptoms of rheumatoid arthritis include soreness, stiffness, aching, and general tiredness.	*Symptoms:* The symptoms of osteoarthritis include joint pain or swelling and pain and stiffness in the morning.
Diagnosis: Doctors diagnose rheumatoid arthritis based on symptoms, a physical examination, and blood tests.	*Diagnosis:* Doctors diagnose osteoarthritis based on symptoms and a physical examination. They may also take X-rays.

Coping with Arthritis

Although there is no cure for arthritis, there are ways to cope with the disease. A doctor can develop an effective treatment plan. Most plans involve a combination of some or all of the following:

- **Medication.** For some types of arthritis, doctors can prescribe medication to slow down the spread of the disease.

- **Painkillers.** Other medications can be taken to ease pain and reduce swelling.

- **Diet.** A balanced diet is necessary to maintain overall health and control weight.

- **Exercise.** Daily exercise helps keep joints flexible and improve muscle strength.

- **Rest.** Getting enough rest is an important way to relieve stress on the affected joints.

- **Heat/cold treatments.** Hot baths or heating pads can help to relieve pain. Cold treatments are sometimes recommended to reduce swelling.

- **Joint replacement.** In severe cases, surgeons can replace a diseased joint, such as a knee or hip, with an artificial one.

Teens and Chronic Illness

During the teen years, you are developing your self-concept and striving for greater independence. For healthy teens, these can be trying times. For a teen with a chronic illness, however, these years can be even more difficult. Teens in such a situation may feel depressed about the illness or develop a negative self-concept. They may feel that they are different from other teens. The support and encouragement of family members and friends can make these trying times a little easier.

Diabetes

Diabetes mellitus, usually called just *diabetes* (dy·uh·BEE·teez), affects about 16 million Americans. About half of these people don't know that they have the condition and are not being treated for it. **Diabetes** is *a disease that prevents the body from converting food into energy.* In people who have diabetes, the body has trouble with the production and use of insulin (IN·suh·lin). **Insulin** is *a hormone produced in the pancreas that regulates the level of sugar in the blood.*

There are two main types of diabetes: insulin-dependent diabetes and non-insulin-dependent diabetes. Insulin-dependent diabetes, also called Type I, generally develops during childhood or adolescence. With this condition, the body produces little or no insulin. Non-insulin-dependent diabetes, also called Type II, affects about 90 to 95 percent of the people who have diabetes. This type of diabetes usually develops in people who are over 40 years old and overweight. With this condition, the body produces insulin but does not use it effectively.

What causes diabetes? People with a family history of the disease have an increased risk of developing it. For non-insulin-dependent diabetes, obesity is a major risk factor. Anyone who has the following symptoms of diabetes should check with a doctor:

■ Excessive production of urine

■ Excessive thirst and hunger

■ Unexplained weight loss

■ Shortness of breath

■ Blurred vision

■ Dry, itchy skin

■ Lack of energy

Coping with Diabetes

There is no cure for diabetes. However, people who have the disease can usually keep it under control and lead normal lives. **Figure 13.9** on the following page shows methods for managing diabetes.

People with diabetes learn how to manage their condition.

Figure 13.9
Managing Diabetes
People who have diabetes must take responsibility for the management of their disease.

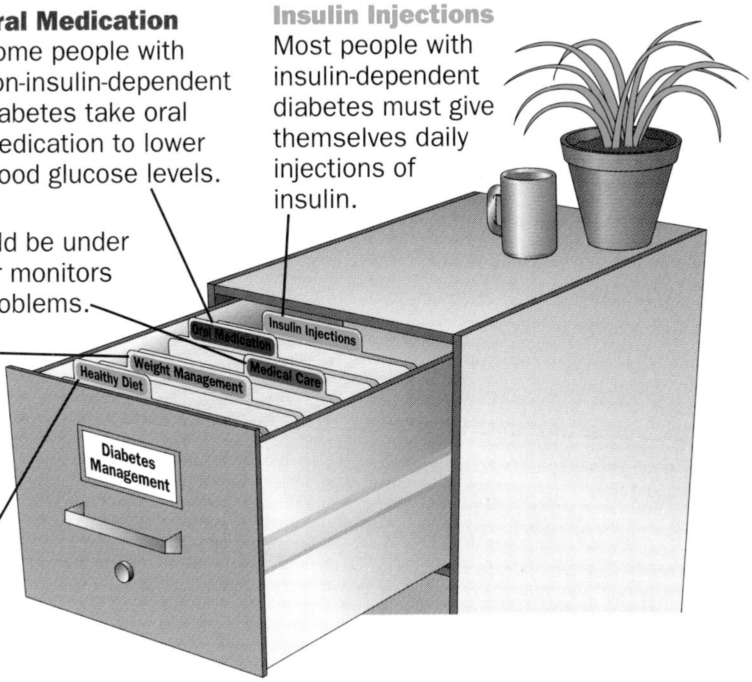

Oral Medication
Some people with non-insulin-dependent diabetes take oral medication to lower blood glucose levels.

Insulin Injections
Most people with insulin-dependent diabetes must give themselves daily injections of insulin.

Medical Care
Anyone who has diabetes should be under the care of a doctor. The doctor monitors the condition and checks for problems.

Weight Management
It is important for people who have diabetes to exercise and maintain a healthy weight.

Healthy Diet
People who have diabetes must monitor their diet to keep the amount of sugar in their blood within safe limits.

Insulin Injections
Oral Medication
Weight Management
Medical Care
Healthy Diet
Diabetes Management

Alzheimer's Disease

Alzheimer's disease affects approximately 4 million people in the United States. **Alzheimer's** (AHLTS·hy·merz) **disease** is *an illness that attacks the brain and affects thinking, memory, and behavior.* The effects of the disease gradually worsen over time. The cause of Alzheimer's disease is unknown. Although this condition usually arises in older people, no one has proven that the condition is caused by the aging process.

Symptoms

Alzheimer's disease causes a loss of live nerve cells in the brain. The affected parts of the brain are those associated with memory and thinking. As a result, a person with Alzheimer's disease may have the following symptoms:

- **Memory loss and mental confusion.** Everyone forgets things, such as a name or telephone number, now and then. A person who has Alzheimer's disease, however, forgets things more often and may not ever remember them again. A person with the disease may also get lost—even in a familiar area—and not know how to get home.

- **Personality changes and mood swings.** It is not unusual for a person's personality to change slightly as he or she grows older. With Alzheimer's disease, however, the change is extreme. The person may become very confused and afraid. Alzheimer's disease may also cause a person to have drastic mood swings. He or she may be calm, then angry, and then tearful—all within a matter of minutes.

- **Altered speech.** Alzheimer's disease may cause a person to forget common words. In place of these words, she or he may use other words that are inappropriate. This can make it very difficult for others to understand what the person is trying to say.

Your Total Health

The Diet Connection ACTIVITY!

A study by Harvard researchers, published in the journal of the American Medical Association in February 1997, found that people who eat a high-starch, low-fiber diet were more likely to develop diabetes. High starch content is found in white rice, white bread, and potatoes. High-fiber alternatives, such as brown rice and whole-grain pasta, breads, and cereals, are much healthier choices. Keep track of how much of these high-fiber foods you eat each day for the next week. If you are eating none or very little, make a plan to change your eating habits.

Did You Know?

Helpful Hounds

For many years, dog guides have been helping people who are visually impaired. These dogs are specially trained to act as their masters' "eyes." Now an organization in the Milwaukee area is training dogs to help people who have Alzheimer's disease. The dogs are taught to let the person's caregiver know if the person is in danger. They also provide comfort and companionship to both the patient and the caregiver.

Coping with Alzheimer's Disease

Researchers have not yet found a cure for Alzheimer's disease. The average life expectancy of someone who has the disease is five to ten years. It is difficult for family members to deal with this type of illness in a loved one. Support groups have been formed to help families deal with the following issues:

■ **Medical concerns.** Family members should find out all they can about any available medication or treatment. They will probably have to help the person with Alzheimer's disease follow the treatment plan.

■ **Practical concerns.** Family members need to know how to care for the person who has Alzheimer's disease, including making the home safe. Eventually, however, the person will need constant care. The family usually must get live-in help or place the person in a health care facility.

■ **Emotional concerns.** Family members must learn how to deal with their emotions regarding the loved one and the disease. They may feel depressed, guilty, or even angry. Learning how to handle these emotions is an important part of dealing with the disease.

A person who has Alzheimer's disease may need help performing everyday tasks.

MAKING HEALTHY DECISIONS
Coping with a Relative Who Has Alzheimer's Disease

Next month Selena's parents will be celebrating their 20th wedding anniversary. Selena and her sister are planning a big surprise party for the occasion. They are going to invite a lot of people, including relatives, friends, and neighbors. The girls have been saving their money for the past six months. They want to make the party really special.

Selena and her sister have a problem, however. They are having trouble deciding whether or not to invite their grandfather to the party. He has Alzheimer's disease, and he needs constant care. He often can't remember who people are—even people he knows well. Sometimes he forgets where he is, and then he becomes very confused and upset. Large numbers of people, especially if he doesn't know some of them very well, sometimes make him irritable.

Selena and her sister would like to invite their grandfather to their parents' party. They love him, and he is their mother's father. However, they don't want to frustrate or upset him. They also realize that someone would have to be with him at all times.

Using complete sentences, answer the following questions on a separate sheet of paper.

Reviewing Terms and Facts

1. **Vocabulary** Define the term *arthritis*. Then use it in an original sentence.
2. **Compare** What is the main difference between *rheumatoid arthritis* and *osteoarthritis?*
3. **Recall** Explain the role of insulin in diabetes.
4. **Identify** List five of the symptoms of diabetes.
5. **List** Name three symptoms of Alzheimer's disease.

Thinking Critically

6. **Suggest** What would you say to a friend who had diabetes, but who didn't want to take her insulin injection?

7. **Infer** Choose one of the diseases discussed in this lesson. Describe the possible effects of the disease on the person who has it and on the person's family or close friends.

Applying Health Concepts

8. **Consumer Health** Look in the Yellow Pages for organizations that offer support groups for people who have arthritis, diabetes, or Alzheimer's disease. Make a list of these organizations, and combine your list with those of your classmates. Post the complete list on the bulletin board.

How should the girls handle this situation? If they invite him, who will take care of him during the party? Selena and her sister decide to use the six-step decision-making process to solve their problem:

1. **State the situation**
2. **List the options**
3. **Weigh the possible outcomes**
4. **Consider your values**
5. **Make a decision and act**
6. **Evaluate the decision**

Follow-up Activities

1. Apply the six steps of the decision-making process to Selena's story.
2. With another student, role-play a scene in which Selena and her sister discuss their problem.
3. Because they want the party to be a surprise, the girls can't ask their parents for advice. Whom else might they ask to help them with their decision?

Chapter 13 Review

Chapter Summary

▶ **Lesson 1** Noncommunicable diseases cannot be spread from person to person. They can be present from birth, result from lifestyle behaviors, or be caused by the person's environment. Heart disease, which includes diseases of the heart and blood vessels, kills more Americans than any other cause.

▶ **Lesson 2** Cancer is a group of diseases that occurs when abnormal cells grow out of control. You can lower your risk of developing cancer by practicing healthy lifestyle behaviors.

▶ **Lesson 3** Many substances in the environment may cause people to have allergic reactions. Some of these same substances cause asthma, a chronic respiratory disease.

▶ **Lesson 4** Arthritis is a disease of the joints. Diabetes is a disease in which the body cannot properly convert food into energy. Alzheimer's disease attacks thought processes, memory, and behavior. Although no cures exist for these illnesses, methods of coping with them are available.

Reviewing Key Terms and Concepts

Using complete sentences, answer the following questions on a separate sheet of paper.

Lesson 1

1. In what way is a *stroke* similar to a *heart attack?*

2. Identify four lifestyle behaviors that can help you lower your risk of heart disease.

Lesson 2

3. Explain the difference between *radiation therapy* and *chemotherapy.*

4. What are four ways in which you can reduce your risk of developing cancer?

Lesson 3

5. What is *asthma?*

6. Explain the purpose of a *bronchodilator.*

Lesson 4

7. List five methods of coping with *arthritis.*

8. Identify the two main types of *diabetes,* and explain the difference between them.

Thinking Critically

Using complete sentences, answer the following questions on a separate sheet of paper.

9. **Deduce** Why do you think heart disease is the number one killer in the United States?

10. **Analyze** Which healthy behavior do you think is the most important for reducing the risk of cancer? Explain your answer.

11. **Synthesize** Why is it a good idea to know what substances you are allergic to?

12. **Infer** In what way is a chronic illness, such as arthritis, different from other illnesses, such as the flu?

Your Action Plan

A healthy lifestyle can help you reduce your risk of developing some types of noncommunicable diseases.

Step 1 Review your private journal entries for this chapter. Do you have any lifestyle behaviors that you would like to change? Decide on a long-term goal that you would like to achieve. For example, you might want to start eating a low-fat diet.

Step 2 Now write down short-term goals that will help you achieve your long-term goal. A short-term goal for reducing fat in your diet might be to replace three high-fat foods you would otherwise eat this week with low-fat choices.

Plan a schedule and a method for reaching each short-term goal. For example, you might decide to try one new low-fat food each week. When you reach your long-term goal, reward yourself for adopting a healthier lifestyle.

In Your Home and Community

1. **Community Resources** Contact an organization in your community that helps people cope with a noncommunicable disease (for example, the American Heart Association or the American Cancer Society). Ask for brochures on ways to reduce the risk of developing the disease or ways to cope with it. Display the brochures.

2. **Health of Others** Talk to your family about the importance of a low-fat, high-fiber diet to reduce the risk of heart disease and cancer. Together, make a list of foods to buy the next time you go to the grocery store. Then develop an action plan to achieve the goal of healthier food choices.

Building Your Portfolio

1. **Interview** Talk to someone you know who has allergies or asthma. Ask the person for tips on how he or she copes with the illness. Audiotape or videotape the interview, and add the tape to your portfolio.

2. **Research and Report** Find out about the latest medical research on arthritis, diabetes, or Alzheimer's disease. Read current articles in newspapers or magazines. Do researchers have ideas about what causes the illness? Are they close to finding a cure? Summarize your findings in a one-page report. Add the report to your portfolio.

3. **Personal Assessment** Look through all the activities and projects you did for this chapter. Choose one or two that you would like to include in your portfolio.

Chapter 14

Preventing Violence and Abuse

Student Expectations

After reading this chapter, you should be able to:

❶ Recognize the causes of violence and know how to prevent violence in your school.

❷ Describe abuse and its effects.

❸ Identify places people can go to for help in stopping abuse.

Teen Chat Group

Charles: Did you hear about that fight at school yesterday? One of the guys had to be taken to the hospital.

Greg: That's the third fight so far this week!

Luis: It was pretty scary. We talked about it in class this morning.

Susan: So what did everyone say?

Luis: We talked about ways we could help stop the fighting, like starting an antiviolence program.

Greg: What exactly is an antiviolence program?

Susan: I just read about one of them yesterday. Students are trained to be peer mediators so that people who have a problem can sit down and talk about it with someone who isn't involved. It helps solve the problem before a fight starts.

Charles: That sounds like a good idea. Let's find out how to start one.

 in your journal

Read the dialogue on this page. Start your private journal entries on preventing violence and abuse by responding to these questions:

▶ What violence prevention programs exist in your school?

▶ Why do you think violence and abuse are problems in our society?

▶ If someone you knew experienced violence or abuse, where would you suggest they go for help?

When you reach the end of the chapter, you will use your journal entries to make an action plan.

Dealing with Violence

This lesson will help you find answers to questions that teens often ask about violence and violence prevention. For example:

▶ **What are the causes of violence?**

▶ **What can I do to protect myself so I do not become a victim?**

▶ **How can I help to prevent violence in my school?**

Words to Know

homicide
hate crime
gang

Violence in Society

The images of violence are all around us—from music lyrics to the daily news reports. Grim stories of beatings, stabbings, gang wars, and family abuse are reported on the news and highlighted in the movies. Violence is a major public health problem in the United States. **Figure 14.1** shows how frequently violent crimes are committed in the nation.

Some people blame the increase in violence on television. By the age of 18, the average teen has viewed 200,000 acts of violence on television. Because some television programs glamorize violence, they may lead people to believe that violence is an acceptable way to settle disagreements.

Other people blame the increase of violent acts on the breakdown of the family, the decline in moral values, and the availability of weapons. Whatever the cause, there are many factors that contribute to the violence in society. In the end, we are all victims—either directly or indirectly.

Figure 14.1
Violent Crime Watch

Violent crime is a problem that affects everyone in our society. A violent crime occurs every 18 seconds. The statistics shown in this figure are for the four main types of violent crime.

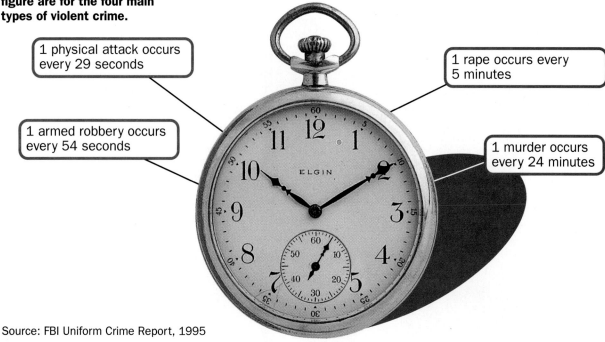

1 physical attack occurs every 29 seconds

1 rape occurs every 5 minutes

1 armed robbery occurs every 54 seconds

1 murder occurs every 24 minutes

Source: FBI Uniform Crime Report, 1995

The Victims of Violence

Who are the victims of violence? Each and every one of us is a victim of the violence in society. To solve this problem, communities, schools, and individuals need to work together.

In the past, an argument might lead to a shouting match or a fistfight. Today, the results may be more tragic. Simple arguments or disagreements might end in gunfire, stabbings, and possibly death. The fact is that violence today is more serious and more random than in the past. Random violence is committed for no particular reason and against anyone who happens to be around at the time. As a result, innocent people may be the victims of violence. Long after the violence has occurred, the victims and their families experience prolonged emotional trauma. In addition, victims may undergo the stress of testifying at long, costly legal trials.

Perhaps you have not been a direct victim of violence. However, you still have felt the impact of violence. Every year, crime in the United States costs an estimated $500 billion. This includes police protection, prisons, lost lives and wages, and medical costs. Even within some schools, security measures have been initiated to prevent violent acts. Locker searches, metal detectors, and security in schools increase costs to schools and communities.

Teens and Violence

The majority of teens are not violent and they do not commit crimes. However, teens are twice as likely as other age groups to be the victims of violence. In fact, the second leading cause of death of all people between the ages of 15 and 24 is homicide. A **homicide** (HAH·muh·syd) is *a violent crime that results in the death of another individual.*

Teens are also more likely than any other age group to commit violent crimes. In fact, more than a third of all violent crime in the United States is committed by young people under the age of 21. What drives these teens to commit such crimes?

in your journal

Do you know someone who has been the victim of a violent crime? In your private journal, describe how you felt when you heard about the crime. Could the victim have prevented the crime? Explain your response.

The Bureau of Justice Statistics has reported that nearly 2,500 people under the age of 18 are killed each year as a result of violent crime. Many were not involved in the confrontation but happened to be nearby when violence erupted.

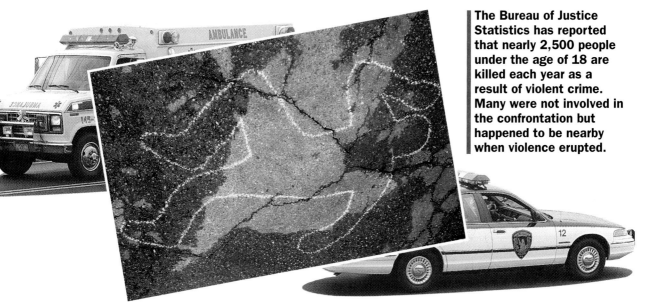

Causes of Violence

People who commit violent acts usually have not learned how to deal with their feelings. Other factors that contribute to violence are discussed below.

Anger

Anger is a normal emotion. Learning how to control it is the most important step in preventing violence. Here are some ways to control your anger.

- Count to ten before you say or do anything.
- Talk to someone you trust and respect about your feelings.
- Exercise to get rid of some of your pent-up feelings.
- Channel your energy into a worthwhile activity.
- Find a nonviolent way to deal with the situation.

Prejudice

Prejudice is an opinion that has been formed without careful consideration. Prejudice is often based on a person's gender, race, religion, or country of origin. Prejudice sometimes leads to **hate crime,** which is an *illegal act against someone just because he or she is a member of a particular group.*

Possession of Weapons

An important relationship exists between access to weapons and the rise in violent crime. As anger increases during a dispute, a weapon may be used as an easy solution. See **Figure 14.2** on the next page.

LIFE SKILLS
Protecting Yourself

*P*eople who commit violent crimes seek out people who look vulnerable. You can reduce the chances of becoming a victim of violent crime by learning to protect yourself. The following tips will help you to stay safe.

In General:

- ▶ Do not look like an easy target. Stand up straight and walk with a confident stride.
- ▶ If someone bothers you, use direct eye contact and a forceful voice and say "Leave me alone," or shout "Fire!"
- ▶ If you are attacked by someone, get away in any way that you can.

Figure 14.2
Causes of Gun-Related Death Among Young People

When young people use guns, the result is often death.

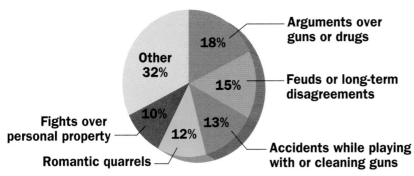

- Other 32%
- Arguments over guns or drugs 18%
- Feuds or long-term disagreements 15%
- Accidents while playing with or cleaning guns 13%
- Romantic quarrels 12%
- Fights over personal property 10%

Source: Center to Prevent Handgun Violence

in your journal

Think about a time when you felt really afraid. How did your body react? Did your hands turn cold? Did you tremble? Did the hair on the back of your neck stand on end? Use your private journal to write about your reactions to the fear you felt.

Peer Pressure

Many teens want to be accepted by a group and will take part in any conflict to show loyalty to the group. Sometimes, pressure from the group causes a teen to do something that goes against his or her own values.

Alcohol and Other Drugs

Alcohol and other drugs can contribute to violence. Substance abuse makes people act in unpredictable and dangerous ways. It can also prevent a person from making good decisions and judgments. Almost half of all violent crimes are committed by people under the influence of alcohol or other drugs.

Outside:

▶ Do not walk alone at night or near alleyways. Walk in lighted areas.

▶ If you think someone is following you, go into a store or other public place.

▶ When entering your house, make sure your keys are ready so that you do not have to fumble for them at the door.

▶ Do not hitchhike or ride in a car with strangers.

▶ If someone wants your money or jewelry and you are in danger, throw your purse, wallet, or jewelry away from you. Then run in the opposite direction.

Inside:

▶ Avoid entering an elevator alone with a stranger.

▶ At home, keep the doors and windows locked. Do not open the door for someone you do not know. Do not tell strangers on the phone that you are home alone.

Follow-up Activity

Using these tips as a checklist, examine the way you protect yourself in general, on the street, and in your home. In what areas are you safety conscious? In what areas do you need to improve? Make an action plan to keep yourself safe.

Gangs and Gang-Related Violence

A **gang** is *a group of people who associate with one another because they have something in common*. Although teen gangs are not all alike, many are involved in criminal activities. Most of the crimes involve some type of violence, intimidation, drive-by shootings, robbery, gang warfare, or rape.

Young people join gangs for many reasons, including racism, poverty, boredom, anger, lack of family support, peer pressure, or the need for companionship. However, there are many safer, noncriminal alternatives to joining a gang.

- If you are lonely or bored, look for a youth group, sports team, or church group in your neighborhood.

- If you are being harassed by gang members and are scared, get help. A family member, community group, school counselor, or police officer can give you support and help protect you.

- If peers are pressuring you, band together with other teens to start a community group that works for positive change.

Stopping and Preventing Violence

Although violence in America is on the rise, communities and individuals are working together to address the risk factors and reduce the incidence of violent crimes. Here is a list of what some communities are doing to make their neighborhoods safer.

- More police on the streets
- Stricter gun laws
- Nighttime sports programs
- Improved lighting in parks and playgrounds
- Neighborhood Watch programs
- Teen curfews
- Tougher punishments for violent crimes

Violence and You

Figure 14.3 on page 397 shows how many students and teachers are victims of violence. Do you, like other students, feel that you would learn more in school if you felt safer? If that is true, then there are many ways that you can work with others to help make your school a safer place.

As a way to remember loved ones and friends who have been victims of violence, people in a community can work together. They can help to make their neighborhoods safer.

Figure 14.3
Violence in School

Violence in schools does not always involve physical injury. Violence also includes shoving another person, sending threatening notes, making physical threats, and offering insults.

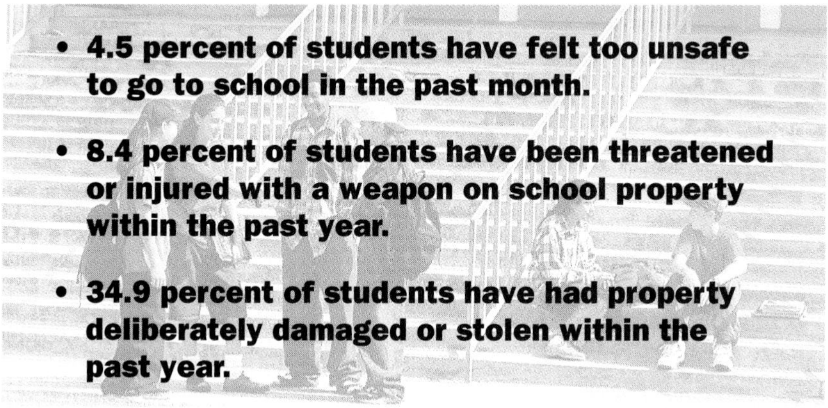

- **4.5 percent of students have felt too unsafe to go to school in the past month.**

- **8.4 percent of students have been threatened or injured with a weapon on school property within the past year.**

- **34.9 percent of students have had property deliberately damaged or stolen within the past year.**

Source: Youth Risk Behavior Surveillance, United States, 1995 (Centers for Disease Control)

Toward Safer Schools

Principals, school board members, teachers, parents, and students are working together to stop violence in the schools. Here is a list of what some schools are trying.

- Peer mediation programs
- Metal detectors
- Violence prevention programs
- Locker searches
- Stricter dress codes
- Video surveillance cameras
- Security guards
- Drug- and gun-sniffing dogs

Schools are also trying to eliminate some of the causes of violence by teaching respect for others and providing counseling.

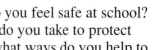

Review
Lesson 1

Using complete sentences, answer the following questions on a separate sheet of paper.

Reviewing Terms and Facts

1. **Vocabulary**   Define the terms *homicide* and *hate crime*.

2. **Give Examples**   Identify ways in which peer pressure might lead a teen to do something she or he would not ordinarily do.

Thinking Critically

3. **Hypothesize**   Why do you think some young people join gangs?

4. **Analyze**   Do you feel safe at school? What actions do you take to protect yourself? In what ways do you help to protect the safety of others?

Applying Health Concepts

5. **Health of Others**   Organize a group to brainstorm ways to prevent school violence. Attend a student council meeting. Share your group's ideas with the students.

6. **Consumer Health**   Find out about movie ratings and warnings on tapes and compact discs. Evaluate the need for them, and share your findings.

TEEN HEALTH DIGEST

CON$UMER FOCU$

Rating TV Programs

In January 1997, six categories of ratings began to appear on network and cable channels. TVY and TVY7 apply only to children's programming. A rating of TVY means that the program is considered suitable for all ages, and a program rated TVY7 is intended for children seven years and older. If an FV accompanies a Y7 symbol, there are scenes of fantasy violence. Other ratings that may accompany the basic ratings are V (violence), S (sexual content), L (coarse language), and D (suggestive dialogue). The rest of the ratings are defined below:

- **TVG:** Material suitable for all audiences.
- **TVPG:** Parental guidance suggested. May contain some coarse language, limited violence, or suggestive sexual dialogue and situations.
- **TV14:** Material may be inappropriate for children under 14. May contain sophisticated themes, strong language, or sexual content.
- **TVMA:** Program is designed to be viewed by mature audiences. May contain profane language and graphic violence or sexual content.

Myths and Realities

The Truth About Abuse

There is plenty of talk about abuse these days. Can you separate the facts from the false statements?

Myth: If a man abuses a young girl sexually, that is rape, but a woman's sexual abuse of a young boy is not rape.

Reality: Any adult who exploits a child sexually is an abuser. No matter what the gender of the abuser or the victim, such an act *is* a form of rape and causes lasting harm.

Myth: People who are sexually abused always go on to abuse others.

Reality: Not true. While it is true that most abusers have histories of being abused, most victims do *not* go on to abuse others. In fact, telling about abuse and getting help often prevents victims from abusing others.

Try This:

For one week, take note of the ratings of various shows you normally watch. Write a short report about your views of the rating system.

People at Work

Helping People

Job: Social worker
Responsibilities: To help people with problems related to poverty, sickness and family matters; to find foster homes for children; to begin legal action in child abuse cases

Education: Four to six years of college
Workplace: A wide range of settings, including schools, hospitals, offices, agencies, jails, and courts
Positive: Social workers can experience the satisfaction that comes from helping others.
Negative: This type of job may seem frustrating when important work cannot be accomplished because agencies lack the money for supplies and services.

Sports and Recreation

A Very Un-Martial Art

Aikido (eye·ki·DOH) is a Japanese martial art that is becoming popular in the United States. Developed originally as a means of self-defense, aikido has as one of its primary purposes the peaceful resolution of conflict.

Even when used as a form of self-defense, aikido retains a non-violent focus. Rather than kicking or pushing opponents, people who practice aikido use their opponents' energy against them to ward off attack. In addition, aikido is primarily cooperative rather than competitive. People who learn this technique seek to match their partners in ability rather than overpower them.

Teens Making a Difference

A Dramatic 47 Seconds

About five years ago Anna Akbari heard a frightening statistic: that a child was abused every 47 seconds. The problem of abuse suddenly became real for her, and she decided to devote her time and talent to educating people about child abuse.

Akbari started a dramatic troupe called 47 Seconds. The troupe performs a mix of music, dance, and drama at schools, churches, and foster parent groups in the Midwest, Akbari's home region. Some of the performers are at-risk teens themselves.

"Our main focus is to let people know there is a way to get help and there are lots of people who care," Anna says.

Try This: Find out what groups in your area give presentations on the topic of abuse and violence. Arrange for one to visit your school.

Understanding Abuse

This lesson will help you find answers to questions that teens often ask about abuse and violence. For example:

▶ **What is abuse and why does it happen?**

▶ **How does abuse affect a person?**

▶ **What can be done to prevent abuse?**

Words to Know

abuse
victim
battery

What Is Abuse?

You may find it difficult to understand how anyone can abuse a child, a family member, another relative, or a stranger. However, abuse in the United States is a significant problem. See **Figure 14.4** for some alarming statistics on abuse.

Abuse (uh·BYOOS) is *the physical, emotional, or mental mistreatment of another person,* and it can take several forms. Abuse may be physical, emotional, sexual, or a result of neglect. It can cause obvious physical wounds, such as bruises, scratches, or broken bones. It can also cause emotional wounds, such as anger, sadness, and fear. Abuse can happen in all kinds of families—from the richest to the poorest, from the most well educated to those with no schooling at all. Abuse can happen anywhere—in the largest cities and in the smallest towns.

Wherever abuse occurs, and whatever form it takes, abuse always does long-lasting damage. It is a crime to abuse another person. This is so important that physicians and teachers are required by law to report suspected cases of abuse. Abuse is never the fault of the **victim**, *the person against whom a crime is committed.*

Figure 14.4
Abuse Statistics

The incidence of abuse in families is evidence of the number of troubled families in our society. These are figures for a single year.

Reported cases of child abuse and neglect in the United States —3.1 million

Estimated number of women physically abused by their husbands or boyfriends—almost 4 million

Estimated number of elderly abused or neglected—820,000

Types of Abuse

There are four major types of abuse. They are physical abuse, emotional abuse, sexual abuse, and neglect. Anyone in a family may be the victim of abuse: a child or adolescent, a husband or wife, a brother or sister, or a grandparent.

Physical Abuse

Physical abuse is mistreatment that results in injury to the body. In some cases, physical abuse results in burns or broken bones. In severe cases, the victims of physical abuse die. The most common form of physical abuse is **battery,** *the beating, hitting, or kicking of another person.*

Emotional Abuse

Emotional abuse is the use of words and gestures to mistreat another person. Angry insults, repeated threats, constant teasing, and harsh criticism are examples of emotional abuse. When people are treated this way over a long period of time, they end up feeling worthless and helpless.

Sexual Abuse

Sexual abuse is any sexual contact that is forced upon a victim. It is a very serious crime. The abuser is often someone the victim knows and trusts, such as a parent, stepparent, older brother or sister, or family friend. When sexual abuse occurs between family members, it is called incest.

The victim of sexual abuse may feel guilty that somehow he or she is responsible for what has happened. However, no matter who the abuser is, sexual abuse is *never the victim's fault*—it is always the abuser's. The person who commits sexual abuse needs professional help. One way to get that help is for the victim to talk to a trusted adult—someone who can assist in arranging for the counseling that is needed.

Neglect

Neglect is the failure to meet the basic physical and emotional needs of a person. Young people need proper food, clothing, and housing to help them grow and develop. They need love and encouragement to help them feel safe and secure. Children who do not have these needs satisfied are neglected.

Teaching young children about child abuse is one way to help prevent it.

Causes of Abuse

All families have problems from time to time. An important key to dealing with these problems is communication. In a healthy family, members learn how to express emotions in a nonviolent way. Often the cause of abuse is that the person does not know how to control his or her own frustrations and emotions, or does not know how to handle problems in a positive way. People who abuse others often do not intend to do harm. Factors that seem to increase the risk that a person will become abusive are listed below:

- History of having been abused as a child
- Alcohol or other drug abuse
- Unemployment and poverty
- Illness
- Divorce
- Feelings of worthlessness
- Emotional immaturity
- Lack of parenting skills
- Inability to deal with anger
- Lack of communication and coping skills

Your Total Health

Stemming the Tide of Abuse ACTIVITY!

Many cases of abuse are related to problems with alcohol or drugs. See Chapter II for more information on where to get help if someone in your family has these problems. Organizations such as Alcoholics Anonymous help people to stop drinking and reduce the chances that they will abuse someone else. Find out about organizations in your community that offer help to alcohol and drug abusers. Share your findings in class.

MAKING HEALTHY DECISIONS
Deciding to Report Abuse

*J*enny is Tasha's best friend. She knows that Tasha's father drinks too much, and when he does, he gets really mean. Several times Tasha has told Jenny about her father's "fits"—how he hollers, throws things, and once put his fist through a door.

This afternoon, in the locker room, Jenny noticed some awful bruises on Tasha's back and arms. At first Tasha explained the cause as a "skating accident." Later, though, she confided to Jenny that her father had beaten her. This was not the first time, either. Tasha made Jenny promise not to tell anyone.

Jenny has to make a decision. She knows that it is important to report abuse. She is afraid that the next beating may be worse. Still, she does not want to break a promise to her best friend. To help her choose the best solution, Jenny will use the six-step decision-making process.

❶ **State the situation**
❷ **List the options**
❸ **Weigh the possible outcomes**
❹ **Consider your values**
❺ **Make a decision and act**
❻ **Evaluate the decision**

Follow-up Activities

1. Apply the six steps of the decision-making process to Jenny's dilemma.
2. Imagine that you are Jenny. Write a diary entry for the day she decides what to do.

Signs of Abuse

A child who has been beaten will usually show signs of physical abuse. The signs of emotional abuse, sexual abuse, and neglect are more difficult to recognize. Some of them are listed here:

- Frequent absences from school
- Poor grades and lack of interest in school
- Dirty or neglected appearance
- Extreme shyness, sadness, or fear
- Aggressive behavior toward others
- Inability to communicate

Effects of Abuse

Abuse is always harmful. It causes damage to the abuser and the victim. Some teens try to escape from abuse by leaving home. Running away, however, often leads to other problems. Runaways usually have no way to support themselves. They have no place to live and no money for food. Life on the street is rough. Some runaways turn to crime. Many runaways become the victims of crime.

People who were abused as children often have low self-esteem, a high level of stress, and other problems. They may find themselves in abusive relationships as adults, and they sometimes become abusers themselves. However, with help, people can break the cycle of abuse.

Teen Issues

Sexual Harassment at School ACTIVITY!

Sexual harassment (huh·RAS·muhnt) is any unwelcome sexual comment, contact, or behavior. This may include jokes, looks, notes, touching, or gestures. Sexual harassment is a type of sexual abuse. It can happen to boys or to girls. Find out if your school has a policy for dealing with sexual harassment.

Review

Lesson 2

Using complete sentences, answer the following questions on a separate sheet of paper.

Reviewing Terms and Facts

1. **Vocabulary**   What is a *victim?*
2. **Vocabulary**   Define the term *battery.* Use it in an original sentence.
3. **Give Examples**   Identify four signs of abuse.

Thinking Critically

4. **Compare and Contrast**   In what ways are neglect and emotional abuse similar? How are they different?

5. **Hypothesize**   Why do you think the effects of abuse are often so deeply felt and so long-lasting?

Applying Health Concepts

6. **Personal Health**   Contact the National Clearinghouse on Child Abuse and Neglect Information. Use some of their most current statistics to create a chart of the various forms of abuse. Share your findings with your class.

Finding Help

This lesson will help you find answers to questions that teens often ask about finding help for abuse victims. For example:

▶ **What help is available for abused and troubled people?**

▶ **Why do some people fail to report abuse?**

family violence
shelter

There are many different types of community programs available to help teens break the cycle of abuse.

Breaking the Cycle of Abuse

The longer abuse continues, the greater the damage will be. The key to breaking the cycle of abuse is reporting it and talking about it. If someone has been abused or is in danger of being abused, it is important for that person to tell someone, such as a family member, a teacher, a school nurse, a doctor, a counselor, or another adult he or she trusts. The victim may be afraid to tell, however, for fear that the information will break up the family, that the abuser will go to jail, or that no one will believe him or her.

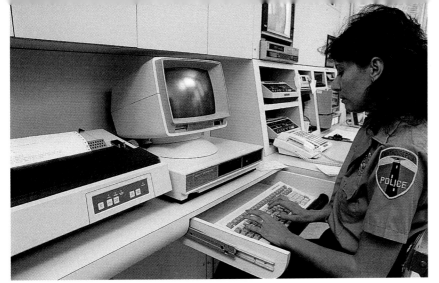

Reporting abuse to law enforcement authorities is one way to get help for both victims and abusers.

Where to Get Help

What kind of help is available for abused children and troubled families? Some of the community resources for dealing with and preventing abuse are described below:

- **Police department.** This is the place to call for help if someone is in immediate danger. In many communities the emergency number for the local police department is 911. Dial 0 to call the operator if you are not sure how to reach the police department in your community.

- **Local hospital.** Hospitals provide emergency medical treatment for people who are injured, hurt, or seriously ill.

- **Family violence shelters.** These are *places where family members in danger of being abused can stay while they get their lives in order.* Counselors at the shelters help family members find solutions to their problems.

- **Family counseling programs.** These programs help family members identify their problems and work together to solve them. School guidance counselors, youth counselors, hospital social workers, and clergy members also provide support to family members on an individual basis or as a group.

- **Support or self-help groups.** In these groups, people have a chance to talk with and listen to others with similar problems. Some support groups are for victims of abuse; others are for abusers. For example, Parents Anonymous is for parents who have abused their children or are afraid that they might begin to do so. Members help one another to understand and change their behavior.

- **Home health visitors.** Some communities arrange for nurses to visit families to help parents improve their parenting skills.

- **Crisis hot lines.** These are telephone services that parents and abused children can call to get help. Some people may be reluctant to talk about their problems to strangers. However, hot line workers have received special training to help people in trouble. All conversations are kept confidential, and the caller does not have to give his or her name.

Cultural Connections

"Space Invaders"

Personal space refers to the space you need between yourself and another person to feel comfortable when you are talking. People from some cultures feel comfortable with less distance between them. People from other cultures may feel comfortable only with greater distances between them. They may feel that people who stand too close are invading their space and showing disrespect. Think of ways to maintain your personal space comfort zone. If you feel that someone is trying to get too close or is touching, patting, or grabbing you, you have a right to ask them to stop. If they do not, walk away or yell for help.

Difficult Issues

Though there are many places to go for help, abuse victims often remain silent. The number of reported abuse cases is much lower than the number of actual cases. Why is this true?

■ **Victims may feel that nobody will believe them.** Witnesses and victims of abuse often don't report abuse because they fear that people will think they're not telling the truth. Children who have been victims of abuse are especially likely to think this way. However, the only way to stop abuse is to report it. If one person doesn't believe you, tell someone else.

■ **People may feel that abuse is a private or personal issue.** Many victims feel uncomfortable sharing something that affects them so personally. For many years, abuse was a subject that no one wanted to talk about. Today, however, the subject of abuse is more openly discussed in the media as well as in the rest of society. Many people have realized how widespread abuse is and that silence only allows it to do more terrible damage.

■ **Males may feel that they cannot or should not be victims.** Some males may feel that reporting abuse is an admission of personal weakness. They may have been told that they should be able to protect themselves. Abusers, however, always have an advantage over their victims. Even when they are not physically stronger, they are usually older or in a position of authority.

■ **Victims may be afraid of their abusers.** Many abuse victims are afraid to come forward because they think their abusers might get even with them for telling, by hurting them or abusing them again. Abusers often tell children that they will be punished if they tell anyone else what has occurred, or that no one will believe them. However, confiding in a trusted adult can often allow the victim to get help—and get away from the abuser.

HEALTH LAB
Abuse and the Media

Introduction: At one time abuse was off-limits as a topic for discussion. Today abuse is a common subject for television shows and for movies, books, and many other media. Some people feel that more widespread coverage has helped a greater number of people to come forward and report incidents of abuse. Other people are concerned that the wrong kinds of media attention will keep people from taking abuse seriously.

Objective: Work with a group of three or four to study the coverage of abuse in the media and hypothesize about how increased coverage has affected the problem of abuse.

Materials and Method: You will need access to newspapers and news magazines, television, radio, and a community library. Within your group, decide which members will cover each of the media to be studied. For one week, examine media reporting on events of that week that concern abuse. Also, search past reports in your assigned area for coverage on incidents of abuse and sources of help for abuse victims.

Observations and Analysis: As you examine media reports on the subject of abuse, analyze their treatment of the subject. Does the reporting seem responsible and thorough? Is

Using complete sentences, answer the following questions on a separate sheet of paper.

Reviewing Terms and Facts

1. **Vocabulary**   What is a *family violence shelter?*

2. **Give Examples**   List three different places where an abuse victim could go for help.

3. **Recall**   List three reasons why people might not report abuse.

Thinking Critically

4. **Analyze**   Why might young children be afraid to tell someone about an abusive parent?

5. **Hypothesize**   Why do you think the number of reported cases of abuse has been increasing in recent years?

Applying Health Concepts

6. **Growth and Development**   Abuse is very harmful to the normal development of a child. Research this subject to find out how people who have been abused deal with and recover from their experiences. Prepare a short report about your findings.

the privacy of victims respected whenever possible? Is there any evidence that the reporting has helped other abuse victims to come forward? Does the report offer any help for other abuse victims? How could the reporting be improved?

Get together with your group, and discuss what you have found. Decide on a way to present your information—as a wall chart or poster, or in some other form. As a class, discuss the difficulties of reporting on such serious and personal matters as well as the need for the media to act in a responsible manner.

Chapter Summary

▶ **Lesson 1** Violence is a major public health problem in the United States, particularly youth violence. Some factors that contribute to violence are anger, prejudice, possession of weapons, poor coping and communication skills, and abuse of alcohol and other drugs.

▶ **Lesson 2** Abuse is the physical, emotional, or mental mistreatment of another person. The four main types of abuse are physical abuse, emotional abuse, sexual abuse, and neglect.

▶ **Lesson 3** To break the cycle of abuse, people must seek help. There are many community programs available that offer help to abused and troubled families.

Reviewing Key Terms and Concepts

Using complete sentences, answer the following questions on a separate sheet of paper.

Lesson 1

1. What is a *gang?*

2. List four ways in which communities are working together to make their neighborhoods safer.

Lesson 2

3. What are the four main types of abuse?

4. What effects can abuse have on a person?

Lesson 3

5. List three people an abused person might go to in order to break the cycle of abuse.

6. What are crisis hot lines?

Thinking Critically

Using complete sentences, answer the following questions on a separate sheet of paper.

7. **Evaluate** How strong an effect do you think violence on television and in movies has on people in our society? Explain your answer.

8. **Explain** How can reporting abuse help the abuser as well as the victim?

9. **Compare and Contrast** Some of the places listed on page 405 offer short-term help, while others offer long-term help. When might short-term help be needed? When might a person seek long-term help?

Your Action Plan

Although violence is present throughout our society, there are many ways to protect yourself from becoming a victim of violence. To do this you will need to make an action plan.

Step 1 Look through your private journal entries for this chapter. What do they tell you about the choices you can make to keep yourself from becoming a victim of violence?

Step 2 Set a long-term goal, such as not getting involved in fights or working to reduce violence in your school or community.

Step 3 Write down at least two short-term goals that will help you reach the long-term goal you have chosen. If your long-term goal is to work to reduce violence in your community, one of your short-term goals might be to find out what violence prevention programs are in place at your school.

Plan a timetable for taking the steps that will help you reach your short-term and long-term goals. When you have reached your long-term goal, you will have the personal satisfaction of knowing that you have protected yourself and others from violence in your community.

In Your Home and Community

1. **Community Resources** Find out about crime prevention programs in your community. The National Crime Prevention Council, 1700 K Street NW, 2nd Floor, Washington, DC 20006-3817, can provide advice on how to start one.

2. **Health of Others** Collect free pamphlets that contain information about places where victims of abuse and violence can go for help. Ask permission to put them in a place where other teens go, such as the school library.

Building Your Portfolio

1. **Local Profile** Collect articles from a newspaper about violence in your area. Put together a scrapbook of the articles, along with suggestions for avoiding the kind of violent act described. Place the scrapbook in your portfolio.

2. **Short Story** Write a story in which a teen helps a younger child who has been abused. Be sure to describe how the teen finds out about the abuse and what he or she does to help. Place a copy of your story in your portfolio.

3. **Personal Assessment** Look through all the activities and projects you did for this chapter. Choose one or two that you would like to include in your portfolio.

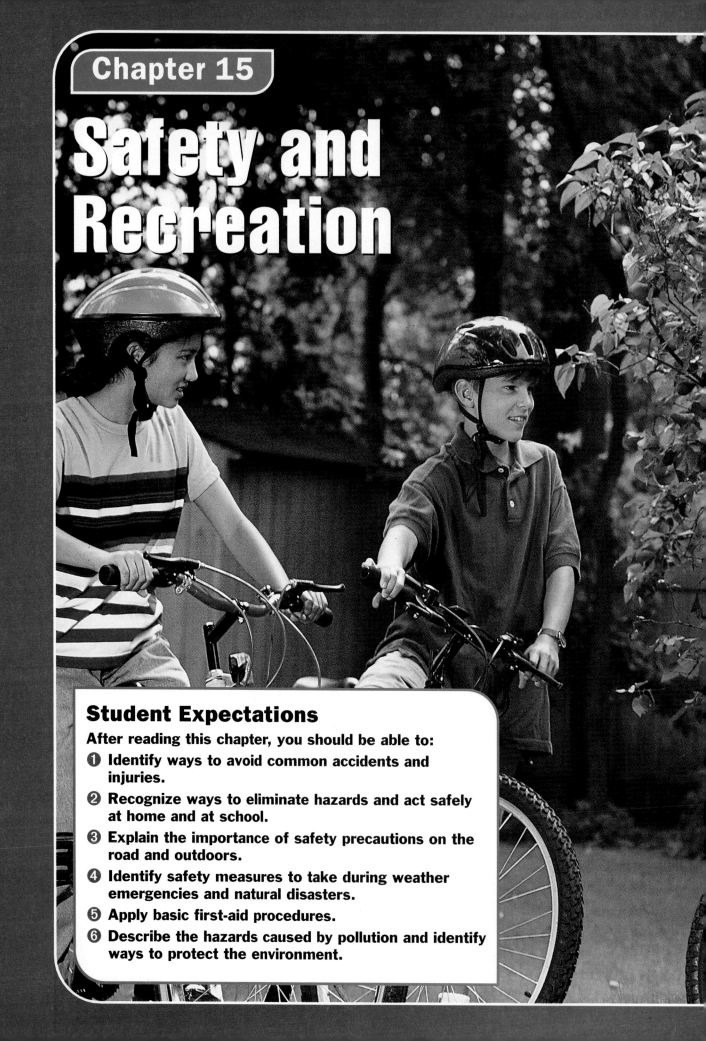

Chapter 15

Safety and Recreation

Student Expectations

After reading this chapter, you should be able to:

❶ **Identify ways to avoid common accidents and injuries.**

❷ **Recognize ways to eliminate hazards and act safely at home and at school.**

❸ **Explain the importance of safety precautions on the road and outdoors.**

❹ **Identify safety measures to take during weather emergencies and natural disasters.**

❺ **Apply basic first-aid procedures.**

❻ **Describe the hazards caused by pollution and identify ways to protect the environment.**

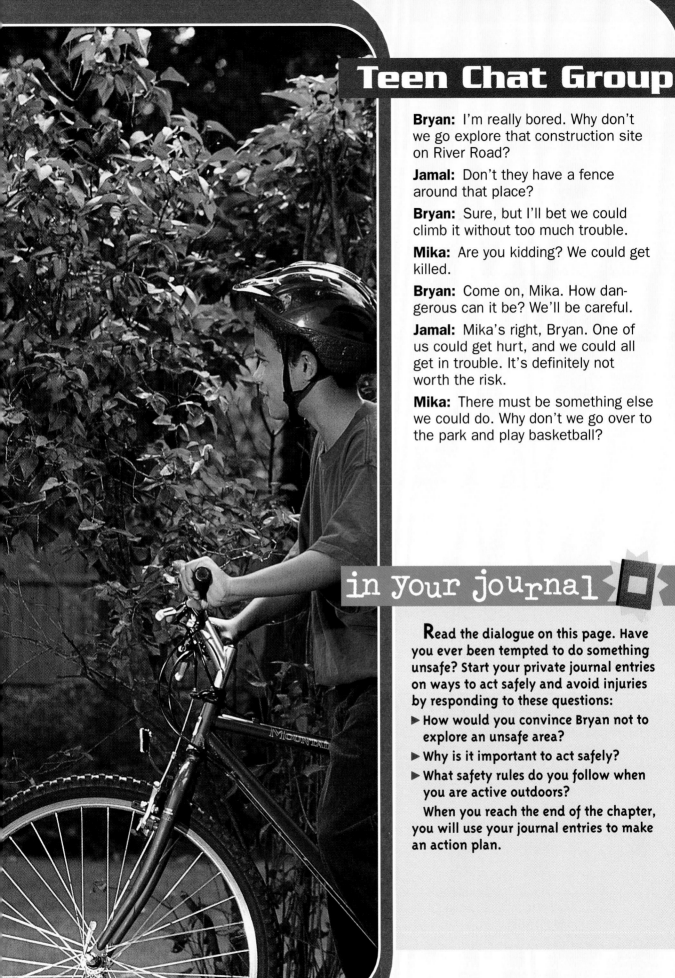

Teen Chat Group

Bryan: I'm really bored. Why don't we go explore that construction site on River Road?

Jamal: Don't they have a fence around that place?

Bryan: Sure, but I'll bet we could climb it without too much trouble.

Mika: Are you kidding? We could get killed.

Bryan: Come on, Mika. How dangerous can it be? We'll be careful.

Jamal: Mika's right, Bryan. One of us could get hurt, and we could all get in trouble. It's definitely not worth the risk.

Mika: There must be something else we could do. Why don't we go over to the park and play basketball?

in your journal

Read the dialogue on this page. Have you ever been tempted to do something unsafe? Start your private journal entries on ways to act safely and avoid injuries by responding to these questions:

▶ How would you convince Bryan not to explore an unsafe area?

▶ Why is it important to act safely?

▶ What safety rules do you follow when you are active outdoors?

When you reach the end of the chapter, you will use your journal entries to make an action plan.

Building Safe Habits

This lesson will help you find answers to questions that teens often ask about avoiding accidents and injuries. For example:

▶ **What does it mean to be safety conscious?**

▶ **Why do accidents and injuries occur?**

▶ **How can I avoid common accidents and injuries?**

Words to Know

safety conscious
accident chain

Safety First

As soon as you were old enough to understand safety rules, a parent or some other family member probably began to teach them to you. For example, you were most likely told not to run into the street, talk to strangers, or play with matches.

Although safety rules are important, you also need to know more. You must become **safety conscious,** which means being *aware that safety is important and careful to act in a safe manner.* Being safety conscious also means that you plan ahead and spot possible hazards. Throughout this book you have learned ways to prevent accidents and injuries by avoiding risk behaviors. Safety consciousness involves using these prevention skills in your everyday habits and actions.

Many young people believe that bad things happen only to *other* people, but this just isn't true. Each year, about 2 million people are hospitalized, and more than 140,000 die, because of accidents and injuries. Many of these people are teens. **Figure 15.1** shows the types of accidents that cause the largest number of deaths in the United States.

Figure 15.1
Leading Causes of Death from Accidents, 1993

Almost half of the deaths of people aged 15 to 24 resulted from accidents. Many of these accidents could be prevented.

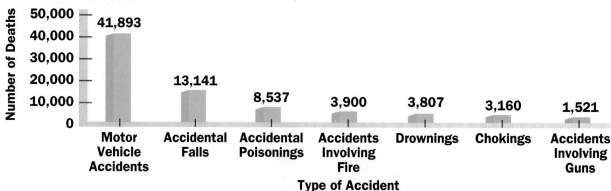

Source: Statistical Abstracts of the United States, 1996

The Accident Chain

Avoiding risks and preventing injuries doesn't mean that you have to give up riding a bike or playing sports. You do need to be careful, plan ahead, and take precautions to protect yourself. These precautions include wearing protective gear and practicing common sense. Most accidents and injuries occur because of carelessness. They are often the result of an **accident chain,** which is *a series of events that include a situation, an unsafe habit, and an unsafe action.* **Figure 15.2** illustrates an accident chain.

Figure 15.2

Example of an Accident Chain

The unsafe actions of both Nicole and her brother Dylan contributed to this accident chain.

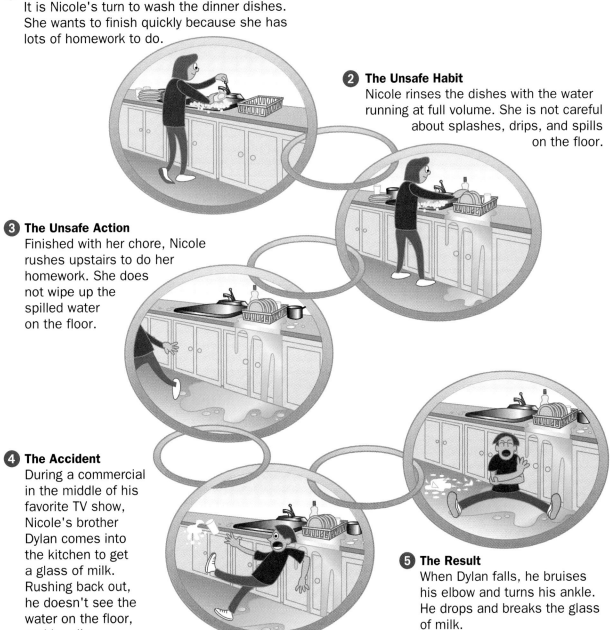

1 **The Situation**
It is Nicole's turn to wash the dinner dishes. She wants to finish quickly because she has lots of homework to do.

2 **The Unsafe Habit**
Nicole rinses the dishes with the water running at full volume. She is not careful about splashes, drips, and spills on the floor.

3 **The Unsafe Action**
Finished with her chore, Nicole rushes upstairs to do her homework. She does not wipe up the spilled water on the floor.

4 **The Accident**
During a commercial in the middle of his favorite TV show, Nicole's brother Dylan comes into the kitchen to get a glass of milk. Rushing back out, he doesn't see the water on the floor, and he slips.

5 **The Result**
When Dylan falls, he bruises his elbow and turns his ankle. He drops and breaks the glass of milk.

Breaking the Accident Chain

Most accidents and injuries can be prevented by breaking the accident chain. For example, either Nicole or Dylan could have acted differently during at least one step in the series of events. If so, Dylan's accident and injury might not have happened (see **Figure 15.3**).

Figure 15.3
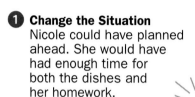
Breaking the Accident Chain
By removing any link from the accident chain, you can prevent most accidents and injuries.

1 Change the Situation
Nicole could have planned ahead. She would have had enough time for both the dishes and her homework.

2 Change the Unsafe Habit
To avoid splashes and drips, Nicole rinses and stacks the dishes carefully. She concentrates on what she is doing.

MAKING HEALTHY DECISIONS
Preventing Accidents While Baby-sitting

*M*rs. Salenas has hired Brandon to baby-sit her four-year-old son, Tommy. She asks Brandon to give Tommy a bath before putting him to bed. Mrs. Salenas gives Brandon the telephone number where she can be reached.

An hour before bedtime, Brandon takes Tommy to the bathroom and starts to turn on the water in the tub. "I do it myself!" Tommy shouts. "I'm big now! You go away."

Brandon has learned in health class that small children can get burned from hot tap water. He also knows that they can easily drown in even a small amount of water. "No, Tommy," he says. "I have to stay with you and make sure that you're safe."

Tommy begins to cry loudly. Brandon doesn't know what to do, so he decides to use the six-step decision-making process.

1 State the situation
2 List the options
3 Weigh the possible outcomes
4 Consider your values
5 Make a decision and act
6 Evaluate the decision

Follow-up Activities

1. Apply the six steps of the decision-making process to Brandon's situation.

2. Role-play a scene in which Brandon acts on his decision.

3. In small groups, discuss other options that Brandon might have chosen.

3 Change the Unsafe Action
Finished with her chore, Nicole checks for spills on the floor and wipes them up.

4 No Accident
Dylan does not rush from the kitchen. He uses a plastic cup instead of a glass for his milk.

5 No Injury
Dylan drinks his milk and enjoys the rest of the show.

in your journal

Have you, or has a member of your family, ever been injured? How might the injury have been prevented? In your private journal, describe a possible injury, and draw a diagram to break it down into the links of an accident chain. Then describe ways in which the chain might have been broken.

Review

Lesson 1

Using complete sentences, answer the following questions on a separate sheet of paper.

Reviewing Terms and Facts

1. **Vocabulary** Define *safety conscious*. Explain how being safety conscious can help you to prevent common accidents and injuries.

2. **List** Name the links in an accident chain.

3. **Restate** How can an accident chain be broken?

Thinking Critically

4. **Explain** What do you think is meant by "safety first"?

5. **Hypothesize** People aged 15 to 24 are involved in more accidents than any other age group. Why do you think this might be true?

Applying Health Concepts

6. **Health of Others** Make a poster to show an accident chain that might occur during a sporting event or bike trip. Include a second illustration that shows how the accident chain could have been broken. Display your poster on the classroom bulletin board.

Safety at Home and in School

This lesson will help you find answers to questions that teens often ask about staying safe at home and at school. For example:

▶ **How can I protect my home from fire?**

▶ **How can I eliminate other common safety hazards at home?**

▶ **How can I avoid accidents and injuries in school?**

Words to Know

flammable
smoke detector
electrocution
electrical overload

in Your Journal

Make a list of all the fire safety rules you can think of in three minutes. As you read this lesson, add to your list.

Safety at Home

Most people feel safest at home. However, even this safest of places has its hazards, or possible sources of harm. In fact, each year millions of people are seriously injured in their own homes. Like other accidents and injuries, most of these that occur at home could be prevented.

Home Fire Safety

According to the American Red Cross, fires cause more deaths than any other type of disaster. The leading causes of home fires include

■ careless cooking habits.

■ cigarette smoking.

■ improperly used or poorly maintained heating devices.

■ improper storage of materials that are **flammable,** ones that are *able to catch fire easily,* such as paint, old newspapers, and rags.

■ overloaded or damaged electrical circuits and wiring.

Figure 15.4 on the next page lists several precautions that will prevent fires in the home.

| Careful cooking habits can help prevent a kitchen fire.

Figure 15.4
Effective Fire Safety Measures

Taking these fire safety measures can help prevent fires, or save lives if a fire should occur.

Action	Reason
❶ Install **smoke detectors**, or *devices that sound an alarm when they sense smoke.* Place a smoke detector outside each sleeping area and on each additional level of the home. Test smoke detectors once a month. Replace batteries at least once a year.	**❶** Many home fires occur in the middle of the night, when everyone is asleep. Smoke detectors save lives by waking people up. The alarm will not sound, however, if the detector's batteries are dead, or if connections inside are dirty or worn. 
❷ Keep stoves and ovens clean. Wipe up spills promptly, and clean the stove thoroughly at least once a week.	**❷** All food ingredients burn. The heat of the oven, the burners, or an open flame can cause spills to catch on fire. Spattered grease or oil can be especially dangerous.
❸ Install a fire extinguisher in the kitchen, away from heat sources and near an exit.	**❸** Oil, grease, and electrical fires are among the most common and most serious kitchen fires. Water cannot be used to put out these types of fires. Instead, a fire extinguisher labeled *ABC* must be used. (See the Life Skills feature in this lesson.)
❹ If anyone smokes, make sure that he or she does not smoke in bed and that ashtrays are completely cold before their contents are thrown away.	**❹** Many home fires have been caused by people who fell asleep while smoking or put smoldering cigarettes into wastebaskets.
❺ Store matches and cigarette lighters in safe places, out of the reach of children. 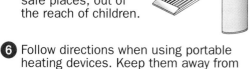	**❺** Children are naturally curious about fire. Many injuries and deaths have occurred because children were playing with matches or cigarette lighters.
❻ Follow directions when using portable heating devices. Keep them away from flammable materials. Unplug the heater before leaving the room.	**❻** Portable heaters are a common cause of home fires. If they come into contact with flammable materials, a fire can start.
❼ Check electrical appliances for loose or damaged cords. Repair or replace damaged appliances and broken outlets. Never run electrical cords under carpets.	**❼** Loose or damaged cords release heat that can cause a fire. The movement of people and the weight of furniture can damage electrical cords that are under rugs, causing wires to be exposed.

Planning an Escape Route

Taking action to prevent fires is one of the most important ways to protect your family and your home. A fire could still occur, however, so you and your family must be prepared.

Work together to plan an escape route for each family member. Since most fatal home fires occur during the night, every escape route should begin in the bedroom. A window with a fire escape or a fire ladder may save a life if the bedroom door is blocked by flames, heat, or smoke.

After all family members understand their escape routes, agree on a place to meet outside your home. That way you can make sure that everyone is safe. All family members should promise that during a fire they will concentrate on saving *themselves*—not their belongings or even pets. Finally, practice your escape plan by holding a family fire drill twice a year.

Did You Know?

Smoke Detectors

According to surveys cited in the "University of California at Berkeley Wellness Letter," as many as half of the smoke detectors installed in homes are not in working order. Batteries should be tested regularly and replaced as needed. All smoke detectors should be replaced after they have been used for ten years.

In Case of Fire

You have learned how to prevent fires. **Figure 15.5** outlines the steps to take if a fire does break out. Knowing what to do ahead of time will help you stay calm and could save your life and the lives of other family members.

Figure 15.5
Effective Steps for Escaping a Fire

If a fire breaks out, follow the escape route that you planned with your family.

1 **Leave quickly.** Get out of the building *before* calling 911 or the fire department.

2 **Before opening a closed door, feel to see if it is hot.** If it is, *do not* open it. There may be flames just outside the door.

3 **If you must exit through smoke, crawl along the floor.** Smoke and hot air rise. Stay as low as possible, breathing in the cleaner air.

4 **If you can't get out, stay in the room with the door closed.** Roll up a blanket and put it across the bottom of the door to keep out smoke. If there is a telephone in the room, call 911 or the fire department. If possible, open the window and yell for help.

5 **If your clothing catches on fire, stop, drop, and roll.** Rolling on the ground will help smother the flames. Never run—the rush of air will fan the flames.

6 **Once outside, go to the prearranged meeting place.** Let everyone know that you are safe. Then someone should go to a neighbor's home and call 911 or the fire department. *Never* re-enter a burning building.

LIFE SKILLS

How to Extinguish Fires Correctly

For a fire to occur, three elements must be present: fuel, oxygen, and heat. To prevent or extinguish a fire, one of these three factors must be eliminated. Most fires must be extinguished by fire fighters. If the fire is small, however, you may be able to put it out yourself. Follow these rules.

1. Use water wisely. Water will extinguish fires in which paper, wood, or cloth is burning. However, *never* use water on the following types of fires:

▶ **Oil or grease fires.** Putting water on burning grease will spread the fire. If grease is burning in a frying pan, turn off the heat, and smother the flames with a lid.

▶ **Electrical fires.** Putting water on an electrical fire can result in **electrocution,** or *death by electrical shock.* A fire extinguisher must be used to put out electrical fires.

2. Install a fire extinguisher. Fire extinguishers are labeled A, B, or C. *Class A* will put out

Preventing Other Injuries at Home

Fires are not the only events that can cause serious injuries or deaths in the home. You and your family must also take care to prevent falls, poisonings, electrical shocks, and accidents involving guns. The following sections will provide this safety information.

Preventing Falls

Falls account for the largest number of nonfatal injuries in homes. Most falls are caused by tripping or slipping. The kitchen, bathroom, and stairs are the most common sites for falls. You can help prevent such accidents in your home by following these rules.

By using a stepladder instead of a chair to reach items on high shelves, you can prevent a fall.

- **Safety in the kitchen.** Wipe up spills promptly. Use a stepladder, not a chair, to reach items on upper shelves. After washing the floor, alert family members, or display a "Caution: Wet Floor" sign.

- **Safety in the bathroom.** Put nonslip strips on the bottom of the tub or shower. Install a secure handgrip on the side of the tub. Anchor rugs with nonslip tape, or use rugs with latex backings.

- **Safety on the stairs.** Do not leave objects on the steps. Keep all staircases well lighted. Check the handrails to be sure that they are stable. If young children live in the house, put gates at the top and bottom of the staircase.

- **Safety in other rooms.** Secure electrical cords to baseboards with tape. Repair or replace all loose or worn carpeting. Arrange furniture so that it is out of heavy-traffic areas.

ordinary fires, such as those involving paper, wood, or cloth. *Class B* should be used for fires involving fast-burning liquids, such as oil, grease, and gasoline. *Class C* will extinguish electrical fires. All-purpose fire extinguishers are labeled *ABC,* meaning they are safe and effective to use on all three types of fires. Follow these tips for the proper use and storage of fire extinguishers.

- ▶ Make sure that your home has at least one ABC fire extinguisher.

- ▶ Install the fire extinguisher in a handy place, away from heat, and near an exit.

- ▶ Read and understand the instructions after purchasing the extinguisher so that you are prepared in case of fire.

- ▶ Check the pressure gauge periodically to make sure that the fire extinguisher is ready to use. If not, it should be recharged or replaced.

- ▶ When using the extinguisher, always aim at the *base* of the flames, not at the top.

Follow-up Activity

Discuss with family members the rules for extinguishing fires safely. If your home does not have a fire extinguisher, urge your parents or other adult members to buy one.

Q: I heard that young children can be poisoned by lead-based paint. How do people prevent this?

A: Most lead-based paint in good condition is not a hazard. However, children can become seriously ill if they breathe dust or eat chips from peeling or crumbling paint that contains lead. Inexpensive kits are available to test the lead content of paint. If lead-based paint is in poor condition, only qualified professionals should handle repairing it.

Unsafe

Safe

To avoid an electrical overload, plug only two electrical appliances into each wall outlet.

Preventing Poisonings

Children are naturally curious, and young children frequently put objects into their mouths. Each year nearly 1 million children under the age of six are poisoned because they have found and swallowed harmful substances. Follow these rules to prevent such tragedies in your home or when you are baby-sitting.

■ Never refer to a child's medicine or vitamins as "candy."

■ Make sure that all medicines have child-resistant caps.

■ Put all medicines or poisonous substances away immediately after use.

■ Keep all cleaning products in their original, labeled containers.

■ Store all potentially poisonous substances in high cabinets, out of children's reach. If possible, keep the cabinets locked.

Preventing Electrical Shocks

Electricity provides energy for heat, lights, cooking, and entertainment. Electricity can be extremely dangerous, however. Improper use or maintenance of electrical appliances, wiring, or outlets can cause severe electric shock and even death. To prevent such injuries at home, follow these rules.

■ Never plug more than two electrical appliances into a wall outlet. More than two may cause an **electrical overload,** *a dangerous situation in which too much electric current flows along a single circuit.* An electrical overload can cause a fire.

■ Never use an electrical appliance near water or if you are wet.

■ Unplug small appliances, such as hair dryers and toasters, when they are not in use. Have broken appliances repaired or replaced.

■ Pull out electrical plugs by the plug itself, *not* by the cord.

■ Have loose or damaged cords repaired or replaced.

Preventing Gun Accidents

In 1994 more than 1,300 people were killed by firearms that were accidentally discharged. Many of those people were children. More than one-third of all American households have guns. If your family or anyone you know keeps guns at home, follow these guidelines.

■ All guns should be treated as if they are loaded.

■ Guns should always be stored unloaded and in locked cabinets. The bullets should be kept in a separate locked cabinet.

■ A gun should never be pointed at anyone.

■ The barrel of a gun should point downward whenever it is being carried.

Safety at School

In some schools, teens may feel the need to protect themselves against violence, some of which may involve guns and other weapons. To be safe at school:

- Cooperate with your school's efforts to keep weapons out of the building. These efforts may include metal detectors and video cameras.

- If you suspect that another student is carrying a gun or any other dangerous weapon, report it to a teacher or school administrator. You can request that your name be held in confidence.

- If someone harasses you, follows you, threatens you, or frightens you in any way, report the incident.

- Don't be a target for theft. Carry only enough money for lunch and other small items. Avoid wearing clothing or jewelry that is very expensive.

- At evening events, such as games, meets, or dances, stay with a group of friends in well-lighted areas. Avoid arguments, and don't take sides in other people's conflicts.

Staying with a group will help keep you and your friends safe.

Review

Using complete sentences, answer the following questions on a separate sheet of paper.

Reviewing Terms and Facts

1. **Vocabulary**   Define the word *flammable*. Give three examples of flammable materials.

2. **Identify**   List five ways to prevent fires in the home.

3. **Outline**   What steps should you take if a fire breaks out in your home?

4. **List**   Identify two ways to prevent falls in the kitchen and two ways to prevent falls in the bathroom.

5. **Identify**   Name five ways to prevent electrical shocks.

Thinking Critically

6. **Explain**   Why is it important to establish and practice a fire escape plan at home? Describe the main elements of an effective plan.

7. **Infer**   Why do you think people should always treat guns as if they are loaded?

Applying Health Concepts

8. **Personal Health**   Evaluate your home for safety. Make a list of any potential safety hazards. With your family, discuss possible changes and improvements that might create a safer home environment.

Safety on the Road and Outdoors

This lesson will help you find answers to questions that teens often ask about safe participation in outdoor activities. For example:

▶ **What should I know about pedestrian safety?**

▶ **What are the basic rules for safety on wheels?**

▶ **How can I be safe in my community?**

▶ **How can I avoid injuries outdoors and in the water?**

Words to Know

pedestrian
hypothermia

Traffic Safety

Can you imagine what would happen on the roads if there were no traffic signals, speed limits, or stop signs? To maintain order and ensure safety, every area enforces traffic laws. The laws must be followed by the drivers of cars, trucks, buses, and motorcycles, as well as by bicycle riders.

Pedestrians, or *people who travel on foot,* must also be aware of traffic laws. They must take responsibility for their own safety on the road. Part of being responsible involves following traffic signs. **Figure 15.6** explains some common signs.

Figure 15.6
Traffic Signs

Understanding the meaning of traffic signs will help you stay safe.

Cars and bicycles must slow down and check for traffic. They must give the right-of-way to pedestrians and approaching cross traffic before proceeding.

Cars and bicycles must wait for the green traffic signal before proceeding. This sign is used at intersections where oncoming traffic receives an early green light.

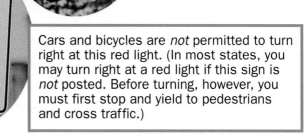

Cars and bicycles are *not* permitted to turn right at this red light. (In most states, you may turn right at a red light if this sign is *not* posted. Before turning, however, you must first stop and yield to pedestrians and cross traffic.)

Pedestrian Safety

Motor vehicle drivers are often encouraged to "drive defensively." For pedestrians, "walk defensively" is excellent advice as well. When walking, be alert, self-protective, and cautious. *Don't* assume that drivers will always obey the laws or follow the traffic signals and signs. Obey traffic signals when crossing the street, and cross only at intersections or crosswalks. Do not walk or run into the street from between parked cars. Drivers may not see you in time to stop. Finally, *never* assume that motorists or cyclists

- can see you.
- know what you plan to do—for example, that you are about to cross the street.
- are paying attention.
- will act in a safe and capable manner.
- will signal before they turn.
- will act according to their signals.

Safety on Wheels

Many people enjoy bicycling, in-line skating, and skateboarding. Not only are these activities fun, but they also provide good exercise. They do involve risks, however. According to the U.S. Department of Transportation, 830 cyclists were killed and about 61,000 were seriously injured in this country in 1995. During the same year, nearly 100,000 in-line skaters were seriously injured. Most were between the ages of 10 and 15. You can have fun and still be safe, however, if you follow these important guidelines.

- **Check your equipment.** Check your bike regularly for cracks in the frame. Make sure that the wheels spin freely. Check to see that the handlebars, seat, chain, and spokes are tight and straight. Be sure that the tires have the correct air pressure and show no leaks or excessive wear.

- **Wear a helmet and other protective gear.** Head injuries are involved in 70 to 80 percent of all bicycle accident deaths. Wearing a helmet reduces the risk of head injury by 85 percent. When in-line skating or skateboarding, wear a helmet, wrist guards, and elbow and knee pads. Doing so will reduce your risk of serious injury by 90 percent.

- **Follow the rules.** Obey traffic laws and follow common sense. Do not use bicycles, skateboards, or in-line skates where they are not permitted, such as on sidewalks. **Figure 15.7** on pages 424 and 425 summarizes other important safety rules.

Checking your equipment will help you prevent accidents and injuries.

Roller Cops

In Amsterdam, the capital of the Netherlands, the streets are very narrow. This has always made it difficult for the police to use cars and vans to capture criminals. Recently several young police officers left their cars at the station and strapped on in-line skates. Skating through the pedestrian malls of the city, they were able to do their jobs better.

Figure 15.7
Be Safe on Skates

Why is it important to follow these safety rules when skating?

- Wear a helmet.
- Wear wrist guards, elbow pads, and knee pads. Light gloves may also be worn to protect your hands.
- Keep your speed under control.
- Don't skate at night, in traffic, or in bad weather.
- Learn how to stop before you start skating.
- Know how to fall properly.

Safety Against Crime

Pedestrians and cyclists must protect themselves not only from injuries but also from violence and crime. Stay away from areas that you think are dangerous or where you feel unsafe. To avoid looking like an easy target, walk with a confident and purposeful step. In addition, follow these tips for safety on the street.

■ **Avoid potential trouble.** At night, do not go out alone. Stay in well-lighted public places and on safe, well-lighted sidewalks. Tell a parent where you are going, what route you are taking, and when you will be home. Do not carry valuables, but always carry some sort of identification. Always carry change or some other means of making an emergency phone call. Do not talk to strangers or approach a stranger who calls to you from a car.

■ **Be smart and aware, and protect yourself.** When standing in line or in other crowded places, be aware of the people around you. If someone stands too close and makes you feel uncomfortable, move away from that person.

■ **Get help when you need it.** If a stranger tries to touch you or says anything that frightens you, scream and run away. Go to a nearby public place and ask for help. Call 911 or the police. Try to remember details about the stranger, such as clothing, physical appearance, and type and color of car.

Figure 15.7 (continued)
Be Safe on Bikes
Why is it important to follow these safety rules when bicycling?

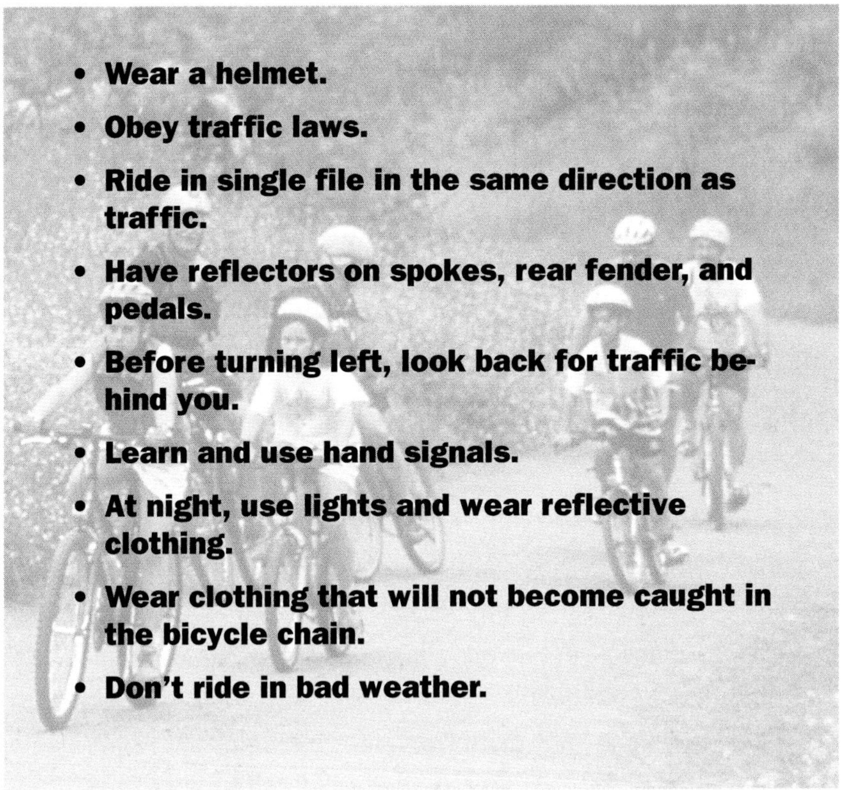

• Wear a helmet.
• Obey traffic laws.
• Ride in single file in the same direction as traffic.
• Have reflectors on spokes, rear fender, and pedals.
• Before turning left, look back for traffic behind you.
• Learn and use hand signals.
• At night, use lights and wear reflective clothing.
• Wear clothing that will not become caught in the bicycle chain.
• Don't ride in bad weather.

in Your Journal

Have the people in your neighborhood formed a group to make the streets safer? If so, describe the actions they have taken. If not, suggest a way to encourage your neighbors to pitch in. What might teens do to help?

Outdoor Safety

Most people enjoy a chance to get outdoors to explore, exercise, or simply enjoy the fresh air. No matter which outdoor activities you choose, ensure your safety with these commonsense rules.

- **Take a buddy.** Outdoor activities are safer and more fun when they're shared. Agree with a friend that you will stay together. In an emergency, you and your friend can help each other.
- **Stay aware.** Learn the signs of oncoming weather emergencies. When necessary, move to safe shelter quickly.
- **Know your limits.** Most outdoor injuries occur when people are tired or try to stretch themselves beyond their abilities. Don't set unreasonable goals for yourself. If you're a beginning swimmer, for example, don't try to swim farther than you can handle.
- **Use your judgment.** Of course you wouldn't dive into a swimming pool before checking to make sure that the pool contained water. Not all safety rules are so obvious, however. Always ask yourself, "Do I have the equipment I need, and am I acting safely?" If you're unsure, ask a parent or other trusted adult.
- **Be sure to warm up and cool down.** Simple stretching exercises will prepare your body for outdoor activities. When you're finished with the activity, cool down slowly with additional stretching.

Dangers in the Wild

Many people are fascinated when they catch sight of an animal in the wild. Wild animals can be dangerous, however, and one reason is the risk of rabies (RAY•beez). This is a severe, often fatal disease, spread by contact with the saliva of an infected animal. To avoid rabies infection and the danger of other injury, never approach an animal in the wild. If an animal seems either dazed or very aggressive, it may be carrying the rabies virus. Leave the area immediately, and then report the incident.

Safety in the Water

Swimming, boating, and diving are pleasant outdoor activities. The most important way to be safe in the water is to know how to swim well. **Figure 15.8** provides additional guidelines for water safety.

Hiking and Camping Safety

Hiking and camping are great ways to exercise and enjoy nature. When you hike or camp, being prepared and acting safely are the keys to preventing injuries. Follow these guidelines.

- Dress appropriately for both the activity and the weather conditions. Wear thick socks and comfortable, sturdy shoes. To prevent blisters, break in hiking shoes ahead of time. Tuck pants into socks to avoid insect bites or stings.

- Take necessary equipment, including a first-aid kit, a flashlight with extra batteries, a supply of fresh water, and a compass.

- Hike on marked trails and camp in specified areas.

- Never camp or hike by yourself. Make sure that family members know your schedule and your route.

- Learn to identify poisonous plants, such as poison ivy and poison oak, so that you can avoid contact with them.

- Make sure that all campfires are extinguished completely. Drench them with water or smother them with sand or dirt.

Figure 15.8
Water Safety

Water activities can be safe, healthful fun if you follow these rules.

Activity	Safety Tips
Swimming	• Swim with a friend and only when a lifeguard or adult is present. • Don't swim when you're tired. • If you ever feel that you are in trouble, do not panic. Wave or call for help. Then take a deep breath and let your body sink vertically beneath the water. Relax. Take several "steps" forward with one leg in front of the other. At the same time, push down with cupped hands and lift your head out of the water. Take a breath and then let your body sink again. Repeat until help arrives.
Diving	• Don't try diving unless you have been taught the proper technique. • Check the depth of the water before diving. Walk into the water first. • Never dive into an above-ground pool or into the shallow end of any pool.
Boating	• Always wear a life jacket. • Know how to handle the boat. • Make sure that the boat is in good working condition.

Winter Sports Safety

Outdoor activities in winter require special safety precautions. Always dress in layered, warm clothing, and stay dry. Protect your hands, head, and feet with snug, warm coverings. If you begin to shiver, go inside and warm up quickly. Such precautions will prevent **hypothermia** (hy·poh·THER·mee·uh), *a sudden and dangerous drop in body temperature.* In addition, remember the tips shown in **Figure 15.9.**

Figure 15.9
Tips for Winter Sports Safety
Here are some tips for enjoying winter sports safely.

A When skating, make sure that the ice is frozen solid. Do not skate on ice that has not been tested for thickness.

B Take lessons before you ski or snowboard. Make sure that your equipment is in good condition and fits you correctly.

C Sled or snowboard only on hills that are away from roads and have no obstacles (such as trees).

D Ski or snowboard only on slopes that you can handle safely. Check the condition of slopes before heading down, and stay alert to condition updates and avalanche warnings.

Review

Lesson 3

Using complete sentences, answer the following questions on a separate sheet of paper.

Reviewing Terms and Facts

1. **List**   Recall six safety rules to follow when bicycling.

2. **Outline**   Describe the steps to take if you feel that you are in trouble while swimming.

3. **Vocabulary**   Define the term *hypothermia.* Then explain how to avoid it.

Thinking Critically

4. **Explain**   What does it mean to "walk defensively"? Why is this an important rule for pedestrians?

5. **Compare**   Give reasons why the buddy system is important in each of these activities: swimming, hiking, going out at night.

Applying Health Concepts

6. **Growth and Development**   Select a sport or outdoor activity mentioned in this lesson that children could participate in. Create a poster that explains the safety rules to young children. Use drawings or magazine clippings to illustrate each rule.

TEEN HEALTH DIGEST

People at Work

A Lifesaving Job

Job: Emergency medical technician (EMT)

Responsibilities: To give on-the-spot emergency medical care to victims of accidents, injuries, and illnesses; to transport victims to the hospital and care for them on the way

Education and Training: EMTs must complete a training course and field training, pass an examination, and be certified in accordance with state regulations.

Workplace: EMTs spend much of their time driving or riding in ambulances.

Positive: An EMT has the personal satisfaction of helping others and even saving lives.

Negative: The work is physically and emotionally demanding; hours are irregular.

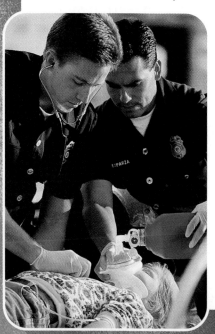

Myths and Realities

The Facts About Safety Belts

Car safety belts save lives. Even so, some people still don't buckle up. Do you know the facts from the myths?

Myth: If a car has air bags, you don't need to wear a safety belt.

Reality: Air bags are truly effective only when used *with* safety belts. Children aged 12 and under should always sit in the back seat, away from air bags. Infants less than a year old should be in the back seat and secured in a rear-facing child safety seat.

Myth: You need to wear a safety belt only on long trips or during highway driving.

Reality: The majority of serious car accidents occur when cars are going less than 40 miles per hour and when occupants are less than 25 miles from home.

Try This:

Use one of these myths, or another that you've heard about safety belts, to make a poster. Point out the truth about the need to buckle up.

Sports and Recreation

Cycling Tips from a Coach

As coach of the U.S. Cycling Team, Chris Carmichael helps young cyclists improve their skills. Here are his top four safety tips for bicycle riders.

- **Wear a helmet.** Helmets help prevent head injuries, the number one cause of cyclists' deaths and serious injuries.

- **Follow the rules of the road.** Cyclists need to follow the same traffic rules as drivers. These rules include riding with traffic and obeying traffic lights and signs.

- **Be visible.** It's the cyclist's responsibility to be seen by motorists. Wear bright clothing, avoid riding at night, and equip your bike with reflectors.

- **Share the road.** Be considerate. "Using hand signals, making eye contact, smiling and waving—just being courteous—all help keep the roads safe for everyone," Chris advises.

CON$UMER FOCU$

Safe Toys for Tots

Q. How can I buy a safe toy for my two-year-old brother?

A. Check the age recommendations on the product label. Because young children put things into their mouths, they can choke on small toys or toys that have removable parts. In addition, stay away from toys made of brittle plastic that may break into sharp pieces.

Teens Making a Difference

Tree Musketeers

When Tara Church and Sabrina Alimahomed were eight years old, they planted a young sycamore tree. They named the tree Marcie the Marvelous. Planting Marcie was so inspiring to them that they went on to form a group they called the Tree Musketeers. Their goal was to plant trees in their hometown of El Segundo, California.

Ten years later, Tree Musketeers has become a nonprofit corporation run *by* teens and *for* teens. The group's projects include Partners for the Planet, a series of national and regional meetings where teens can share ideas on how to help the environment, and Tree House, in which teens are converting a vacant lot into an environmental learning area.

About her work Tara has stated, "My wish is to make other teens see that every single one of them is extremely important and extremely powerful in their ability to effect change. It all starts with just one individual's determination to make a difference."

Try This: *Marbles are an example of unsafe toys for small children. What others can you think of? Make a warning list to share with your family and neighbors.*

Safety in Weather Emergencies

This lesson will help you find answers to questions that teens often ask about how to stay safe during weather emergencies. For example:

▶ **What should I do in case of a flood?**

▶ **What are the basic safety rules for surviving an earthquake, tornado, or hurricane?**

▶ **What should I do if I am caught in a blizzard or thunderstorm?**

Words to Know

> **earthquake**
> **aftershocks**
> **tornado**
> **tornado watch**
> **tornado warning**
> **hurricane**
> **blizzard**

 in your journal

What weather emergencies and natural disasters are most common in your area? In your journal, write about what you might do to help others in your community who were affected by such a natural disaster.

Weather Emergencies and Natural Disasters

Floods, earthquakes, and violent storms can strike without warning, causing tremendous damage. These weather emergencies and natural disasters cannot be prevented. Therefore, people should learn the most effective ways to protect themselves before, during, and after a natural disaster. Many of the same protective measures apply in all weather emergencies and natural disasters. These measures include the following.

■ **Be prepared.** Assemble a disaster supplies kit with your family. It should contain a first-aid kit, canned food and a can opener, and bottled water. Also include a battery-operated portable radio, one or more working flashlights (check them regularly), and a supply of extra batteries.

■ **Stay alert to information.** The National Weather Service monitors the progress of storms and weather emergencies. Listen to the radio or watch television to receive news bulletins and advisories about oncoming storms.

■ **Stay calm and be smart.** During a weather emergency, the worst thing you can do is to panic. Pay attention to news bulletins. Do not hesitate to evacuate your home if you are instructed to do so.

Floods are the most common natural disaster. They often occur after heavy rain or snow, a hurricane, or a break in a dam or levee.

Floods

Floods can happen almost anywhere and at any time. People who live in low-lying coastal regions or river valleys are at greatest risk. Floods may be caused by severe rainfalls or damage to dams.

During a flood, never try to walk, swim, ride a bike, or ride in a car through the water. Stay tuned to National Weather Service news bulletins and follow their advice. Although many floods take hours or days to develop, a flash flood can occur in minutes. **Figure 15.10** explains the three types of flood advisories broadcast by the National Weather Service. Follow these guidelines.

- Do not walk in flooded areas. Drowning poses a severe risk, as does electrocution caused by downed power lines.

- Because flood waters often pollute the water supply, do not drink tap water. Drink bottled water instead.

- If you have been evacuated, do not try to return to your home until you are advised that it is safe to do so.

- Once you have returned home, discard contaminated food. Disinfect anything that has come into contact with the flood waters.

Figure 15.10
Flood Advisories

The National Weather Service issues three types of flood advisories: flood or flash flood watch, flood warning, and flash flood warning.

Type of Advisory	Meaning	What to Do
Flood or Flash Flood Watch	A flood is possible in your area. Stay tuned.	Move valuables to higher levels of your home. Listen to the radio. Watch for rising water and other signs of flash flooding. Keep your disaster supplies kit with you, and prepare to evacuate.
Flood Warning	Flooding is already occurring or will occur soon in your area.	Follow the advice of the National Weather Service and local officials. If told to evacuate your home, do so as quickly as possible. Move to higher ground, away from rivers, streams, and creeks.
Flash Flood Warning	Sudden, violent flooding is already occurring or will occur soon in your area.	Evacuate immediately. Follow the guidelines listed above for flood warnings, but act quickly.

Earthquakes

An **earthquake** is *a violent shaking of the earth's surface.* In the United States, earthquakes are most common along the Pacific Coast, but they can occur elsewhere. An earthquake is usually not a single event. Following the initial shaking, several **aftershocks,** or *secondary earthquakes,* often occur. **Figure 15.11** on the next page provides guidelines for personal safety during an earthquake.

The Richter Scale

Q: What is the Richter Scale?

A: The Richter (RIK·ter) Scale is a method of recording the amount of ground motion caused by earthquakes. It was developed in 1935 by an American scientist named Charles F. Richter. It rates the ground motion on a scale of 1 to 10, with 10 representing the maximum force. An earthquake with a magnitude of 4.5 usually causes minor damage, while one with a rating of 6 can be very destructive. Major earthquakes are those with a magnitude of 7 or more.

Figure 15.11
Protecting Yourself During an Earthquake

Most injuries and deaths that occur during an earthquake are caused by falling objects or crumbling buildings.

If you are indoors . . .

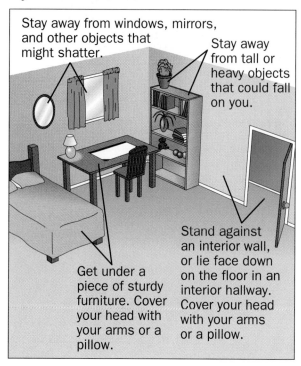

Stay away from windows, mirrors, and other objects that might shatter.

Stay away from tall or heavy objects that could fall on you.

Get under a piece of sturdy furniture. Cover your head with your arms or a pillow.

Stand against an interior wall, or lie face down on the floor in an interior hallway. Cover your head with your arms or a pillow.

If you are outdoors . . .

Stay away from trees, buildings, or power lines. They may fall.

Find a clear, open area. Drop to the ground and protect your head with your arms.

Tornadoes

A **tornado** is *a whirling, funnel-shaped windstorm that drops from the sky to the ground.* Of all types of storms, tornadoes can cause the most severe destruction. States in the Midwest and states bordering the Gulf of Mexico have more tornadoes than other regions of the United States. Tornadoes most often occur during the spring and summer. **Figure 15.12** on the next page explains how tornadoes develop.

The National Weather Service monitors the possibility of tornadoes and issues two types of news bulletins. If *weather conditions indicate that a tornado may develop,* a **tornado watch** is issued. If your area receives a tornado watch, turn on a battery-powered radio for further updates, and prepare to take shelter. The Weather Service may also issue a **tornado warning.** This means that *a tornado has been sighted and people in the area are in immediate danger.* If you receive a tornado warning, take shelter at once.

■ **Where to go.** The safest place to be is underground—in a cellar or basement. If you can't get underground, go to an interior room or hallway. If you are outdoors, lie in a ditch or flat on the ground. Stay away from trees, cars, and buildings.

■ **What to do.** Cover yourself with whatever protection you can find, such as a mattress or heavy blankets and clothing. Then stay where you are. Tornadoes move along a narrow path at about 25 to 40 miles per hour. The storm will pass quickly.

Mobile Homes

Mobile homes, because of their relatively light weight, are particularly vulnerable to severe damage from tornadoes. If you live in a mobile home, evacuate immediately at the first mention of a tornado watch. Go as quickly as possible to a nearby building.

Figure 15.12
How a Tornado Develops

Winds within the spiral of a tornado often swirl at more than 200 miles per hour.

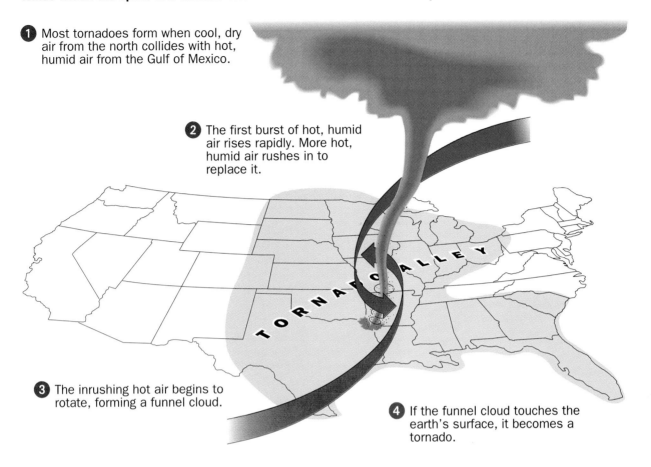

1 Most tornadoes form when cool, dry air from the north collides with hot, humid air from the Gulf of Mexico.

2 The first burst of hot, humid air rises rapidly. More hot, humid air rushes in to replace it.

3 The inrushing hot air begins to rotate, forming a funnel cloud.

4 If the funnel cloud touches the earth's surface, it becomes a tornado.

Hurricanes

A **hurricane** is *a strong windstorm with driving rain that originates at sea.* Hurricanes begin in tropical areas and often move toward land and along the coast. A whirling, circular cloud mass, a hurricane has its fiercest strength in the area surrounding the center. The center of the hurricane itself, called its eye, remains calm.

Hurricanes most often occur during the late summer and early fall, and coastal areas receive the greatest damage. However, strong winds and driving rain often extend to interior areas as well. The National Weather Service can often determine a storm's path well in advance. Listen to news bulletins, and follow these guidelines.

■ Safeguard your home. Board up windows and doors. Bring inside any items such as outdoor furniture and bicycles.

■ If local officials advise you to evacuate, do so immediately.

■ If no evacuation is advised, remain indoors. Be prepared for power loss.

■ Don't be fooled by the eye of the hurricane. As the eye passes overhead, the storm may appear to be over. It is not. Stay indoors until news bulletins notify you that the storm has passed.

Cultural Connections

Storm Names

In the United States and other regions of the Northern Hemisphere, hurricanes swirl in a counterclockwise direction. In the Southern Hemisphere, they swirl in a clockwise direction. These southern storms are often called cyclones (SY·klohnz). Similarly, hurricanes that originate in the western Pacific, equal in strength and characteristics to Atlantic storms, are often called typhoons (ty·FOONZ).

Blizzards and Thunderstorms

Blizzards and thunderstorms are more common and usually less violent than hurricanes and tornadoes. They can still pose serious risks, however. A **blizzard** is *a very heavy snowstorm with winds of up to 45 miles per hour.* During a blizzard, follow these safety rules.

- If possible, stay inside. Be prepared for power loss.

- If you are outside, keep moving, and reach shelter as quickly as possible. Keep your nose, mouth, and ears covered. Because it is easy to get lost during a blizzard, pay attention to landmarks along the way.

Thunderstorms usually pass quickly with only minor damage. However, lightning has the potential for extreme danger. Protect yourself by following these safety guidelines.

- Stay inside, or seek shelter. Be prepared for power loss. To avoid electric shock as well as damage to electric appliances, unplug them. Do not use the telephone or running water until the storm has passed.

- If you are caught outdoors, squat low to the ground in an open area. Keep away from electric poles and wires, tall trees, water, and metal objects.

If you are swimming or boating when a thunderstorm approaches, get to land immediately, and seek shelter.

Lesson 4 Review

Using complete sentences, answer the following questions on a separate sheet of paper.

Reviewing Terms and Facts

1. **Describe** What actions should you take *after* a flood?

2. **Identify** List two ways to protect yourself if you are inside during an earthquake and two ways to protect yourself if you are outside.

3. **Compare** Explain the difference between a *tornado watch* and a *tornado warning.*

4. **Vocabulary** Define the term *hurricane.* During what time of year do hurricanes most often occur?

5. **Recall** What safety rules should you follow during a blizzard?

Thinking Critically

6. **Compare and Contrast** How are hurricanes and tornadoes similar? How are they different?

7. **Analyze** Why is it so important to be prepared *before* a weather emergency strikes?

Applying Health Concepts

8. **Personal Health** Write a plan of action for your family in case of a natural disaster most common to your area. Include details about where in your home you might be safest. Share the plan with your family.

First Aid

This lesson will help you find answers to questions that teens often ask about how to administer first aid. For example:

▶ **What should I do first in an emergency?**

▶ **What is the proper technique for rescue breathing?**

▶ **What techniques help someone who is choking?**

▶ **How can I help someone who has been poisoned or burned?**

First Steps

Illness and injury can occur at any time. If a person becomes seriously ill or injured, someone else must step forward to provide immediate emergency care. Time is often critical and may mean the difference between the victim's recovery and his or her death. It is important for everyone to know basic first-aid techniques. **First aid** is *the immediate care given to someone who becomes injured or ill until regular medical care can be provided.* If someone needs first aid, take these steps.

■ Recognize that an emergency exists.

■ Call for help or dial 911.

■ Provide immediate ABC care (see **Figure 15.13**) until medical help arrives.

Words to Know

first aid
cardiopulmonary
    resuscitation
    (CPR)
rescue breathing
choking
abdominal thrusts
chest thrusts
first-degree burn
second-degree
    burn
third-degree burn
fracture

Figure 15.13
The ABCs of First Aid

In an emergency situation, move the victim *only* if he or she is not safe. Check the ABCs until help arrives.

A = Airway
Check the person's airway to make sure that it is not blocked. If it is blocked, it must be cleared. Gently roll the person onto his or her back. Tilt the head back as you lift up on the chin. This will open the airway.

B = Breathing
Look, listen, and feel to make sure that the person can breathe. Look for the rise and fall of the chest. Listen for the sound of air moving in and out of the mouth and nose. Feel for exhaled breath on your hand or cheek. If the person is not breathing, perform rescue breathing (see **Figures 15.14** and **15.15**).

C = Circulation
Press two fingers on either side of the person's neck to check for a pulse. If you feel a pulse, continue with rescue breathing. If you do not feel a pulse, the person needs **cardiopulmonary resuscitation (CPR)**. This is *a first-aid procedure to restore breathing and circulation.* To perform CPR, a person must have special training. Call to passersby to find someone who has CPR training. In the meantime, continue with rescue breathing.

To perform cardiopulmonary resuscitation (CPR), a person must be trained. Done incorrectly, this procedure can cause severe injuries. The American Red Cross and other community agencies give courses in CPR.

Breathing Emergencies

If a person is not breathing, he or she will survive for only a few minutes unless help is provided. If the person is not breathing but has a pulse, you need to perform rescue breathing. **Rescue breathing** is *a substitute for normal breathing, in which someone forces air into the victim's lungs.* **Figure 15.14** shows how to perform rescue breathing on adults and children. **Figure 15.15** on the next page shows how to perform rescue breathing on infants.

Figure 15.14
Rescue Breathing for Adults and Children

Knowing how to perform rescue breathing can help you save a life. Although not shown here, special masks and latex gloves are often used by emergency workers for this procedure.

❶ Tilt the person's head back. To do this, place one hand under the chin and gently lift up. At the same time, place your other hand on the person's forehead and gently press down.

❷ With your fingers, pinch the person's nostrils shut. Take a deep breath and place your mouth over his or her mouth, forming a seal. Give two slow breaths, each about 1½ seconds long. Breathe only until the chest gently rises.

❸ For an adult or child 8 years or older, continue this procedure by giving one slow breath every 5 seconds for 1 minute. For a child 1–8 years old, give one slow breath every 3 seconds for 1 minute. After each breath, remove your mouth to allow the person to exhale.

❹ Using your hands to keep the person's head tilted back, check for signs that the person is breathing on his or her own. Look for the rise and fall of the chest. Listen for the sound of exhaling. Then feel the person's neck for a pulse. If the person has not started breathing, or if you do not feel a pulse, continue rescue breathing. Check the breathing and pulse after each minute.

Figure 15.15
Rescue Breathing for Infants

When performing rescue breathing on infants, it is important to be very gentle. Although not shown here, special masks and latex gloves are often used by emergency workers for this procedure.

1 Gently tilt the child's head back slightly—not as far back as you would tilt an adult's head. Support the head with both hands. Do *not* pinch the nostrils shut.

2 Take a breath and place your mouth over the infant's nose and mouth, forming a seal. Give two slow, long, very gentle breaths. Each breath should last about 1½ seconds. Remove your mouth and wait 3 seconds. Repeat, giving 1 slow breath every 3 seconds. Remove your mouth after each breath to allow the child to exhale.

3 Check the child's pulse. Look, listen, and feel with your cheek for signs that he or she is breathing. If not, repeat rescue breathing. After each minute, recheck the pulse and breathing signs.

Severe Bleeding

The victim is now stable—he or she has a pulse and is breathing. Medical help has been called and is on the way. You must now check for any injuries that may involve severe bleeding. Remember that whenever blood is present, there is a risk of HIV transmission. The use of latex gloves can minimize this risk. To stop or slow the victim's loss of blood, use one of the following three methods.

- Cover the wound with a clean cloth and press firmly against the wound with your hand. If the cloth becomes soaked with blood, add a second cloth. Do not remove the first one, however.

- Elevate the wound above the level of the heart. Elevation will force the blood to move uphill, thus slowing its flow. If you think that the injury might also involve a broken bone, however, do not move or elevate it.

- If bleeding does not stop, use your other hand to apply pressure to a main artery leading to the wound. Squeeze the artery against a bone. **Figure 15.16** shows the location of these arteries and the points at which you should apply pressure.

After the bleeding has stopped, cover the wound with a clean cloth to prevent infection. Remain with the victim until professional medical help arrives.

Figure 15.16
Pressure Points

The dots on this drawing indicate the pressure points for the main arteries.

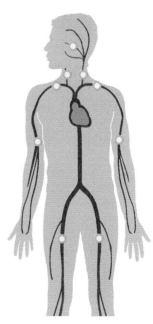

If a Person Is Choking

Choking is *a condition that occurs when a person's airway becomes blocked.* Every year nearly 4,000 people in the United States die from accidental choking. When a person is choking, an obstruction prevents air from entering the lungs. If the obstruction is not removed, the person can die in just a few minutes.

Be alert to signs that a person is choking. Clutching at the throat is the universal sign for "I am choking." The person may also wheeze, have difficulty speaking, or turn red or blue in the face. Immediate first aid is needed.

For an adult or older child who is choking, use **abdominal thrusts.** This procedure consists of *quick, upward pulls into the diaphragm to force the obstruction out of the airway.* For an infant or young child who is choking, use **chest thrusts.** These are *quick presses into the middle of the breastbone to force the obstruction out of the airway.* Both of these procedures are shown in **Figure 15.17** below.

in your journal

Every family should post a list of emergency telephone numbers in an easy-to-find location in the home. These numbers include the poison control center, fire department, other local health and rescue agencies, and close neighbors and relatives. Make sure that such a list is posted by every phone in your house.

Figure 15.17
First Aid for Choking Victims

Why do you think first aid for a choking adult is different from first aid for a choking infant or young child?

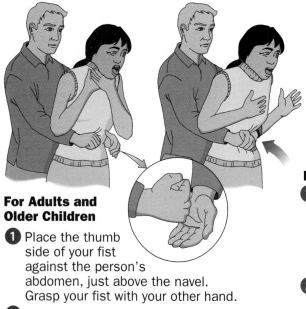

For Adults and Older Children

❶ Place the thumb side of your fist against the person's abdomen, just above the navel. Grasp your fist with your other hand.

❷ Give quick, upward thrusts. Continue until the person coughs up the object. If necessary, have the person lie down, face up, and begin rescue breathing.

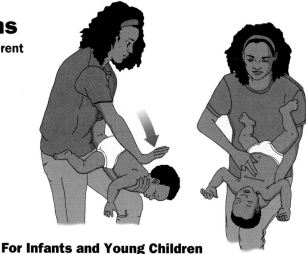

For Infants and Young Children

❶ Hold the child in one arm. While supporting the child's head with your hand, point the head down. Give the child five blows with the heel of your hand, between the shoulder blades. If the object is not dislodged, proceed to chest thrusts (step 2).

❷ Turn the child over onto his or her back, supporting the head with one hand. With two or three fingers, press into the middle of the child's breastbone—directly between and just below the nipples—four times. Once the object is dislodged, begin rescue breathing if necessary.

Poisoning, Burns, and Other Emergencies

Be prepared to help out in all kinds of emergencies. Always start by checking the ABCs of first aid. Then follow the steps described in **Figure 15.18** on the next page.

Figure 15.18

First Aid for Other Emergencies

Each type of emergency requires a different type of first aid.

Type of Emergency	First-Aid Treatment
Poisoning	Call 911 or a poison control center and follow directions carefully. Save the container of poison. Check the victim's breathing and pulse once a minute. Perform rescue breathing if needed. Keep the victim warm and still.
Burns	A **first-degree burn** is *a burn in which only the outer layer of the skin is burned and turns red.* A **second-degree burn** is *a serious burn in which the burned area blisters.* For these types of burns, cover the burned area with cool water (not ice) for 10 to 15 minutes. Then wrap loosely in a clean, dry dressing. Do not pop blisters or peel loose skin. Elevating the burned area may reduce pain. A **third-degree burn** is *a very serious burn in which all layers of the skin are damaged.* For this type of burn, call 911 or an ambulance. Victims of these burns, which are usually caused by fire, electricity, or chemicals, need immediate medical help. Do *not* apply cold water to the burn or attempt to remove burned clothing. While waiting for medical help, keep the victim still, and have him or her sip fluids.
Broken bones	*A break in a bone* is a **fracture.** Have the victim remain still while you wait for medical help. Apply a cold pack, but do not attempt to move the injured part. Moving broken bones can cause further injury.
Sprains and bruises	Tell the victim not to use the injured part of the body. Elevate it, and apply cold packs for 24 hours.

Review

Using complete sentences, answer the following questions on a separate sheet of paper.

Reviewing Terms and Facts

1. **List** What three steps should be taken if someone needs first aid?
2. **Restate** Explain clearly the ABCs of first aid.
3. **Recall** When would you use abdominal thrusts on a victim, and when would you use chest thrusts?
4. **Identify** List and describe the three levels of burns.
5. **Vocabulary** Define the term *fracture.* How should a fracture be treated?

Thinking Critically

6. **Compare and Contrast** How are the rescue breathing techniques for adults similar to and different from those for infants?
7. **Hypothesize** If someone has been poisoned, why is it important to save the container of poison to show to the medical team?

Applying Health Concepts

8. **Health of Others** With one or two classmates, create a skit about one of the emergencies discussed in this lesson. Use dialogue, narrative, and movement to show correct and effective first aid.

Protecting Our Planet

This lesson will help you find answers to questions that teens often ask about protecting the environment. For example:

▶ What causes air pollution, and what can I do about it?

▶ What causes water pollution, and what can I do about it?

▶ How can I cut down on trash and other waste materials?

Words to Know

pollution
Environmental
  Protection
  Agency (EPA)
Occupational
  Safety and
  Health
  Administration
  (OSHA)
fossil fuels
acid rain
sewage
conservation
biodegradable

Science Connection

Endangered Animals   ACTIVITY!

Many wild animals in the United States are endangered species. They have become endangered for several reasons, including pollution and destruction of the wilderness. Find out which species of animals and plants are endangered in your area. Write a brief report on your findings.

Pollution and the Environment

Your environment consists of all the living and nonliving elements that surround you. In a local sense, your environment includes your neighborhood, family, friends, and pets. It also includes trees, flowers, the air you breathe, the water you drink, and animals such as squirrels and birds. In a global sense, your environment includes the sun, world populations, natural resources, and wild animals. Because we all share this global environment, we all have a responsibility to protect it.

People haven't always protected the global environment. Many human actions and lifestyles have caused environmental problems. One major problem is **pollution,** or *dirty or harmful substances in the environment.* Fortunately, the governments of many nations are working to fight and prevent pollution. The **Environmental Protection Agency (EPA),** for example, is *an agency of the United States government that is committed to protecting the environment.*

Another government agency working in this area is the **Occupational Safety and Health Administration (OSHA).** OSHA is *a branch of the U.S. Department of Labor whose job is to ensure the protection of American workers.* OSHA's responsibilities include creating and enforcing regulations to lessen hazards, such as carcinogens, in workplaces.

EPA regulations have helped to protect such endangered species as the American bald eagle.

Air and Water Pollution

Most air pollution results from the burning of **fossil** (FAH·suhl) **fuels,** which are *the oil, coal, and natural gas used to provide energy.* People use fossil fuels to operate motor vehicles and factories and to provide heat and electricity to homes and other buildings. When fossil fuels are burned, poisonous gases are released into the atmosphere. These gases mix with moisture in the atmosphere to form **acid rain.** This is *rain that is more acidic than normal.* Over time, acid rain can harm forests by changing the chemistry of the soil. It can also contaminate fresh water supplies.

Most water pollution results from chemical wastes from factories, oil spills, and sewage. **Sewage** (soo·ij) is *garbage, detergents, and other household wastes that are washed down drains.* These waste materials can pollute drinking water and kill plants and animals in rivers, oceans, and lakes. In addition, polluted drinking water can lead to very serious human diseases, including cholera and typhoid fever.

What You Can Do

No single person can solve all the problems that threaten the global environment. However, each person can help. We can all work to prevent air and water pollution. We can also do our part in **conservation,** or *the saving of natural resources.* These resources include oil, natural gas, and water. You can start by following the guidelines presented in **Figure 15.19.**

Did You Know?

Free Bikes

To encourage people to use bicycles instead of cars for short trips, some cities have begun "free bike" programs. Officials in Boulder, Colorado, and Austin, Texas, have placed specially marked bicycles throughout these cities. Anyone can use the bikes. When riders get to their destinations, they must leave the bikes unlocked and out in the open. In this way, people can take turns using the bicycles.

Figure 15.19
Preventing Pollution
There are many ways to help in the fight against air and water pollution.

To Help Prevent Air Pollution

- Carpool with others, or use public transportation.
- Ride your bike or walk to nearby activities.
- Never start smoking. Cigarette smoke pollutes not only your body but also the environment of those around you.
- Conserve energy. Turn off lights when you leave a room. Turn off televisions, radios, and computers when you are not using them. If you are cold, put on a sweater rather than turn up the heat.

To Help Prevent Water Pollution

- Use biodegradable soaps, detergents, and bleaches. Biodegradable (by·oh·di·GRAY·duh·buhl) products can be *easily broken down in the environment.*
- Have leaky faucets repaired so that water is not wasted. Take short showers. Don't leave the water running while washing dishes or brushing your teeth.
- Be protective of oceans, streams, rivers, and lakes. Don't litter, and do pick up any litter that you see.

Protecting the Land

Along with air and water, the land is a natural resource that is threatened by pollution. In the United States alone, people throw away hundreds of millions of tons of trash and garbage every year. Much of it goes to landfills—huge pits where waste materials are dumped and buried. Eventually most of the trash will break down into tiny particles in the soil. However, a number of commonly used materials take many years to break down.

Land pollution is dangerous to human beings in many ways. Homes are sometimes built on top of old landfill sites that have been contaminated by hazardous wastes. Forests and agricultural lands are often contaminated as well. When forests and wilderness areas are destroyed, wild animals and plants are threatened. When agricultural land is destroyed, our food supply is threatened.

What You Can Do

People can fight the problem of land pollution by changing their waste disposal habits. Individuals need to cut down on the amount of trash and garbage they create. **Figure 15.20** lists some strategies to follow.

Figure 15.20
Ways to Fight Land Pollution

By following the "Three Rs"—reduce, reuse, recycle—people can significantly cut back the amount of trash being created.

Strategy	Definition	Tips
Reduce	Cut down on the amount of trash and garbage you throw away.	Use your own baskets or cloth bags to carry groceries home. Avoid using disposable plates, cups, tableware, or napkins. Use cloth towels instead of paper towels. Buy products in bulk—they use less packaging per individual item. Do not buy items with unnecessary packaging, such as tomatoes that come in a plastic tray *and* are covered by plastic wrap.
Reuse	Find a practical use for an item that you might otherwise throw away.	Wash glass and plastic food containers, and use them for storage. Reuse plastic or paper bags when you go grocery shopping, or use them as trash bags. Donate good clothing that you no longer use to charity. Save worn-out clothing to use as cleaning rags. When possible, have broken items repaired rather than throw them away.
Recycle	Change an item in some way so that it can be used again.	Most communities have recycling programs. Find out which items are recycled in your area, how they should be separated, and how they are collected. Commonly recycled items include aluminum and tin cans; green, brown, and clear glass bottles; plastic containers; newspapers, magazines, and telephone books; paper and cardboard; and batteries.

Using complete sentences, answer the following questions on a separate sheet of paper.

Reviewing Terms and Facts

1. **Restate** What are the roles of the EPA and OSHA in the protection of the environment and public welfare?

2. **Recall** Name three *fossil fuels*. How are fossil fuels used?

3. **Explain** How is acid rain formed?

4. **Identify** List three common causes of water pollution.

5. **Vocabulary** Define the term *conservation*. Then use this term in an original sentence.

Thinking Critically

6. **Analyze** Why is it so important to protect our environment from pollution?

7. **Predict** What might happen if people don't reduce, reuse, and recycle?

Applying Health Concepts

8. **Consumer Health** Next time you go grocery shopping, examine the packaging of all the products you buy. Make a list of all the types of packaging you encounter and the environmental advantages and disadvantages of each one. At the bottom of the page, suggest ways in which poor packaging could be improved.

HEALTH LAB
The Dangers of Water Pollution

Introduction: Water pollution is hazardous to many types of wildlife, including water birds. These birds have oil on their feathers. Because the oil does not mix with water, it acts as a natural raincoat, preventing water from soaking into the feathers. This protective coating makes birds lighter and helps them stay afloat. The oil also insulates the birds, keeping them warm.

Waste materials such as detergents are sometimes dumped into rivers and lakes. Fertilizers can also end up in lakes when they wash off lawns in a heavy rain. Some of the chemicals destroy the birds' natural foods. Others break down the oil on their feathers. When this happens, water soaks into the feathers and makes the birds heavier. Often they can no longer swim or fly.

Objective: With a partner, observe how water pollution can endanger wildlife.

Materials and Method: You will need 1 cup of fresh water; a 1-quart clear glass bowl; 1 teaspoon cooking oil (to represent the oil on a duck's feathers); 2 teaspoons powdered dishwashing detergent (to represent a water-polluting chemical); and a long-handled wooden spoon.

Pour the water into the bowl, and add the oil. Look at the oil. Does it appear to be mixing with the water? Using the long-handled spoon, gently stir in the detergent. Be careful not to let the detergent come into contact with your skin or eyes.

Observations and Analysis: What changes occurred after the detergent was added? Explain why. Use your observations to write a paragraph describing how detergents that get into waterways could harm wildlife.

Chapter 15 Review

Chapter Summary

▶ **Lesson 1** Most accidents and injuries are caused by a chain of circumstances. Changing unsafe habits and actions can break the chain.

▶ **Lesson 2** Following safety procedures and eliminating hazards can prevent injuries in the home. At school, be alert and aware.

▶ **Lesson 3** Pedestrians and bicycle riders should follow the rules of the road. Following safety guidelines will help you avoid injuries outdoors.

▶ **Lesson 4** During weather emergencies and natural disasters, act quickly, seek shelter, and take safety precautions to protect yourself.

▶ **Lesson 5** Effective first aid involves recognizing an emergency, calling for medical help, and providing immediate care for the victim.

▶ **Lesson 6** Everyone can help to protect the environment by reducing pollution of the air, water, and land.

Reviewing Key Terms and Concepts

Using complete sentences, answer the following questions on a separate sheet of paper.

Lesson 1

1. Give an example of an accident chain.

2. Give an example of a situation in which changes in habits could prevent an injury.

Lesson 2

3. Why is it dangerous to use water on an electrical fire?

4. Define the term *electrical overload*. How can this hazard be prevented?

Lesson 3

5. What is a *pedestrian?*

6. List five rules to follow when using skateboards and in-line skates.

Lesson 4

7. How are *earthquakes* and *aftershocks* related?

8. Describe a *tornado*. Where do tornadoes most often occur?

Lesson 5

9. Explain the difference between CPR and rescue breathing.

10. What are the signs that a person is choking?

Lesson 6

11. How are *pollution* and the environment related?

12. What is a *biodegradable* product?

Thinking Critically

Using complete sentences, answer the following questions on a separate sheet of paper.

13. **Analyze** How can safety consciousness help you prevent accidents and injuries?

14. **Synthesize** Suppose that you are hiking in the woods and see a thunderstorm approaching. What should you do?

15. **Infer** If you came upon a serious car accident, what action would you take first? Why would you do this?

16. **Explain** Why should everyone take some degree of responsibility for protecting the environment?

Your Action Plan

You can prevent many injuries by being safety conscious at home, at school, and outdoors. This chapter has provided many tips for staying safe.

Step 1 Review your private journal entries for this chapter. Highlight points that will enable you to remember and practice safety precautions at home, at school, and outdoors. What habits or actions should you change to reduce your risk of injury?

Step 2 Set a long-term goal that will improve your personal safety. For example, you might decide to make your home as safe as possible from fire.

Step 3 Next, write down short-term goals that will help you achieve your long-term goal. A short-term goal could be to create a checklist for possible hazards around the house or to find out where a fire extinguisher might be purchased.

Create a schedule for reaching each short-term goal. Review your schedule regularly to make sure that you are on track. When you have reached your goal, consider becoming safety conscious in a different area of your life.

In Your Home and Community

1. **Health of Others** Draw a floor plan of your home, including bedrooms, doors, windows, hallways, and stairs. Indicate two escape routes for each family member. The escape routes should begin at each bedroom. Share the plan with the members of your family. Then practice your escape plan by conducting a family fire drill.

2. **Community Resources** Invite an emergency medical technician or a police officer to speak to your class. Ask the person to demonstrate common first-aid techniques. Also ask the speaker about safety tips for preventing accidents and injuries.

Building Your Portfolio

1. **Persuasive Essay** Do you feel that bicycle riders, like drivers, should have to pass a test before using public roads? Take a stand on this issue, and write a one-page essay that supports your views. Put the essay in your portfolio.

2. **Report of an Event** Find newspaper articles about weather emergencies and natural disasters. Select one event, and pretend that you are there. Describe what actions you would take. Add the articles and your description to your portfolio.

3. **Personal Assessment** Look through all the activities and projects you did for this chapter. Choose one or two that you would like to include in your portfolio.

Glossary

The Glossary contains all the important terms used throughout the text. It includes the **boldfaced** terms listed in the "Words to Know" lists at the beginning of each lesson and that appear in text, captions, and features.

The Glossary lists the term, the pronunciation (in the case of difficult terms), the definition, and the page on which the term is defined. The pronunciations here and in the text follow the system outlined below. The column headed "Symbol" shows the spelling used in this book to represent the appropriate method.

Pronunciation Key

Sound	As in	Symbol	Example
ă	hat, map	a	abscess (AB·sess)
ā	age, face	ay	atrium (AY·tree·uhm)
a	care, their	ehr	capillaries (KAP·uh·lehr·eez)
ä, ŏ	father, hot	ah	biopsy (BY·ahp·see)
ar	far	ar	cardiac (KAR·dee·ak)
ch	child, much	ch	barbiturate (bar·BI·chuh·ruht)
ĕ	let, best	e	vessel (VE·suhl)
ē	beat, see, city	ee	acne (AK·nee)
er	term, stir, purr	er	nuclear (NOO·klee·er)
g	grow	g	malignant (muh·LIG·nuhnt)
ĭ	it, hymn	i	bacteria (bak·TIR·ee·uh)
ī	ice, five	y	benign (bi·NYN)
		eye	iris (EYE·ris)
j	page, fungi	j	cartilage (KAR·tuhl·ij)
k	coat, look, chorus	k	defect (DEE·fekt)
ō	open, coat, grow	oh	aerobic (e·ROH·bik)
ô	order	or	organ (OR·guhn)
ò	flaw, all	aw	palsy (PAWL·zee)
oi	voice	oy	goiter (GOY·ter)
ou	out	ow	fountain (FOWN·tuhn)
s	say, rice	s	dermis (DER·mis)
sh	she, attention	sh	conservation (kahn·ser·VAY·shuhn)
ŭ	cup, flood	uh	bunion (BUHN·yuhn)
u	put, wood, could	u	pulmonary (PUL·muh·nehr·ee)
ü	rule, move, you	oo	attitudes (AT·i·toodz)
w	win	w	warranty (WAWR·uhn·tee)
y	your	yu	urethritis (yur·i·THRY·tuhs)
z	says	z	hormones (HOR·mohnz)
zh	pleasure	zh	transfusion (trans·FYOO·zhuhn)
ə	about, collide	uh	asthma (AZ·muh)

Abdominal thrusts Quick, upward pulls into the diaphragm to force an obstruction out of a person's airway. (page 438)

Abstinence Refusing to participate in unsafe behaviors or activities. (page 255)

Abuse (uh·BYOOS) The physical, emotional, or mental mistreatment of another person. (page 400)

Accident chain A series of events that includes a situation, an unsafe habit, and an unsafe action. (page 413)

Acid rain Rain that is more acidic than normal. (page 441)

Action plan A series of steps for reaching a goal. (page 54)

Addiction (uh·DIK·shuhn) A physical or psychological need for a drug or other substance. (page 283)

Adolescence (a·duhl·E·suhns) Time of life between childhood and adulthood. (page 176)

Adrenaline (uh·DRE·nuhl·in) A hormone that increases the level of sugar in the blood, which gives the body extra energy. (page 220)

Advertisement A message designed to get consumers to buy a product or service. (page 61)

Aerobic (e·ROH·bik) **exercise** Nonstop, rhythmic, vigorous activity that increases breathing and heartbeat rates. (page 121)

Aftershocks Secondary earthquakes that may occur after an initial earthquake. (page 431)

AIDS (acquired immunodeficiency syndrome) A deadly disease that interferes with the body's ability to fight infection. (page 353)

Alcohol A drug created by a chemical reaction in some foods, especially fruits and grains. (page 296)

Alcoholism An illness caused by a physical and mental need for alcohol. (page 299)

Allergen (AL·er·juhn) A substance that causes an allergic reaction. (page 373)

Allergy An extreme sensitivity to a substance. (page 373)

Alternatives Other ways of thinking or acting. (page 322)

Alveoli (al·VEE·uh·ly) Microscopic air sacs in the lungs where gases are exchanged. (page 277)

Alzheimer's (AHLTS·hy·merz) **disease** An illness that attacks the brain and affects thinking, memory, and behavior. (page 383)

Amphetamine (am·FE·tuh·meen) A strong stimulant drug that speeds up the nervous system. (page 304)

Anabolic steroids (a·nuh·BAH·lik STIR·oydz) Synthetic compounds that cause muscle tissue to develop at an abnormally high rate. (page 158)

Anaerobic (an·e·ROH·bik) **exercise** Intense physical activity that requires short bursts of energy. (page 121)

Angioplasty (AN·jee·uh·plas·tee) A surgical procedure in which an instrument with a tiny balloon attached is inserted into an artery to clear a blockage. (page 365)

Anorexia nervosa (an·uh·REK·see·uh ner·VOH·suh) An eating disorder in which a person has an intense fear of weight gain and starves himself or herself. (page 145)

Antibodies Proteins that attach to antigens, keeping them from harming the body. (page 337)

Antigens (AN·ti·jenz) Substances that send your immune system into action when your body is invaded by germs. (page 337)

Antihistamine A medication that relieves the symptoms of an allergic reaction. (page 374)

Anxiety disorder A disorder in which real or imagined fears keep a person from functioning normally. (page 229)

Arteriosclerosis (ar·tir·ee·oh·skluh·ROH·sis) Hardening of the arteries. (page 364)

Artery A type of blood vessel that carries blood away from the heart to all parts of the body. (page 123)

Arthritis (ar·THRY·tuhs) A disease of the joints marked by painful swelling and stiffness. (page 380)

Assertive Having the determination to stand up for yourself in a firm but positive way. (page 321)

Asthma (AZ·muh) A chronic respiratory disease that causes tiny air passages in the lungs to become narrow or blocked. (page 375)

Astigmatism (uh·STIG·muh·tiz·uhm) An eye condition in which images are distorted, causing objects to appear wavy or blurry. (page 77)

Atherosclerosis (a·thuh·roh·skluh·ROH·sis) A condition in which fatty substances build up on the inner lining of arteries. (page 364)

Bacteria (bak·TIR·ee·uh) Tiny one-celled organisms, some causing disease, that live nearly everywhere. (page 333)

Battery The beating, hitting, or kicking of another person. (page 401)

Benign (bi·NYN) Not cancerous. (page 367)

Biodegradable (by·oh·di·GRAY·duh·buhl) Easily broken down in the environment. (page 441)

Blizzard A very heavy snowstorm with winds of up to 45 miles per hour. (page 434)

Blood pressure The force of blood pushing against the walls of the blood vessels. (page 126)

Body composition The proportions of fat, bones, muscle, and fluid that make up body weight. (page 120)

Body language Nonverbal communication that includes posture, gestures, and facial expressions. (page 241)

Body Mass Index (BMI) A measure of weight based on comparing body weight to height. (page 141)

Body system A group of organs working together to carry out related tasks. (page 196)

Brain The information center of the nervous system, which receives and screens information and sends messages to other parts of the body. (page 308)

Bronchi (BRAHN·ky) Two tubes that branch from the trachea, one to each lung. (page 276)

Bronchodilator (brahn·koh·dy·LAY·ter) Medication that relaxes the muscles around the bronchial air passages. (page 376)

Bulimia nervosa (boo·LEE·mee·uh ner·VOH·suh) An eating disorder in which a person repeatedly eats large amounts of food and then purges. (page 145)

Burnout A sense of exhaustion caused by exerting too much energy for too long a time. (page 167)

Calories (KA·luh·reez) Units of heat that measure the energy available in foods. (page 95)

Cancer A disease that occurs when abnormal cells grow out of control. (page 367)

Capillary The smallest blood vessel, which provides body cells with blood and connects an artery with a vein. (page 123)

Carbohydrates (kar·boh·HY·drayts) The starches and sugars that provide the body with most of its energy. (page 96)

Carbon monoxide (KAR·buhn muh·NAHK·syd) A colorless, odorless, poisonous gas produced when tobacco burns. (page 272)

Carcinogen (kar·SI·nuh·juhn) A substance in the environment that causes cancer. (page 369)

Cardiopulmonary resuscitation (CPR) A first-aid procedure to restore breathing and circulation. (page 435)

Cardiovascular (KAR·dee·oh·VAS·kyoo·ler) **system** Another name for the circulatory system. (page 123)

Cartilage (KAR·tuhl·ij) Strong, flexible tissue that covers the ends of bones and also supports some structures. (page 130)

Cavity A hole that begins in a tooth's enamel. (page 70)

Cell The basic unit, or building block, of life. (page 196)

Central nervous system (CNS) The brain and the spinal cord. (page 308)

Chemotherapy (kee·moh·THEHR·uh·pee) The use of chemicals to destroy cancer cells. (page 370)

Chest thrusts Quick presses into the middle of the breastbone to force an obstruction out of a person's airway. (page 438)

Chlamydia (kluh·MI·dee·uh) A bacteria-caused STD that may affect the reproductive organs, urethra, and anus. (page 351)

Choking A condition that occurs when a person's airway becomes blocked. (page 438)

Cholesterol (kuh·LES·tuh·rawl) A waxlike substance used by the body to build cells and make other substances. (page 99)

Chromosomes (KROH·muh·sohmz) Threadlike structures within a cell that carry the codes for inherited traits. (page 199)

Chronic (KRAH·nik) Present continuously or on and off over a long time. (page 362)

Circulatory system The group of organs and tissues that transport essential materials to body cells and remove their waste products. (page 123)

Cirrhosis (suh·ROH·sis) Scarring and destruction of liver tissue. (page 297)

Colon (KOH·luhn) The large intestine, which is a storage tube for solid wastes. (page 113)

Commitment A pledge or promise. (page 150)

Communicable (kuh·MYOO·ni·kuh·buhl) **disease** A disease that can be passed from one person to another. (page 332)

Communication The exchange of thoughts, feelings, and beliefs among people. (page 240)

Comparison (kuhm·PEHR·i·suhn) **shopping** Comparing products, evaluating their benefits, and choosing the products that offer the best value. (page 68)

Competition Rivalry between two or more individuals or groups trying to reach the same goal. (page 152)

Compromise A method in which each person gives up something in order to reach a solution that satisfies everyone. (page 244)

Conditioning Training to get into shape. (page 159)

Conflict A disagreement between people with opposing viewpoints. (page 260)

Consequences The effects or results of actions. (page 32)

Conservation The saving of natural resources. (page 441)

Consumer (kuhn·SOO·mer) Anyone who buys goods and services. (page 60)

Contagious period The length of time when a particular disease can spread from person to person. (page 344)

Contract (Kuhn·TRAKT) To shorten, often referring to muscle function. (page 130)

Cool-down Gentle exercise that lets your body adjust to ending a workout. (page 138)

Cornea (KOR·nee·uh) The clear section that lets in light at the front of the eye. (page 76)

Criteria (kry·TIR·ee·uh) Standards on which to base a decision. (page 48)

Cross-training Any fitness program that includes a variety of physical activities to promote balanced fitness. (page 161)

Cumulative (KYOO·myuh·luh·tiv) **risks** Related risks that increase in effect with each added risk. (page 41)

Dandruff Flaking of the outer layer of dead skin cells on the scalp. (page 75)

Decibel The unit for measuring the loudness of sound waves. (page 79)

Decision making The process of making a choice or finding a solution. (page 46)

Defense mechanism (di·FENS MEK·uh·nizm) A short-term way of dealing with stress. (page 222)

Dehydration (dee·hy·DRAY·shuhn) Excessive loss of water from the body. (page 155)

Depressant (di·PRE·suhnt) A drug that slows down the body's functions and reactions, including heart and breathing rates. (page 305)

Depression A mood disorder involving feelings of hopelessness, helplessness, worthlessness, guilt, and extreme sadness that continue for periods of weeks. (page 229)

Dermis (DER·mis) The inner layer of skin that contains blood vessels, nerve endings, and hair follicles. (page 73)

Diabetes (dy·uh·BEE·teez) A disease that prevents the body from converting food into energy. (page 382)

Diaphragm (DY·uh·fram) Large dome-shaped muscle below the lungs that draws air in and pushes air out. (page 276)

Diet All the things you regularly eat and drink. (page 92)

Digestion (dy·JES·chuhn) The process by which the body breaks food down into smaller components that can be absorbed by the bloodstream and sent to each cell in the body. (page 108)

Digestive (dy·JES·tiv) **system** A series of organs that work together to break down foods into substances that your cells can use. (page 108)

Discount store A store that offers special reduced prices. (page 68)

Disease A condition that interferes with the proper functioning of the body or mind. (page 332)

Distress Stress that keeps you from doing the things you need to do or that causes you discomfort. (page 219)

Drug A nonfood substance taken into the body that can change the structure or function of the body or mind. (page 301)

Earthquake A violent shaking of the earth's surface. (page 431)

Eating disorder An extreme eating behavior that can lead to serious illness or even death. (page 145)

Electrical overload A dangerous situation in which too much electric current flows along a single circuit. (page 420)

Electrocution Death by electrical shock. (page 418)

Embryo (EM·bree·oh) The name for an organism from fertilization to about the eighth week. (page 197)

Emotions Feelings such as love, joy, or fear. (page 4)

Empathy The ability to identify and share another person's feelings. (page 243)

Endocrine (EN·duh·krin) **system** Glands throughout your body that regulate body functions. (page 182)

Endorsement (en·DOR·smuhnt) A statement of approval. (page 63)

Endurance (in·DUR·uhnts) The ability to perform vigorous physical activity without getting overly tired. (page 121)

Environment (en·VY·ruhn·ment) All the living and nonliving things that surround you. (page 9)

Environmental Protection Agency (EPA) An agency of the United States government that is committed to protecting the environment. (page 440)

Epidermis (e·puh·DER·mis) The outermost layer of skin. (page 73)

Excretion (ek·SKREE·shuhn) The process by which the body gets rid of liquid waste materials. (page 112)

Excretory (EK·skruh·tor·ee) **system** The system that removes wastes from the body and controls water balance. (page 112)

Exercise Physical activity that develops fitness. (page 118)

Exercise frequency How often a person works out each week. (page 139)

Exercise intensity How much energy a person uses when working out. (page 139)

Extend To lengthen, often referring to muscle function. (page 131)

Family The basic unit of society. (page 245)

Family violence shelter A place where family members in danger of abuse can stay while they get their lives in order. (page 405)

Fatigue Extreme tiredness. (page 221)

Fats Sources of energy that also perform other functions, such as vitamin storage and body insulation. (page 97)

Fertilization (fer·til·i·ZAY·shuhn) The joining of a male sperm cell and a female egg cell to form a new human life. (page 190)

Fetus (FEE·tuhs) The name for the developing child from about the ninth week until the time of birth. (page 197)

Fiber The part of grains, fruits, and vegetables that the body cannot break down. (page 98)

First aid The immediate care given to someone who becomes injured or ill until regular medical care can be provided. (page 435)

First-degree burn A burn in which only the outer layer of the skin is burned and turns red. (page 439)

Fitness The ability to handle the physical work and play of everyday life without becoming overly tired. (page 118)

Flammable Able to catch fire easily. (page 416)

Flexibility The ability to move joints fully and easily. (page 123)

Fluoride (FLAWR·eyed) A substance that helps teeth resist decay. (page 70)

Food Guide Pyramid A guide for making healthful daily food choices, developed by the U.S. Department of Agriculture. (page 93)

Fossil (FAH·suhl) **fuels** Oil, coal, and natural gas used to provide energy. (page 441)

Fracture A break in a bone. (page 439)

Friendship The relationship between people who like each other and who have similar interests and values. (page 249)

Fungi (FUHN·jy) Primitive life forms that cannot make their own food. (page 333)

Gang A group of people who associate with one another because they have something in common. (page 396)

Gene The basic unit of heredity that determines the traits you inherit from your parents. (page 199)

Generic (juh·NER·ik) **products** Goods sold in plain packages at lower prices than brand name goods. (page 68)

Genital herpes (JEN·i·tuhl HER·peez) An STD caused by a virus that produces painful blisters in the genital area. (page 352)

Germ A microorganism that causes disease. (page 332)

Gland A group of cells, or an organ, that produces a chemical substance. (page 182)

Glucose (GLOO·kohs) A sugar that is the body's main source of energy. (page 102)

Gonorrhea (gah·nuh·REE·uh) A bacteria-caused STD that affects the genital mucous membrane and sometimes other body parts, such as the heart or joints. (page 352)

Grief Sorrow caused by the loss of something precious. (page 205)

Gynecologist (gy·nuh·KAH·luh·jist) A doctor who specializes in the female reproductive system. (page 192)

Habit A pattern of behavior repeated frequently enough to be performed almost without thinking. (page 34)

Hallucinogen (huh·LOO·suhn·uh·jen) A drug that distorts moods, thoughts, and senses. (page 305)

Hate crime An illegal act committed against someone just because he or she is a member of a particular group. (page 394)

Hazard A potential source of danger. (page 41)

Head lice Parasitic insects that live in the hair and cause itching. (page 75)

Health A combination of physical, mental/emotional, and social well-being. (page 4)

Health insurance (in·SHUR·uhns) A plan in which people pay a set fee to an insurance company in return for the company's agreement to pay some or most medical costs. (page 84)

Health maintenance (MAYN·tuh·nuhns) **organization (HMO)** A form of managed health care that offers its members the services of many different types of health care providers. (page 84)

Heart attack Condition that occurs when the blood supply to the heart slows or stops and the heart muscle is damaged. (page 364)

Hepatitis (he·puh·TY·tis) A liver inflammation, caused by a virus, characterized by yellowing of the skin and the whites of the eyes. (page 342)

Heredity (huh·RED·i·tee) The passing on of traits from biological parents to children. (page 9)

Histamines (HIS·tuh·meenz) Chemicals in the body that cause the symptoms of an allergic reaction. (page 374)

HIV (human immunodeficiency virus) The virus that causes AIDS. (page 353)

Homicide (HAH·muh·syd) A violent crime that results in the death of an individual. (page 393)

Hormones (HOR·mohnz) Chemical substances, produced by glands, which help to regulate the way the body functions. (page 176)

Hurricane A strong windstorm with driving rain that originates at sea. (page 433)

Hygiene (HY·jeen) Cleanliness. (page 19)

Hypertension (hy·per·TEN·shuhn) Condition in which a person's blood pressure stays at a level that is higher than normal; also called *high blood pressure.* (page 364)

Hypothermia (hy·poh·THER·mee·uh) A sudden and dangerous drop in body temperature. (page 427)

Immune (i·MYOON) **system** A combination of body defenses made up of cells, tissues, and organs that fight off germs and disease. (page 336)

Immunity The body's ability to resist the germs that cause a particular disease. (page 339)

Individual sports Physical activities you can take part in by yourself or with a friend, without being part of a team. (page 151)

Infancy (IN·fuhn·see) The first year of a baby's life. (page 201)

Infection Condition that occurs when germs get inside the body, multiply, and damage body cells. (page 332)

Influenza (in·floo·EN·zuh) A communicable disease typically characterized by fever, chills, fatigue, headache, muscle aches, and respiratory symptoms. (page 341)

Infomercial (IN·foh·mer·shuhl) A longer television commercial whose main purpose appears to be to present information rather than to sell a product. (page 63)

Inhalant (in·HAY·luhnt) A substance whose fumes are breathed in to produce mind-altering sensations. (page 305)

Insulin (IN·suh·lin) A hormone produced in the pancreas that regulates the level of sugar in the blood. (page 382)

Intoxicated (in·TAHK·suh·kay·tuhd) Drunk. (page 315)

Invulnerable Not able to be hurt. (page 320)

Iris (EYE·ris) The colored part of the eye. (page 76)

Joint A place where two or more bones meet. (page 128)

Kidney One of a pair of bean-shaped organs that filter water and waste materials from the blood. (page 112)

Lens (LENZ) The part of the eye that focuses light on the retina. (page 76)

Life-altering Capable of changing a person's day-to-day existence. (page 38)

Life-threatening Possibly causing death. (page 36)

Ligament (LI·guh·ment) A strong band of tissue that holds a bone in place at a joint. (page 130)

Liver The body's largest gland, which secretes a liquid called bile that helps to digest fats. (page 111)

Long-term goal A goal that you plan to reach over an extended length of time. (page 53)

Lymphatic (lim·FA·tik) **system** A secondary circulatory system that helps the body fight germs and maintain its fluid balance. (page 337)

Lymphocytes (LIM·fuh·syts) Special white blood cells in the lymph that are important in fighting off germs and disease. (page 337)

Mainstream smoke Smoke exhaled by a smoker. (page 290)

Malignant (muh·LIG·nuhnt) Cancerous. (page 367)

Managed care A health care plan that emphasizes preventive medicine and works to manage the cost and quality of health care. (page 84)

Mass media Media that can reach large groups of people, such as newspapers, books, television, movies, and the Internet. (page 61)

Media The various methods for communicating information. (page 61)

Mediation (mee·dee·AY·shuhn) Resolving conflicts by using a neutral person to help reach a solution that is acceptable to both sides. (page 265)

Medicaid (MED·i·kayd) A public health insurance program for low-income families and individuals. (page 85)

Medicare (MED·i·kehr) A federal government health insurance program that provides health insurance to people who are 65 years old and over. (page 85)

Medicine A drug that is used to treat an illness or relieve pain. (page 301)

Melanin (ME·luh·nuhn) A substance made by cells in the epidermis that gives skin its color. (page 73)

Menstruation (men·stroo·WAY·shuhn) The flow of the uterine lining material from the body. (page 191)

Mental health Your ability to deal in a reasonable way with the stresses and changes of everyday life. (page 210)

Minerals Substances that strengthen the muscles, bones, and teeth; enrich the blood; and keep the heart and other organs operating properly. (page 97)

Mononucleosis (MAH·noh·noo·klee·OH·sis) A virus-caused disease characterized by swelling of the lymph nodes in the neck and throat. (page 342)

Mood disorder A disorder in which a person undergoes changes in mood that seem inappropriate or extreme. (page 229)

Mortality (mor·TA·luh·tee) Death. (page 39)

Muscle endurance The measure of how long a group of muscles can exert a force without tiring. (page 4)

Muscular system The body system that consists of tissues that move parts of the body and operate internal organs. (page 128)

Narcotic (nar·KAH·tik) A drug that relieves pain and dulls the senses. (page 305)

Negotiation (ni·goh·shee·AY·shuhn) The process of discussing problems face-to-face in order to reach a solution. (page 265)

Neuron (NOO·rahn) One of the cells that make up the nervous system. (page 307)

Neutrality (noo·TRA·luh·tee) Not taking sides when others are arguing. (page 265)

Nicotine (NIK·uh·teen) An addictive drug found in tobacco. (page 272)

Noncommunicable disease A disease, such as asthma and cancer, that cannot be spread from one person to another. (page 332)

Nonverbal communication All the ways in which you can get a message across without using words. (page 241)

Nonviolent confrontation Resolving a conflict by peaceful methods. (page 264)

Nurture To provide for the physical, emotional, mental, and social needs of a person. (page 246)

Nutrient density The amount of nutrients in a food relative to the number of calories. (page 104)

Nutrients (NOO·tree·ents) The substances in foods that your body needs in order to grow, have energy, and stay healthy. (page 95)

Nutrition (noo·TRI·shuhn) The body's process of taking in food and using it for growth and good health. (page 92)

Obesity Condition in which a person weighs 20 percent more than his or her ideal weight. (page 142)

Objective Based on facts. (page 41)

Occupational Safety and Health Administration (OSHA) A branch of the U.S. Department of Labor whose job is to ensure the protection of American workers. (page 440)

Ophthalmologist (ahf·thahl·MAH·luh·jist) A physician who specializes in the structure, functions, and diseases of the eye. (page 77)

Optic (AHP·tik) **nerve** A bundle of nerve fibers that send messages from the eye to the brain. (page 76)

Optometrist (ahp·TAH·muh·trist) An eye care professional trained to examine the eyes for vision problems and to prescribe corrective lenses. (page 77)

Organ A body part made up of different tissues joined together to perform a function. (page 196)

Osteoarthritis (ahs·tee·oh·ar·THRY·tuhs) A chronic disease, common in elderly people, that results from the breakdown of cartilage in the joints. (page 380)

Ovaries (OH·vuh·reez) The female reproductive glands. (page 190)

Overcommitment Obligating yourself to more people or projects than you have time or energy to follow through on. (page 167)

Overtraining Exercising too hard or too often, without enough rest in between. (page 161)

Pancreas (PAN·kree·uhs) A gland that helps the small intestine by producing pancreatic juice, a blend of enzymes that breaks down proteins, carbohydrates, and fats. (page 111)

Passive smoker A nonsmoker who breathes secondhand smoke. (page 290)

Pedestrian A person who travels on foot. (page 422)

Peer pressure The influence that your friends have on you to believe and act like them. (page 251)

Peers People close to your age who are similar to you in many ways. (page 251)

Peripheral (puh·RIF·uh·ruhl) **nervous system (PNS)** All the nerves outside the central nervous system, which connect the brain and the spinal cord to the rest of the body. (page 308)

Personality An individual's special mix of traits, feelings, attitudes, and habits. (page 212)

Physical fatigue Extreme tiredness of the whole body. (page 221)

Physiological (fi·zee·uh·LAH·ji·kuhl) **dependence** A type of addiction in which the body itself feels a direct need for a drug. (page 284)

Pituitary (pi·TOO·i·tehr·ee) **gland** Gland, located at the base of the brain, that produces several hormones that control other glands. (page 183)

Plaque (PLAK) A thin, sticky film that contributes to tooth decay. (page 70)

Plasma (PLAZ·muh) A yellowish fluid; the watery part of the blood. (page 125)

Pollen A powdery substance released by certain plants. (page 373)

Pollution Dirty or harmful substances in the environment. (page 440)

Pores Tiny openings in the skin. (page 73)

Precaution An action taken to avoid danger. (page 41)

Prejudice (PRE·juh·dis) A negative and unjustly formed opinion, usually against people of a different racial, religious, or cultural group. (page 261)

Preschooler A child between the ages of three and five. (page 202)

Prevention Taking steps to make sure that something unhealthy does not happen. (page 14)

Primary care provider A doctor or other health professional who provides checkups and general care. (page 83)

Proteins (PROH·teenz) Essential nutrients used to build and repair body cells and tissues. (page 96)

Protozoa (proh·tuh·ZOH·uh) One-celled, animal-like organisms. (page 333)

Psychological (sy·kuh·LAH·ji·kuhl) **dependence** An addiction in which the mind sends the body the message that it needs more of a substance. (page 285)

Psychological fatigue Extreme tiredness caused by a person's mental state. (page 221)

Puberty (PYOO·ber·tee) The time when you start to develop certain physical characteristics of adults of your own gender. (page 177)

Pulmonary (PUL·muh·nehr·ee) **circulation** Circulation that carries blood from the heart, through the lungs, and back to the heart. (page 124)

Pupil (PYOO·puhl) The dark opening in the center of the iris that allows the right amount of light to enter the eye. (page 76)

Quackery (KWAK·uh·ree) The sale of worthless products and treatments through false claims. (page 66)

Radiation (ray·dee·AY·shuhn) **therapy** A treatment for some types of cancer that uses X-rays or other forms of radioactivity. (page 370)

Recovery The process of becoming well again. (page 325)

Refusal skills Ways to say no effectively. (page 23)

Reproduction (ree·pruh·DUHK·shuhn) The process by which living organisms produce new individuals of their kind. (page 186)

Reproductive (ree·pruh·DUHK·tiv) **system** Body organs and structures that make possible the production of offspring. (page 186)

Rescue breathing A substitute for normal breathing in which someone forces air into an accident victim's lungs. (page 436)

Respiratory system The set of organs that supply the body with oxygen and rid the body of carbon dioxide. (page 276)

Responsibility The ability to make choices and to accept the results of those choices. (page 28)

Retina (RE·tin·uh) The light-sensing part of the inner eye. (page 76)

Rheumatoid (ROO·muh·toyd) **arthritis** A chronic disease characterized by pain, inflammation, swelling, and stiffness of the joints. (page 380)

Risk behavior An action or choice that may cause injury or harm to you or others. (page 14)

Safety conscious Aware that safety is important, and careful to act in a safe manner. (page 412)

Saliva (suh·LY·vuh) A digestive juice produced by the salivary glands in the mouth. (page 109)

Saturated fats Fats found mostly in meats and dairy products. (page 99)

Schizophrenia (skit·zoh·FREE·nee·uh) A serious mental disorder in which a person's perceptions lose their connection to reality. (page 230)

Second-degree burn A serious burn in which the burned area blisters. (page 439)

Secondhand smoke Air that has been contaminated by tobacco smoke. (page 290)

Self-assessment Careful examination and evaluation of your own patterns of behavior. (page 14)

Self-concept The view that you have of yourself. (page 214)

Self-esteem Confidence in yourself. (page 53)

Self-management The ability to take care of your overall health and to take control of your behavior and actions. (page 22)

Semen (SEE·muhn) A mixture of sperm and fluids produced by the male reproductive system. (page 187)

Sewage (SOO·ij) Garbage, detergents, and other household wastes that are washed down drains. (page 441)

Short-term goal A goal that you can reach right away. (page 53)

Sidestream smoke Smoke that comes from the burning tip of a cigarette. (page 290)

Skeletal system The framework of bones and other tissues that support the body. (page 128)

Small intestine A coiled tube, about 20 feet long, where most of the digestive process takes place. (page 111)

Smoke detector A device that sounds an alarm when it senses smoke. (page 417)

Specialist (SPE·shuh·list) A doctor trained to treat particular types of patients or health matters. (page 83)

Sperm The male reproductive cells. (page 187)

Spinal cord A long bundle of neurons that relays messages to and from the brain and all parts of the body. (page 308)

STD (sexually transmitted disease) A disease spread from person to person through sexual contact. (page 350)

Stimulant (STIM·yuh·luhnt) A drug that speeds up the body's functions. (page 303)

Stomach A muscular organ in which some digestion occurs. (page 110)

Strength The ability of your muscles to exert a force. (page 120)

Stress Your body's response to changes around you. (page 220)

Stressor Something that triggers stress. (page 220)

Stroke Condition that occurs when part of the brain is damaged because the blood supply to the brain is cut off. (page 364)

Subjective Coming from a person's own views and beliefs, not necessarily from facts. (page 41)

Suicide Intentionally killing oneself. (page 230)

Support system A network of people available to help when needed. (page 233)

Syphilis (SI·fuh·lis) A bacteria-caused STD that can affect many parts of the body. (page 352)

Systemic (sis·TE·mik) **circulation** Circulation that sends oxygen-rich blood to all the body tissues except the lungs. (page 124)

Tact The quality of knowing what to say to avoid offending others. (page 242)

Tar A thick, dark liquid that forms when tobacco burns. (page 272)

Target heart rate The number of heartbeats per minute a person should aim for during vigorous exercise for cardiovascular benefit. (page 139)

Tartar (TAR·ter) Plaque that has hardened on teeth, threatening gum health. (page 70)

Team sports Organized physical activities with specific rules, played by opposing groups of people. (page 151)

Teen hot line A special telephone service that teens can call when feeling stressed. (page 233)

Tendon (TEN·duhn) Strong, flexible, fibrous tissue that joins muscle to muscle or muscle to bone. (page 130)

Third-degree burn A very serious burn in which all layers of the skin are damaged. (page 439)

Tissue A group of similar cells that do a particular job. (page 196)

Toddler A child between the ages of one and three. (page 202)

Tolerance (TAHL·er·ens) Situation in which the body becomes used to a drug and needs greater amounts to get the desired effect. (page 324)

Tornado A whirling, funnel-shaped windstorm that drops from the sky to the ground. (page 432)

Tornado warning A news bulletin warning that a tornado has been sighted and that people in the area are in immediate danger. (page 432)

Tornado watch A news bulletin warning that weather conditions indicate that a tornado may develop. (page 432)

Trachea (TRAY·kee·uh) The tube in the throat that takes air to and from the lungs. (page 276)

Tuberculosis (too·ber·kyuh·LOH·sis) A bacteria-caused disease that usually affects the lungs. (page 342)

Tumor (TOO·mer) A group of abnormal cells that forms a mass. (page 367)

Unsaturated fats Liquid fats that come mainly from plants. (page 99)

Uterus (YOO·tuh·ruhs) A pear-shaped female organ in which a developing child is nourished. (page 190)

Vaccine (vak·SEEN) A preparation of dead or weakened germs that is injected into the body to cause the immune system to produce antibodies. (page 339)

Values The beliefs that guide the way a person lives, such as beliefs about what is right and wrong and what is most important. (page 22)

Vein (VAYN) A type of blood vessel that carries blood from all parts of the body back to the heart. (page 123)

Verbal communication Using words to express yourself, either in speaking or in writing. (page 241)

Victim The person against whom a crime is committed. (page 400)

Virus (VY·ruhs) The smallest and simplest life form, causing a wide range of diseases. (page 333)

Vitamins Substances that help to regulate the body's functions. (page 97)

Warm-up Gentle exercise you do to prepare your muscles for vigorous activity. (page 138)

Warranty A company's or a store's written agreement to repair a product or refund your money if the product does not work properly. (page 68)

Wellness An overall state of well-being involving regular behaviors that have a positive result over time. (page 6)

Withdrawal Unpleasant symptoms that occur when someone stops using an addictive substance. (page 283)

Abdominal thrusts/presiones abdominales Presiones rápidas hacia arriba para forzar la salida de un objeto que esté bloqueando las vías respiratorias.

Abstinence/abstinencia Negarse a comportarse o tomar parte en actividades peligrosas.

Abuse/abuso El maltrato físico, emocional o mental de otra persona.

Accident chain/cadena de accidentes Una serie de sucesos que incluyen una situación, una costumbre peligrosa y una acción peligrosa.

Acid rain/lluvia ácida Lluvia que es más ácida de lo normal.

Action plan/plan de acción Una serie de pasos para alcanzar una meta.

Addiction/adicción La necesidad física o mental de una droga u otra substancia.

Adolescence/adolescencia El período de vida entre la niñez y la adultez.

Adrenaline/adrenalina Una hormona que aumenta el nivel de azúcar en la sangre, lo cual da energía adicional al cuerpo.

Advertisement/anuncio Un mensaje diseñado para hacer que los consumidores compren un producto o servicio.

Aerobic exercise/ejercicio aeróbico Actividad rítmica y vigorosa que aumenta la velocidad de la respiración y de los latidos del corazón.

Aftershocks/ondas posteriores Terremotos secundarios que ocurren después del terremoto principal.

AIDS (acquired immunodeficiency syndrome)/SIDA (síndrome de inmunodeficiencia adquirida) Una enfermedad mortal que interfiere con la habilidad del cuerpo de defenderse contra infecciones.

Alcohol/alcohol Una droga creada por una reacción química en ciertos alimentos, especialmente frutas y granos.

Alcoholism/alcoholismo Una enfermedad causada por la necesidad física y mental de consumir alcohol.

Allergen/alergeno Una substancia que causa una reacción alérgica.

Allergy/alergia Sensibilidad extrema a una substancia.

Alternatives/alternativas Diferentes maneras de pensar o actuar.

Alveoli/alvéolos Sacos microscópicos en los pulmones, donde se intercambian gases.

Alzheimer's disease/enfermedad de Alzheimer Una enfermedad que ataca el cerebro y afecta el razonamiento, memoria y conducta.

Amphetamine/anfetamina Una droga estimulante fuerte que acelera el sistema nervioso.

Anabolic steroids/esteroides anabólicos Compuestos sintéticos que hacen que el tejido muscular se desarrolle con rapidez anormal.

Anaerobic exercise/ejercicio anaeróbico Intensa actividad física que requiere arranques de energía.

Angioplasty/angioplastia Una operación quirúrgica en la que un instrumento con un globo diminuto se introduce en una arteria para desatascar algo que la bloquea.

Anorexia nervosa/anorexia nerviosa Un trastorno alimenticio en que la persona tiene miedo intenso de ganar de peso y se priva de alimentos.

Antibodies/anticuerpos Proteínas que se pegan a los antígenos, impidiendo que éstos le hagan daño al cuerpo.

Antigens/antígenos Substancias que hacen que el sistema de inmunidad reaccione cuando el cuerpo es invadido por gérmenes.

Antihistamine/antihistamínico Una medicina que alivia los síntomas de una reacción alérgica.

Anxiety disorder/trastorno de ansiedad Un trastorno en el que el temor de problemas reales o imaginarios no deja que la persona funcione normalmente.

Arteriosclerosis/arteriosclerosis Endurecimiento de las arterias.

Artery/arteria Un tipo de vaso sanguíneo que lleva sangre del corazón a todas partes del cuerpo.

Arthritis/artritis Una enfermedad de las articulaciones caracterizada por inflamación y rigidez.

Assertive/resuelto Que tiene la determinación para actuar con confianza y firmeza, de manera positiva.

Asthma/asma Una enfermedad crónica que hace que se estrechen o se atasquen las diminutas vías respiratorias en los pulmones.

Astigmatism/astigmatismo Una condición del ojo en que las imágenes se deforman, haciendo que los objetos aparezcan ondulados o borrosos.

Atherosclerosis/aterosclerosis Una condición en que substancias grasosas se acumulan en las paredes internas de las arterias.

Bacteria/bacterias Organismos diminutos de una sóla célula que viven en casi todas partes, algunos de los cuales causan enfermedades.

Battery/golpeadura Golpear o dar patadas repetidas a otra persona.

Benign/benigno Que no tiene cáncer.

Biodegradable/biodegradable Que se descompone fácilmente en el medio ambiente.

Blizzard/nevasca Tormenta de nieve fuerte, con vientos que llegan a 45 millas por hora.

Blood pressure/presión arterial La fuerza de la sangre presionando contra las paredes de los vasos sanguíneos.

Body composition/composición del cuerpo La proporción de grasa, hueso, músculo y fluido que contiene el cuerpo.

Body language/lenguaje corporal Comunicación no verbal que incluye la postura, los gestos y las expresiones faciales.

Body Mass Index (BMI)/Índice de masa corporal (IMC) Una medida del peso del cuerpo basada en una comparación del peso con la estatura.

Body system/sistema corporal Un grupo de órganos que trabajan juntos para ejecutar tareas relacionadas.

Brain/cerebro El centro de información del sistema nervioso que recibe y revisa información y envía mensajes a otras partes del cuerpo.

Bronchi/bronquios Dos tubos que salen de la traquea y conducen a los pulmones.

Bronchodilator/broncodilatador Medicina que relaja los músculos alrededor de los bronquios.

Bulimia nervosa/bulimia nerviosa Un trastorno alimenticio en que la persona consume grandes cantidades de comida seguida de purgantes.

Burnout/agotamiento Sentirse extenuado por haber gastado demasiada energía durante demasiado tiempo.

Calories/calorías Unidades de calor que miden la energía que contienen los alimentos.

Cancer/cáncer Una enfermedad causada por el crecimiento incontrolado de células anormales.

Capillary/capilar El tipo de vaso sanguíneo más pequeño, que proporciona sangre a las células y conecta una arteria con una vena.

Carbohydrates/carbohidratos El azúcar y las féculas que le proporcionan al cuerpo la mayor parte de su energía.

Carbon monoxide/monóxido de carbono Un gas sin color, sin olor y venenoso que se produce al quemarse el tabaco.

Carcinogen/carcinógeno Una substancia en el medio ambiente que produce cáncer.

Cardiopulmonary resuscitation (CPR)/resucitación cardiopulmonar Un procedimiento de primeros auxilios para restaurar la respiración y circulación.

Cardiovascular system/sistema cardiovascular El sistema circulatorio.

Cartilage/cartílago Un tejido fuerte y flexible que cubre las terminaciones de los huesos y soporta ciertas estructuras.

Cavity/cavidad Un hueco que se empieza a formar en el esmalte del diente.

Cell/célula La unidad básica o bloque formativo de la vida.

Central nervous system (CNS)/sistema nervioso central (SNC) El cerebro y la espina dorsal.

Chemotherapy/quimioterapia El uso de substancias químicas para destruir células cancerosas.

Chest thrusts/presiones torácicas Presiones rápidas en el centro del esternón para forzar a que salga algo que esté bloqueando las vías respiratorias.

Chlamydia/clamidia Una enfermedad causada por una bacteria, que se transmite sexualmente y afecta los órganos de reproducción, la uretra y el ano.

Choking/asfixia La condición que ocurre cuando las vías respiratorias de una persona están bloqueadas.

Cholesterol/colesterol Una substancia parecida a la cera que el cuerpo usa para crear células y otras substancias.

Chromosomes/cromosomas Estructuras en forma de hilos dentro de la célula que contienen los códigos de las características hereditarias.

Chronic/crónico Que está presente o reaparece repetidamente durante un largo período de tiempo.

Circulatory system/sistema circulatorio El grupo de órganos y tejidos que transportan materiales esenciales a las células y se llevan los desechos de éstas.

Cirrhosis/cirrosis Condición en la que los tejidos del hígado presentan cicatrices y destrucción.

Colon/colon El intestino largo, donde se almacenan los desechos sólidos.

Commitment/compromiso Una promesa u obligación.

Communicable disease/enfermedad contagiosa Una enfermedad que se puede transmitir de una persona a otra.

Communication/comunicación El intercambio de pensamientos, sentimientos y creencias entre personas.

Comparison shopping/compras comparadas Comparar productos, evaluar sus beneficios y escoger los que ofrecen el mejor valor por el precio.

Competition/competencia Rivalidad entre dos o más personas o grupos que están tratando de alcanzar la misma meta.

Compromise/transigir Un modo de resolver diferencias en que cada persona renuncia a algo que desea para llegar a un acuerdo que satisfaga a todos.

Conditioning/preparación física Entrenamiento para ponerse en forma.

Conflict/conflicto Un desacuerdo entre personas con puntos de vista opuestos.

Consequences/consecuencias Los efectos o resultados de los actos.

Conservation/conservación El ahorro de recursos naturales.

Consumer/consumidor El que compra bienes y servicios.

Contagious period/período de contagio El período de tiempo en que se puede transmitir una enfermedad de una persona a otra.

Contract/contraer Hacerse más corto, a menudo se refiere a los músculos en función.

Cool-down/enfriamiento Ejercicios suaves que permiten que el cuerpo se acostumbre a dejar de ejercitarse.

Cornea/córnea La parte transparente anterior del ojo que permite que pase la luz.

Criteria/criterios Principios en que se basa una decisión.

Cross-training/entrenamiento variado Cualquier programa de ejercicio que incluya distintos tipos de actividades físicas para estar en buena condición física balanceada.

Cumulative risks/riesgos acumulativos
Riesgos relacionados cuyos efectos aumentan con cada riesgo que se añade.

Dandruff/caspa Escamas que forman las células muertas de la capa externa del cuero cabelludo.

Decibel/decibel La unidad que se usa para medir el volumen de las ondas del sonido.

Decision making/tomar decisiones El proceso de hacer una selección o hallar una solución.

Defense mechanism/mecanismo de defensa Una forma temporal de manejar el estrés.

Dehydration/deshidratación Pérdida excesiva de agua por el cuerpo.

Depressant/depresor Una droga que disminuye las funciones y reacciones del cuerpo, incluyendo el ritmo del corazón y la respiración.

Depression/depresión Un trastorno del ánimo en el que una persona se siente indefensa, despreciable, culpable, sin esperanza y extremadamente triste durante períodos que continuan varias semanas.

Dermis/dermis La capa interna de la piel que contiene vasos sanguíneos, terminaciones nerviosas y folículos pilosos.

Diabetes/diabetes Enfermedad que impide que el cuerpo convierta alimentos en energía.

Diaphragm/diafragma Músculo grande en forma de domo, situado debajo de los pulmones, que aspira y despide el aire.

Diet/dieta Todo lo que comes y bebes con regularidad.

Digestion/digestión El proceso corporal de descomponer los alimentos en componentes más pequeños para que la sangre los pueda absorber y llevar a cada célula del cuerpo.

Digestive system/sistema digestivo Una serie de órganos que trabajan juntos para descomponer los alimentos en substancias que las células puedan usar.

Discount store/tienda de descuento Una tienda que vende mercancía a precios rebajados.

Disease/enfermedad Una condición que interfiere con el funcionamiento normal del cuerpo o la mente.

Distress/angustia Estrés que impide que hagas lo que tienes que hacer o que te causa molestia.

Drug/droga Una substancia no alimenticia que al tomarse puede causar cambios en la estructura o funcionamiento del cuerpo o la mente.

Earthquake/terremoto El sacudimiento violento de la superficie de la Tierra.

Eating disorder/trastorno alimenticio Costumbres de alimentación exageradas que pueden causar enfermedades graves o muerte.

Electrical overload/sobrecarga eléctrica Una situación peligrosa en que demasiada corriente eléctrica fluye a través de un solo circuito.

Electrocution/electrocución Muerte causada por una descarga eléctrica.

Embryo/embrión El nombre de un organismo desde la fertilización hasta la octava semana.

Emotions/emociones Sentimientos como el amor, la alegría o el miedo.

Empathy/empatía La compenetración o habilidad de identificarse y compartir los sentimientos de otra persona.

Endocrine system/sistema endocrino Las glándulas del cuerpo que regulan sus funciones.

Endorsement/aprobación Una declaración de aceptación o consentimiento.

Endurance/resistencia La habilidad de hacer actividades físicas vigorosas sin cansarse demasiado.

Environment/medio ambiente Todas las cosas vivas y no vivas que te rodean.

Environmental Protection Agency (EPA)/Agencia de Protección Ambiental Una agencia del gobierno de los Estados Unidos que está encargada de proteger el medio ambiente.

Epidermis/epidermis La capa más externa de la piel.

Excretion/excreción El proceso mediante el cual el cuerpo se deshace de los desechos líquidos.

Excretory system/sistema excretorio El sistema que despide los desechos del cuerpo y controla el balance del agua.

Exercise/ejercicio Actividad física que aumenta la buena forma física.

Exercise frequency/frecuencia del ejercicio El número de veces en que una persona hace ejercicios semanalmente.

Exercise intensity/intensidad del ejercicio La cantidad de energía que una persona consume al ejercitarse.

Extend/extender Estirar, a menudo se refiere a la función muscular.

Family/familia La unidad básica de la sociedad.

Family violence shelter/refugio para familias maltratadas Un sitio donde personas en peligro de ser abusadas por otros miembros de su familia pueden quedarse mientras que ponen sus vidas en orden.

Fatigue/fatiga Cansancio extremo.

Fats/grasas Fuentes de energía que también cumplen otras funciones, como el almacenamiento de vitaminas y el aislamiento térmico del cuerpo.

Fertilization/fertilización La unión de un espermatozoide masculino y un óvulo femenino para formar una vida nueva.

Fetus/feto El organismo desde la novena semana hasta el momento del nacimiento.

Fiber/fibra La parte de los granos, frutas y vegetales que el cuerpo no puede descomponer.

First aid/primeros auxilios El cuidado inmediato que se da a una persona herida o enferma hasta que se le pueda proporcionar ayuda médica regular.

First-degree burn/quemadura de primer grado Una quemadura en que sólo la capa exterior de la piel se quema y enrojese.

Fitness/buena condición física La habilidad de tomar parte en el trabajo y las diversiones de la vida diaria sin cansarse demasiado.

Flammable/inflamable Que se quema con facilidad.

Flexibility/flexibilidad La habilidad de mover las articulaciones completa y fácilmente.

Fluoride/fluoruro Substancia que ayuda a que los dientes resistan las caries.

Food Guide Pyramid/Pirámide de los alimentos Una guía para seleccionar alimentos sanos diariamente, diseñada por el Departamento de Agricultura de EE.UU.

Fossil fuels/combustibles fósiles Petróleo, carbón y gas natural usados para proporcionar energía.

Fracture/fractura Una rotura en el hueso.

Friendship/amistad La relación entre personas que simpatizan y tienen intereses y valores similares.

Fungi/hongos Seres vivos primitivos que no pueden hacer sus propios alimentos.

Gang/pandilla Un grupo de personas que se relacionan porque tienen algo en común.

Gene/gene La unidad básica de la herencia que determina las características que heredas de tus padres.

Generic products/productos genéricos Productos que se venden en envolturas sencillas y a menor precio que los de marca.

Genital herpes/herpes genital Una enfermedad transmitida sexualmente, causada por un virus, que produce ampollas dolorosas en el área genital.

Germ/germen Un microorganismo que causa una enfermedad.

Gland/glándula Un grupo de células o un órgano que produce una substancia química.

Glucose/glucosa El tipo de azúcar que es la fuente principal de energía del cuerpo.

Gonorrhea/gonorrea Una enfermedad transmitida sexualmente que es causada por una bacteria que afecta la membrana mucosa genital y a veces otras partes del cuerpo, como el corazón o las articulaciones.

Grief/pena Tristeza profunda causada por la pérdida de algo muy querido.

Gynecologist/ginecólogo Médico que se especializa en el sistema reproductor femenino.

Habit/hábito Un patrón de conducta que se repite con gran frecuencia, casi sin pensar.

Hallucinogen/alucinógeno Una droga que altera el estado de ánimo, los pensamientos y los sentidos.

Hate crime/crimen por odio Un acto ilegal cometido en contra de alguien, sólo porque pertenece a un grupo en particular.

Hazard/peligro Una amenaza posible.

Head lice/piojos Insectos parasíticos que viven en el pelo y causan picazón.

Health/salud Una combinación de bienestar físico, mental/emocional y social.

Health insurance/seguro de salud Un plan en el que la gente paga una cantidad fija a una compañía de seguros la cual, a cambio, paga algunos o la mayoría de sus gastos médicos.

Health maintenance organization (HMO)/organización para el mantenimiento de la salud Un tipo de servicio de salud controlado que le ofrece a sus miembros distintas clases de servicios de salud.

Heart attack/ataque al corazón Una condición que se presenta cuando el flujo de sangre al corazón disminuye o se para, dañando el músculo cardíaco.

Hepatitis/hepatitis Una inflamación del hígado, causada por un virus, en que la piel y esclerótica del ojo se ponen amarillas.

Heredity/herencia La transferencia de rasgos de los padres biológicos a sus hijos.

Histamines/histaminas Substancias químicas en el cuerpo que causan los síntomas de una reacción alérgica.

HIV (human immunodeficiency virus)/VIH (virus de inmunodeficiencia humana) El virus que causa el SIDA.

Homicide/homicidio Un crimen violento que resulta en la muerte de una persona.

Hormones/hormonas Substancias químicas, producidas por glándulas, que ayudan a regular las funciones del cuerpo.

Hurricane/huracán Tormenta de fuertes vientos y lluvia que se origina en alta mar.

Hygiene/higiene Limpieza.

Hypertension/hipertensión Una condición en que la presión arterial de una persona se mantiene a niveles más altos de lo normal; también se llama presión alta.

Hypothermia/hipotermia Una disminución repentina y peligrosa de la temperatura del cuerpo.

Immune system/sistema de inmunidad Las defensas del cuerpo combinadas, compuestas de células, tejidos y órganos que combaten gérmenes que causan enfermedades.

Immunity/inmunidad La habilidad del cuerpo de resistir los gérmenes que causan una enfermedad en particular.

Individual sports/deportes individuales Actividades físicas en que puedes participar solo o con un amigo, sin formar parte de un equipo.

Infancy/infancia El primer año de vida de un ser humano.

Infection/infección La condición que se produce cuando gérmenes invaden el cuerpo, se multiplican y dañan las células.

Influenza/influenza Una enfermedad contagiosa, caracterizada por fiebre, escalofríos, fatiga, dolor de cabeza, dolores musculares y síntomas respiratorios.

Infomercial/comercial informativo Un anuncio de televisión largo cuyo propósito aparenta ser informar en vez de vender un producto.

Inhalant/inhalante Una substancia cuyos gases se respiran para obtener sensaciones alucinantes.

Insulin/insulina Una hormona producida en el páncreas que regula el nivel de azúcar en la sangre.

Intoxicated/embriagado Borracho.

Invulnerable/invulnerable Que no puede ser lastimado.

Iris/iris La parte coloreada del ojo.

Joint/articulación Un lugar en donde se unen dos o más huesos.

Kidney/riñón Uno de la pareja de órganos en forma de frijol que filtran el agua y los desechos de la sangre.

Lens/cristalino La parte del ojo que enfoca la luz en la retina.

Life-altering/que cambia la vida Capaz de modificar la vida diaria de una persona.

Life-threatening/amenaza a la vida Que puede causar la muerte.

Ligament/ligamento Una banda de tejido fuerte que sostiene el hueso en su sitio en una articulación.

Liver/hígado La glándula más grande del cuerpo que secreta un líquido llamado bilis que ayuda a digerir las grasas.

Long-term goal/meta a largo plazo Una meta que piensas alcanzar durante un largo período de tiempo.

Lymphatic system/sistema linfático Un sistema circulatorio secundario que ayuda al cuerpo a defenderse de gérmenes y a mantener el equilibrio de fluido.

Lymphocytes/linfocitos Glóbulos blancos especiales en la linfa que son importantes en la defensa contra gérmenes y enfermedades.

Mainstream smoke/humo directo El humo inhalado por el fumador.

Malignant/maligno Canceroso.

Managed care/asistencia médica manejada Un plan para el cuidado de la salud que hace hincapié en la medicina preventiva y trata de controlar el costo y la calidad de la asistencia médica.

Mass media/medios de comunicación de masas Medios de comunicación que llegan a gran número de personas, como periódicos, libros, televisión, películas y la Internet.

Media/medios de comunicación Los distintos métodos de comunicar información.

Mediation/mediación La resolución de conflictos por medio de una persona imparcial que ayuda a llegar a una solución aceptable para ambos bandos.

Medicaid/Medicaid Un programa público de seguro médico para familias pobres.

Medicare/Medicare Un programa de seguro médico del gobierno que proporciona seguro a personas mayores de 65 años.

Medicine/medicina Una droga que se usa para tratar enfermedades o aliviar el dolor.

Melanin/melanina Una substancia producida por las células de la epidermis que dan el color a la piel.

Menstruation/menstruación La eliminación de material de las paredes del útero.

Mental health/salud mental La habilidad de ocuparse, de manera razonable, del estrés y los cambios de la vida diaria.

Minerals/minerales Substancias que fortalecen los músculos, huesos y dientes; enriquecen la sangre y ayudan a que el corazón y otros órganos funcionen debidamente.

Mononucleosis/mononucleosis Una enfermedad causada por un virus, caracterizada por inflamación de los nódulos linfáticos en el cuello y la garganta.

Mood disorder/trastorno del estado de ánimo Un trastorno en que la persona cambia de humor de manera inapropiada o extrema.

Mortality/mortalidad La muerte.

Muscle endurance/resistencia muscular Una medida de la cantidad de tiempo durante el cual un grupo de músculos puede trabajar sin cansarse.

Muscular system/sistema muscular El sistema del cuerpo que consiste en tejidos que mueven las distintas partes del cuerpo y hacen funcionar los órganos internos.

Narcotic/narcótico Una droga que alivia el dolor y entorpece los sentidos.

Negotiation/negociación El proceso de discutir un problema cara a cara para llegar a una solución.

Neuron/neurona Una de las células que componen el sistema nervioso.

Neutrality/neutralidad No ponerse de parte de nadie cuando otros están en desacuerdo.

Nicotine/nicotina Una droga que se encuentra en el tabaco que causa adicción.

Noncommunicable disease/enfermedad no contagiosa Una enfermedad, como el asma o cáncer, que no se puede transmitir de una persona a otra.

Nonverbal communication/comunicación no verbal Todos los modos de comunicar un mensaje sin palabras.

Nonviolent confrontation/confrontación no violenta Resolver un conflicto por medios pacíficos.

Nurture/criar y cuidar Ocuparse de las necesidades físicas, emocionales, mentales y sociales de una persona.

Nutrient density/densidad de nutrientes La cantidad de nutrientes que contiene un alimento en proporción a la cantidad de calorías.

Nutrients/nutrientes Las substancias en los alimentos que el cuerpo necesita para crecer, tener energía y mantenerse sano.

Nutrition/nutrición El proceso corporal de tomar alimentos y usarlos para crecer y mantener buena salud.

Obesity/obesidad La condición de estar el 20 porciento o más sobre el peso ideal.

Objective/objetivo Basado en los hechos.

Occupational Safety and Health Administration (OSHA)/Administración de Salud y Seguridad Ocupacional Una rama del Departamento de Trabajo que protege la seguridad de los trabajadores estadounidenses.

Ophthalmologist/oftalmólogo Un médico que se especializa en la estructura, función y enfermedades del ojo.

Optic nerve/nervio óptico Un grupo de fibras nerviosas que envían mensajes del ojo al cerebro.

Optometrist/optometrista Un profesional de la salud que está preparado para examinar la vista y recetar lentes correctivos.

Organ/órgano Una parte del cuerpo que comprende distintos tipos de tejidos que hacen una función particular.

Osteoarthritis/osteoartritis Una enfermedad crónica, común en los ancianos, que es el resultado de la degeneración del cartílago de las articulaciones.

Ovaries/ovarios Las glándulas reproductoras femeninas.

Overcommitment/demasiados compromisos Comprometerse a cumplir con más personas o proyectos de los que uno puede por falta de tiempo o energía.

Overtraining/entrenamiento excesivo Ejercitarse con demasiada fuerza o frecuencia, sin descanso suficiente.

Pancreas/páncreas Una glándula que ayuda al intestino delgado, a través de la producción de jugo pancreático, el cual está formado por una mezcla de varias enzimas que descomponen las proteínas, carbohidratos y grasas.

Passive smoker/fumador pasivo Una persona que no fuma pero inhala humo secundario.

Pedestrian/peatón Una persona que viaja a pie.

Peer pressure/presión de contemporáneos La presión que tus amigos ejercen sobre ti para que creas y actúes igual que ellos.

Peers/contemporáneos Personas de la misma edad que se parecen a ti en muchas maneras.

Peripheral nervous system (PNS)/sistema nervioso periférico Todos los nervios fuera del sistema nervioso central que conectan el cerebro y la espina dorsal al resto del cuerpo.

Personality/personalidad La mezcla de rasgos, sentimientos, actitudes y hábitos de un individuo.

Physical fatigue/fatiga física Cansancio extremo de todo el cuerpo.

Physiological dependence/dependencia fisiológica Un tipo de adicción en que el cuerpo tiene una necesidad directa de una droga.

Pituitary gland/glándula pituitaria Glándula situada en la base del cerebro que produce distintas hormonas que controlan otras glándulas.

Plaque/placa Una película pegajosa que contribuye a las caries dentales.

Plasma/plasma Un líquido amarillento; la parte líquida de la sangre.

Pollen/polen Una substancia en forma de polvo, despedida por ciertas plantas.

Pollution/contaminación Substancias sucias o dañinas en el medio ambiente.

Pores/poros Pequeñas aberturas en la piel.

Precaution/precaución Una medida que se toma para evitar peligro.

Prejudice/prejuicio Una opinión negativa e injusta, generalmente en contra de personas de otro grupo racial, religioso o cultural.

Preschooler/niño preescolar Un niño entre las edades de tres y cinco años.

Prevention/prevención Tomar medidas para asegurarse de, que no suceda algo que no es saludable.

Primary care provider/profesional primario de la salud El médico u otro profesional de la salud que proporciona chequeos médicos y cuidado general.

Proteins/proteínas Nutrientes esenciales que se usan para crear y reparar las células y tejidos del cuerpo.

Protozoa/protozoos Organismos de una célula, semejantes a animales.

Psychological dependence/dependencia psicológica Una adicción en que la mente envía mensajes al cuerpo comunicándole que necesita más de una substancia.

Psychological fatigue/fatiga psicológica Cansancio extremo causado por el estado mental de una persona.

Puberty/pubertad El período en que comienzas a desarrollar las características físicas de los adultos de tu sexo.

Pulmonary circulation/circulación pulmonar La circulación que lleva la sangre del corazón, a través de los pulmones y de regreso al corazón.

Pupil/pupila La abertura oscura en el centro del ojo que permite que la cantidad de luz apropiada entre en el ojo.

Quackery/curanderismo La venta, por medio de engaños, de productos y tratamientos que no valen nada.

Radiation therapy/radioterapia Tratamiento para ciertos tipos de cáncer que utiliza rayos X u otro tipo de radiación.

Recovery/recuperación El proceso de ponerse bien de nuevo.

Refusal skills/habilidad de negarse Modos efectivos de decir que no.

Reproduction/reproducción El proceso por el cual los organismos vivos producen otros de su especie.

Reproductive system/sistema reproductor Los órganos y estructuras del cuerpo que hacen posible producir hijos.

Rescue breathing/respiración de rescate Forzar aire en los pulmones de la víctima de un accidente que no puede respirar normalmente.

Respiratory system/sistema respiratorio El conjunto de órganos que proporcionan oxígeno al cuerpo y eliminan el bióxido de carbono.

Responsibility/responsabilidad La habilidad de tomar una determinación y de aceptar las consecuencias.

Retina/retina La parte del ojo sensible a la luz.

Rheumatoid arthritis/artritis reumatoidea Una enfermedad crónica, caracterizada por dolor, inflamación y rigidez de las articulaciones.

Risk behavior/conducta arriesgada Un acto o selección que puede causar lesiones o daño a uno mismo o a otros.

Safety conscious/consciente de la seguridad Que se da cuenta de la importancia de la seguridad y actúa con cuidado.

Saliva/saliva El líquido con enzimas digestivas producido por las glándulas salivales de la boca.

Saturated fats/grasas saturadas Grasas que se encuentran principalmente en carnes y productos lácteos.

Schizophrenia/esquizofrenia Un trastorno mental serio en el que las percepciones de la persona pierden su conexión con la realidad.

Second-degree burn/quemadura de segundo grado Quemadura grave que forma ampollas en el área quemada.

Secondhand smoke/humo secundario Aire que está contaminado por el humo del tabaco.

Self-assessment/autoevaluación
Examinación y valoración minuciosas de los patrones de conducta de uno mismo.

Self-concept/autoimagen La manera en que te ves a ti mismo.

Self-esteem/autoestima Confianza en ti mismo.

Self-management/manejo personal La habilidad de ocuparte de tu salud total y controlar tu conducta y actos.

Semen/semen Una mezcla de espermatozoides con los fluidos producidos por el sistema reproductor masculino.

Sewage/aguas residuales Basura, detergentes y otros desechos caseros que se llevan las tuberías de desagüe.

Short-term goal/meta a corto plazo Una meta que puedes alcanzar rápidamente.

Sidestream smoke/humo indirecto Humo que procede de un cigarrillo prendido.

Skeletal system/sistema esquelético El armazón de huesos y otros tejidos que sostienen el cuerpo.

Small intestine/intestino delgado Un tubo enrollado, de unos 20 pies de largo, donde se produce la mayor parte de la digestión.

Smoke detector/detector de humo Un aparato que hace sonar una alarma cuando descubre humo.

Specialist/especialista Un médico que ha estudiado para tratar determinados tipos de pacientes o problemas de la salud.

Sperm/espermatozoides Las células reproductoras masculinas.

Spinal cord/espina dorsal Un largo conjunto de neuronas que transmite mensajes entre el cerebro y todas las otras partes del cuerpo.

STD (sexually transmitted disease)/enfermedad transmitida sexualmente Una enfermedad que se pasa de una persona a otra a través del contacto sexual.

Stimulant/estimulante Una droga que acelera las funciones del cuerpo.

Stomach/estómago Un órgano musculoso en que ocurre parte de la digestión.

Strength/fuerza La capacidad que tienen tus músculos para producir un efecto.

Stress/estrés La reacción del cuerpo a los cambios a su alrededor.

Stressor/estresante Algo que provoca el estrés.

Stroke/embolia Condición que se produce cuando parte del cerebro queda dañado porque disminuye el flujo de sangre a éste.

Subjective/subjetivo Que proviene de las opiniones y creencias de una persona y que no necesariamente está basado en los hechos.

Suicide/suicidio Matarse intencionalmente.

Support system/sistema de apoyo Una red de personas dispuestas a ayudar cuando sea necesario.

Syphilis/sífilis Una enfermedad transmitida sexualmente, causada por una bacteria, que afecta muchas partes del cuerpo.

Systemic circulation/circulación sistémica Circulación que lleva sangre rica en oxígeno a todos los tejidos del cuerpo, menos a los pulmones.

Tact/tacto La habilidad de saber lo que se debe decir para no ofender a los demás.

Tar/alquitrán Un líquido espeso y oscuro que se forma al quemarse el tabaco.

Target heart rate/ritmo deseado del corazón El número de latidos del corazón, por minuto, que una persona debe tratar de alcanzar durante el ejercicio vigoroso, para obtener beneficio cardiovascular.

Tartar/sarro Placa dental que se ha endurecido en los dientes, amenazando la salud de las encías.

Team sports/deportes en equipo Actividades físicas organizadas, con reglas particulares, practicadas por grupos opuestos de personas.

Teen hot line/línea de emergencia para adolescentes Un servicio telefónico especial a donde los adolescentes pueden llamar cuando sienten estrés.

Tendon/tendón Tejido fibroso, fuerte y flexible que une un músculo a otro o a una articulación.

Third-degree burn/quemadura de tercer grado Una quemadura muy grave en que todas las capas de la piel quedan dañadas.

Tissue/tejido Un grupo de células similares que tienen una función en particular.

Toddler/niño pequeño Un niño entre uno y tres años.

Tolerance/tolerancia Situación en que el cuerpo se acostumbra a una droga y necesita mayores cantidades para obtener el efecto deseado.

Tornado/tornado Tormenta de viento, en forma de torbellino, que cae del cielo a la tierra.

Tornado warning/aviso de tornado Un boletín de noticias comunicando que un tornado se acerca y que la gente del área corre peligro.

Tornado watch/alerta de tornado Un boletín del estado del tiempo anunciando que un tornado se puede estar formando.

Trachea/tráquea El tubo en la garganta por donde el aire entra y sale de los pulmones.

Tuberculosis/tuberculosis Una enfermedad causada por bacterias que generalmente afecta los pulmones.

Tumor/tumor Una masa de células anormales.

Unsaturated fats/grasas no saturadas Grasas líquidas que provienen principalmente de plantas.

Uterus/útero El órgano femenino en forma de pera en que se desarrolla y nutre un niño antes de nacer.

Vaccine/vacuna Una preparación de gérmenes muertos o debilitados que se inyecta en el cuerpo para hacer que el sistema de inmunidad produzca anticuerpos.

Values/valores Las creencias que guían la manera en que una persona vive, como creencias sobre el bien y el mal y lo que es importante.

Vein/vena El tipo de vaso sanguíneo que lleva la sangre de todas partes del cuerpo de regreso al corazón.

Verbal communication/comunicación verbal El uso de palabras, escritas o habladas, para expresarse.

Victim/víctima La persona contra quien se comete un crimen.

Virus/virus Los seres vivos más pequeños y simples, que causan una gran variedad de enfermedades.

Vitamins/vitaminas Substancias que ayudan al cuerpo a regular sus funciones.

Warm-up/calentamiento Ejercicios suaves que se hacen para preparar el cuerpo para hacer ejercicios vigorosos.

Warranty/garantía La promesa escrita de un fabricante o una tienda de reparar un producto o devolver el dinero al comprador, si el producto no funciona debidamente.

Wellness/bienestar El estado general de buena salud, que incluye patrones de conducta que a la larga tienen buenos resultados.

Withdrawal/retirada Síntomas desagradables que se producen cuando alguien deja de usar una substancia a la que está adicto.

Index

Note: Page numbers in *italics* refer to art and marginal features.

Fitness programs, 136–40
  aerobics vs. strength training, 138
  choice of exercises for, 136, *136*
  cool-down, 138
  frequency/intensity of exercise, 139
  goals for, 135, 136, *139*
  progress, checking, 140
  and safety, 137, *137*
  stretching, *138*
  and target heart rate, 139
  warm-up, 138
Fitness testing, 162–63
Flexibility, 122
Floods, 431, *431*
Flossing, 71, *71*
Flu (influenza), *278*, 341, *341*, 349
Fluoride, 70
Folic acid, *365*
Food allergies/allergens, *6*, 373
Food and Drug Administration (FDA), *41*, 302
Food Guide Pyramid, *93*, 93–95, 103
Formaldehyde, in tobacco smoke, *273*
Fractures, *439*
Friends/friendships, 249–53
  choosing, 256
  defined, 249
  influence of, on health, *10*
  and peer pressure, 251–53, *252*
  qualities of, 250
  self-assessment form for evaluating, 250
Fruit(s), 107
  antioxidants in, 195
  and cancer prevention, 371
  preserving vitamins in, *99*
  rinsing, 107
Fruit Group, recommended daily servings for, *93, 94*
Fungi, *333*

Gallbladder, 111
Gangs, 396
Genes, 199
Genital herpes, 352
Germs, 332–34, *333*
  defined, 332
  spreading of, 334, *334*
Giantism, *185*
Glands, 183, *183*
Gliding joints, *129*
Glucose, 102
Goals, 52–55
  and action plans, 54, *55*
  career, *52*
  conflicting, *53*
  long-term, 53, *54*
  reasons for having, 52
  and self-esteem, 53
  short-term, 37, 53

Goiter, 185
Gonorrhea, 352
Government, and health care, 85
Grandparents, 248
Grape juice, *365*
Grease fires, extinguishing, *418*
Greeting others, 34, *34*
Gretzky, Wayne, 258
Grief, dealing with, 205
Gun accidents, preventing, 420
Guns, and violence, *394, 395*
Gynecologists, *83*, 192

Habits, 34–38
  addictions vs., 36
  analyzing, 36–37
  and avoiding risks, 42
  breaking, 38
  changing harmful, 36–38
  customs vs., *36*
  defined, 34
  forming healthful, 35, *35*, 347
  identifying, 36, *286*
  life-altering, 38
  life-threatening, 36
  and repetition, 36
  safe, 412–14
Hair, 74–75
  caring for, 75
  problems with, 75
  structure of, *74*
Hair follicles, *73, 74*
Hallucinogens, 305
Hammer (of ear), 78, *78*
Handwashing, 12, *19, 345*
Hard contact lenses, *78*
Hate crimes, 394
Hazards, 41, *41*
Head lice, 75
Health
  assessing your, 14–15
  defined, 4
  and environment, 9
  and heredity, 9
  improving your, 16–18
  influences on, *8*, 8–11, *10, 11*
  mental/emotional. *See* Mental/emotional health
  physical, 4, 19–20, *119*
  responsibility for others', 31, *31*
  responsibility for your own, *29*, 29–30
  and self-esteem, 217
  social, 5, 22–23, *119*
  taking charge of your, 19, 44
  total, *6, 6*
  and weight, 142, *142*
  wellness vs., 6
Health care, 82–85
  cost of, 84
  facilities for, *83*
  government programs, 85

  insurance, 84
  managed care, 84
  medical specialists, *83*
  and prevention, 82
  primary care providers, 83
  by specialists, 83, *83*
  and treatment, 82
Healthful habits, 35, *35*
Health information, being a consumer of, 62–63
Health insurance, 84
Health risks. *See* Risks
Health triangle, *119*
Heart, *124*
  alcohol's effect on, *297*
  and exercise, 127, *127*
  muscle in, 130
Heart attack, *364*
Heart disease, 363, *364, 365*–66
  risk for, 45
Heart rate, target, 139
Heart transplants, 365
Help, getting, 232–35, *233*
HELP criteria, 48
Helping others, 23, *23*
Hepatitis, *342*
Heredity, 9, 199
  and noncommunicable diseases, 363
Hernia, 188
Heroin, 305
Herpes, genital, 352
Hiking safety, 426
Hinge joints, *129*
Histamines, 374
HIV (human immunodeficiency virus), 353–55
Home, safety at, 416–20
Homicide, 393
Homocysteine, *365*
Honest, being, 47
Hormones, 176, 182, *183, 184*
Hospice, 83
Hospice workers, 194
Hospital emergency rooms, *83*
Hot lines
  crisis, 405
  teen, *233*
Human development, 196–200. *See also* Life stages
  after fertilization, 197, *197*
  birth, 198
  and cell-to-system structure, 196, *196*
  and fetal environment, 199, *200*
  and heredity, 199
Hurricanes, 433
Hurt pride, 261
Hygiene, 19
Hyperactivity, sugar and, 106
Hypertension, *364*
Hypnotics, 305

Illegal risks, 40
Illness, as family challenge, *247*
Image ads, 63
"I" messages, 242
Immune system, 336–39, *337*
Immunity, 339
Immunization, 339
Individual sports, 151
Infancy, 201, *201*
Infants
    choking first aid for, *438*
    rescue breathing for, *437*
    speaking to, by parents, *198*
Infections, 193, 309, 332–34
Infectious diseases, contagious vs.,
    351
Infertility, 193
Influenza. *See* Flu
Infomercials, 63
Information, health, 62–63, *346*
Informational ads, 63
Information resources, 21, *21*
Ingredients, product, *67*
Inhalants, 305
Inhaling, *277*
Injuries
    skeletal/muscular, 133
    sports, 157
Inner ear, 78, *78*
Insects, allergens from, *373*
Instructions, product, *67*
Insulin, 382
Insurance, health, 84
Interferon, 337
Internet, *10*
Intoxication, *315*
Iris, *76*
Isopropyl alcohol, *296*

Jaeger, Andrea, 44
Japan, *344*
Job loss, as family challenge, *247*
Jogging, 121
Joints, 128
Jumping rope, *120,* 121

Kids' Stuff Foundation, 44
Kwan, Michelle, 12

Labels
    Nutrition Facts, 100, *101*
    reading product, 66, *67*
Land pollution, 442, *442*
Law, substance abuse and the, 318
Leadership skills, 30–31
Lead paint, *420*
Left atrium (of heart), *124*
Left ventricle, *124*
Lemieux, Mario, 378
Lens (of eye), *76*
Leukemia, *368*
Lice, head, 75

Life-altering habits, 38
Life changes, and stress, 223
Life stages, *201–3,* 201–4
    adolescence, 203
    adulthood, 203, *203*
    childhood, 202
    death, 204
    infancy, 201
Lifestyle, 120–21, 346
    and noncommunicable diseases,
        363
Life-threatening habits, 36
Ligaments, 130, *130*
Listening, 243
Liver, 111
    and alcohol, *111*
    alcohol's effect on, *297*
Long-term goals, 53, *54*
Loud sounds, hearing damage from,
    79
Low-fat snacks, *143*
LSD, 305
Lung cancer, *278, 368*
Lungs, *124, 276, 277,* 376–77
Lymphatic system, 337
Lymphocytes, 337
Lymphoma, *368*
Lynch, Nnenna, 164

Macrophages, 337, *338*
Magazine articles, advertising in, *63*
Mainstream smoke, 290
Male reproductive system, 186–89
    caring for, 188
    parts of, *187*
    problems of, 188–89
Males, physical changes of adoles-
    cence in, *177*
Malignant tumors, 367
Managed care, 84
Marijuana, 303, *303*
Mass media, 61
Meal planning, 102–5
Measles, 341
Meat, Poultry, Fish, Dry Beans, Eggs,
    and Nuts Group, recommended
    daily servings for, *93, 94*
Media. *See also* Advertising/adver-
    tisements; Television
    abuse and, 406–7
    defined, 61
    influence of, on health, *10*
    mass, 61
Media literacy, 20–21
Mediation, 265
Medicaid, 85
Medicare, 85
Medications, and pregnancy, *200*
Medicine, defined, 301
Melanin, 74
Menstruation/menstrual cycle, 191,
    191, 192

Mental disorders, 228–31
    anxiety disorders, 229
    causes of, 229
    getting help for, 232–35, *233*
    and handling problems, 228, *228*
    mood disorders, 229
    schizophrenia, 230
    teen suicide, 230–31, *234*
    treatment of, 230
    warning signs of, 232
Mental/emotional health, 5, 20–22,
    210–13. *See also* Mental disor-
    ders; Self-esteem
    assessing your, 15
    defined, 210
    fitness and, *119*
    and personality, *212,* 212–13
    and positive outlook, *210–11*
    and substance abuse, 316, *316*
Mental growth, during adolescence,
    178
Mental health professionals, *233*
Mental needs, providing for, by fam-
    ily, 246
Messier, Mark, 258
Metamphetamine, *304*
Methanol, *296*
    in tobacco smoke, *273*
Microorganisms, 332
Middle ear, 78, *78*
Milk, Yogurt, and Cheese Group,
    recommended daily servings for,
    93, 94
Mobile homes, and tornadoes, *432*
Mononucleosis, *342*
Mood disorders, 229
Morphine, 305
Mortality, defined, 39
Motor neurons, *307*
Motor vehicle accidents, *412*
Mouth, digestion in, 109, *109*
Moving, as family challenge, *247*
Mucous membranes, 336
Multiple sclerosis, 309
Mumps, *189,* 341
Muscles/muscular system, *131*
    and bones, *132*
    caring for, 133
    contraction, 130
    defined, 128
    extension, 131
    pairs, muscle, 131, *132*
    soreness in, after exercise, *162*
    types of, *130*
Music, for exercising, *122*
Music therapists, 226

Narcotics, 305
Natural disasters
    earthquakes, 431, *432*
    floods, 431, *431*
    weather emergencies, 432–34

TSE. *See* Testicular self-examination
Tuberculosis, *278, 342*
Tumors, 367
Typhoons, *433*

Ultraviolet rays, 74
Unit pricing, *66*
Unsaturated fats, 99
Urethra, 187, *187*
Urologists, *83*
U.S. Department of Agriculture
    (USDA), 93
Uterus, *190,* 191, *191,* 193
Uvula, 109, *109*

Vaccination, 343, *343*
Vaccines, 339, *343*
Vagina, *190,* 191, 193
Vaginitis, 193
Values
    and decision making, 47–48, *49*
    defined, 22, 213
    and family, 246
    of friends, 250
    and peer pressure, *252*
    and purchasing decisions, *61*
Vegetables, 107
    antioxidants in, 195
    and cancer prevention, *370*
    preserving vitamins in, *99*
    rinsing, 107
Vegetable Group, recommended
    daily servings for, *93, 94*
Veins, *123*

Ventricles, *124*
Verbal communication, 241, *241*
Vestibule (of ear), *78*
Victims, of abuse, 400, 406
Violence, 392–97
    causes of, 394–95
    gang-related, 396
    preventing, 396
    random, 393
    and schools, 397, *397*
    in society, 392
    and teens, 393
    victims of, 393
Viruses, 333, *333*
Vision problems, 77–78. *See also*
    Eyes
Vitamin D formation, by skin, *72*
Vitamins, preserving, in fruits and
    vegetables, *99*
Volunteering, *30,* 45, 81, 106

Walking, as exercise, 121
Warm-up, 138
Warnings, *48*
    product, *67*
Washing hands, 12, *19, 345*
Water, drinking, 155, 156
Water pollution, 441, *441,* 443
Water safety, 426, *426*
Water workout, 134
Weapons, and violence, 394, *395*
Weather, and exercise, 137
Weather emergencies, 432–34
Weight, and circulatory system, 127

Weight-bearing exercise, 106–7
Weight management, 44, 45, 141–45
    and body mass index, 141, *142*
    and calories, 143, *143*
    eating disorders, 145
    and exercise, 143
    and health, 142, *142*
    and nutrition, 143
    obesity, 142
    through exercise, 98
    tips for, *144*
    and wellness, 141
Wellness
    defined, 6
    health vs., 6
    high level of, 6
    range of, *7*
    sports and, *154*
    and weight management, 141
Wheels, safety on, 423, *424*
White blood cells, 125, *125,* 126,
    337
Whiteheads, 74
Winter blues, *229*
Winter sports safety, 427, *427*
Withdrawal, 283, 325
Womb, *190*
Wood alcohol, *296*

Yoga, *19, 131*
Y.O.U.T.H. *See* Youth Organization
    Unites to Help
Youth Organization Unites to Help
    (Y.O.U.T.H.), 45

Credits